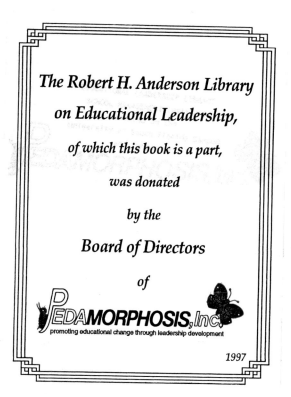

COMMUNITIES
AND THEIR
SCHOOLS

DON DAVIES, editor

MIRIAM CLASBY
LUVERN L. CUNNINGHAM
PEGGY ODELL GONDER
JOHN I. GOODLAD
JOHN HARTER
BARBARA L. JACKSON
THOMAS J. LABELLE
JACK D. MINZEY
ROBERT SCHWARTZ
DAVID SEELEY
HARVEY J. TUCKER
DAVID B. TYACK
ROBERT E. VERHINE
HARMON ZEIGLER

MCGRAW-HILL BOOK COMPANY

New York   St. Louis   San Francisco
London   Paris   Tokyo   Toronto

Thomas H. Quinn and Michael Hennelly were the editors of this book. Elaine Gongora was the designer. Thomas G. Kowalczyk supervised the production. It was set in Century Schoolbook by University Graphics, Inc. Printed and bound by R. R. Donnelley and Sons, Inc.

Library of Congress Cataloging in Publication Data

Main entry under title:

Communities and their schools.

  (A Study of schooling in the United States)
  "Conducted under the auspices of IDEA."
  Includes index.
  1. Community and school—United States—Addresses, essays, lectures. I. Davies, Don. II. Institute for Development of Educational Activities. III. Series: Study of schooling in the United States.
LC221.C65   370.19′31′0973   80-26125
ISBN 0-07-015503-8

1 2 3 4 5 6 7 8 9 DODO 8 7 6 5 4 3 2 1

The following persons assisted in the early planning for this volume and contributed valuable insights and directions. We wish to thank them for their time and effort. The resulting book, however, is the responsibility of the authors and A Study of Schooling and may not reflect the opinions of those listed below.

Thomas J. La Belle
University of California,
  Los Angeles

Don Davies
Boston University

Melvin Seeman
University of California,
  Los Angeles

Jack Minzey
Eastern Michigan University

Berlin Kelly
National Institute of Education

Raymond Terrell
California State University,
  Los Angeles

William Moynihan
Colgate University

Kenneth A. Tye
IMTEC

Paul E. Heckman
University of California,
  Los Angeles

The following persons were affiliated with the Research Division of the Institute for the Development of Educational Activities.

Lucy Blackmar

Audrey Clarke

Charles Wall

Judith Golub

This book is one of the volumes commissioned as background information for A Study of Schooling. The Study is an in-depth examination of representative elementary, junior high, and senior high schools located in several regions of the United States. The Study focuses on the school as a whole and includes the curriculum, the student and adult experiences in the school, and relationships with the community. Results of the research are presented in subsequent reports and a summary volume.

John I. Goodlad
Principal Investigator

A STUDY OF SCHOOLING IN THE UNITED STATES

SUPPORTED BY

The Danforth Foundation
International Paper Company Foundation
The JDR³ᵈ Fund
Martha Holden Jennings Foundation
Charles F. Kettering Foundation
Lilly Endowment, Inc.
Charles Stewart Mott Foundation
National Institute of Education
The Needmor Fund
Pedamorphosis, Inc.
The Rockefeller Foundation
The Spencer Foundation
United States Office of Education

Conducted under the auspices of | I | D | E | A | , a division of
the Charles F. Kettering Foundation.

CONTENTS

PREFACE

Some colleagues and I, several years ago, began an inquiry entitled, A Study of Schooling in the United States. The purpose was to increase our understanding of an institution many people believe should be doing a better job. Efforts to improve it in recent decades have produced a mixed bag of wins and losses. Most of these efforts have concentrated on some visible part of the whole: teacher education, the curriculum, counseling, testing, and so on. They were guided by the assumption that specific interventions, accompanied by some new funds, would do the job.

Our earlier studies of educational change, part of a growing literature on this subject, had brought to the fore several notions about school improvement that nourished the genesis of A Study of Schooling. Important among these was and is the idea that a school is a unique institution. It does not manufacture or process things. Nor does it sell goods and services, nor seek to make a profit for owners or investors. Rather, a school provides a setting for interactions between two groups of people, one of which is supposed to help the other gain access to the knowledge and tools humankind has developed and to the rules by which at least some humans seek to live. It seemed to us, therefore, that failure to comprehend this institutional uniqueness and the actual functioning of a school could lead readily to incorrect or misleading diagnoses of its problems and needs. In order to seek to change something, we believe, it is necessary first to understand it.

We chose to study a small sample of schools—just 38 in seven communities in seven regions of the United States. We gathered, then, a very large amount of information about a group of schools appearing to be representative of different types of elementary and secondary schools—this in preference to gathering information on just a few aspects of many schools. We obtained data from administrators, teachers, students, parents, and others, and observed carefully and extensively in classrooms.

We did not test hypotheses. We sought to gain insights. These insights have provoked the generation of many hypotheses about schools that had not crossed our minds before.

Ultimately, we must seek to make sense out of data: formulate conclusions, draw implications, make judgments. In the process, standards or norms are used. To the extent that differing norms came into play, differing judgments result. It was our intention from the beginning to provide the kind of data that would enlighten the issues of schooling and the dialogue about these issues in which differing norms came into juxtaposition. This process, we hoped, would lead to improved diagnoses and more enlightened processes of improving schools.

We wanted our own processes of drawing conclusions and formulating recommendations to be enriched by whatever research and sound judgment might already be available. We had hoped to enlist specialists in all areas of our inquiry for purposes of compiling succinct summaries of the issues in each area and the best knowledge-based analyses of these issues. We defined about a dozen aspects of schooling for which we wanted these compilations.

By this time, however, our hands were full with the complex, expensive, task of studying this many schools in depth. It was necessary to turn all of our resources to this most important task. We were able to commission only three of the accompanying volumes we had hoped to secure in many additional fields. Two of these have been published: *Schooling for a Global Age* (1979), and *Arts and the Schools* (1980). This volume, *Communities and Their Schools*, is the third and last in the series.

One of the outcomes of our earlier studies of school change and improvement was a growing belief that schools are being asked to do too much. Not only have they been asked to take over some of what families once did, they carry their additional burdens without the full collaboration of household, church, press, and school that once prevailed. Schools cannot do the full job of educating required. We need educative communities. It is to the issues and tasks of community-wide educating and the role of the schools in a configuration of educating institutions that most of *Communities and Their Schools* is directed.

On behalf of the several philanthropic foundations and governmental agencies providing financial support to A Study of Schooling, I thank all these persons who contributed to the present volume. These include both the several persons brought together to plan it (see p. iii) and the writers. Charles D. Wall provided initial direction to both groups. The liaison role was picked up later by Paul E. Heckman. Judith S. Golub provided many substantive suggestions and editorial advice. Special thanks are due Don Davies, editor of the volume.

Currently, several volumes based on data from A Study of Schooling are being written. All of these place the data within the context of issues central to the conduct of schooling in the United States. Several technical reports bringing together data on selected aspects of schooling are available from the Charles F. Kettering Foundation, 5335 Far Hills Avenue, Dayton, Ohio 45429.

John I. Goodlad
Principal Investigator
December, 1980

INTRODUCTION

DON DAVIES
Institute for Responsive Education

*To create alternative forms of schools responsive to the
pluralistic character of American society will demand a new
frame of mind on the part of those involved. . . . The basic
goals of a democratic common school can be reinterpreted for
our era, and the institutions of public education once again
changed, if Americans have the wisdom and the will.*
—David Tyack, in Chapter 1

*Communities and a sense of community will continue to
wither as long as our institutions . . . are preoccupied with
their own survival rather than with the human conditions
and needs they are supposed to serve. More than money, we
need a different way of viewing the problem— an alternative
perspective.*
—John Goodlad, in Chapter 11

A new frame of mind . . . a different way of viewing the problems of schools and communities. These are the chief contributions of this volume. The book arrives near the beginning of the decade of the 1980s. Communities are withering. Schools are in deep trouble. Resources are limited. The old definitions and formulations appear sterile. There is a strong incentive to seek fresh and more useful ways of thinking about and understanding schools and communities and the complex political and ecological web that binds them. This is our objective. To move toward it, we assembled a collection of talented scholars and writers with diverse backgrounds and points of view. Represented are historians, political scientists, economists, anthropologists, educational administrators and philosophers, teachers, citizen organization leaders, community educators, and government officials. We have provided ourselves with the broad canvas that the topic of school-community relations and the diversity of authors requires.

The result, of course, is a pastiche rather than a single artist's drawing. But the medley is both a virtue and a necessity, as it reflects the variability of ways of looking at schools and communities revealed in A Study of Schooling, of which this book is a part.* There *are* differences between and among large and small schools in small towns and large cities located in urban, suburban, and rural areas. There *are* differences between and among students, parents, teachers, administrators, school board members, scholars, practitioners, liberals, conservatives, and radicals. There *are* differences between and among social classes, races, the sexes, and ethnic groups. Understanding these differences—the confusion and richness of American pluralism—can, itself, lead to fresh ways of looking at often abstract concepts such as "community," "the goals of education," and "school-community interaction."

The book also reflects the contradictions, conflicts, and uncertainties revealed in A Study of Schooling. These pertain to the ends and means of education, the meaning and definition of community, and the processes of decision making and resource allocation. The most obvious and striking contradiction woven through the pages which follow is that between the rhetoric of the American dreams of equality and equity and the resistance of institutions and communities to move toward greater equality of opportunity and greater equity in services and influence. The classic struggles in Boston and New York depicted by David

---

*For a discussion of the Study of Schooling, see John I. Goodlad, Kenneth A. Sirotnik, and Bette Overman, "An Overview of 'A study of Schooling.'" *Phi Delta Kappan*, vol. 61, no. 3, November 1979, pp. 174–178.

Seeley and Robert Schwartz are two examples of this fundamental contradiction. The efforts of the federal government—both courts and legislature—to resolve the equality/equity contradictions have had powerful impact on school-community relations in the 1960s and 1970s. This impact is reflected in Harmon Zeigler's discussion in Chapter 2 of the review step in the policy process; in my own Chapter 4 discussion of government-mandated mechanisms for citizen participation; and, most especially, in Chapter 6 by Barbara Jackson, in which she describes and illustrates the effects of federal intervention on governance structures.

Uncertainty about the meaning and definition of community is also reflected in these pages. For example, Barbara Jackson points to the differences in the way "community" is defined and the way the definition shapes the political and educational reality. In one instance, in the federally-sponsored Urban-Rural School Development Program, it is a geographic area—the area served by a particular school. In another instance, "community" is comprised of people with shared beliefs and values about schools. In yet another setting, Boston, "community" is taken to mean people who have in common being black or poor and who seek increased control over a school. All three "definitions" of community are used and found useful by the authors. Differing definitions of community schools and community education are also explored.

However, the book before you, with all of its diversity, does have a pattern and a plan. The reader who is willing to proceed with us from front cover to back will discover a design in regard to both chronology and content.

The opening chapter provides the historical context. David Tyack leads us from the unstructured pluralism of American education in the 1840s, through establishment of the primacy of the common, public schools, to the reform efforts of the late 19th and early 20th century to "take the schools out of politics," and to apply the ideas and technology of corporations to the schools. He then brings us to the present, sketching the turbulent effects of new participants (e.g., the urban poor, the courts), and new constraints (e.g., collective bargaining, declining enrollments) in the 1960s and 1970s. He demonstrates the durability over time of important contradictions.

With the historical context briefly but firmly drawn, the remainder of Parts I and II are based largely on the issues, events, and practices of the 1960s and 1970s. This 20-year period has been marked both in this country and abroad by burgeoning interest, activity, and varied, sometimes conflicting, new efforts to reshape school-community interaction.

The major focus in Part I is on the political relationships between communities and their schools—governance, decision making, citizen participation, and teacher influence. This dominance reflects the view of many of the authors and myself that decisions about communities and their schools are, in fact, political—they have to do with "who gets what when" and with the choices about whose values are to be reflected in the schools.

After Tyack's historical view of governance issues, Harmon Zeigler and Harvey Tucker, in Chapter 2, strive to answer the question, "Who governs the schools?" They undertake a painstaking analysis of the six successive and distinct steps in the process of policy making or governance. They draw on their own work, especially a survey of a national sample of school districts and an intensive data-gathering effort in eleven public school districts. The data reveal professional domination of all aspects of policy making and an insulation of educational policy making from community politics. Zeigler and Tucker assert the inapplicability of the professional-expert model of decision making in issues such as desegregation and resource allocation and predict stronger external challenges to this model. The challenges can further lessen the influence of communities on school policies. The theme of the limitations on local schools and communities is renewed.

In Chapter 3, David Seeley and Robert Schwartz tell a tale of two cities, New York and Boston, to identify the chief governance problem—excessive bureaucratization—and two solutions to it, decentralization and community control. Community control in New York City is not presented, as has often been done, as an experiment that failed but as an idea that was not really tried. The failure of a major effort to reform and decentralize school governance in Boston is tied to the conflict over court-ordered desegregation. The authors end on the hopeful note that both city school systems have produced not only new leaders but new types of leadership which may create school systems more appropriately responsive to community needs.

Chapter 4, which I wrote, deals with citizen participation by outlining the forms and functions of citizen participation and proposing six criteria to aid the reader in thinking about and judging proposals carrying the label citizen participation. Drawing on field studies by the Institute for Responsive Education and others, the chapter concludes that current forms of participation in decision making are not working well in terms of these criteria and suggests two promising directions—developing school-based governance and fostering citizen-initiated community organizations working on a broad range of social and economic concerns. I suggest that new ways of thinking about participation are required.

Luvern Cunningham describes and analyzes one important new form of citizen participation—third-party problem solving. In Chapter 5, Cunningham draws on experience in eight cities to identify nine functions of such groups ranging from convening and mediating to catalyzing and implementing new policies. Cunningham, reacting to other often trivial forms of participation, stresses increasing effectiveness of activities rather than extending the number of persons involved. His way of thinking about school-community relations envisions citizen participation based on thoughtfully developed and understood premises and on theories of problem solving and institutional change.

Moving on to Chapter 6, the reader will find a rich variety of case material from several federal programs designed to foster citizen participation and alter school governance structures. Barbara Jackson's chapter "Federal Intervention and New Governance Structures" dramatizes the interlacing of changes in the goals of schools, the content and style of educational programs, and changes in governance structures in such federal programs as the Urban League's Street Academies under the Experimental Schools Program and the Urban/Rural School Development Program.

Jackson places this material in the context of the federal government's role to protect and advance the interests of the have-nots in the society, especially poor black people and other minority group members. A profound shift in the federal role was based on the recognition that problems were no longer local in the urbanized and industrialized society of the late 20th century. She posits that in order to recapture a "sense of community" and protect the interests of the least powerful in the society, ways must be found to connect the individual and the government through organizations in which people can learn and practice self-government. Her view that the federal government's efforts in the 1960s and early 1970s were often appropriate and successful suggests a different way of thinking about the role of the federal government in school-community relations.

In Chapter 7, David Stern and John Harter tackle some issues involved in the emergence in the 1960s and 1970s of strong teacher organizations and collective bargaining and the impact of these developments on school governance and school-community relations. The authors urge a new way of thinking about the relationships between the economic demands of teacher unions and declining public support for the schools. They suggest "productivity bargaining" as one mechanism but reject simplistic and technical measures of productivity. Stern and Harter call for students, citizens, parents, and other taxpayers— along with teachers—to share the responsibility for deciding how productivity should be defined, measured, and related to economic benefits for teachers. "Productivity bargaining" in education would involve citizens, teachers, and administrators in a valuable process of defining outcomes and rewards which would help to restore and sustain good relations between educators and the public.

Governance is the focus, then, for the first two thirds of the book. The focus in Part II shifts to other kinds of interactions—community education in the United States and overseas and school-community resource exchanges. These are neither apolitical nor insignificant aspects of our topic. The three chapters in Part II contribute strongly to that basic goal of finding a new frame of mind and alternative perspectives.

The community education efforts in non-industrialized nations described by Thomas LaBelle and Robert Verhine in Chapter 8 stand in contrast to the descriptions of activities in Jack Minzey's chapter on American community education and provide a comparative and international perspective to the primarily domestic issues discussed elsewhere in this volume.

LaBelle and Verhine establish five models of community schools, each representing five distinctive goals: (1) to increase educational access; (2) to enhance learning; (3) to foster the transition from study to work; (4) to serve as community centers; and (5) to strengthen nationalism and socioeconomic development. The descriptive cases highlight the impact of economic considerations and cultural, political, and ideological traditions on the ends and means of community education and on governance issues as well. The analysis of the cases invites and suggests comparisons to the other chapters in the book, even though some of the undertakings in other societies represent choices no longer available to us or culturally or politically appropriate. The opportunities for cross-fertilization and cross-national exchanges emerge as one fruitful way of achieving new frames of mind and different ways of viewing the problems of school-community relations. Perhaps the most salient contribution to the book's search for such new ways of thinking is the authors' conclusion that the schools are impotent to "lead the community" unless the wider society, through political, cultural, and social patterns, is prepared to both assign the school such responsibility and to support its efforts. LaBelle and Verhine warn that efforts to foster different and closer school-community relations often flounder when these efforts are contrary to the interests of local elites or the nation-state or when the wider society does not itself value institutions which are based on the primacy of individual and institutional collaboration.

In Chapter 9, Jack Minzey presents a comprehensive overview of community education in the United States which rests on the premise that American society should and could assign much larger responsibilities to schools. Minzey describes community education as a process of relating all the resources of the community to community needs. He assumes the collaborative mode which LaBelle and Verhine suggest is imperative. Minzey speculates that the most likely unit to recapture the lost sense of community and build a creative, participatory society is the school district: "The country will be divided into thousands of school districts, each responsible for the realization of natural and human resources within a relatively small area." Minzey's chapter describes exemplary practices in community education and offers practical suggestions to those interested in developing such an approach.

Peggy Odell Gonder picks up on this practical note. In Chapter 10, she outlines a wide range of imaginative ways to enrich student experiences by tapping community resources. Gonder discusses volunteer programs, school-business cooperation, government-initiated efforts to involve parents in the learning process such as Head Start and Title I, school-community contracts, the community as a "textbook" as in the Foxfire projects. This chapter is one of the few places in the book where emphasis is given to students. A variety of examples of programs to foster new roles for youth are described. The limited resources theme, which occurs so often in our book, also appears here as the motivation for a variety of resource exchange programs such as in Cambridge, Massachusetts, where school nursing services and neighborhood health centers have been combined.

Part III moves us to the future, providing two very different perspectives, in order to stimulate those *new frames of mind* and *different ways of viewing the problem* we are seeking.

John Goodlad, who directed A Study of Schooling, formulates provocative alternative visions in Chapter 11. His thesis is that schools are in varying degrees "learning communities" with unique potential for developing a sense of community. He seeks limits on the school, defined both as concept and place, contesting the view that the school should embrace the whole of educating. He calls, rather, for the school to do "educationally within the community ecosystem that which no other system is equipped to do." His ecological perspective offers a fresh way of thinking about schools and communities. "An ecological perspective turns attention not just to relationships between individuals and one institution, but to the health of the relationships among individuals and institutions." Goodlad's coda for this volume is the proposition that the most promising direction for the future is in strengthening these relationships.

Miriam Clasby, in the twelfth and final chapter, explores the limits of localism and the growing impact of external national and international forces on school-community relations. She challenges the myths that local communities or local educators do control the schools and that schooling is one of our best hopes for individual, community, and national well-being. She warns that unless considerations for schooling in a community are placed within new contexts of education in the larger society, they run the danger of unwittingly affirming a past that no longer exists. Careless perpetuation of the myth of local control and of schools as preparation for an ever-brighter future for all "can only help propel us headlong into that world described by Thomas Pynchon in *Gravity's Rainbow* where community exists only as 'shared victimhood.'"

The emphasis on promising directions and new approaches to school-community relations that characterizes most of our book is an effort to counteract the alienation and despair that result if one accepts without a struggle this concept of our future as one "shared victimhood." In fact, the most important feature of the book is its emphasis on promising practices and new approaches. These are put forward as first steps toward addressing some critical social problems: reducing the isolation of schools in a community; offsetting bureaucratic rigidities; developing complex interconnections among local, state, and national groups; building networks of resources at various levels of the system; challenging unexamined values; and introducing a wide range of examples of power-sharing appropriate in an interconnected society. Although activities vary widely in specific features, they are linked by common qualities of initiative, inventiveness, reflectiveness, commitment, and often courage and persistence.

No single design and certainly no panacea emerge from these pages. There are instead multiple threadings—from the community into the school, from the schools out toward the local arena and larger society, upward and downward through local, state, and national levels. There are also indications of multiple and diverse pressures to reshape current practices. Each of the chapters is, nevertheless, in some way incomplete; together they produce only a partial record of recent developments. More significantly, many emphasize micro-level efforts which hint at, but do not directly address, macro-level structural constraints.

And, in fact, the book is incomplete. There are two important omissions. The first is educational finance. While Stern and Harter deal directly with economic issues and other chapters refer to economic restraints, there is no fully developed report on the economic exchanges between schools and committees and no attention to the court-impelled strivings toward more equitable spending among school districts within a state and the impact of increased state assumption of public school financing on local school-community relations. Similarly, there is no chapter devoted to the emergence of litigation as a prime form of citizen influence on the schools and the dominant role that legal structures now play in many aspects of school-community relations.

Each reader will, no doubt, note other gaps, omissions, and failures to emphasize one thing or another. Despite these limitations, we do believe that the book will, in fact, contribute to a *new frame of mind* and *to different ways of viewing the problems*. Beyond the specifics of the topics and examples, the book testifies to the capability of citizens from widely different sectors of the society; students and adults sorting out issues, structures, goal strategies; forging alliances for common purpose; using the topic of the schools to see and act upon those contradictions in the society so clearly revealed by the inadequacies of the schools. This is, in fact, a new way of thinking about the present and future of school-community relations.

A grant from the Charles Stewart Mott Foundation supported the preparation of this book. This book, in turn, is one of a series of publications on issues and practices in education and schooling written in conjunction with A Study of Schooling, referred to earlier. The Study, nearing completion as this manuscript goes to press, was funded at various stages by the following: Danforth, International Paper Company, Jennings, Kettering, Mott, Rockefeller, and Spencer Foundations; the JDR[3rd] Fund, the Needmore Fund, and Pedamorphosis, Inc.; the National Institute of Education, and the U.S. Office of Education.

1

GOVERNANCE AND GOALS:
Historical Perspectives on Public Education

DAVID B. TYACK
Stanford University

Who runs American schools, and to what end? Wisdom begins and ends in admitting that there are no definitive answers to these questions. Once I was asked to "explain" American education—on ten minutes' advance notice—to a group of perceptive journalists from Asia. As we talked, I discovered that these foreign visitors found some features of our system perplexing if not contradictory. Consider these puzzles:

- American schools are highly decentralized in formal structures of control—we have fifty states and about 15,000 separate local districts—yet classrooms from Maine to Hawaii show remarkable similarities.

- In theory, the public school is to be public in control, equitable in support, and socially comprehensive. Yet in practice "public control" is hard to define and even harder to accomplish, financing of schools often reflects grossly unequal tax bases, and pupils are frequently segregated by ethnicity and social class.

- Schooling supposedly provides equality of opportunity to all children and access to the best jobs, but the people who make it to the top of the educational and occupational systems are mostly the children of those who already occupy favored positions in the society.

- Political scientists often describe the governance of schools as a "closed system" in which educators make the crucial decisions that lay school boards merely rubber-stamp, but educational leaders often complain that they are highly vulnerable and constantly have to worry about public opinion.

There are several ways to examine these real or apparent contradictions. The way I shall pursue here is to explore the governance and goals of education historically. As ideals and institutions develop over time, they tend to incorporate disparate and even conflicting elements. To understand legacies with which we live today, it helps to untangle their origins, to analyze ideas and practices now familiar but once problematic and new. I shall explore the development of a complex web of politics that has bound schools to their communities and to the local, state, and national governments. In addition, I shall analyze how educational purposes emerged, persisted, changed, or disappeared as schools adapted to transformations in the economic, social, and political structure of American society.

THE COMMON SCHOOL MOVEMENT OF THE NINETEENTH CENTURY

Most historians agree that the common school movement of the mid-nineteenth century is the major turning point in the history of public schooling in this country. Prior to 1840, when the crusade for public education gained momentum, the typical attitude of the public toward education resembled a common attitude today toward religion: attend the school of your choice. There was an enormous variety of schools to choose from, as there are churches today. Many foreign visitors—Alexis de Tocqueville is only the best known—commented on Americans' zeal for education. Most of the early state constitutions proclaimed the value of diffusing knowledge among the people. States gave subsidies to all kinds of schools from Harvard University to charity schools for city urchins. And the non-system of education worked rather well, at least for whites. It has been estimated that in 1830 about 35 percent of children from 5 to 19 were enrolled in some school. In 1840, about 90 percent of white adults were literate, placing the United States in the forefront of education at that time, together with Scotland, Sweden, and Germany.

Even in the handful of states that had rudimentary "public schools" (that is, publicly controlled and financed), the methods of governance and finance were extremely heterogeneous. One common form of education was the proprietary school: a teacher instructed children for a price, and the controls and opportunities were those of a business in a market economy. The teacher either satisfied the customers and made money or went out of business. Another model was the school incorporated by the state and governed by private trustees; the rapidly multiplying academies and colleges fit this pattern. Students typically paid tuition, but since these institutions were often presumed to serve the public interest, states or localities sometimes subsidized them and wealthy individuals provided scholarships for deserving youth. The charity school for the education of the poor, often sponsored by churches or benevolent societies, constituted another familiar educational genre. In any case, during the early nineteenth century, there were few sharp lines between "public" and "private" education. Even in "public" schools parents often paid tuition (called "rate-bills"). Schools commonly reflected the pluralism of the society and tended to perpetuate differences of religion, ethnicity, social class, and occupational status. Americans thought education was a good thing, but they turned mostly to voluntary agencies or families to provide the money and the control.

In the middle decades of the nineteenth century reformers like Horace Mann wanted to translate this generalized faith in education into support of one particular institutional form: the public school—free, financed by state and local government, controlled by lay boards of education, mixing all social groups under one roof, and offering education of such quality that no one would desire private schooling. To a remarkable degree these crusaders for the common school succeeded in their quest (more so than any other major reformers of a period that was a seedtime of social change). So sharp were the outlines of the common school by the 1860s—clearly different from private schools and having internal coherence as an institution—that a British visitor could write a book about the free school *system* of the United States. Funds spent on public schools comprised only 47 percent of all expenditures for education in 1850; by 1900, they had become 79 percent. With the exception of the growing Catholic parochial schools, the public schools held almost a monopoly on elementary education.[1]

Who were the common school reformers, what were their major concerns, and how did they operate? Here it is useful to distinguish the campaign for public education in the urbanized East from the creation of common schools in the sparsely settled regions of the Western states.

In the Eastern cities the men who led the common school crusade were mostly members of professional and business groups, joined by leading schoolmen. They saw public education as the key answer to troubling new problems created by urbanization, industrialization, immigration, and the democratization of the suffrage. Poverty, crime, intemperance, violence, and human suffering were increasingly visible in the manufacturing centers and crowded and heterogeneous commercial cities. Such conditions contradicted articles of faith cherished by the reformers: the perfectibility of man, the need for orderly self-government, the doctrine of equality of opportunity through self-help, and the responsibility of individuals for the welfare of others in their community. Basically conservative, these reformers believed that the common school offered the most humane form of social control and the safest form of social renewal.

In frontier settlements, on the other hand, a large proportion of the common school evangelists were ministers—often joined by other professional leaders—who were bothered by disintegration of standards of behavior and learning in the individualistic frontier. They sought to recreate the kinds of integrative institutions and patterns of education they had known in the East. They wished to create communities around the core institutions of school and church.

In both settings the crusaders for public education agreed that social stability and individual welfare alike required a uniform public school that could assure common standards of literacy, morality, and citizenship in the rising generations. In their opinion, the old hodgepodge of schools could not accomplish that; only an efficient common school would suffice. The best-known common school reformers were state superintendents such as Horace Mann of Massachusetts, Henry Barnard of Rhode Island, John Pierce of Michigan, and John Swett of California. They had very little formal power. Mann, for example, was authorized only to collect statistics, diffuse information about educational innovations, "suggest" improvements in schooling to the State Board and legislature, and organize meetings of teachers, school board members, and "friends of education generally." The last item contained the key to his influence: exhortation and evangelism for an educational celestial city.

After the departure of the charismatic early leaders, state departments of education probably made little impact on practice during the nineteenth century. The office was ridiculously understaffed; in 1890 the median size of state departments of education (including the superintendent) was two (about one official for 100,000 pupils).[2] Superintendents collected statistics (usually rather badly) and sometimes disbursed funds. Because of poor communication networks between the capital and the local districts and the lack of real political or organizational clout, state superintendents were mostly figureheads. Legislatures might pass laws—for example compelling school attendance—but without effective networks for implementation the laws were frequently dead letters.

If the state governments had minimal impact on the day-to-day operation of education, the influence of the federal government was almost imperceptible to most school boards and educators. Some federal funds did flow to the states from the sale of the public domain, and periodically requests for statistics came from the U.S. Bureau of the Census and the U.S. Bureau of Education (after its founding in 1867). Some Republican Congressmen had hoped to carry out their party's policy of "Unification and Education" in the years after the Civil War by creating agencies that would require states to meet a federal standard of excellence in universal schooling and by providing federal funding to carry out this plan. But the plans for federal aid were never passed, and such strong resistance arose to any kind of federal oversight of education that the Department of Education enacted in 1867 was reduced the next year to a Bureau and its funding and staff were cut.

Throughout most of the nineteenth century real control of public education rested in the hands of local lay board members and, in some places, trusted local educators. As Mann found when he tried to standardize certain features of schooling in Massachusetts—one of the most sophisticated and densely settled of the states—local elected officials often resented any suggestion of centralization. In sparsely settled regions each community wanted its own school nearby, under its own eye and thumb. For example, in Iowa a group of farmers, irate because their children had to walk too far to school, one night secretly used a team of oxen to move the schoolhouse a mile closer. States might create normal schools to train teachers or set certification standards, but local boards usually hired whomever they pleased. States might prescribe subjects or textbooks, but local parents and teachers made do with whatever came to hand. The "system" was very loosely structured; what held it together at all was a general consensus on the importance of literacy and moral and civic instruction. Schools institutionalized the values shared in the community, including in most cases a pan-Protestant religion. In rural or village neighborhoods patrons built the schools with their own hands, boarded the teachers in their own homes, and visited the schoolrooms on Friday afternoons to hear their own children recite, spell, and declaim the verities of the *McGuffey Readers*. School committee members performed almost all the functions that administrators would later assume.

In the cities there was a growing tension between lay control by activist board members and an emerging bureaucratization of schools. In the early stages of the common school, some cities had one-room schools with local trustees as in the countryside, but it became obvious to some leaders that haphazard village patterns made planning and coordination difficult. Some shapers of the nineteenth century urban school systems were fascinated with the new organizational forms appearing in manufacturing, commerce, and the railroads. In factories, for example, they saw a division of labor and a pattern of supervision which seemed to create predictable results by efficient methods. A parallel development within education was age-graded classrooms with a systemwide consecutive curriculum, administered by building principals and the district superintendent. Some of these new managers realized that efficient planning of large enterprises required information flowing in reliable ways through set communication channels; school officers tried to keep statistical track of the burgeoning numbers of pupils, used achievement tests for promotion of students from grade to grade, and began to keep bureaucratic records and to set organizational rules. So fixed did these standard operating procedures become by the 1870s that critics began to complain that urban school systems were becoming inflexible machines.

This attempted rationalization of the schooling process in city systems, however, was often hindered by what leading schoolmen and lay reformers regarded as an archaic mode of school governance. The village pattern of active lay administration of schools persisted in many cities. Central school boards were often enormous, steadily increasing in size as new wards of the city grew by accretion around the central districts. In a majority of nineteenth-century cities, local ward boards retained important duties, such as hiring teachers and awarding contracts for supplies and even new buildings. The norms of school committee behavior reflected the rural and village systems of lay administration. Boards considered it their right and obligation to decide almost all substantive questions, including hiring all staff, purchasing supplies, and determining curriculum and methods of discipline. Since the board or committee of the whole did not have time to look into such matters as the selection of a furnace or the proper way to teach penmanship, it commonly divided into subcommittees that handled such details. Board members tended to regard superintendents as clerks or factotums, hired to enforce regulations and to mind the shop.

Honest and civic-minded board members tended to take an activist view of their functions. At times important cultural issues of religion and ethnicity entered local school politics. Desiring to represent the views of their ward constituents, board members often argued about such issues as the teaching of foreign languages in elementary schools or the use of the King James Bible. And of course the rapid expansion of schools offered corrupt politicians rich opportunities for graft, as in the heyday of the Tweed Ring in New York City.

Although the citizens of small communities had direct access to policy making in education and at least some lay groups had influence over the pluralistic politics of schooling in cities, during the nineteenth century there were certain groups that lacked such power. Native Americans, for example, had little say over the education of their children, for an obscure official in the Bureau of Indian Affairs in Washington might have more power in the stroke of his pen than the most august tribal leader on a reservation. Likewise, after the relatively brief period of political influence of blacks in reconstruction governments in the South, black Americans found themselves once again subject to the caste system and dependent on the good will of their former white masters. When state after state disenfranchised the Negro at the turn of the twentieth century, white legislatures and local boards built up the system of white schools by starving the black schools. In 1931, after decades of disinheriting the Negro educationally, the South as a whole spent $45.63 on each white student as compared with $14.95 on each black; many counties had much greater disproportions (one in South Carolina, for example, allotted $8.00 to each Negro child compared with $178 for each white). In such communities blacks had no formal political control whatever, since power was vested in all-white boards and superintendents.[3]

For the great mass of white Americans, however, the nineteenth century was a time when at least some of the basic aims of the common school were achieved. Looking back at the end of the nineteenth century, the U.S. Commissioner of Education found cause for pride. By then about 70 percent of persons aged 5 to 18 years were enrolled in some kind of school; the absolute number of pupils in public education had grown to 15,000,000; and of every 100 students in all kinds of educational institutions, 95 were in elementary schools, 4 in secondary, and 1 in a postsecondary school. A typical young American of 1898 had about five years of schooling. To the average parent or school person of the nineteenth century the basic functions of schooling were relatively clear-cut: to equip students with academic skills and to give them a moral and political socialization that would enable them to participate in society as industrious, temperate, honest citizens. All this could be accomplished in a brief time and by simple means: a few years of elementary schooling under the influence of earnest teachers. Few educators saw schools as a means of channeling children into niches in the economy, for most believed that a modest education coupled with self-help, ambition, and good character would assure success. The school simply was to give each child corrective nurture and an equal starting point for the race of life. Few stopped to ask if the race was rigged.[4]

"TAKING THE SCHOOLS OUT OF POLITICS": NEW GOVERNANCE, REVISED GOALS, 1890–1950

As we have seen, a basic theme of the common school movement had been *public* as opposed to *private* control and support of education. By the end of the nineteenth century many school leaders and their allies among business and professional elites thought that there was entirely too much public control of education. Under the banner of "taking the schools out of politics" they formed political and professional alliances to centralize the governance of urban schools in small boards elected at large (thereby abolishing ward boards), to consolidate rural schools, and to make local practices conform to state educational standards. The central result was greatly to lessen the influence of citizens over the schools in their neighborhoods. This was deliberate, for the centralizers did not trust the people to run the schools. One of their key leaders, Nicholas Murray Butler of Columbia University, put it this way: it was as foolish to speak of "democratization of the treatment of appendicitis" as to speak of "the democratization of schools. . . . The fundamental confusion is this: Democracy is a principle of government; the schools belong to the administration; and a democracy is as much entitled as a monarchy to have its business well done."[5]

Education was a matter for experts to direct. The job of the board of education was mainly to select a good superintendent and then to delegate most decisions to him (the male pronoun fits, for practically all superintendents were men). But not just any board would do: the members should be "successful men," professionals, businessmen, folks who knew that a school system should be run in a business-like fashion like a corporation. When scholars examined the social background of school board members during this period, they found that indeed they were mostly people from the higher echelons of their communities.[6]

The campaign to centralize control of urban schools in small boards succeeded for the most part. In 1893 in the 28 cities with populations over 100,000 the average size of the school board was 21.5 (and many of the cities at that time had ward boards in addition with dozens or even hundreds of members); by 1913 the central boards averaged 10 members, by 1923 only 7. By the 1920s decentralized ward boards had mostly disappeared.

The slogan of "taking the schools out of politics" was, of course, misleading. The centralizers wanted power to *their* people. Later, in a quite different context, the arch-segregationist Senator Theodore Bilbo said that "all this talk about taking the schools out of politics is a huge joke to intelligent people. It means nothing except to take the schools out of your politics and put them in my politics."[7] The chief goal of the centralizers was to create a relatively closed system that transformed "political" issues largely into "administrative" questions to be decided by experts. Wallace Sayre has argued that it was understandable that educators would want to develop these "serviceable myths" in order to create autonomy within a bewildering field of political forces:

> Education is a unique governmental function.... Educators are the only proper guardian of the educational function; their autonomy in this guardianship is essential to the public interest.... The community, when it confronts educational questions, should be an unstructured audience of citizens. These citizens should not be influenced in their responses to educational questions by their structured associations in organizations: not as members of interest groups of any kind (save perhaps in parents' groups) or as members of a political party. The unstructured community will be wisest in its responses to educational questions when it listens to the educators, to the "experts" in education....[8]

Parallel to this movement to centralize control of city schools was the twentieth-century campaign to consolidate rural one-room schools into larger graded elementary schools and to merge small high schools into consolidated ones. As we have seen, the rural schools were very closely tied to their local communities: in many sparsely settled regions there were several times more school trustees than teachers. In 1900 there were about 200,000 one-teacher schools; in 1930 almost 150,000;

and in 1950 approximately 60,000. The number of separate school districts declined from 127,531 in 1930 to 83,718 in 1950 and 16,960 in 1973.

Consolidation of small schools, then, was a far slower process than centralization of city schools, and it aroused more fervent controversy. Rural people wanted to run their schools and to have them nearby. The school was a significant symbol and source of community. Educators, however, often believed that rural people did not know what was best for them.[9] One of these reformers wrote in 1914 that "because the rural school is today in a state of arrested development, burdened by educational traditions lacking in effective supervision, controlled largely by rural people, who, too often, do not realize either their own needs or the possibilities of rural education ... the task of reorganizing and redirecting rural education is difficult, and will necessarily be slow."[10] Another said that the rural schools needed the expert leadership found in city schools: "It is the lack of captains and colonels of larger grasp and insight that is today the greatest single weakness of our rural and village educational army."[11]

It was to the state that the centralizers and consolidators usually turned in order to correct the deficiencies of urban or rural school districts. State legislatures granted cities new charters and passed laws encouraging or requiring small districts to combine. State departments of education grew rapidly, especially during the 1920s, reaching a median size of 28 in 1930 (the largest staff—New York's—had 594 members). Not only did legislatures now pass manifold regulations—setting standards in teacher certification, school ventilation, methods of "pupil accounting," scope and sequence in curriculum, and the like—but they also began to have the administrative machinery to enforce them. Certain state requirements such as laws enjoining teachers to inculcate patriotism or kindness to dumb animals were doubtless more exhortatory than operationally defined, but frequently state departments of education gained leverage over the local districts when laws linked state financial aid to average daily attendance or to compliance with state standards.

The centralization of city schools under small boards with cosmopolitan outlooks, the consolidation of rural schools, the imposition of uniform state standards—all served to make schools less provincial and more alike in their practices. In addition, in the twentieth century, educational organizations grew enormously in size and provided local educators with an opportunity to share ideas. The National Education Association, for example, which typically had only 3,000–5,000 members during the nineteenth century, reached the 100,000 mark in 1922. Educational specialties multiplied—counselors, vocational educators, secondary and elementary principals, attendance officers—and almost all had their own organizations, giving members a sense of being part of a common national guild. Regional accrediting associations also helped to determine—and often freeze—the new uniform standards. National curriculum commissions produced important statements of purpose and practice, the most famous of which was probably the "Cardinal Principles of Secondary Education" (1918). Despite continuing local and regional variations, then, there were strong forces pushing toward national standardization.[12]

Along with the managerial and structural revolutions that were taking place in American education came some subtle revisions of goals. In the twentieth century, school leaders did not explicitly disavow the earlier ideals of the common school. Indeed, those who admired John Dewey made "democracy" one of the key words in the educational litany. But leaders who prided themselves on being hardheaded, especially the "scientists" and those who were part of the managerial revolution, began to develop two doctrines that changed thinking about the functions of schooling. The first was a kind of biological or social determinism, and the second was the notion that schools should serve as a screening and channeling mechanism—that is, that they had a crucial role in deciding children's later life chances.

By the early twentieth century, many educators were becoming convinced that American society was divided into classes. They noticed that certain immigrant groups, especially, were clustered in the working class, and thought it likely that such social distinctions would persist. This had important implications for education. We should, said one leading spokesman, "give up the exceedingly democratic idea that all are equal, and that our society is devoid of classes," and instead realistically adapt schooling to the likely life chances of students.[13] Blacks, especially, needed a practical and industrial education to fit them for their probable work. The development of intelligence tests seemed to underscore the wisdom of this sociological determinism and to give it biological justification. Scholars like Lewis Terman seemed to demonstrate that those on the bottom of the social system—groups like Southern Italian workers, for example—were genetically inferior, as judged by IQ tests. There were, of course, many who disagreed with the pseudoscientific reasoning of those who argued the logic of a social or biological determinism, but "racial" theories and cultural chauvinism were common among educators.

Whether they agreed with any of the varieties of determinism or not, as the twentieth century progressed educators began to see that schooling was beginning to occupy a much greater role in the lives of students than previously. One reason was that students stayed in school far longer. The median number of years of school attendance nearly doubled from 1870 to 1950. Another reason was that employers were beginning to require educational credentials for entry into many white-collar positions, such as high school graduation for such "women's jobs" as telephone operator and secretary and teacher, or college degrees for the high technical and managerial jobs which men largely monopolized. Increasingly school people thought it their duty to select and channel students into educational programs that would fit their probable destination in life. The contest for mobility, in other words, now began in school. Although talented lower-class individuals surely did use education to rise in social status, study after study showed that differentiation within high schools largely reflected divisions of class, ethnicity, and sex in the outside society.[14]

During the period from 1890 to 1950, then, there were important revisions of goals and shifts in patterns of governance that tended to standardize schooling in the United States. These developments help to explain the puzzles with which this essay began: uniformities in a decentralized system; the tendency of schools to perpetuate the existing socioeconomic status of pupils rather than provide upward mobility; the troubles citizens have in influencing supposedly "public" education; and the ways in which a professedly democratic institution reflects the ethnic segregation and the economic and sexual inequalities of the larger society.

But it would be a distortion to suggest that this is all there is to the story of public education during those years. In the majority of small and medium-size communities the schools probably were in fact not "closed systems" politically but were responsive to the communities they served. It is revealing to note that until the 1960s most writers on the relationship between communities and schools regarded educators as too vulnerable to community influence, not too insulated. In fact the liberal educator Myron Lieberman reflected this general opinion when he wrote in 1960 that local control of schools was the chief reason for "the dull parochialism and attenuated totalitarianism" of American education.[15] It was the large cities, with their many divisions of specialists and tiers of officials, that tended to have bureaucracies well buffered from public pressure, not the smaller communities which were often (in Willard Waller's phrase) "museums of virtue" that socialized children according to the positive values and approved evasions of the local residents. The literature on teachers and administrators in such small systems hardly shows them to be impervious to their communities. Indeed, there is much to the argument that the bolder educators did the children a favor in helping to liberate them from the provincialism of their parents.

As for the goals of schooling, the contradiction we sense between promise and performance comes in part from the persistence and refinement of democratic aims during the period from 1890 to 1950. Alongside the determinists, who thought it natural that schools would largely reflect or even reinforce the inequalities of the larger society, were many educators who struggled to reveal the contradictions precisely to reform education and fulfill the dream of a *common* school. These were people like George Counts who exposed the elitism of school boards and the selective character of high schools; Newton Edwards, who decried the grossly unequal funding of schools across the nation; Horace Mann Bond, who taught Americans the grim facts about the education of blacks; Robert Havighurst, who analyzed how social class bias deformed the operation of public schools; and countless teachers and administrators who believed in the democratic purposes of schooling and tried to practice what Mann and Dewey had preached.

CHALLENGES AND REFORMULATIONS, 1950–1970

The contradictions between the dream of the common school and the actualities of public schooling became increasingly apparent in the years following the *Brown* desegregation decision in 1954. In the 1960s American education entered a time of great change and turbulence. Dozens of popular books etched in sharp lines the pathologies of public education. Scholarly studies poured from the presses with abundant documentation of the failures of the schools to serve the children of the poor and of oppressed minority groups. Proposals for reform, new plans for governance, and actual interventions followed one another with kaleidoscopic speed: integration, compensatory education, performance contracting, decentralization, community control, accountability, vouchers, and even deschooling. What began as a reaffirmation of traditional faith in education in the war on poverty and in the civil rights movement sometimes ended in bitter rejection of the dream as a cruel illusion.

In the 1960s the entry of new actors into educational policy making disturbed the relative tranquility of school governance during the previous two generations. In 1969 the political scientist Stephen Bailey wrote that "reviewing traditional—even recent—literature about American school boards is a strange and unsettling experience. . . . The described value systems and life styles of school boards, and the perceptions of reality of the authors who have written about them, seem romantically archaic and irrelevant." Reading the standard studies, he continued, "is a little like studying modern geography with a pre–World War II textbook, and a pre–World War I atlas."[16] At center stage in the 1950s scenario were the school board and the superintendent. Local interest groups occasionally entered the dialogues. In the wings, giving faint signals, was the state department of education. The school lawyer was the man who defended the board when a parent slipped on the icy steps of the school and sued the district. Now and then people debated abstractly about the dangers of federal control *if and when* the Congress decided to give federal aid. Yearly the board decided how much of a raise it could afford to give the teachers. Ethnic issues were often perceived as problems in "intergroup relations" to be solved by adjustments in curriculum.

In the 1960s traditional goals and governance were sharply challenged by new participants, new constraints, and new opportunities. In cities, especially, groups that had once been at the fringes of decision making now wanted to share the power—notably teachers, minority groups, and students. Teachers demanded collective negotiations not only about salary but often about management and curriculum as well. The American Federation of Teachers and the National Education Association competed with one another for the loyalty of militant teachers; strikes became commonplace. Members of minority groups, especially blacks, used various strategies to influence educational policy, including court cases, boycotts, and more militant actions, as in the momentous strike and decentralization crisis in New York City in 1968–69. Disappointed with the results of years of effort to desegregate schools, some blacks opted instead for community control. Ethnic self-determination and pride sparked campaigns for affirmative action in hiring minorities, for new bilingual programs, and for courses in ethnic history. Students in many kinds of communities contested the authority of school administrations to restrict dress and forms of expression and pressed for changes in school regulations and curriculum. Lawyers supported by federal legal aid grants took many school districts to court for violation of students' constitutional rights.

In the years following the *Brown* decision the state and federal court systems became a significant arena of educational policy making. Policies which had been within the traditional prerogatives of state or local boards of education now were challenged as violations of civil rights statutes or constitutional guarantees. Desegregation cases in both South and North forced major changes in the assignment of pupils and staff. Lawyers successfully attacked the way educators classified students as "retarded." Judges like Skelly Wright of Washington, D.C., placed districts under court order to modify methods of tracking pupils, allocating of money, and assigning of teachers. Suits brought under Title VIII of the Civil Rights Act attacked unequal funding of athletic programs for girls and other kinds of sexual discrimination. In

Tinker and subsequent cases, the Supreme Court broadened the rights of expression and clarified due process for students (as in requiring hearings for suspension of students). In the famous Bible and prayer decisions, the Supreme Court also banned the ceremonial uses of religion in public schools.

Of course, judicial decisions from *Brown* onwards did not enforce themselves—schools still segregated students, principals still opened assemblies with the Lord's prayer, administrators still banned student publications—but activist lawyers and courts did much to change established practice in education. As a consequence, legal action became a significant constraint on standard operating procedures in schools and on traditional domains of school governance.

With the Elementary and Secondary Education Act of 1965 (ESEA) the Congress broke a century-long legislative logjam that had blocked large-scale federal aid to local school systems. Earlier aid to vocational education or to specific programs under the National Defense Education Act of 1958 did set precedents, but the scale and nature of the 1965 act created a far greater impact on local districts than previous federal programs had. Federal expenditures for education jumped tenfold from 1958 to 1968, in the latter year constituting about 10 percent of the public costs for schooling. The largest sums were targeted through Title I of ESEA for improving the education of "the disadvantaged," and other funds were available for innovative projects in local districts. The United States Office of Education began to become, for the first time, a significant part of the governance of American education, though its powers remained circumscribed. In 1950 it had a staff of only about 300 and a budget of $40 million; in the 1960s the bureaucracy was substantially reorganized under Commissioner Francis Keppel and ballooned in size and budget. It no longer simply collected statistics, issued reports, and supervised or consulted in scattered programs. Rather, it became a channel for vast sums and an interpreter of the intent of Congress and the executive branch. Now officials at the state level and in local districts pored over federal guidelines, prepared proposals for funds, and sent back reports to Washington in steady streams.[17]

Amid all the changes of actors in educational politics and the shifts in ideology, however, the local district board and administration remained the key pressure point for outside forces impinging on education and the translator of these influences into practice in classrooms. At times it seemed, said Stephen Bailey, that "by the time the Federal government, state education departments, local professional staffs, militant teacher organizations, John Birch societies, textbook and hardware salesmen, black parents and Panthers, and the local media have completed their macabre Whirling-Dervish dance, local school boards appear to be nothing but awkward wallflowers perversely held responsible for the success of the party."[18] The politics of education had indeed become a jarring mix of conflicting forces and values, overlapping jurisdictions, legal constraints and mandates, and traditionally powerless groups seeking new influence.

Still, school boards and administrators had influence over critical decision making. How did they respond to new policy initiatives?

In a society in which part-time reformers and interest groups seek to change institutions, the full-time officials in the bureaucracies and the lay trustees most closely involved still have considerable latitude in reaction, ranging from enthusiastic implementation to partial cooptation to quiet sabotage to open conflict. For example, if a state legislature passed a law requiring instruction in the evils of liquor, a teetotalling superintendent and board might make temperance central in the health curriculum, while another school system might comply only in a token way if at all. One school board might welcome the *Brown* decision as a help in performing its moral duty to desegregate, yet another might vow never to mix the races despite the law of the land. In a system so loosely linked as the federal-state-local network of educational governance, a variety of responses are in fact possible. How have the new challenges, constraints, and opportunities since 1960 affected the routines that were established during a period of relative calm?

Political scientists have examined the politics of education intensively only during the last fifteen years. Hence most empirical studies deal chiefly with the recent era of turbulence. As indicated in Chapter 2, most of the research on local school governance reaches the same conclusions: superintendents and their staffs retain control over most initiation of policy; school boards normally serve to legitimate the decisions of professionals; and the norms of "non-political" participation and discussion in school issues remain strong. The authors of the most comprehensive recent study of local governance—L. Harmon Ziegler, M. Kent Jennings, and G. Wayne Peak—conclude that the evidence they discovered in eighty-three representative communities across the nation demonstrates that the turn-of-the-century reforms "succeeded only too well" in their goal of "taking education out of politics." They found minimal competition for school board membership. Indeed, more than half the reelected incumbents were uncontested, and a common pattern of recruitment was for present members to coopt new members from among their acquaintances. Open board conflict with the superintendent was rare and, where it existed, the school administrator usually won. Some students of large city bureaucracies, in particular, have argued that the superintendent and middle management tend to control policy formation through their near monopoly over information about the schools and their power to set or limit agendas. When administrators disagree with school board decisions, they can often sabotage implementation.[19]

Of course, political scientists also have analyzed the conflicts that erupted between boards and superintendents. Michael Kirst and Frederick Wirt call local school politics an arroyo, a creek bed that is normally dry but that can suddenly fill with a flashflood created by storms of protest over desegregation, sex education, school finance, or some other volatile public issue.[20] Lawrence Iannacconne describes local school politics as mostly a closed system, but one that episodically shifts as superintendents are replaced in response to changes in community demands.[21]

In a perceptive analysis of recent writings on local governance, William Boyd notes that there is a sharp contradiction between what he calls the "rubber stamp" view of the functioning of school boards and the "beleaguered superintendent" interpretation. Critics who portray educational decision making as a closed system dominated by professionals argue that "this state of affairs is not only undemocratic, but, because it favors the status quo and attention to the vested interests of educators, is also a leading reason for the failure of public education to respond adequately to the . . . changing needs of the many publics it is supposed to serve." By contrast, he notes, many administrators see themselves as vulnerable to "a variety of interest groups and forces that not infrequently threatens to neutralize their ability to provide any effective kind of leadership."[22]

Boyd argues that it is dangerous to generalize about professional autonomy and that the influence of the superintendent differs according to the issue and according to the size and socioeconomic composition of the community. As Ziegler found, lay boards can often challenge the professionals more successfully in small communities (when the need arises, which is infrequent) than in big city bureaucracies (which have substantial ability to play factions off against each other or to use pocket vetoes within the system). Likewise, as Boyd and others observe, boards are more willing to delegate internal curricular matters to the superintendent than external matters of widespread public concern, like busing. Often communities of high social status have values congruent with those of the school managers and elect board members who have skills in mediating conflicts. Overt conflict of boards with superintendents in suburbs is more likely to take place in working-class communities, whose goals may diverge from those of the school administrators, than in prosperous communities that value expertise and consensus.

This last point on congruence of values raises an important qualification of the supposed "autonomy" of school managers. As Boyd stresses, one reason there does not appear to be much dissonance between boards and superintendents may well be that the administrators are, in effect, good politicians responsive to the board and to the community. They sense the "zone of tolerance" of alternative policies permitted within the community. By anticipating the reaction of the board, superintendents advance only those proposals that have a good chance of acceptance. This sort of anticipatory consensus is not the same thing as traditional arbitration of policies through partisan politics, but it is not an insulated expertise either. When superintendents see some of their peers fired for exceeding the "zone of tolerance," it enforces an unwritten rule: don't take those risks. From the time of Horace Mann forward, leading spokespeople for education have also stressed the need to avoid controversies that would rend the public school consensus.

As a result of this adaptive behavior, the schools may have been at least partially responsive to communities even in the absence of active citizen participation in policy making in education. Indeed, a recent study of public agencies finds schools less "closed," more receptive to innovation, than other sectors such as health and welfare councils, urban renewal agencies, or bodies planning mental health service.[23] The strategy of adaptive response by school professionals may also help to explain why American education has largely innovated by accretion, by adding new subjects or processes or staff to the existing structures. A common reaction of local boards and superintendents to community criticism in the 1960s, as earlier, was to preserve the system's basic operating procedures, power, and structure, while adding new minority teachers or administrators, courses in black history, or drug abuse programs. To those who believe in government by consensus, administered by experts, the cooptation of dissident groups is a natural, indeed admirable, technique of inclusion, while preserving the basic power alignments intact. To those who wish to alter the balance of power in education or to induce basic change, reform by accretion falls far short of the goal.

Many political scientists would like to politicize local school districts in order to increase the responsiveness of schools, but the educational effects of doing so must be carefully analyzed. Most of the writing on that subject thus far has been exhortatory or apocalyptic. Examples of politicization can be chosen to prove whatever points one wishes—for example, South Boston (local white resistance to desegregation), Charleston, West Virginia (opposition to godless, communistic textbooks), or the Rough Rock Demonstration School (in which native

Americans tried to shape schooling to Navaho needs). Until recently liberal commentators on local governance have tended to agree with Myron Lieberman's comment (quoted earlier) that community control of schools was the chief reason for "the dull parochialism and attenuated totalitarianism" of American education. With the rise of concern for political participation of excluded groups in the 1960s and with the new studies on school politics as a "closed system," the pendulum of liberal opinion has swung toward greater responsiveness to local political groups.

Seen in the shifting historical context of goals and governance, the events of the last fifteen years in public education have highlighted some new features, to be sure, but many of the issues being debated today are perennial ones in political and educational theory. This suggests that there are no easy answers and no responses adaptable to all times and places.

In my opinion, it is a hopeful sign that many policy makers in education, both lay and professional, are giving up the notion that there is one best system of schooling. To create alternative forms of schools responsive to the pluralistic character of American society will demand a new frame of mind on the part of those involved. There are many obstructions in the way of innovation: state codes that restrict freedom; administrators and teachers who sabotage the new because they fear it; alienated students who destroy even what they have helped to create; parents who distrust change. But time and skill can diminish such obstacles when the prime constituencies—the students, parents, and teachers—realize that together they can create meaningful choices. The basic goals of a democratic common school can be reinterpreted for our era, and the institutions of public education once again changed, if Americans have the wisdom and the will.

NOTES

1. Albert Fishlow, "Levels of Nineteenth Century Investment In Education," *Journal of Economic History,* vol. 26, pp. 418–436, December 1966.

2. National Education Association, *Studies in State Educational Administration,* No. 9, 1931, NEA, Washington, D.C., 1931, pp. 5–6.

3. Robert G. Newby and David Tyack, "Victims without 'Crimes': Some Historical Perspectives on Black Education," *Journal of Negro Education,* vol. 40, pp. 192–206, Summer 1971.

4. William T. Harris, "Elementary Education," in Nicholas M. Butler (ed.),

Monographs on Education in the United States, J. B. Lyon, Albany, N.Y., 1900.

5. Speech to Chicago Merchants' Club, reprinted in *Public Schools and Their Administration: Addresses Delivered at the Fifty-Ninth Meeting of the Merchants' Club of Chicago,* Merchants' Club, Chicago, 1906, p. 40.

6. George S. Counts, *The Social Composition of Boards of Education,* University of Chicago Press, Chicago, 1927.

7. Quoted in Reinhard H. Luthin, *American Demagogues: Twentieth Century,* Beacon, Boston, 1954, p. 61.

8. Wallace Sayre, "Additional Observations on the Study of Administration: A Reply to 'Ferment in the Study of Organization,'" *Teachers College Record,* vol. 60, pp. 74–75, October 1958.

9. David Tyack, "The Tribe and the Common School: Community Control in Rural Education," *American Quarterly,* vol. 24, pp. 3–19, Spring 1974.

10. Quoted in Ellwood P. Cubberley, *Rural Life and Education: A Study of the Rural-School Problem as a Phase of the Rural-Life Problem,* Houghton-Mifflin, Boston, 1914, pp. 306–307.

11. Ibid., p. 183.

12. Edgar B. Wesley, *NEA, the First Hundred Years: The Building of the Teaching Profession,* Harper and Bros., New York, 1957.

13. Ellwood P. Cubberley, *Changing Conceptions of Education,* Houghton-Mifflin, Boston, 1909, pp. 56–57.

14. George S. Counts, *The Selective Character of American Secondary Education,* University of Chicago Press, Chicago, 1922.

15. Myron Lieberman, *The Future of Public Education,* University of Chicago Press, Chicago, 1960, p. 36.

16. Stephen K. Bailey, "New Dimensions in School Board Leadership," in William E. Dickinson (ed.), *New Dimensions in School Board Leadership: A Seminar Report and Workbook,* National School Boards Association, Evanston, Ill., 1969. p. 97.

17. Michael W. Kirst, "The Growth of Federal Influence in Education," in C. Wayne Gordon (ed.), *Uses of the Sociology of Education,* 73rd Yearbook of the National Society for the Study of Education, Chicago, 1974.

18. Bailey, op. cit., p. 97.

19. L. Harmon Ziegler and M. Kent Jennings with G. Wayne Peak, *Governing American Schools,* Duxbury Press, North Scituate, Mass., 1974.

20. Frederick M. Wirt and Michael W. Kirst, *The Political Web of American Schools,* Little Brown, Boston, 1972.

21. Lawrence Iannaccone, *Politics in Education,* Center for Applied Research in Education, New York, 1967.

22. William L. Boyd, "The Public, the Professionals, and Educational Policy-Making: Who Governs?" *Teachers College Record,* vol. 77, pp. 539–547, May 1976, p. 542.

23. Ibid., pp. 574–575.

2

WHO GOVERNS AMERICAN EDUCATION:
One More Time

HARMON ZEIGLER
Center for Educational Policy and Management
University of Oregon

HARVEY J. TUCKER
Texas A & M University

O nce a barren wasteland of political science, educational governance has profited within the past few years by the appearance of a variety of empirical studies.[1] Naturally, in an area so recently subject to investigation, many ambiguities remain. To subsume these ambiguities under the question of "Who governs" is to invite even more confusion, for it is by no means clear what is meant by the act of governing.

Traditional definitions of governance, such as Lasswell's "Who Gets What, When, and How" or Easton's "Authoritative Allocation of Values" are helpful primarily as foci or organizing concepts, as they are too general to serve as operationally precise guides for research. This chapter will attempt to organize evidence according to a model of the governance process thought of in terms of six successive and distinct steps: (1) proposal development, (2) executive recommendation, (3) legislative action, (4) supplementary change, (5) implementation, and (6) review. With some modifications, this six-step model can be used to describe the normal decision-making process at all levels of government. Our goal, of course, is to restrict the discussion to school governance.

While using this six-step model as an organizing notion, our focus will be on participation in the governing process. The question, broadly stated, is: how *insulated* is the decision-making process? This question has become the focus of an intense debate and deserves additional explication.[2] Again, there is a need for further definition. The potential participants in school district decision making are: (1) the school board, (2) the superintendent, (3) the central administrative staff, (4) other professionals (teachers, principals, etc.), (5) the public, and (6) other governments.

The range of participants may vary among the various steps of the policy-making process. By considering both the six potential participants and the six stages of the governmental process, we hope to reach some defensible conclusions about "who governs?"

SOURCES OF ORIGINAL DATA

The first source of original data reported in this paper is a study of school governance, conducted in 1968, which was based on a national sample of public school districts. A major report of findings was published in 1974 under the title, *Governing American Schools*.[3]

NOTE: Some of the research reported in this paper was supported by the Research and Development Division, Center for Education and Policy Management, University of Oregon, funded under a contract with the National Institute of Education, Department of Health, Education, and Welfare.

Briefly, the *Governing American Schools* inquiry was based on a national survey of school districts proportionate to the size of the school population. A sample of 83 school boards was designated. Out of a potential pool of 541 board members, successful interviews were obtained with 490, a response rate of 91 percent. Interviews were conducted in person and lasted, on the average, well over an hour.

The school board sample was supplemented with samples of superintendents and the public. The response rate for superintendents was also extremely high: interviews were obtained with 81 of 83 candidates. A mass public sample was incorporated from the 1968 election study conducted by the Survey Research Center. The range of respondents across the districts in no instance exceeded 23, and the average was 8.5. Survey cases were weighted according to criteria explained in *Governing American Schools*.

The *Governing American Schools* project, while enjoying the advantages of generalizability from a national sample, suffered the unavoidable limitations of survey research. The attempt of the 1968 study to describe the functioning of school governance faced three interrelated problems:

1. The observations reported by respondents quite often were in conflict.

2. Individual recall of behavior was often inaccurate.

3. The discrepancy between reported and actual behavior was exacerbated because recollections involve interactions with others (e.g., school board members' interactions with superintendents, members of the public, etc.)

Because of these and other limitations, questions of school governance can only be partially studied by survey research.

In an attempt to fill the gaps left by previous research, a longitudinal comparative research project—titled *The Responsiveness of Public Schools to Their Clientele*—was conducted.[4] This study included both systematic observation of events and periodic recording of participants' perceptions. During the nine-month 1974–75 academic year, data were collected on the flow of communications and decisions in eleven public school districts in the United States and Canada. The data set consists of three major elements:

1. Objective records of all statements and decisions made at central school board meetings, meetings of the superintendent and his administrative cabinet, and other formally constituted media of public exchange (e.g., regional board meetings, public hearings, etc.)

2. School board members, superintendents, and other senior administrators were interviewed regularly to record their perceptions of presentations made by members of the public at meetings and private communications about school policy from members of the public. Those who made presentations at public meetings were interviewed concerning their perceptions of how they had been received by school district officials at the meeting. They were also asked about any previous contacts.

3. An opinion survey on school policy was conducted among samples of the public, interest group leaders, and among the school board and senior administrators in each school district.

Given the decision to attempt a comprehensive description of communications, only a limited number of school districts could be studied. An attempt was made to select a sample of districts which would reflect, albeit incompletely, the variety of districts in America. Districts included fall across the range of possible sizes, locations, demographic attributes, formal decision rules and informal decision processes, and expected degree of conflict during the observation period.

Data from these two studies are reported throughout the rest of this chapter. For convenience, the first will be referred to as the *Governing* study and the second as the *Responsiveness* study.

PROPOSAL DEVELOPMENT

Proposal development begins when the need for action is articulated and one or more policy alternatives are suggested. Proposal development can originate with either governmental or nongovernmental individuals or groups within the educational system or can originate outside a specific decision-making unit. Indeed, many of the problems currently encountered by local school districts are the result of proposal development occurring at the federal level. Whatever the source, however, proposal development requires that preferences be translated into *demands* which require a *response*. Hence, the question of "responsiveness," so currently in vogue, can be understood as asking which demands, out of all those placed upon a school system, are selected for a response.[5]

As the term "development" implies, there is more to this step than the mere expression of a preference or desire. Proposal development involves making a communication to school district officials which they can understand and take action on. Thus, proposal development includes preparation of a formal proposal for consideration by appropriate officials. The result of proposal development is the setting of the agenda (which demands will be responded to), a formal commitment by the school district to consider particular policy alternatives.

Agenda setting is the opening round in the struggle for influence, and by no means an inconsequential one. As Schattschneider has commented, "political conflict is not like an intercollegiate debate in which the opponents agree in advance upon a definition of the issues. As a matter of fact, *the definition of alternatives is the supreme instrument of power.*"[6] Control of the agenda, then, is analogous to, say, choice of a battleground in war. A group or individual will always select an advantageous battleground.[7]

Participation in agenda setting seems largely a *professional* monopoly in education with minimum involvement by the school board or the public. In the *Governing* study, it was found that, in about two-thirds of the districts, the superintendent (and, in some cases, his/her staff) was *solely* responsible for setting the formal agenda for board meetings.

In the *Responsiveness* study, we defined agenda setting at school board meetings in terms of introducing a topic for discussion. While in most school districts the formal agenda document is controlled exclusively by school administrators and board members, this less restrictive definition makes it possible for all actors to participate in agenda setting. Indeed, district patrons and the general public are always invited to attend school board meetings and make their views known. The distribution of initiation of discussions among our six potential participants in school district decision making is presented in Table 1.

Even by this more liberal definition of agenda setting, educational professionals dominate all other actors. On the average, superintendents initiate nearly half of all discussions; and educational professionals account for nearly 70 percent of the agenda. School board members control 24 percent of agendas, members of the public 7 percent, and representatives of other governments less than 1 percent.

The direct setting of the agenda for school board policy making is quite insulated from those outside the school establishment. Clearly, the administration occupies a powerful "gatekeeping" position. The administration is in a position to establish an agenda which will mini-

TABLE 1 AGENDA-SETTING AT SCHOOL
BOARD MEETINGS

	MEAN	LOW	HIGH
Superintendent	47%	18%	73%
Central Administrative Staff	19	1	43
School Board	24	9	57
Other Professionals	3	0	9
Public	7	1	33
Other Governments	*	0	1

*Less than one percent.

mize controversy and maximize routine decision making. That is, superintendents and other professionals can set an agenda which emphasizes technical problems requiring administrative, rather than board, resolution. While Boyd asserts that "there is reason to believe that many, perhaps even most, school administrators are inclined to be cautious in their policy initiations and reluctant to test the boundaries of their influence,"[9] it is highly significant, from our perspective (whether or not he is empirically correct), that he concedes the control of the agenda to the administration.

The matter merits further consideration. In addition to the problem of a public body—the school board—yielding its agenda-setting authority to its nominal employee, one puzzles about how much public participation can be initiated when the public enters the game after the issues have been defined.

One should not take the insulation of nonprofessionals from direct participation in the proposal-development step as evidence of a conspiracy. The public's knowledge of schools is substantially less than that of school authorities. In our mass public sample, which supplemented our school board and superintendent sample, we found that one-third of the public could not name any problems facing their school district. Among those who noted problems, the great majority could cite but one. Among this segment, the problem was generally vague and diffuse (such as "bad teachers"). In contrast, school authorities cite problems with much greater certainty, specificity, and frequency.[10] Clearly, then, the mass public has little more than a rudimentary knowledge of the issues or, more important, the *potential* issues within their schools.

The generally low level of public knowledge should not be equated with disinterest. There is evidence to suggest that the public would like more access information about education. Moreover, the high level of community involvement in isolated, episodic issues suggests a substantial reservoir of public interest, although it is only occasionally manifest. The problem is that the mass public only responds to selected, developed issues rather than participating in the generation of issues. To illustrate, of all the potential issues which might arise within the schools, perhaps the most important are those concerning the very substance of schools: the educational program, or curriculum. Indeed, all other issues are in some sense secondary to this fundamental issue. Yet, to the mass public, issues relating to the educational program have a very low salience. Only a tiny fraction, fewer than one in thirty cites problems directly or even generally concerning the educational program. In contrast, school board members and superintendents cite curriculum problems with up to fifteen times greater frequency.[11] The gap in saliency occurs because members of the mass public do not have the expertise to discuss or resolve most curriculum issues. They lack, for example, the vocabulary educational professionals and school board members employ in their consideration of curriculum. The problem is not one of disinterest, but of frozen access.

According to traditional democratic theory, political influence—in this case agenda setting—follows lines of legal authority. The public elects a school board to make policy. The board appoints a superintendent to administer policy. Thus, administrators follow the mandates of legislators who follow the instructions of their constituents. The major source of power is electoral support, and the norm of policy making is responsiveness to public demands and preferences. This model suggests frequent participation in agenda setting by school board members and other lay people. Yet, at least in the formal meetings of school boards, this is not the case.

Another, perhaps more apt model, focuses on professional expertise as the essential element in decision making. In this chain of influence the major source of power is information; the norm is deference to expertise. Problems are brought to the attention of the school board by the publicly proclaimed experts: the superintendent and his or her staff.

The role of the public in proposal development under this latter model has been discussed in a variety of recent essays on "administrative representation."[12] The idea is that since the superintendent is the dominant policy actor, he or she can, through a variety of informal contacts (keeping an ear to the ground), adequately represent the views of the public to the board.[13] Such a notion is intriguing. After all, if the superintendent *is* in fact representing diverse community needs, then the relative quiescence of the public and of school boards is of no concern. Perhaps superintendents receive sufficient communication from the public in forums other than public meetings to represent its desires and preferences. However, our research casts doubts upon this view.

Superintendents do receive a considerable volume of private communications concerning school policy. The private communications to all board members exceed (54 to 46 percent) these received by the superintendent. However, the superintendent receives far more private communications than any single board member. More significantly, virtually all privately articulated demands occur after the presentation of an agenda item. In addition, superintendents tend to communicate with groups and individuals with a decidedly "establishment" tinge,[14] and most communications are in support of a position announced by the superintendent. Eighteen percent of the private communications received by the superintendents in the *Responsiveness* study were in disagreement, 34 percent were in agreement, and the remainder were either neutral or without issue content. This finding is consistent, of course, with numerous other examinations of private communications to public decision makers. On the basis of this evidence, it seems fair to conclude that, if superintendents hear largely from supportive constituents, their "representative net" is rather small. As a substitute for public dialogue, private communication is inadequate.

To sum up the proposal development phase of our model: (1) Proposal development is clearly dominated by superintendents; (2) The active role of school boards and members of the public is substantially below that indicated by traditional democratic theory; (3) While superintendents receive sufficient volume of private communications to make a model of "administrative representation" plausible, the quality of those communications does not support a democratic model of administrative representation.

EXECUTIVE RECOMMENDATION

Once a formal proposal has been submitted by one of the actors in a political system, it is usually reviewed by the office of the chief executive. The basic legal mandate of governors, mayors, and school superintendents originates in the administrative oversight function. However, the accepted role of the chief executive has expanded from supervision of decision implementation to include responsibility for screening policy proposals before they come to the legislative body. The importance of executive recommendation has grown along with the increased centralization of technical and information resources in the executive branches of government.

The executive recommendation step consists of interaction between the source of a proposal and the office of the chief executive, deliberation and consideration of the proposal and alternatives, and recommendation of a policy to the legislative body. When proposal development originates within the executive branch—which is the norm in school districts—the interaction consists of negotiation between the executive office and the initiating department. When proposals originate within government but outside the executive branch, with other governments, or with nongovernmental individuals and groups, executive agency personnel are included in executive recommendation deliberations as expert consultants. Whatever the origin of a policy proposal, the goal of the executive recommendation step is to eliminate "bad" proposals and to modify "good" proposals in order to make them relevant, effective, and (perhaps most important) acceptable to all parties.

In educational governance, executive recommendations are expected and honored. Indeed, it appears only reasonable that those who set the agenda should also recommend appropriate policy actions. As is clear from studies of municipal, state, and federal government, the prominence of executive recommendations hardly makes school district governance unique. Our *Responsiveness* study revealed that superintendent preferences are explicit for 66 percent of the votes taken by school boards.

The frequency and importance of executive recommendation stem from a variety of sources. The most important is professional expertise. Although superintendents act as the chief executives of units of government, their basic resource is expertise rather than more traditional political skills, for example, bargaining. It is a curious anomaly in American popular attitudes that while the concept of local lay control of schools is so highly valued, the educational expert is accorded greater deference than perhaps any other professional in public life. As a recent survey concluded, "if the apparent weight of public opinion had its way, school boards would lose much of their present authority."[15] Schools of high quality are universally desired, and the quality of the educational program is thought to be best assured by placing it under the control of an expert.

Superintendents also are called on to make policy recommendations because they will ultimately be charged with implementing decisions. Their opinions are sought not only to tap expertise but also to include consideration of policy execution. This second purpose is extremely important because school boards must, of necessity, grant wide latitude to chief executives in the actual implementation of the programs they pass. Even more so than other legislative bodies, school board members are part-time, amateur, volunteer officials. They have neither the resources nor the time to pass legislation in such detail that administrators can merely follow instructions. Executive review gives superintendents an opportunity to explain how they intend to follow through after the school board acts.

Another reason that superintendents are called upon to make policy recommendations is that they are the only actors who are presumed to be overseeing an integrated program. Others focus on limited spheres. While all assert that the interests of the children come first, administrators, teachers, parents, and other groups enter the policy-making process when their own interests are at stake. The superintendent is expected to weigh conflicting input from segments of the school district and to present a balanced, comprehensive program. School boards rely on the superintendent to present a program that does not contain elements which are mutually exclusive or in conflict, and that is appropriate to the district's financial and personnel resources.

Executive recommendations are also sought from the superintendent because he or she enjoys significant political power in the traditional sense. The superintendent is the single most visible representative of the school system. The average citizen can more readily name his superintendent of schools than his U.S. Congressman, to say nothing of elected school board members. Unlike individual board members, administrators, principals, teachers, or parents, the superintendent's constituency is the entire school district. The mass popular identification of government with its chief executive makes the superintendent the "tribune of the people." Although they are rarely popularly elected, superintendents have a base of popular and elite support which they can use as a resource in the decision-making process.

Contrary to the professional maxim that superintendents should not engage in "politics," superintendents are political actors with political powers. As in other units of government, school district governance involves conflict. For many superintendents, political conflict presents a crucial paradox: when conflict occurs, the technical skills so diligently developed not only are of no value, they are a liability. Trained in an ideology which defines conflict as pathological and consensus as the most legitimate basis for a decision, superintendents may find conflict more painful than other executive officers. A defensive, hostile response to criticism may then generate more intense conflict. Thus, superintendents with doctorate degrees (the most ideologically committed) and little on-the-job experience reported substantially higher levels of decision-making conflict than other superintendents. Those with either less education or more experience (which mediates the negative influence of education) were able to manage conflict with more skill.[16]

In two of the districts we examined for an entire academic year, the superintendent's contract subsequently was not renewed. In neither case was there a public discussion of administrative problems or any appreciable dissent by the board from the superintendent's policy position.[17] The norm of unity, of concealing disputes from public scrutiny, operates to prevent broadening the arena of conflict. Nevertheless, the board, while not publicly challenging the superintendent, simply replaced him.

In such cases, the basic resource of the superintendent—expertise—is not negotiable. Because superintendents rely upon expertise rather than more traditional political skills, when this resource is declared inapplicable, the superintendent's power base is destroyed. It is no surprise that issues not solvable by technical skills, such as busing and school closures made necessary by declining enrollments, are so troublesome to superintendents. As American schools move from an era of expanding resources to one of scarce resources, the essentially political issue of resource distribution will become dominant. School boards will continue to turn to superintendents for recommendations. Superintendents must use both their political and technical resources as the task of conflict management becomes more prominent in school district governance.

LEGISLATIVE ACTION

If proposal development is characterized in terms of agenda setting, executive review should be characterized as agenda refining. Legislative action, then, is the process of making authoritative decisions concerning the items of the policy agenda. We now turn our attention to public school board meetings, for it is here, after superintendent and staff set the agenda and recommend a policy alternative, that formal decisions are made.

The primary function of legislative sessions of school boards is decision making. As Table 2 summarizes, our study of school board meetings found that an average of nearly three-fourths of all discussions are intended to be concluded with some sort of formal decision. As the wide range of proportion of discussions intended for decision indicates, school boards differ in the character of their legislative sessions. Some boards combine decision making and public hearing functions; others conduct separate meetings for public hearings.

Table 2 also shows that school boards successfully reach decisions when they are intended, and that the vast majority of decisions are made by a formal vote.

We have already seen that superintendents and their staff members dominate agenda setting for school board meetings. However, school boards permit and encourage participation from all six of our potential participants during their legislative sessions. Tables 3 through 6 summarize participation at legislative sessions of school boards.

In Table 3 the unit of analysis is the discussion, and the percentages given represent the proportion of discussions in which at least one member of a category of actors made at least one statement. As one would expect, school board members participate to a high degree. Superintendents participate, on the average, in less than half the discussions (it should be noted that the range is from 18 to 71 percent). Central administrative staff participate in 35 percent, and other profes-

TABLE 2   PURPOSE AND RESOLUTION OF
DISCUSSIONS AT SCHOOL BOARD MEETINGS

	MEAN	LOW	HIGH
Decision Intended	74%	47%	97%
Decision Reached When Intended	90	58	99
Decision By Vote	86	72	97

TABLE 3 PARTICIPATION IN DISCUSSIONS AT SCHOOL BOARD MEETINGS

	MEAN	LOW	HIGH
School Board	93%	84%	100%
Superintendent	43	18	71
Central Administrative Staff	35	18	63
Other Professionals	17	11	25
Public	20	6	42
Other Governments	1	0	2

sionals in 17 percent. A member of the "school establishment" participates in virtually every discussion. The "outsiders" are the public and representatives of other governments. They participate, on the average, in one out of five discussions.

Table 4 presents another definition of participation. Here the unit of analysis is the statement and the figures represent the percentage of statements made by each group of actors based on all statements made at school board meetings. Again, a picture of school officials talking among themselves emerges. Less than 10 percent of all statements are made by the public and other government officials.

A low level of public participation is only partially demonstrated by these data. Equally important is what is said. If public participation is visibly policy-laden, then the low aggregate participation may be misleading. To gain an idea of the content of public input, we categorized each communication according to whether the participant made a *demand* (either in favor or in opposition to a proposed policy) or sought *information* about a proposed or existing policy. Demand articulation from non-official sources is a key ingredient in democratic political theory. Political scientists typically assume a model of governance which begins with the articulation of preferences. Hence, the response to such requests is a key variable in evaluating the performance of public bodies.

However, such a model is inappropriate for school governance. Public participation is typically informational; few demands are made, as

TABLE 4 PROPORTION OF STATEMENTS MADE AT SCHOOL BOARD MEETINGS

	MEAN	LOW	HIGH
School Board	60%	47%	74%
Superintendent	12	7	18
Central Administrative Staff	13	7	28
Other Professionals	6	4	9
Public	9	2	16
Other Governments	*	0	1

*Less than one percent.

TABLE 5   TYPES OF STATEMENTS MADE AT SCHOOL BOARD MEETINGS

	DEMAND FAVOR	DEMAND OPPOSED	REQUEST INFO	SUPPLY INFO
Superintendent	15%	2%	7%	75%
School Board Member	25	4	30	45
Staff Official	11	1	3	85
Line Official	11	2	2	85
Public	17	11	13	58
Government Official	8	6	2	84

indicated by Table 5. Clearly, public meetings are not an occasion for demand articulation and response. By monitoring "public" discussion (such as letters to the editor, television coverage, etc.), we were able to chart the policy preferences of active citizens. Such demands do exist, and they rise and fall with the level of controversy. They are not, however, visible at public meetings. Indeed, as the level of controversy increased, the agenda and discussions of boards became even more heavily laden with routine matters. The norm of unity prevails.

On the other hand, private communications are substantially more policy-laden. More than half of such communications are classified as demands. Yet, since such communications normally occur after agenda setting and are supportive of the course of action intended by the administration, they are an inadequate substitution for a genuine public dialogue.

After the agenda has been set and discussion completed, some sort of decision is in order. Table 6 examines who makes formal policy proposals considered by the school board. This is different from the question of agenda setting because the person who initiates discussion may or may not make a policy proposal. We define a proposer as the first person who articulates a proposal which is decided upon—favorably or negatively—by the school board. Although most boards require that a formal motion be made by a school board member, our definition is less

TABLE 6   POLICY PROPOSALS MADE AT SCHOOL BOARD MEETINGS

	MEAN	LOW	HIGH
School Board	65%	25%	97%
Superintendents	26	1	69
Central Administrative Staff	6	*	23
Other Professionals	1	0	6
Public	2	0	9
Other Governments	*	0	1

*Less than one percent.

restrictive. All six categories of participants are potential policy proposers.

School board decision making is even more insulated from the public by this measure of participation. Persons outside the school district establishment account for an average of less than 3 percent of policy proposals. In no district do outsiders make as many as 10 percent of proposals. Generally speaking, two-thirds of policy proposals are originally articulated by school board members and the other one-third by the superintendent and his staff. Clearly, by design or chance, the public is insulated from direct participation in decision making at the legislative action step.

Our *Governing* study indicated that, with exceptions, the superintendent had his way. That is, opposition by the board to the recommendations of the administration was reported in a minority of districts. Further, such opposition was likely to be unsuccessful. However, these findings were based on the responses of school board members, rather than those of the superintendent. Board members were asked to estimate the probability of the superintendent eventually achieving his policy alternative in the face of board opposition.[18] Here we encounter the same problem as was observed with agenda setting. That is, if a superintendent estimated the probability of success as low, would he not avoid a confrontation? Boyd is a conspicuous advocate of this position.[19] If this notion is correct, then the superintendent's estimate of victory in the face of opposition should be lower than the board's. However, when asked a question identical to the one asked the board, superintendents gave more optimistic estimates. Fifty-four percent of the board sample believed that the superintendent would "win" against board opposition, compared with 79 percent of the superintendents.[20] We suspected, then, that the "anticipated response" sanction was exaggerated. If superintendents were confident they could win, why should they be cautious?

However, in view of the fact that by matching board and superintendent responses by district we discovered substantial variance in percentages, the question was pursued by recording the roll-call votes of the school board in our longitudinal *(Responsiveness)* study. As Table 7 shows, the superintendent was either asked for or volunteered a pol-

TABLE 7 VOTING DECISIONS AT SCHOOL BOARD MEETINGS

	MEAN	LOW	HIGH
Decisions Made By Voting	86%	72%	97%
Unanimous Votes	85	62	99
Superintendent Position Known	66	5	89
Superintendent Position Adopted	99	95	100

icy recommendation for two of every three voting decisions. In some districts, the superintendent was substantially less active in recommending policy than in others. Indeed, one indicator of community conflict is the policy-passive behavior of the superintendent. Nevertheless, the norm is for the superintendent to make a recommendation. Table 7 also shows that adoption of superintendent recommendations, usually unanimously, is also the norm.

School boards react to their superintendents, much in the manner of Congress reacting to the initiative of the "chief legislator," the President. The basic resource of the board is its representative capacity, yet few boards have been able to escape superintendent domination. The superintendent's professional expertise and control of information resources are major factors, yet a more fundamental factor is the board's image of its role. As Dykes says, "What the school board does depends in large measure on the board's view of itself in relation to its responsibilities."[21]

A majority of American school board members perceive their role as being consistent with the values of professional educators. Lipham and his colleagues found that 90 percent of all school board members thought that they should not speak for segments of the community; yet slightly over one-fourth of the citizens thought this was a good idea.[22] Our *Governing* study supported this view. Rather than serving as a conduit to channel popular views to administrators, boards define their job as "selling" the administration's program to segments of the community. School boards fail to assert their representative function partly because they find it difficult to do so, and partly because they choose not to do so.

SUPPLEMENTARY CHANGE AND IMPLEMENTATION

The next two stages in the governance process are substantially less public than the preceding stages. The legislative action step produces a formal document which is an order from the school board to school district employees. Only a small proportion of these orders are meant to be implemented immediately. There is typically a lag time between legislative action and implementation. For example, because of the academic calendar, curriculum decisions made in May will not take effect for months.

The rationale for this delay between legislative action and implementation is threefold. First, it gives time for the development of implementation procedures by school district administrators. Second, it provides for a transition period between old and new programs during which time affected parties can be informed of changes. Third, it provides a final opportunity for minor adjustment, major change, or even revocation prior to implementation.

The *supplementary change* step involves changes made by the school board after legislative action and before implementation. However, supplementary change in school districts is rare. A major reason why decisions are rarely returned to the school board agenda is that superintendents, unlike governors or mayors, do not have the right to veto legislative decisions. The legal position of the superintendent would make such authority impossible. Again, too, the reality of the distribution of influence between board and superintendent makes a veto power absurd, since virtually all board policies are proposed by the superintendent. What reason for a veto could exist? Consequently, in school governance, changes in policy before implementation tend, more than in other governance situations, to be incremental and technical, involving at most a few central office staff and perhaps participation by affected teachers and principals.

In rare cases of particularly conflictual decisions, pressures from external sources may achieve reconsideration, but such examples—although they create the illusion of widespread conflict—are not part of the normal routine of governance. More typically, supplementary change decisions enhance the domination of the superintendent over the school board. A recurring example is school boards acquiescing to administration proposals to transfer funds in the course of a fiscal year. The entire budget, the district's "master plan," has been debated and resolved months before. The superintendent requests additional funds for favored programs late in the fiscal year when the alternative to increased funding is program cutback or elimination. By changing routine decisions to "crisis" decisions, superintendents can use the supplementary change step to reverse earlier adverse decisions or increase the probability of "victory" over the school board.

Implementation, an activity of low visibility limited to school district employees, is similarly dominated by professionals. Indeed, it is at the implementation phase of governance that linkages between policy intent and policy achievement can be most easily modified by professional hostility. The most apt example is the "new militancy" of teachers. Typically, teachers' organizations have virtually no influence upon educational policy. Compared to other professions, teachers have been less politically active and more reluctant to challenge the authority of superiors. However, even during their passive period, teachers shaped the educational process within the classroom, the level at which most constituent satisfaction or dissatisfaction could be expected.

As employees of the district, teachers were expected to implement district policy. In fact, they were free to implement or not, unless their noncompliance was so flagrant as to call it to the attention of administrative superiors. Organizationally impotent, teachers enjoyed substantial autonomy in the delivery of educational services to the client. This is not to say that they were not, if the occasion arose, subservient to administrators. Indeed, most teachers believed that administration, either at the building or central office level, was more capable of making pedagogical decisions than they were. However, as districts increased in size, because of both growth and consolidation, administrative supervision became more difficult.

This same increase in complexity also created an administrative bureaucracy which, in turn, created a plethora of regulations teachers were, at least nominally, expected to follow. Guthrie points out, "As school systems grew and came under the dominance of expert managers, teachers lost their ability to communicate freely with their employers, school trustees, or even with the superintendent and his staff."[23] Alienation from work, as a consequence of bureaucratic expansion, contributed to the growth of teacher unions and led to increased systematic teacher involvement in the policy proposal phase of governance.

Money is the primary issue when teachers bargain collectively. However, written agreements, which now govern more than half of the nation's public school teachers, also frequently specify working conditions.[24] Both of these "bread and butter" items, which have quite properly been regarded as belonging to the implementation phase, have obvious policy implications. Money impacts on policy formation, even if teachers are not (and they typically are not) involved in districtwide budget making. Additionally, working conditions may be linked, at least indirectly, to policy implementation. Thus, for instance, some contracts include under working conditions the controversial topic of teacher evaluation. Finally, a growing number of contracts are overtly policy-oriented. For instance, contracts increasingly provide for teacher representation on groups that set curricular policy, select textbooks, and recommend educational programs.

It seems likely that overtly policy-linked items will increase in their negotiability. Corwin, for instance, has concluded that a desire for more influence over school policy and disagreement with central-level decision making seem to account for most of the dissatisfaction underlying increased teacher militancy.[25] The more demands for influence are granted, the greater will be the escalation of such demands. Ultimately, the entire policy-proposal phase could be encompassed in the bargaining between the teacher organization and a professional bargainer representing the board and administration.

Such a development would not radically alter the distribution of influence between board and superintendent, but it would substantially reduce the now dominant policy-proposal function of the administration. Pierce, for example, argues that while the demand for lay participation did little to break administrators' control over schools, collective bargaining did quite a lot.

"It was not until teachers began to organize and use collective bargaining to gain more control over educational policy that the monopoly of the school administration began to crumble."[26] An important point is that collective bargaining not only threatens administrative dominance, it also reduces even further whatever policy initiation remains with school boards.

Although, as we have noted, collective bargaining agreements are laden with policy, they are normally regarded as personnel negotiations and thus conducted privately. Public disclosure of bargaining positions or strategies is an unfair labor practice. Hence, not only is public scrutiny impossible, the board and superintendent find it necessary to hire a negotiator. Neither administration nor board members can follow the proceedings. Both may lose control of policy under such circumstances, allowing policy-proposal functions to be assumed by people without any vestige of public accountability.

Although collective bargaining obviously is a major problem for school districts, it is a problem so concealed from public or board scrutiny that no accountability is feasible. In our study of eleven school districts, we searched in vain for any discussion of collective bargaining at board or administrative cabinet meetings. When administrators assumed control of policy, there was at least the possibility of a board veto, although it rarely occurred. Now, even such weak constraints are removed. The distinction between policy and implementation, already blurred because "administrative implementors" make policy, is further blurred because "delivery agents" are acquiring policy responsibilities. Thus, the chain of accountability is further weakened.

REVIEW

The final step in the policy-making process is review and evaluation of past decisions and programs. Of necessity, review must follow implementation. But as we shall see, the review process is continuous and, for some actors, is concurrent with other steps in the policy-making process. Internal review is undertaken by school board members and district employees. External review involves participation by those outside the governmental unit.

There are two major types of internal review: executive review and legislative review. Most executive review occurs within the context of the executive recommendation step, with participation limited to school district administrators. This process is personified in most large districts by an administrator in charge of research and evaluation. There is also an ongoing process of executive review in the context of policy implementation management. On the micro level, principals review the performance of teachers. On the macro level, superintendents meet with their cabinets to assess districtwide programs.

Evaluation involves comparing actual performance with an expected performance or goal. The summary goal of public schools is to educate children. There are, however, a number of indicators of success: enrollments, promotions, test scores, student-teacher ratios, etc., and another set of indicators relating benefits to costs. Furthermore, many evaluation indicators are technical or extremely detailed and therefore difficult for the untrained and uninitiated to interpret.

Legislative review occurs within the context of the legislative action step. Because school board members are part-time, amateur, and volunteer, they have neither the time nor the expertise to carry on an effective review and evaluation program. The time lag between legislative authorization and implementation and assessment can be several years—and several school boards—which further impedes the effectiveness of legislative review in school districts.

State legislatures are increasingly turning to outside experts to help them review and evaluate programs. There does not seem to be a parallel trend in school districts. School boards do not have staff research support and have not secured experts independent of executive employees to aid them in the review process. School boards have relied on their own limited expertise and the expertise of lay members of the public who attend meetings and contact them in private. As a result, legislative review is weak in school districts.

External review of school district policies involves actors from other governments. As we have seen, participation of representatives of other governments is extremely rare. However, as the popular and professional administrative literature attests, this participation is extremely important when it does occur. Although external review can come from the executive and judicial branches of state and federal government, judicial review is presently of greater concern to school districts.

Ironically, judicial review is, in a sense, much less isolated from the general public than are the steps in the policy-making process which occur entirely within the school district. The courts are always responsive to the extent that suits are either accepted for consideration or rejected, and those accepted are subject to decision. The courts cannot table, bury in committee, ignore, or otherwise avoid the matters they accept for consideration. While gaining a place on the judicial agenda may be difficult, those who do so are assured that some action will be taken.

The well-known result is that minority groups, whose limited access and influence in the local school district reduce incentive to work at that level of government, have requested the intervention of state and federal authorities on their behalf. Certainly the issue of equality of educational opportunity looms large in the review process. Both the maze of litigation surrounding federally mandated busing and the litigation involving finance reflect this concern. The defense in such cases usually invokes the principle of local control as a justification for not achieving equal educational opportunity. Indeed, local control has even achieved statutory legitimacy. Title IV of the Elementary and Secondary Education Act states, "The school. . . . is most effective when the school involves the people of that community in a program designed to fulfill their education needs." But, to date, the principle of equality of opportunity has taken precedence over that of local control. Local options have given way to standardized procedures and programs enforced by the courts.

One conspicuous public debate involves the *Serano* and *Rodrigues* decisions. The impact of *Serano* was widely viewed as threatening local control, while *Rodrigues* was viewed as restoring local control. In fact, the former interpretation is more accurate. Federal courts are certainly likely to avoid school finance issues since *Rodrigues,* but state courts are not. Additionally, the impact of both decisions is likely to shift the burden of financial reform to the state legislature which can expect its remedies to be subject to judicial review. Thus, continued litigation concerning educational equality will have the effect of removing the local board (and even the superintendent) from the policy process.

The thrust of legal challenges, whether financial or with regard to racial imbalance, is against local participation. Since the largest source of school revenue is local property taxes, wealthy districts can spend more than poor districts. Thus, equality of financial resources for education can only be achieved by statewide distribution programs. Further, since there is substantial variation in the wealth of states, the goal of equality may ultimately require a national system of school finance. As state and federal governments assume more control over financing education, opportunity for local populations to influence educational policy by voting for or against budgets will diminish, as will the opportunity for local admnistrators to set budgetary priorities.

The courts seem to be moving toward an unrealistic separation of policy making and spending. The two clearly cannot be separated. Further, there is a spill-over effect from increased litigation. Administrators, finding their districts involved in litigation, can seek judicial remedies for board actions viewed as unreasonable. Thus, cases of superintendents successfully challenging board decisions not to renew their contracts and lower-level administrators challenging similar decisions (especially those regarding reassignment) are becoming more prevalent. The upshot is that judicial review weakens the policy-making authority of all officials at the local level. Additionally, minority groups, who correctly perceive more access to nonlocal decision arenas, use external review to augment their influence. Such augmentation, achieved at the expense of local officials, further insures their insulation.

CONCLUDING REMARKS

We have used a six-step model of school district governance to examine the role of six potential types of participants in the policy-making process. Different actors are eligible to participate at different steps; and the process is least insulated, in theory, from those outside the school district establishment at the proposal development and legislative action steps. However, few outsiders do participate directly. Furthermore, at each step in the policy-making process, administrators—especially superintendents—dominate school board members. Empirical data support neither a traditional model of governance from democratic theory, nor a democratic model of administrative representation. The answer to the question, "Who governs public schools?" is "Superintendents and their professional staffs."

Such a conclusion is, certainly, not without exceptions. Superintendents have to manage conflict, and some fail. Hence, superintendent turnover is a topic attracting increasing attention. Still, the fact that superintendents can be (and are) removed does not negate our argument. Indeed, the mere fact that the only solution to superintendent dominance is removal is testimony to our argument. The belief that boards should either support or remove superintendents poses extreme alternatives for boards and makes a "normal" bargaining process even more difficult. We estimate that superintendents spend less than four hours per week in private communications with boards, hardly indicative of a sustained process of negotiation and compromise.

More effective challenges to administrative dominance are likely to come from efficiently organized teachers and, especially, from forces originating from outside the local district. Such challenges, however, serve only to exacerbate the insulation of educational policy making from community politics.

NOTES

1. See William Boyd, "The Public, The Professionals, and Educational Policy-Making: Who Governs?" *Teachers College Record,* vol. 77, no. 4, pp. 539–577, May 1976; and Paul E. Peterson, "The Politics of American Education," in Fred N. Kerlinger (ed.), *Review of Education,* F. E. Peacock Publishers, Inc., Itasca, Ill., 1974, for excellent reviews of the literature.

2. Both the Boyd and Peterson papers, for example, challenge the notion of insulation as advanced in L. Harmon Zeigler and M. Kent Jennings, with the assistance of G. Wayne Peak, *Governing American Schools,* Duxbury Press, North Scituate, Mass., 1974.

3. Ibid. The reader is referred to that volume for a detailed account of the research design and data collection procedures. Other reports from the *Governing American Schools* study include: L. Harmon Zeigler and M. Kent Jennings, "Response Styles and Politics: The Case of the School Boards," *Midwest Journal of Political Science,* vol. 15, no. 2, pp. 290–321, May 1971; L. Harmon Zeigler and M. Kent Jennings, "Interest Representation in School Governance," *Urban Affairs Annual Review,* 1972; L. Harmon Zeigler and Michael O. Boss, "Racial Conflict in American Public Education," *Sociology of Education,* vol. 47, no. 3, pp. 319–36, June 1974; L. Harmon Zeigler, "The Decision-Making Culture of American Public Education," *Political Science Annual,* vol. 5, Bobbs-Merrill, 1974; L. Harmon Zeigler and Michael O. Boss, "Pressure Groups and Public Policy: The Case of Education," in Robert N. Spadaro, Thomas R. Dye, Robert T. Golembiewski, Murray S. Stedman, and L. Harmon Zeigler, *The Policy Vacuum,* D. C. Heath and Co., Lexington, Mass., 1975; L. Harmon Zeigler, "School Board Research: The Problems and the Prospects," in Peter J. Cistone (ed.), *Understanding School Boards,* D. C. Heath and Co., Lexington, Mass., 1975; L. Harmon Zeigler, Michael O. Boss, Harvey J. Tucker and L. A. Wilson, II, "Professionalism, Community Structure, and Decision-Making School Superintendents and Interest Groups," *Policy Studies Journal,* vol. 4, no. 4, pp. 351–62, Summer, 1976; and L. Harmon Zeigler and Michael Boss, "Experts and Representatives: Comparative Bases of Influence in Educational Policy-Making," *Western Politics Quarterly,* vol. 30, no. 2, pp. 255–63, June 1977. The basic data files and accompanying codebook for this study are available through the Inter-University Consortium for Political Research, the University of Michigan, Ann Arbor.

4. For a report of the findings see Harvey J. Tucker and L. Harmon Zeigler, *Professional Versus the Public: Attitudes, Communication, and Response in Local School Districts,* Longman, Inc., New York, 1980.

5. There are, of course, other definitions of responsiveness. Our definition assumes that responsiveness is best understood as a reaction to expressed demands. Others, however, define responsiveness as the degree of congruence between policy and community expectations, whether articulated or not. For a discussion of the merits and pitfalls of various definitions, see L.

Harmon Zeigler and Harvey J. Tucker, *The Quest for Responsive Government,* Duxbury Press, North Scituate, Mass., 1978.

6. E. E. Schattschneider, *The Semi-Sovereign People,* Holt, New York, 1960, p. 68.

7. This analogy is suggested in Roger W. Cobb and Charles D. Elder, *Participation in Politics: The Dynamics of Agenda-Building,* The Johns Hopkins University Press, Baltimore and London, 1972.

8. These findings should not necessarily obscure some of the more subtle aspects of agenda setting. In some districts the superintendent shared agenda-setting responsibility with the central office staff. In other districts the agenda is established for the board by the superintendent, yet established for him by his central office staff. Our observations of administrative cabinet meetings uncovered districts in which the superintendent routinely accepted the agenda of his staff. In such cases the superintendent, who appeared publicly as the "expert," was himself deferring to other nominally subordinate experts. In these cases, where the superintendent, in effect, represents the agenda priorities of the staff to the board, the lines of authority and accountability are most blurred.

9. Boyd, op. cit., p. 31.

10. Some of these data were reported in Zeigler and Jennings with Peak, *Governing American Schools,* op. cit. A more extensive analysis was undertaken by Michael O. Boss who tragically died before his manuscript was complete. These remarks are drawn from Boss's incomplete notes.

11. This analysis is taken from Boss's notes. It was found that the more a district spends (as indicated by per-pupil expenditures), the higher the salience of curriculum issues to the public. Further, the salience of curriculum issues among the public seems more volatile than with decision makers. Hence, the correlation between per-pupil expenditures and citing of curriculum problems is higher (.41) with the public than with the board (.24) and superintendent (.11). In suburban schools, fully 77 percent of the public cites curriculum problems, a percentage which exceeds that of the board and administration. Thus, although the education program is of low salience, it need not be so.

12. See, for example, Dale Mann, *The Politics of Administrative Representation,* D. C. Heath and Co., Lexington, Mass., 1976.

13. See M. Kent Jennings, "Patterns of School Board Responsiveness," in Cistone (ed.), op. cit., pp. 246–249 for an explanation of this idea.

14. Zeigler and Jennings with Peak, *Governing American Schools,* op. cit., pp. 95–105 discussed the dominance of supportive groups in the communication pattern of school boards. Boss found superintendents to be even less diverse.

15. National School Boards Association, *The People Look at Their School Boards,* Research Report 1975-1, p. 31.

16. The idea of a defensive response is developed in Robert L. Crain, *The Politics of School Desegregation,* Aldine Publishing Co., Chicago, 1968, pp. 115–124. The data about superintendents, education, and conflict management skills are found in Zeigler, Boss, Tucker, and Wilson, op. cit., p. 360.

17. As a district becomes embroiled in such a controversy, public discussion diminishes but private discussion is enhanced. The conflict management skills of the superintendent are not displayed publicly. Only his failure becomes a public information after the fact.

18. Zeigler and Jennings with Peak, *Governing American Schools,* op. cit., p. 164.

19. Boyd, op. cit., p. 31.

20. These data are explained in Boss's unpublished notes.

21. Archie Dykes, *School Board and Superintendent: Their Effective Working Relationships,* Interstate Printers and Publishers, Danville, Ill., 1964, pp. 132–133.

22. James M. Lipham, Russell T. Gregg, and Richard A. Rossmiller, "The School Board as an Agency for Resolving Conflict," Educational Resources Information Center, Bethesda, Md., 1967.

23. James W. Guthrie, "Public Control of Schools: Can We Get It Back?" *Public Affairs Report,* Vol. 15, p. 3, June 1974.

24. National School Boards Association, *The Impact of Collective Bargaining on Curriculum & Instruction,* Research Report 1975-2, p. 6.

25. Ronald G. Corwin, "The Organizational Context of School Board-Teacher Conflict," in Cistone (ed.), op. cit., pp. 31–158.

26. Lawrence C. Pierce, "Teachers' Organizations and Bargaining: Power Imbalance in the Public Sphere," in National Committee for Citizens in Education, *Public Testimony on Public Schools,* McCutchan Publishing Corp., Berkeley, 1975, p. 124.

3

DEBUREAUCRA-TIZING PUBLIC EDUCATION:
The Experience of New York and Boston

DAVID SEELEY
Public Education Association of New York

ROBERT SCHWARTZ
Office of the Mayor, Boston*

*Currently Assistant Director for Program on Law and Public Management, National Institute of Education, Washington, D.C.

Americans familiar with urban education in recent years can quickly match key words with New York and Boston. For New York the word is "community control." For Boston it is "desegregation." At the height of the upheavals in the two cities over these issues, the press dutifully recorded the daily comings and goings of Rhody McCoy, Albert Shanker, Louise Day Hicks, and Judge Garrity. Ocean Hill-Brownsville and South Boston High became household words. Historians have begun to chronicle the battles fought, won, and lost.

While community control and desegregation are often seen as opposing movements in minority communities—the one separatist and the other integrationist—they are actually part of the same civil rights movement: the effort to eliminate the caste system or second-class citizenship for minorities and to allow them to enjoy the same rights and privileges as other Americans. The community control movement concerns the right to have some say over the education of their children, and desegregation focuses on the right to have their children go to school without the continuing badge of discrimination and segregation.

However, the battles in both cities were also part of another longer-term issue: the effort to debureaucratize the schools. This is a struggle which may be only in its early stages and may go on for some years before history will be able to judge its success or failure. It is an important issue in its own right, independent of its entanglement with racial politics in New York, Boston, and other major cities. To understand the issue of debureaucratizing the schools, one must look at what has been happening to American public education in the perspective of a longer span of history and in terms of the fundamental structure of urban school systems. Only then can one look beneath the surface and realize that while one city seemingly had a racial battle over community control and the other a racial battle over desegregation, in both cities the racial issues were played out within a related process of reformulating basic educational and organizational structure.

THE PROBLEMS OF BUREAUCRATIZATION

American public schools, which began as one of the most democratic of institutions and virtual extensions of grassroots communities, are now widely criticized as unresponsive and in some cases even "oppressive" to their clients. There is growing recognition that a major reason for this increasing alienation of schools from their communities is their organizational structure: the professionalized government bureaucracy. However valid a bureaucracy may be for organizing an army or a factory, there is serious doubt as to its suitability for organizing education—at least in our society.

UNRESPONSIVENESS

School bureaucracies are considered "unresponsive" for two reasons: they are unresponsive to changes in the society because they are too rigid and inflexible, and they are unresponsive to the clients of the schools because bureaucratic officials tend to give their first loyalty to the "system" rather than to the individual client.

Bureaucratic rigidity is an age-old problem observed by Max Weber and all students of bureaucracy from the time they were first studied. The inflexibility of bureaucracies is but the negative aspect of one of bureaucracy's strengths. What enables an army or a factory to organize large masses of people and resources to accomplish organizational goals is the rational ordering of behavior according to fixed rules, procedures, timetables, job descriptions, hierarchical authority, etc.—in other words all the basic elements of a bureaucratic system. These produce work habits, expectations, and internal rewards that are the source of both efficiency in carrying out a prescribed pattern of activity and inflexibility in changing it.

Unresponsiveness to clients is partly the result of this inherent inflexibility. If the efficiency of the system is derived from following fixed rules and procedures, one can say that the system is *designed* to be unresponsive. But unresponsiveness to clients involves another element as well. School bureaucracies are supposedly governed by boards of education, which as representatives of the clients of the system presumably should be able to demand responsiveness at least to themselves. But, as Zeigler and Tucker pointed out in the previous chapter, all the evidence shows that school bureaucracies tend to run school boards rather than the other way around. In terms of de facto power, the part-time lay board members are no match for the officials of the bureaucracy, who have more expertise, longer tenure, and full-time involvement in their work. In short, once we have set up bureaucracies, even if presumably under democratic control from the top, it is unrealistic to expect much responsiveness to forces from the outside.

DISRESPECT FOR MINORITIES

In addition to their unresponsiveness, school bureaucracies have also come under attack in recent years for their failure to recognize democratic pluralism. Again, this is but a negative aspect of what used to be seen as a virtue of our public school system when its mission was to "Americanize" a nation of immigrants. When assimilation was the goal, the bureaucratic ideal of "treating everyone the same" was functional. Now there is a concern for respecting and preserving a diversity of cultural backgrounds, and the abstract-rational value base of the bureaucracy finds itself at odds with these new purposes.

The contradiction goes deeper than just the conflict over ethnic heritage. The movement for the past several decades has been toward greater respect for "individual differences" of all kinds: different learning styles, different rates of development, handicapping conditions, the "gifted," etc. Research is beginning to reveal the violence that is done not only to the value system but to the academic development of children of varied backgrounds who are "processed" by a supposedly "value neutral" school bureaucracy that is often rife with covert ethnic, class, religious, and philosophical biases. If one of the prime values of bureaucracy is uniformity—and indeed it is one of its strengths—then there is an inherent contradiction between the bureaucratic model of organization and real respect for individual and diverse cultural, social, and value orientations.

ANTI-EDUCATIONAL

The problems of our present school bureaucracies might be forgiven if they were effective in their mission of education. But there is increasing evidence that the bureaucratic organizational model, as it has developed over time, works against educational quality and effectiveness. It is not hard to see why since it denigrates the two key people in the educational process—the teacher and the learner.

Bureaucracy and professionalism are like oil and water; they don't mix. One is based on hierarchical authority, the other on the authority of expertise. One emphasizes the ability of supervisors to control the behavior of subordinates, the other emphasizes individual responsibility to carry out a professional mission. In bureaucracy the teacher is at the "bottom" of the system, whereas in educational terms the teacher should be the heart of the process.

By the nature of a bureaucracy, control from above is exercised through policies and rules, and for practical reasons these have to be easily enforceable. A teacher can teach best, however, not by following rules but by interacting intelligently and creatively with a group of students. The result of bureaucracy at its silliest is the system which cares more whether teachers have their shades drawn to the prescribed level than whether children are learning. And the same forces that produce such ludicrous examples operate pervasively to deaden the ability of teachers to teach.

It is not that bureaucracies cannot use professional workers effectively under certain circumstances. General Motors can hire engineers and lawyers and put them to work productively to assist the business of making cars and money. When the goals are clear and accountability strong, professional skills can often be combined with a bureaucratic organization to good effect. But in our large school bureaucracies we seem to have the worst of both worlds. Teachers and principals proclaim their professionalism in order to avoid accountability from above, but then they act as "employees" who need do only what they are told. Unfortunately, they are seldom told anything clear and concise about their most important work—teaching children—and they probably can't or shouldn't be.

The downgrading of the teacher in the bureaucratic hierachy is bad enough. The student is in even worse shape: children are not seen as part of the educational system at all. Instead, the student is the "client" of the system—the person "served" by the system—or sometimes the "target" of the educational program.

This may seem rational enough, if the system is a hierarchically organized group of employees, each with a specific job to do, each trained and supervised to do that job, and controlled by a set of rules and policies that are a condition of employment. The students, their families, and the community are quite naturally seen as "outside" such a system. Students are, after all, unpredictable and varied and not subject to the disciplines of employment, and their families and communities are even further outside the "span of control" of the bureaucratic order.

The trouble is that such concepts work against the fundamental spirit of the educational process. Students are the most important "producers" in education; they have to do most of the work in producing learning. They must be perceived as an integral part of the process, not as the "targets" of the process. Everyone else in the educational system—teachers, principals, counselors, librarians—are best thought of as facilitators of student learning. Children are not like raw material that needs processing, that can be stacked and sorted and efficiently dealt with by a mechanical bureacracy. Education is a matter of growth and development of complex individuals, who not only vary from one another but from one minute to the next.

Albert Hirschman has pointed out that organizations often fail to make sufficient use of "resources and abilities that are hidden, scattered, or badly utilized."[1] The greatest "hidden resource" in schools is students themselves, who, if they are seen as outside the system—even a well-intentioned system—are less likely to be engaged in helping to produce their own learning. Frank Reissman has urged that we shift from a compensatory model to a "strength" model in urban education.[2] But the bureaucratic organizational conception is not comfortable dealing with the "strength" of those it is "serving," since this strength is outside its control mechanisms. It is more comfortable conceiving of students as passive and inert, available for its ministrations.

Not only do bureaucratic educational systems like those in New York and Boston (and many other places) tend to underutilize or misuse teaching and learning resources, but their natural reactions to ineffective education often make matters worse. When parents complain of poor education and demand "accountability" from the system, there is a tendency to increase bureaucratic control from the top, which may well cause further misuse and abuse of teachers and learners and thus produce even worse educational results. There is a tendency to add more administrators, supervisors, and central office staff, which not only diverts available resources from the classroom but may increase interference with the teaching-learning process. One study, for instance, shows that the higher the proportion of administrators to teachers, the lower the academic achievement.[3]

All in all, the bureaucratic system of organization is a monstrosity from an educational point of view. It oppresses teachers and administrators as well as students. As James Shields puts it, there is something inherent in the nature and ethos of bureaucratic organizations as they have evolved in America that causes them to "sanitize" and thereby impoverish the lives of people they touch.[4]

EDUCATIONAL BUREAUCRACIES TODAY

It can be said that the first country school that developed beyond a single classroom was to some extent a "bureaucracy" and that our local school "bureaucracies" have served us tolerably well for many decades. Why all of a sudden in the 1960s was there such a fuss about bureaucracy?

It is important to realize that public school systems today are substantially different from those of a hundred years ago. School systems are much bigger and more centralized. The number of school districts has been reduced from over 100,000 to about 15,000 over the past thirty years. This means that only about one-eighth as many people are involved in school board decision making, and they are trying to make decisions for ever larger systems. Education has become far more complex; those who run a school system need to know about law, finance, measurement, curriculum, collective bargaining, etc. The school bureaucracies have become far more professionalized and entrenched, and their professional employees have their own politically powerful unions and ties to national organizations. Additional bureaucracies have proliferated at the state and federal level, and complex relationships with interlocking rules, regulations, and responsibilities have developed between the different layers of educational bureaucracy. The upshot of these changes is that whereas school systems a hundred years ago were to a large extent instruments for *carrying out* community will, they are increasingly becoming instruments for *closing out* community will. Even many smaller systems, which need not have gone this way, have adopted bureaucratic organizations emulating the large city systems, the models for "modern" school management.

The kind of bureaucratic school organization that developed over the past hundred years may have been functional in accomplishing some of society's goals during that period: greatly expanding the number of schools, systematizing a national education program, assimilating millions of immigrants, and creating a more unified nation. However, there is no need to belittle the past accomplishments of American education in order to conclude that the organizational structure that developed through this period of growth is not suitable for many of the tasks of the years to come: increasing the quality of education, bringing into the educational process at ever higher levels large segments of the population which have been given little more than basic literacy in our present school systems (and sometimes not even that), recognizing and respecting the values of individuals and individual subcultures, and reintegrating the experiences of the school with the broad array of potential learning experiences outside the school, such as the media, employment, cultural institutions, volunteer work, learning within the family, and so on.

It is ironic that cities like New York and Boston found themselves confronted with such unresponsive, inflexible, and politically unaccountable school organizations at the very time they were also confronted with an array of important public policy issues in education: Who should be taught what? How will it be financed? How should school programs be adjusted to take account of changes in the family, the media explosion, changes in life style and community values, changes in work and the economy, changes in social class and caste, the shrinking of the world community? Just as the body politic in the nineteenth century shaped a public school system to meet the perceived needs of the day, so the body politic now must reshape public education systems to meet the projected needs of the coming decades. Our present school organizations, which were to some extent purposely constructed to close out political influences, obstruct rather than facilitate this reshaping process.

Since the 1960s there has been a great increase in the number of citizen advisory committees at all levels of the educational system to try to respond to this need for increased public involvement. In addition to these consultative bodies, which serve as adjuncts to the present school decision-making structure, reforms were started in the 1960s which attempted to change the basic structure itself. These reforms, variously labeled "decentralization," "community control," or "shared power," are now widely proclaimed as "failures," especially by spokesmen of the educational establishment. But a fair reading would have to conclude that they were "failures" not in the sense that they were tried and found wanting but that *efforts to try them failed.* They failed, in part, because many people saw them primarily as civil rights or race issues rather than as part of an effort to deal with the important issue of debureaucratizing the schools.

Let us look at the experience of the two cities of New York and Boston where attempts were made to change the structure of the school system and see what lessons they may have for the future in dealing with the problems of school bureaucracy.

THE NEW YORK EXPERIENCE

In the early 1960s, the deterioration of the public schools in New York City reached alarming proportions. Three political forces—liberalism, civil rights, and unionism—helped shape the response in terms of decentralization and community control. There were three areas of the city where schools were especially ineffective and parents most angry about it. Here, in the summer of 1967, under the prodding of Mayor Lindsay and civil rights forces, the school system established the three famous experimental decentralized districts: I.S. 201 in East Harlem, Ocean Hill-Brownsville in Brooklyn, and the Two Bridges in the Lower East Side. Simultaneously Mayor Lindsay, legislative leaders, and State Education Commissioner James Allen pressed for legislation that would decentralize the entire school system. The push and shove over these proposals included agonizing battles in three successive legislatures, one of the longest and most bitter teacher strikes in history, the rending asunder of the civil rights coalition, attacks on foundations in general and the Ford Foundation in particular for its funding of the demonstration districts and the involvement of its President, McGeorge Bundy, as head of the Mayor's decentralization panel (which produced The Bundy Report: *Reconnection for Learning*), and finally a watered-down decentralization law in 1969. Throughout the debates, however, the agenda remained decentralization and community control.

There was a movement in the black community that might have led in a different direction. Some parent and community groups, convinced that the public schools were not serving their children, set up alternative schools with private funds, creating pressure to finance these efforts with public funds. A landmark court decision might have provided the legal framework for such a policy. A 1958 New York case, *In re Skipwith*, held that the compulsory school attendance law could not compel parents to send their children to inferior ghetto schools where they would be subjected to substandard education and discrimination. It can be argued that it is not enough merely to allow dissatisfied parents in these circumstances to keep their children out of school, but that the state has an obligation to pay for a nondiscriminatory alternative. Such a solution, while logical and desirable from the point of view of disaffected parents and educators, would clearly have created a radical change in the basic structure of public education.

Any potential movement in the direction of public support for alternative community schools came to naught, however. The liberal faith in the *idea* of public schools, if not in their current performance, and the strong opposition to any kind of public subsidy for private schools were such that political realists in the 1960s never gave serious thought to nongovernmental alternatives as a way to deal with the educational crisis. Efforts instead took the direction of trying to make the public school system more politically accountable to parents and the public through decentralization and community control. This proposal was more consistent with the values of liberalism, civil rights, and unionism. Yet, strong crosscurrents within and between these political values shaped the community control movement and in the end very nearly destroyed it.

Liberalism was certainly comfortable with the idea of improved accountability. There had been complaints for years about the "unresponsiveness" of the school system and the rigidity, if not pathology, of the bureaucracy at "110 Livingston Street," the school system headquarters. Liberal reformers were perennially trying to make the system more accountable. The idea of local school boards (i.e., political rather than merely administrative decentralization) was a proposal within the orthodox liberal democratic tradition. Liberalism in New York City, however, still had considerable faith in social justice through government bureaucracy. As applied to public school policy, the New York liberal tradition favored a citywide school board, a "professional" bureaucracy and a scientific-expert approach to education—all of which militated against localism. During the debates on decentralization there was much fear expressed of "balkanizing" the city and "lowering standards." If ghetto parents complained that these much vaunted "standards" were little in evidence in their schools, many answered that the solution was to improve and strengthen the bureaucracy, not to weaken it by increasing the involvement of "nonprofessionals."

Even though minority grievances provided the major impetus for dismantling the central bureaucracy, the civil rights movement itself contained crosscurrents that weakened the push for local control. The major civil rights organizations were linked politically, ideologically, and financially with the liberal and union establishment. Some organizations that supported the civil rights movement were able to support community control only after bitter internal fights, and then they often did so only halfheartedly. Some groups, such as the Urban Coalition, were effectively neutralized by anti-community control forces from within. The opponents of increased local control were also quick to argue that it would lead to increased segregation and was therefore "anti-civil rights." The fact that the I.S. 201 demand for local autonomy came after the school system failed to integrate the school only strengthened the fear that community control represented a movement away from liberal civil rights ideals. The idea that blacks and Puerto Ricans ought to have as much right to control their schools as did the white middle class did not cut much ice with a liberal establishment that still had faith in large government bureaucracies and public employee unions.

In the end the school staff unions, especially the United Federation of Teachers, were the prime opponents of community control and the major force which shaped the "decentralization" law into a continuation of the mostly centralized system which has prevailed in New York since 1970. Yet in the beginning the union leadership was not averse to considering some form of greater community decision making. There is no inherent contradiction between unionism and local control; employees of locally controlled schools can be just as unionized as those in large centralized systems, as can be readily seen in thousands of smaller school districts across the country. Union leaders in fact argued that they would be *more* powerful in a decentralized system, since they would have centralized power whereas the parents' and citizens' power would be fragmented.

Nevertheless there were reasons why the unions in New York were opposed to more powerful local school boards. For one thing, while an employee organization's power as a *union* (derived through the threat of strike) might be as strong or stronger under decentralization, its *political* power (derived through electoral politics) might be weakened. The union had learned how to influence central board decisions through the political process; there was no guarantee that it could exercise similar control over local boards. Furthermore, power might shift within the unions. School-level local union leaders might become more important if teachers no longer had to look only to their citywide leaders to represent their interests in the decision-making process.

Ironically, the union, which had started in part as a protest against the mindless and degrading way in which the bureaucracy treated teachers, had become a major defender of the status quo. Many of its prime values were linked to a centralized bureaucratic system: citywide seniority and transfer rights and civil service hiring, firing, and tenure procedures. Given the racial breakdown of the contesting parties, with the most militant advocates of community control being blacks and Puerto Ricans and the school staff being the most "lily white" of any major city in the country, in the end the sheer fear of losing jobs, tenure, and seniority under community control was the prime factor leading the unions into strong opposition. The debate became a racial issue. The opponents of decentralization were able to turn the issue into one of blacks versus whites, instead of bureaucratic control versus community control. As usual the whites won.

WHAT HAPPENED?
The result of the push and shove of these contradictory forces was the abortive "Decentralization" law of 1969—a bill so far removed from the original ideas of community control that many of its advocates boycotted the elections for community school board members, while others simply became apathetic, cynical, and all the more convinced that nothing would change in the New York City schools. Control over personnel and money—in other words, the keys to control over the schools—was left almost entirely in the hands of the central authorities. The system for electing local school boards was so elaborate and complicated that few community leaders had much hope that any but the most organized and highly financed organizations could win. As many as seventy candidates might run for a district board with no local media and no way for the average voter to know about the candidates or the issues.

The teachers union claimed that the bill was 80 percent the way it wanted it, and this is a fair estimate. It is also a fair representation of the respective strengths of the political forces involved, for as we have seen, despite all the sound and fury of the struggle, there was neither cohesive political organization nor consistent ideology behind the community control movement. What has happened since 1970 when the first community school boards were elected has been a mixture of success and failure, increased community involvement in some places and increased apathy and discouragement in others, lively educational innovation and renewal in some areas and dreary continuation of bureaucratic inertia or even corruption and scandal in others.

In a system as large as New York—it is larger than the school systems of 39 of the states—there is room for some of everything. The press coverage has done little justice to the hundreds of talented and dedicated community school board members, parent leaders, teachers, and administrators who have been working hard to improve education for children under the confused new structure. Nor has it reported on more than a few of those who have taken advantage of the confusions of the system, with its lack of clear-cut accountability at any level, to feather their own nests, build their political power, or more typically just to coast along with the same unproductive practices that existed before decentralization.

If one asks if community control worked, the first answer must be that it has not yet been tried. Yet, the struggle of the 1960s started a movement that is still developing today. Many people did not accept defeat and ever since the law was passed have been working in various ways and at various levels to make the system more accountable to its clients. It may turn out that the 1969 Decentralization law was not the end of the fight for community control but only a milestone in a much longer journey by the public to regain control over its public schools.

The most obvious efforts to extend community power were of course in the school board elections. While some boycotted the elections out of disgust at the hypocrisy of the new law, others set to work to do their best to elect parent and community candidates. While the efforts were often discouraging when competing with the money and organization of established groups, there were more successes than many realized— enough to keep the movement going and to develop new leaders when old ones grew tired and discouraged. It is true that the unions increased their local political activities and organization to gain control over the local boards, but there has also slowly developed a contervailing parent and community political sophistication and organization, and many of those supported by the unions have also been supported by parent groups and when elected are not just "UFT board members." In the third community school board elections in 1975, when the Alliance for Children tied together under one banner the local campaigns of parent and community groups in 26 of the 31 districts (now there are 32), 45 percent of the Alliance-endorsed candidates won, compared to 55 percent of the UFT supported candidates. In a number of districts parent and community representatives have gained a majority voice despite the superior funding of union candidates.

Even the much-discussed low participation in the elections is not an unmixed story. While there are many good reasons why voters do not take the trouble to vote in the special community school board elections, including the community boards' minimal power and the great difficulty of finding out about the candidates and issues, the fact is that several hundred thousand people have voted in each of the elections— many of whom have never participated in any municipal election before. In the 1977 elections, when participation citywide dropped to its lowest level of 8 percent, the participation actually increased in over half the districts, many of them minority districts. Nationally, a 5 percent or 10 percent voter turnout for school board elections is not uncommon, even for boards which have much more power to affect children's education than those in New York City.

Next to school board elections, the most visible means used to extend and expand community power under the new structure has been litigation. From the beginning the central authorities followed the normal bureaucratic path of holding on to as much power as they could under the ambiguous provisions of the new law. The central board adopted a sort of "supremacy doctrine," holding that its policies automatically overrode community board decisions. This sweeping assertion of centralized power was upheld by the courts in view of the wording of the law. Nevertheless the community boards continued to bring the central board to court and on several occasions won. District 2 in Manhattan won the right of community school boards to control their own school lunch program, and District 3 in Manhattan won the right for them to decide on the content of Title I programs. While these victories were small in comparison to the overwhelming power of the central bureaucracy to thwart the implementation of even those rights won in court, the litigation also proved a training ground for community leaders, who learned that power does not shift easily and can be won only by skill, persistence, and pressure on many points.

Perhaps the most significant litigation concerned the community boards' power to appoint staff, particularly school principals and administrators. The Decentralization law had left the selection of school staff tied to the citywide Board of Examiners, which had long been a target of reformers and civil rights groups. At the time the law passed, only 1 percent of the schools had licensed minority principals— by far the worst record of any large city in the country. Pressure to break out of this bureaucratic stranglehold was a central objective of the community control movement, and the failure to achieve it in the legislature was a major source of disappointment with the new law. After the bill was passed, however, the combined efforts of a number of civil rights and civic organizations succeeded in enjoining the Board of Examiners tests in federal court on the grounds of racial discrimination. As a result, community boards have been able to appoint principals and other administrators on the basis of state certification, and the number of minority appointments has increased significantly, to approximately 15 percent. Even more important, community boards have had more freedom to seek a "new breed" of principal—more community-oriented and more willing to be held accountable for producing results.

As of this writing, the struggle is entering a new phase with a new Chancellor, himself the former president of one of the community school boards, who was installed by a Mayor who won his election over the active opposition of the municipal unions, including the school staff unions. It is not clear yet what Chancellor Macchiarola will do with decentralization. On the one hand he has a much better sense of tough and accountable central management than his predecessors, which might lead in the direction of a certain amount of "recentralization." On the other hand he has been much more accessible to community organizations and has installed an almost entirely new top staff at 110 Livingston Street who follow his example in this regard. Among his first acts was to reverse the previous Board of Education's opposition to the proposal of groups like the Public Education Association, the United Parents Association, and twenty-two other civic and civil rights organizations (joined together as the Educational Priorities Panel) to press for reallocation of funds from central bureaucracy to direct services to children. Over $50 million has been shifted over the past three years. He also denied "automatic" tenure to seventy-nine principals and assistant principals in an unprecendented step toward staff accountability. The Chancellor has also vigorously defended the Community School Districts as an important intermediate level of participation and supervision, pointing out that there is no way for a central bureaucracy to monitor 900 schools.

Perhaps most significant of all, although still in the planning stages, is the movement of the new administration toward "school site management." The idea of requiring greater accountability at the school level, long advocated by groups like the City Club and the Public Education Association, is gaining momentum from three quarters. First, the Urban Coalition has worked with the unions, Board of Education, principals, and parent civic groups to negotiate a plan for comprehensive participatory school-based planning which went into effect in a substantial sample of city schools in the fall of 1979. Meanwhile, the New York State Board of Regents' "New York City Project" has also led to a consensus among an even wider spectrum of city education forces to move toward school-level accountability with the participation of parents, teachers, and students at the school site. Lastly, Chancellor Macchiarola's chief educational planner, Ronald Edmonds, has developed a School Improvement Plan which is designed to operate school by school, respecting their idiosyncratic differences but holding them to account for producing results.

All in all, the struggle to debureaucratize the New York City schools is, at best, in its infancy. After a disastrous setback in the racial politics of the 1960s, it has been creeping forward in the intervening decade. It possibly has a brighter future under the new Chancellor, but only time will tell.

THE BOSTON EXPERIENCE

School activists around the country watched the decentralization struggle play itself out in New York. The common assumption from the time
the Ford Foundation put its money into the three demonstration districts at least through the publication of the Bundy Commission
Report was that the movement toward decentralization and community control was national. It was felt that the ideas being tested in New
York would have an impact on the way every older American city might
reshape its organizational structure to deliver educational services to
an increasingly poor and minority population. A decade later, it is clear
that the New York experience did have a substantial influence nationally. It sufficiently frightened other school officials and politicians so
that only one other major city—Detroit—can be said to have even
approximated the watered-down decentralization experiment that was
ultimately implemented in New York.

Most other cities took only a few steps toward administrative decentralization, for example the creation of district superintendents or the
formation of advisory-only parent councils at the school or district
level. It is not that the underlying causes and problems that surfaced
in East Harlem or the Ocean Hill section of Brooklyn were absent in
comparable sections of Chicago, Philadelphia, Boston, or St. Louis. On
the contrary, the same alienation and distrust of the school bureaucracy, the same loss of faith in the system's capacity or willingness to
meet its professed commitment to either desegregation or equal treatment, pervaded the black and Hispanic communities in virtually all
urban centers. But with the exception of Detroit, where a marriage of
convenience between anti-busing whites and community control–oriented blacks succeeded in winning legislative approval of a bill creating
regional school boards within the city, black community control advocates were unable to win the kind of political allies necessary to get
school boards or legislatures to follow New York's lead. After the New
York experience, not only did the major national foundations become
gun-shy about intervening in the structure and politics of urban school
systems, but—more critically—so did the vast majority of elected officials. The political price paid by John Lindsay for his efforts to redistribute power away from professionals and toward black and Hispanic
parents was all too obvious to other mayors across the country. The
lesson was a simple one: stay away from schools—and especially stay
away from tampering with the existing power structure of school
systems.

In Boston, where blacks constituted less than 20 percent of the population and where no minority person had been elected to the five-

member School Committee in this century, there was never any serious political prospect of decentralization throughout the turbulent sixties. The futility of trying to get the all-white School Committee to share power with community people was apparent even to the most optimistic activists. There was one small-scale attempt to enable parents and other residents to participate in the running of two all-black middle schools which the system had essentially given up on, but that experiment failed for want of any real commitment to it on the part of the School Committee (see Chapter 6). Otherwise, black political energies were channeled into three areas: the creation of a network of *private* community-controlled schools; the development of two substantial voluntary busing programs, one within the city, the other to the suburbs; and the passage of legislation requiring the Boston School Committee to desegregate its schools.

By the early seventies, however, in the face of the continued unresponsiveness of the central school bureaucracy, the attention of Boston's black activists and white reformers began to swing back to the School Committee itself and the need for fundamental changes in the political structure governing the schools. Although the one-way busing programs and alternative schools created a few years earlier continued to exist, outside financial support for these efforts became increasingly problematic, and the energy level of the founders began to wane. As for the legislative mandate to desegregate its schools, the Boston School Committee managed successfully to evade, stall, and ultimately defy all attempts by the State Board of Education to secure compliance with even the first step required by the law: the filing of an acceptable plan to reduce the growing number of racially imbalanced schools in the city.

In early 1973, under the auspices of Mayor Kevin H. White, a broad-based group of reformers came together to see if it could agree on a plan for restructuring the School Department. The Mayor's situation in 1973 was strikingly different from that of John Lindsay in New York in 1967. White had just handily defeated, for the second time, Louise Day Hicks, the former School Committee Chairperson and leader of the anti-busing forces. Although it was clear that there was overwhelming popular support for the School Committee's refusal to desegregate, it was equally clear that there was substantial public skepticism about the performance of the School Committee in matters educational and financial. Although there was no imminent crisis prompting the Mayor's intervention, as there had been in New York, it was only a matter of time before the Supreme Judicial Court of Massachusetts would order the School Committee to obey the state law; or, failing that, that a suit recently brought in Federal District Court by the NAACP would come to trial.

Joining the Mayor's representatives at the planning table were leaders from the Chamber of Commerce, the Legislative Black Caucus, social service agencies, neighborhood associations, Title I parent councils, Community School Council, and, most promisingly, the Boston Teachers Union. The group, at its initial meetings, quickly came to a shared diagnosis of the problems that any structural reform plan should address. Problems included:

- *The size and representativeness of the School Committee.* The Boston School Committee consisted of five members elected at large, a "reform" engineered in 1905 by Yankee elites to remove the schools from ward-based politics increasingly dominated by Irish newcomers. Ironically, the Irish so mastered the politics of at-large elections that the School Committee had for the last twenty years become almost their exclusive preserve.

- *The relative impotence of the Superintendent of Schools vis-à-vis the School Committee.* The turn-of-the-century Yankee reformers had envisioned that a five-member citywide school Committee would essentially function as a Board of Directors to a strong Superintendent operating as a chief executive would in a large corporation. However, this vision had been corrupted over time to the point where the Superintendent was only one of five executives reporting directly to the School Committee.

- *The absence of any provision for citizen participation in decision making at the local level.* Although the mid-nineteenth century ward-based School Committee was no doubt unwieldy, it did have the advantage of encouraging participation at the neighborhood level, both through the Committee structure itself (which at one point grew to 118 members!) and through a separate Primary School Committee with citizen-monitors appointed for each school. As the School Committee moved from district elections to the at-large system, and then reduced its size from twenty-four members to five, no replacement mechanisms were created to provide grassroots participation.

- *The lack of any clear accountability structure for either the expenditure of funds or the delivery of educational services.* One aspect of the accountability problem has already been alluded to in the description of the erosion of the Superintendent's authority by the School Committee. Equally serious was the blurring of responsibility for the budget created by a special Boston-only statute which limits the School Committee's fiscal autonomy without making it completely dependent on the Mayor. By allowing the School Committee to appropriate whatever it spent the previous year but requiring Mayoral approval for any increase in expenditures, the statute virtually guaranteed a climate of finger-pointing and buck-passing with the public not knowing whom to hold responsible.

By contrast with New York, both the historical climate within which the reform plan developed and the analysis upon which it was based led to avoidance of the term "community-control." The inevitable consequences of developing a school reform plan in the wake of the Ocean Hill-Brownsville controversy was that the planners had to bend over backwards to point up the dissimilarities between the two cities and, consequently, between the two plans. Although decentralization was a key feature of the Boston plan, the rhetoric surrounding the plan spoke of "partnership" and "power-sharing" rather than control.

The Boston reformers believed they had learned several lessons from the New York experience which they incorporated into their own planning. First, the scale of the decentralized units in New York (20,000–30,000 students per district) seemed overwhelming from a Boston perspective. Given the goal of increased citizen participation and increased accountability for learning at the local level, the Boston plan established districts that were approximately one-tenth as large as New York's. The Boston districts were created in two forms: first, a separate district for each high school; and second, a separate district for each middle school or junior high school and its elementary feeder schools. There were thirty-six districts in the proposed plan.

The second lesson from New York was that efforts had to be made to keep the teachers union involved throughout the change process if the plan were to stand a chance of success politically and, if successful, were to be implemented without being sabotaged. A third of the seats on each of the proposed councils were set aside for teachers elected by their peers (the other two-thirds to be divided among parents and students on the high school councils, parents and other district residents on the middle school councils). Additionally, all transfer and seniority rights of current teachers were explicitly protected in the Boston plan. The effect of these provisions in the plan was to neutralize the teachers union. Given the New York experience, this seemed a substantial victory.

A third lesson from New York led to perhaps the most radical feature of the Boston reform plan: namely, the outright abolition of the Boston School Committee. If the decentralized councils were to have substantial power to determine for their own schools how money should be spent, what should be taught, and who should be hired to teach and administer, then the New York experience confirmed that to leave intact a central board that had formerly exercised those powers unilaterally would serve only to invite a power struggle over every attempt by a local council to exercise its new prerogatives. Therefore, the Boston planners proposed the replacement of the independently elected School Committee with a Citywide Advisory Committee consisting of delegates elected from the local councils. The Citywide Advisory Committee's chief responsibilities would be coordination and consultation. It would have virtually no decision-making authority. Thus while avoiding the label "community control," the plan actually contemplated more local autonomy than the New York City Legislation.

If the Boston school reform plan had been solely a decentralization plan, in all likelihood it would today be law. But because the plan abolished the School Committee and dealt with the fiscal accountability problem by making the School Department a line department of City government answerable to the Mayor, the political controversy surrounding the Boston plan focused on the issue of Mayoral control rather than community control. Although virtually the same set of actors supported the change in Boston as had supported the New York Plan—blacks and Hispanics, liberals, the media, academics, the Mayor—and opposition in Boston was much weaker because of the neutrality of the teachers union, the Boston plan failed in the political arena. Eager to avoid having a delicately crafted plan carved up in the legislature as the Bundy Commission plan had been in Albany, the Boston planners sought to enact their plan through the Home Rule provisions of Massachusetts law. By filing their bill first with the Boston City Council and getting it approved by the Council and Mayor prior to its submission to the legislature, the Boston planners thought they could force the legislature to vote the bill up or down without amendment since the Home Rule statute requires the enactment of Home Rule bills exactly in the form passed by the local government.

Unfortunately, within a week of the plan's submission to the City Council three other plans to change the structure of the School Committee surfaced, each devoid of any decentralizing features. The City Council decided to pass the problem along to the voters by drawing up a Home Rule bill containing all four plans and requiring a two-stage referendum process before any change could become law. The City Council enacted the enlarged Home Rule bill in the fall of 1973, and the Mayor, both branches of the legislature, and the Governor all approved the bill before the end of the year. However, it was not until November 1974 that the final step in the change process was to occur: a binding referendum in which Boston voters were asked to choose between the decentralization plan (which had handily defeated the three rival proposals in a Spring referendum) and the status quo.

By November 1974, however, a whole new set of dynamics existed.

What had seemed distant when the planners first met eighteen months before was now reality: there was a Federal Court order to desegregate the Boston schools. As the rest of the country watched in horror, Boston seemed poised at the brink of civil war, with the inevitable consequence that all issues other than busing disappeared from public view. The Mayor, whose active campaigning on behalf of the referendum had been assumed by the planners, was totally consumed with the public safety side of desegregation. The anti-busing forces, now at their political peak, saw the peacekeeping Mayor as the enemy and seized upon the School Committee referendum as a test of their political muscle. Since the reformers were by and large prodesegregation, it was relatively easy for the anti-busers to characterize the reform plan as an attempt by the Mayor, the blacks, and white liberals to continue the work of the Federal Court by taking the school system away from the School Committee which had fought the "good" (i.e., anti-busing) fight for nearly a decade. In an election climate in which a vote for change was defined as an endorsement of busing, it is little wonder that the School Committee referendum was defeated. What is remarkable is that the margin of defeat was only three to two.

If the Boston School reform experience could be summed up solely in terms of a failed referendum fight, it would hardly be worth recounting at such length. But, as often happens in this kind of political reform effort, the reformers, by defining the problem and laying out at least the broad outlines of a solution, broke a trail which others would later follow. Within a few months, Federal District Judge W. Arthur Garrity appointed a panel of Masters to draw up a long-term desegregation plan for Boston. The plan the Masters submitted contained a sufficient measure of decentralization to provoke the complaint from the anti-busing leaders that the Court should not order what the voters had only recently rejected. Nonetheless, the Judge was persuaded by the Masters' argument that meaningful desegregation could not occur unless accompanied by improvement in education and that this would require a substantial administrative and political reorganization. Consequently, the Judge ordered that the School Department be decentralized into nine districts, each to be administered by a community superintendent. He also created an elaborate three-tiered network of parent advisory councils, whose chief function would be to monitor the progress of desegregation at the school, district, and central-office levels. Although the Judge had no authority to grant these councils any powers other than advisory ones, he took advantage of a policy already adopted by the School Committee to involve the councils in the screening of candidates for principalships and all other senior administrative positions.

The top management reform provisions in the defeated referendum plan had to wait until 1978 to resurface. This time the leadership came from the School Committee itself, which had undergone a gradual but unmistakable move toward moderation. With the election in 1977 of John O'Bryant, the first black member to serve since the creation of the five-member Committee in 1905, the Committee began publicly to acknowledge the need to remove itself a bit from the day-to-day operations of the schools and allow the Superintendent to run the department. Early in 1978 the School Committee president appointed a Task Force on Reorganization. The Task Force, at least three of whose members had served on the Mayor's school-reform planning group five years earlier, divided its work into two phases. It decided to tackle the problem of reorganizing the top of the school department first, especially concentrating on strengthening the office of the superintendent. This was viewed as the most urgent aspect of reorganization, given the fact that the School Committee was just beginning to search for a new superintendent and doubted its ability to attract talented outside candidates under the existing ground rules. Consequently, a Home Rule bill was drafted which for the first time clearly established the superintendent as the School Department's chief executive, eliminated the Board of Superintendents (another nineteenth century invention) and created a new set of senior management positions whose occupants serve at the pleasure of the superintendent. This bill was enacted with great speed, taking effect on September 1 simultaneous with the appointment of Dr. Robert Wood, former President of the University of Massachusetts and Secretary of HUD, as the first "outsider" to be appointed Superintendent of Schools in Boston in anyone's memory.

Although the reorganization Task Force was supposed to be reconvened in the fall of 1978 to begin the second phase of its work—strengthening the district-level decentralization—as of this writing that has not happened. The new Superintendent, however, has pressed ahead on his own to abolish approximately one hundred central office positions and begin the transfer of responsibility and accountability for as many functions as feasible to the nine district offices. Although it is far too early yet to ascertain the parameters of the superintendent's commitment to decentralization, there has been no discussion to date of strengthening the powers of the district councils. Thus, although some elements of the original reform plan are now in place—a decentralized administration, a strengthened superintendency, local councils—the School Committee remains intact, although discernibly more moderate; the blurred financial responsibility between the Mayor and School Committee remains unresolved; and the local councils remain advisory only. The reform scorecard in Boston is therefore incomplete, but the direction is slowly, and one hopes surely, in the direction of further debureaucratizing of the system.

CONCLUSION

This tale of two cities is disappointing for those who hope for a speedy response to the need for debureaucratizing school governance structure. In both cities, although the need was pressing, the existing bureaucratic interests not only dragged their feet but, thanks to exploitation of the race issue, up to now they have substantially thwarted the move to develop a fully responsive system.

The story, however, may follow the scenario of many other social and political movements: a strong challenge to the status quo, followed by a strong reaction to defend existing interests and patterns, followed in turn by a period of regrouping during which the initial needs for change reassert themselves and new ways are found to meet them. As we move toward the 1980s we find both systems not only with new leadership but a new *type* of leadership that is more responsive and less wedded to old bureaucratic values. In both cities a new political climate is demanding changes, perhaps as much or more so than in the 1960s, but with a less flamboyant and disruptive political style and a more careful political and administrative strategy.

There are signs in both cities, and elsewhere in the country, that the needed changes may be underway. If the movement toward change is successful, urban public education could be entering a major period of renaissance. If the forces defending the status quo reassert themselves to block the change process, however, it is possible that parents then will increasingly shift their loyalties away from public education and turn to solutions like vouchers and tax credits to help them get their children educated in non-public schools. If this happens, public education will have been done in not so much by its enemies as by the unresponsiveness of its own establishment.

NOTES

1. Albert O. Hirschman, *The Strategy of Economic Development*, Yale University Press, New Haven, 1958, p. 5.

2. Frank Riessman, *The Inner City Child*, Harper and Row, New York, 1976, pp. 88–103.

3. Charles E. Bidwell and John D. Kasarda, "School District Organization and Student Achievement," *American Sociological Review*, vol. 40, February 1975.

4. James J. Shields, Jr., "Steps for School Reform: An Agenda for Education for Democratic Political Community," *Educational Studies*, vol. 6, no. 3/4, 1975, p. 151.

4

CITIZEN PARTICIPATION IN DECISION MAKING IN THE SCHOOLS

DON DAVIES

Boston University and
Institute for Responsive Education

Hard times and conflict produce social inventions of lasting importance. Workable regulation of the securities industry followed the stock market crash of 1929. Collective bargaining as a device for conflict resolution emerged only after decades of labor unrest. Urban strife in the mid-1960s led to the community economic development corporation, a new mechanism for comprehensive planning and development in economically deprived communities.

Public schooling in the 1980s may be in a similar condition of crisis and opportunity. The times are hard. The need for changes in school finance and governance is clear. And, inevitably, there will be conflict over competing policy proposals to bring about such changes. This decade offers an opportunity for social inventiveness that can help create new and more satisfying forms and styles of community-school relationships. Capitalizing on this opportunity requires fashioning a variety of workable ways for parents and citizens to participate with educators in the governance of schools.

Three realities that characterize our time create pressure to open up school governance. First, there is the reality of limited resources. Austerity puts the heat on taxpayers, public employers, and employees alike and makes the intensely political resource allocation process the major educational issue. In this process the source of public employee (educators) power lies not in professional expertise but rather in political resources. A crucial resource is community support. Thus the character of community school relations shapes these political resources.

Second, our era is characterized by an increasing federal and state role in financing local schooling and influencing school policies. As Harmon Zeigler points out, this increasing state and federal support and influence threaten to diminish opportunities for both local educators and local citizens to influence school policies.[1] Inventing mechanisms to maintain an authentic federalist system in school politics requires the consent and participation of both educators and the public.

Third, both the resource allocation and the policy-making processes are dominated by fragmented interest groups operating in a political system that is not well interconnected and is subject to both inaction and corruption. Within such a context every education policy issue can become both divisive and immobilizing. Decision makers, whether professional or lay, are caught in a whirl of conflicting pressures. Feeble and ad-hoc arrangements for citizen participation are hardly adequate under such circumstances. The pressure for an increased capacity for conflict management points to the need for durable and broad-based mechanisms for participation. These pressures make it more likely that both citizens and educators will be willing to invent and implement more effective forms and functions of citizen participation in the schools.

My purpose in this chapter is to provide guidance to citizens and educators as they consider alternative ways of responding to these pressures. This guidance is offered from a position which seeks both increased citizen participation in school decision making and the maintenance and strengthening of public schools. The following pages will:

- Propose several criteria for making judgements about citizen participation
- Delineate the functions and current forms of citizen participation in the schools
- Describe the interrelationships between and among forms, functions, the issues in which citizens participate, and the nature of the participants
- Identify and comment on a few promising practices and directions

To ease the way of the reader through this chapter a word about definitions may be helpful. Citizen participation is not a unitary concept but rather an all-purpose phrase like "equal opportunity" and "local autonomy" that covers a multitude of confusions and confliciting meanings. From the nation's beginnings, citizen participation has been an important value expressed in the wide variety of individual and collective ways in which citizens have taken part in political and civic life. It has encompassed voting, serving on public agency committees, attending town meetings, and joining voluntary associations. Citizen participation is also a term invoked widely in popular educational writing and talk to signify a variety of ways that parents are involved in school affairs including taking part in parent associations or booster clubs, raising money for school purposes, tutoring or volunteering services that aid the school program, helping one's own children at home, and attending school-sponsored events.

For the purposes of this chapter, citizen *participation* is defined as citizen influence (or attempts at influence) in educational decision making in the most significant areas of school affairs: budget, personnel, and programs. Other kinds of parent and citizen activities in school affairs will be termed *involvement*. In this chapter's lexicon, "citizen" means parents and community residents who are not school employees or students.

CRITERIA FOR JUDGING CITIZEN PARTICIPATION

In citizen participation as in education in general, more is not necessarily better; change is not necessarily progress. One person's reform can be another's poison; one group's "success" can be another's "disaster."

Criteria are needed to help think clearly about the vast array of activities and events in a field characterized by polemics, inflated claims, and conflicting goals. Such criteria should also serve as the basis for judgements about directions to be taken.

The six criteria presented here are informed by current studies and theoretical analyses but are ultimately derived from my own values and biases about citizen participation. They are, in fact, ways of making these biases and judgments operational.

CRITERION ONE: MAINTENANCE OF A HEALTHY PUBLIC SCHOOL SYSTEM

Does the policy or activity contribute to maintaining a healthy, viable, publicly controlled system of education for children from the widest of backgrounds? This is the first question that should be asked and positively answered about present and proposed forms of citizen participation. This criterion is rooted in a belief that a publicly controlled system of common schools is necessary for social cohesion, equal access to educational opportunity, and continued progress toward achieving a stable democratic society. It rests also on the belief that a system of publicly controlled schools cannot adequately perform these functions unless it serves a broad range of persons across social and economic classes. This is to say that a public school system which serves exclusively, or nearly so, children of the poor and working class is doomed to second-class economic and political support and social status and will worsen existing class and racial inequities and barriers.

To apply this criterion does not imply that citizen participation should not be directed to altering the structure and content of the school system in profound ways. In fact, the maintenance of a healthy public system of schooling probably requires reform. Without changes in many areas of the school, the erosion of public support and the narrowing of its constituency will continue. A protectionist stance which fails to recognize the inadequacies of the present system is not likely to succeed in the long run. To apply this criterion metaphorically: participation that rocks the boat is necessary and desirable; participation that seeks to sink the boat should be resisted.

CRITERION TWO: MORE EQUITABLE DISTRIBUTION OF POWER

Does the policy or activity contribute to increasing access to power for those now least powerful: the poor, the working class, and members of racial and ethnic minority groups? This criterion is of central importance in judging citizen participation in the schools. It rests on the belief that our society's most important unfinished work is to eliminate maldistribution of resources, justice, and opportunities. Public education and citizen participation are necessary tools for this work, even though there are severe limitations on the contributions each can make.

Citizen participation is a central part of the democratic formula, a means to hold government and institutions accountable to the public and a means to integrate the individual into the community and the broader society. Seen in this way participation must be equitably distributed across the lines of race, class, or sex, or participation itself will contribute to uneven concentrations of power and resources.

However, equity in participation has never been achieved. It was not even a serious and explicit goal of our public policy until the civil rights movements and the anti-poverty programs of the 1960s and early 1970s. At that time, both private protest and government policy drew new people into participating in many areas of school policy making.

One legacy of that civil rights and War on Poverty era has been the institutionalization of mechanisms designed to encourage citizen participation through a variety of federal and state mandates: Title I Parent Advisory Councils (PAC), Follow-Through Councils, and Bilingual PAC's are but a few examples. The record of this institutionalized participation, however, has been mixed.

From the heyday of the late 1960s, there has been a decline in participation in school affairs by low-income and minority people in the cities in the late 1970s. Our studies also show that many of the government-mandated groups have failed to attract and hold the participation of minority and low-income representatives.[2] These groups, often middle-class and professional in style of operation and orientation, naturally tend to appeal to middle-class parents. In addition, the costs in time and out-of-pocket expenses are obviously more of a burden for low-income people, and often language is a barrier as well.

On the other hand, the preceding era of "maximum feasible participation" has given us some instructive examples. First, it has taught us that participation is not neutral. As noted above, one group's success is another group's disaster. When, as in New York City in the middle-to-late 1960s, low-income and minority people did make claims upon and exercise influence in school policy making, much controversy and professional resistance were engendered.

Second, and on the more positive side, in New York and other cities high levels of activity and the creation of active and vocal citizens' organizations demonstrated that poor and working class people could participate and influence educational policy. When there were opportunities for genuine participation, as in the New York City demonstration community control districts, poor people showed that they would and could participate with both frequency and impact.[3]

Finally, participation in groups concerned about school issues has been shown to be an effective form of leadership training and motivation for further involvement in civic and political affairs. This is another reason why the policies or activities designed to foster participation should be judged on the basis of whether or not they provide access to those who are now the least powerful and the least involved in civic affairs.

CRITERION THREE: CONSISTENCY WITH POLITICAL AND ORGANIZATIONAL REALITIES

Does the policy or the activity take into account the political culture and traditions in a particular setting and the organizational characteristics of schools? This criterion dictates that social inventiveness be accompanied by flexibility and sensitivity to local contexts. Experience suggests that in citizen participation as in other areas it is impossible and unwise to seek to invent the one best system and apply it indiscriminately as a quick fix.

POLITICAL REALITIES

The political culture of a city or town profoundly affects how citizens can participate; forms and strategies that work in one place don't work in another.

The political culture is affected by such factors as: (1) distribution of economic power and resources; (2) racial, ethnic, and class composition and migration and residential patterns; (3) adaptability of government structure to changing needs and demands; (4) degrees of centralization and decentralization in governmental structure; (5) openness and representativeness of elected and appointed officials; (6) public-private sector relationships; and (7) styles of influence and decision making.

In a city such as Atlanta, two of the most effective organizations in school affairs—one working class, one affluent middle class—work quietly and behind the scenes, eschewing confrontation or public criticism of officialdom, following what they describe as "the Atlanta way." In contrast, in San Francisco, public challenges and confrontation between citizen groups and school officials are the norm.

ORGANIZATIONAL REALITIES

Organized citizen participation efforts—whether citizen-initiated or mandated—that fail to take into account the political culture of their setting can hardly expect to be effective. In the same way, strategies and mandates for institutionalized citizen participation must take into account the realities of schools as complex formal organizations—their structure, standard operating procedures, and informal folkways. For example, schools, like other organizations, tend to resist change and to do so dynamically. School systems are also "loosely coupled" institutions in which authority is widely and sometimes ambiguously dispersed. Schools, as organizations, are heavily influenced by a subsystem of informal norms and traditions that are difficult for outsiders such as parents to understand and deal with. There are also important differences between and among schools and school systems in size, budget making, relationships to state and federal authorities, decision-making procedures, and in labor relations laws and practices.

The organizational characteristics of schools—those they have in common and those on which there is wide variation—are seldom understood or adequately taken into account by government agencies which foster citizen participation by requiring advisory committees. This failure is one of the causes of the difficulties of implementation of most mandated forms of citizen participation. Similarly, citizen-initiated efforts to participate in school affairs often fail because they are not grounded adequately in these organizational realities.

CRITERION FOUR: IMPROVED PROFESSIONAL/PUBLIC RELATIONSHIPS

Does the policy or activity contribute to improved communication and working relationships between professionals in the schools and those they serve—students, parents, and other community residents who use school services? Just as society requires institutions, institutions require competent professionals—individuals with competence, training, specialized knowledge, and commitment to service. The number of professions and professionals has mushroomed during this century with the proliferation of knowledge and increasing affluence of the society fueling the demand for specialized human services of all kinds. With the growth of professions have come some counterproductive tendencies: fragmentation, the erection of barriers between and among specialized groups, the unwillingness of professional groups to protect the public against malpractice by not involving the people they serve in efforts to police their own ranks, and the extension of professional prerogatives into areas of values and judgment where these prerogatives are not justified.

In the schools, the increasing professionalization of teachers, administrators, and other specialists has undoubtedly contributed to improved quality of services for children. But too often this professionalism has become distorted into excessive protectionism, erecting high barriers to legitimate rights of citizens to decision making about the education of their own children.

School professionals often see citizen participation as the enemy of professionalism. It need not be. It can be the basis for both power sharing and political alliances. Citizens sometimes see professionalism as their enemy. Properly conceived as putting expertise at the service of the public and accountable to it, there need be no inherent contradiction between professionalism and citizen participation.

A number of factors have contributed to the misguided notion that professionalism and citizen participation are inevitably on a collision course. Some reasons are historical and stem from participation initiatives which fail to take into account the realities of schools as complex organizations. Initiatives which fail to take these into account will often pit lay citizens and professionals against each other. Another reason stems from the mistaken assumption that school governance and professional-lay relationships are a zero-sum game: more power and access to citizens means (it is assumed) less power and access to professionals. This need not be the case. A major study of the federally funded Urban-Rural program concluded that:

> ... *sharing* power *increases* power. The total for school improvement is enhanced by bringing hitherto disenfranchised persons into the process. Further it is demonstrated that the traditional authorities may find a source of legitimacy for their actions that was heretofore lacking.[4]

A third reason stems from professionals' mistaken notion that citizen participation initiatives such as mandated advisory committees are designed primarily, and even exclusively, to benefit parents at the expense of professionals. Again this need not be the case. An evaluation study of the impact of California's Early Childhood Education Program and its mandate for advisory committees found that the presence of these committees not only provided more access for parents but also more access for teaching staff hitherto excluded from areas of school policymaking.[5] Moreover, bureaucracy, while it can "protect" professionalism against the conflicting claims and demands of the environment, actually, in the long run, works against the exercise of professional skill; strict hierarchy does not recognize and allow for the creative application of technical skill. Hence any efforts, whether citizen-initiated or mandated, which broaden the base of decision making also create more space for the creative and collaborative exercise of professional expertise.

Therefore, this criterion is an important one to apply to citizen participation in the schools. Such participation can be expected to contribute to improved communication and relationships between professional educators and those they serve. This is not to suggest that school employees and the public do not have different interests to be served and that all conflict between these interests can be avoided. Nor is it to suggest that citizen organizations should allow their goals or strategies to be determined by professionals or their right to participate to be abridged. It is to suggest that one outcome that can be expected from citizen participation in education is more productive exchanges between school professionals and those they serve.

CRITERION FIVE: DIVERSITY AND COHESION
Does the policy or activity contribute to achieving a reasonable balance between diversity and cohesion in the society and in the educational system? American society depends on the maintenance of a balance between local, parochial, and group interests, on the one hand, and societal and national interests on the other. This balance is ever-challenged, ever changing, and always at the heart of political decision making and controversy. The educational system is often a prime battleground, as in the case of the continuing struggle over bilingual and bicultural education and school desegregation.

This is a difficult criterion to apply. It is probably neither desirable nor possible to apply it singly to each proposed policy or organization or activity. Rather, it is best applied to the aggregate of public policies—the policy system—proposed to encourage citizen participation. It is legitimate to expect that a policy system should contribute both to diversity and cohesion and to the process of mediating between the two.

For example, such a system might encourage decentralization of decision making to the school level; provide access to the policy process at the school and district level to groups representing neighborhood, racial, ethnic, or other particular interests; offer state—and district—level goal setting and monitoring to protect broad social interests; strengthen Federal programs to meet nationally determined priorities and obligations such as the implementation of school desegregation or the rights of handicapped children or those of limited English-speaking ability; and recognize the importance of the courts in protecting individual and class interests vis-à-vis societal interests.

These examples suggest that diversity and cohesion are indeed inseparable. Public policy support and recognition of these diverse claims upon the public schools will, in the long run, create cohesion and build support for and strengthen public schooling by eliminating motivations to seek educational service elsewhere.

The strongest insurance for a good balance between local and societal interests is citizen participation itself. There is substantial evidence that when people are barred from real influence over the conditions that affect their lives, they tend to become more inward-focused, more alienated from public processes. On the other hand, studies have shown that participation contributes to social cohesion: participants were far more likely than non-participants to actively subscribe to democratic values, to recognize the value of give and take, and, thus, to recognize the legitimacy of other interests and of the process for reconciling those interests.[6] In short, participation has a moderating effect on participants: viewpoints become less polarized and more open to compromise. This does not mean, however, that participation breeds satisfaction with the *status quo*, with specific policies, practices, and institutions.

To pursue an earlier metaphor, a policy system which recognizes and provides access for diversity engenders social cohesion by promoting participation which "rocks the boat" rather than that which seeks to sink it.

CRITERION SIX: SIGNIFICANT PROBLEMS AND REAL RESULTS

Does the proposed policy or activity allow citizens to participate on problems and issues of significance to them and to have a real-world impact? This is the most practical and easiest criterion to apply. It simply focuses on the significance of the activity, as determined by the participants themselves, and on the results of that activity: Does it make any difference on matters that are important?

In part, this criterion is implicit in our definition of *participation* as distinct from *involvement*. Even more importantly, it is a necessary consequence of seeing citizen participation as a way of strengthening public commitment to the maintenance of a healthy public school system.

Citizens participate because they care. As revealed in recent Gallup Polls, they want to have a say in significant issues: school program, budget, personnel, and discipline.[7] Unfortunately, much of the current activity labeled citizen participation appears to revolve around an agenda imposed by professionals or government agencies or to be trivial in nature. In many other instances, the participatory activities, especially those mandated by local, state and Federal authorities, appear to be window dressing, and are not expected to have important results and seldom do. Triviality of content and lack of results explain the limited enthusiasm on the part of large numbers of citizens to devote time and resources to the process.

From this follow several policy implications. First, window-dressing participation far from successfully coopting participants and protecting the status quo works against social cohesion. A study of the effects of advisory council participation in New York City showed that those parents who were involved on "window-dressing" councils performing trivial public-relations functions ended up being *more* alienated from the schools than those parents who did not participate at all. On the other hand, citizens on councils which dealt with real issues did not always agree with official school policies but were nevertheless more supportive of the schools and recognized the legitimacy of the policy-making process though they did not always agree with its outcomes.[8]

Second, triviality of content is not always a result of conscious manipulation. It may result from the organizational realities of schools. Participation taking place at a level where few significant issues are dealt with and few important decisions are made cannot help but be trivial. For example, if few if any decisions are made at the school site, it makes little sense to establish a committee for citizen participation in decision making at that level. If many key issues are resolved at the state level, citizens who cannot organize to influence state-level decisions will continue to be powerless.

Finally, lack of results can also be attributed to structural factors. Many citizen participation mechanisms are mandated with broad but vague advisory functions. Being advisory and having vague objectives make it difficult for such groups to accomplish very much. Real and significant participation with identifiable accomplishments is the result of having clear and specific goals and functions. It has been discovered that the success of citizen organizations is closely related to having clear and concrete goals that are both stated and communicated to all parties.[9] Specificity of goals appears to be a prerequisite to doing significant work and getting results.

NON-RELEVENT CRITERIA

It is reasonable and productive to apply these criteria to current and proposed forms of citizen participation. Without criteria, the idea that doing something is always better than doing nothing may swamp citizen participation in confusion.

However, it is both unreasonable and impossible to apply these criteria in a strict and mechanical way. They are, of necessity, general and as such subject to widely varying application. In fact, the most effective ways of discrediting the concept of citizen participation in education is to claim and seek to prove that it will have a profound impact on economic, social, and educational problems that stubbornly resist solutions. Having grandiose expectations that new forms of citizen participation will have sweeping results that can be convincingly and accurately measured guarantees that those new forms will fail.

There is one commonly recognized criterion that should decidedly not be applied to making judgements about citizen participation: pupil achievement as measured by standardized tests. There is an unfortunate and naive expectation that student achievement will be advanced by nearly any form of parent or citizen participation: "We want to improve reading scores of children in low income areas so we will require a parent advisory committee." The effectiveness of the new committee will thus be judged on the basis of the fluctuations in reading scores. This way of thinking dooms parent participation to being judged a failure.

With this warning about the limitations of citizen participation and the measurement of its results, it is appropriate to turn to the functions and forms of participation.

FUNCTIONS AND FORMS OF CITIZEN PARTICIPATION

The Institute for Responsive Education has developed a nine-part classification scheme that encompasses the functions it identified in a national study for the National Institute of Education. These categories are not mutually exclusive. They are as follows:

1. *Information.* Includes receiving information from the schools and providing information to the media, community agencies, citizen organizations, and residents.

2. *Service.* Includes services to children such as tutoring or program enrichment; services to parents such as child care or counselling; and services to school staff such as classroom assistance, bus monitoring, or raising money for school purposes.

3. *Advising and Decision Making.* Advising and decision-making functions cut across the areas of budget, personnel, program, facilities, student discipline, and extracurricular activities.

4. *Planning and Development.* A wide variety of activities are included in this category ranging from goal setting to proposal writing to helping produce or review instructional materials.

5. *Research and Evaluation.* Gathering data about school and community problems and assessing the quality of school programs are the most common activities included under this category.

6. *Monitoring/Reporting.* Citizen monitoring of school desegregation, which requires reporting to the school board and the court, is one example of this function. It is sometimes ad hoc and private, sometimes continuing and public.

7. *Training.* This includes training others (students, parents, community residents, school staff) and being trained for a particular role (e.g., monitor or community researcher).

8. *Advocacy.* Protection of individuals or groups of clients or constituents is an advocacy function. Litigation is often one aspect of this function.

9. *Electoral Politics.* This function includes running for office or supporting individuals for elective office including school councils or school boards. Additional electoral activities are voter registration and providing information about elections and candidates.

These functions are performed in a wide variety of formats. The most important differentiation in form is between individual and collective participation.

INDIVIDUAL PARTICIPATION
Individual participation in or influence on educational policies takes several major forms. Voting for local and state officials and in elections affecting taxes, bonds, and other policy matters is the best and most obvious example. Individuals also influence educational policy by making choices about where they will live and where their children will attend school. Individual choice among schools, however, is often open only to those who can afford it. Choices include electing a private or parochial school including a private alternative school designed with a particular style or clientele in mind; choosing one public school rather than others within a public school system, including magnet and public alternative schools; or leaving one district to move to another, as in the phenomenon of "white flight" from school desegregation.

Such individual participation is always in a context of public policies which constrain the choices: tax policies which offer or deny financial incentives for choosing private schools, flexible or rigid transfer policies, school desegregation requirements, differential taxpayer costs across districts and states.

VOUCHER PLANS
The most interesting and controversial policy proposal pertinent to this form of individual participation is the voucher plan. Voucher plans were proposed in the late 1960s and early 1970s with private foundation and federal government support to encourage choice as a legitimate form of individual participation. These proposals produced a flurry of controversy and widespread opposition by both education interest groups and many of the organizations representing the interests of minority and low-income Americans. The idea was tried in only one place, the Alum Rock school district in California. The evaluations were largely negative and federal funds were withdrawn.[10]

In the late 1970s the voucher idea has reemerged, fueled by the taxpayers' revolt and public dissatisfaction with the cost and results of public schooling. The idea appeals to some because it offers an opportunity for more direct influence and is likely to produce more measurable results than organizing to change school policies.[11]

A well-constructed voucher plan may meet four of the six criteria proposed earlier, but on two the plan is seriously deficient. It appears almost inevitable that such a plan will weaken rather than help to maintain and reform the public school system. It will lead to increased segregation of children by race and class and will lead to less rather than more access to power by those groups now least powerful. If plans such as the one currently being considered in California were to be implemented, it is likely that the public schools would serve primarily children of the poor and working class.

LITIGATION

Still another form of individual participation currently of great importance is litigation. Most observers would agree that in the past thirty years the faltering political system has created a vacuum which has been filled by the courts. For example, unable to produce legislative action to desegregate public schools, blacks turned to the courts and obtained remedies. Parents of handicapped children, who were unable to get state educational services for their children through the education agencies or the legislature, went to court instead and achieved their objective. Litigation is a time-consuming form of individual citizen participation in educational decision making. But, for low-income and minority people especially, the courts offer more direct access to influence than the usual organizational forms of political participation, which are dominated by the middle class.

Hence, on the criterion of increasing access to power for the least powerful, litigation has scored high in recent years. On other criteria, case-by-case, remedy-by-remedy judgments must be made. However, one problem with litigation as a policy-influencing tool is that it can result in legal remedies but cannot insure that the substance or the spirit of the remedy is actually carried out. For example, the Court can place black or handicapped children in nonsegregated schools or classes, but it cannot insure that the administrators and teachers will be caring, competent, and fair.

COLLECTIVE FORMS OF PARTICIPATION

This section focuses on the type of citizen participation which currently involves the greatest controversy and confusion and where the greatest promise may lie: citizen organizations seeking to participate in educational decision making.

Since the early 1970s, there has been a great upsurge in the number of parent and citizen groups aimed at participating in decision making. There are two basic forms:

1. *Mandated:* those that are created or mandated by local, state or federal government action and function within the structure of the public school system.

2. *Citizen-initiated:* those that are begun and controlled by parents or citizens and that function primarily as private associations outside of the official school structure.

These two basic forms vary significantly, even though there is often an overlapping of functions and memberships. The first three described below are mandated organizations.

FEDERALLY MANDATED ORGANIZATIONS
Since 1971, nearly every federal education program affecting the elementary and secondary schools has included a mandate for citizen participation. As noted previously, these are partly a legacy of the War on Poverty requirements for "maximum feasible participation." Purposes that federal policymakers say they have in mind as they create new participatory forms are: training for parent/citizen leadership and ameliorating concerns about excessive federal domination in local school affairs.

The participation requirement in education programs since 1971 differ markedly from those of the 1960s. Both Head Start and Follow Through were a part of the Economic Opportunity Act of 1964 and both provide a *policy-making* role for parents through membership on policy boards. Education programs since 1971 (both new laws or amendments to 1960s laws) require evidence of *consultation* with client representatives in proposal preparation and mandate the establishment of advisory committees. The Office of Education administers ten programs that require a continuing advisory committee at the local level. Some of these specify a single committee for the entire school district; some call for committees in each individual school participating in the program. For example, in Title I of the Elementary and Secondary Education Act, Parent Advisory Committees are required at both the building and the district level. In almost all cases, however, the authority assigned to these committees is ambiguous and with just two exceptions is advisory only. The policy boards in local Follow Through Programs and, since 1978, community councils in the Teacher Corps Program have policy-making as well as advisory roles.

In addition to establishing such special program advisory committees through the legislative and executive branches, the federal court system has legitimized citizen participation by including citizens' committees as part of its remedies for school segregation. These have been established in a number of cities undergoing federal court-ordered desegregation. Such committees usually take the form of citywide bodies charged with information, monitoring, and reporting functions. In Boston, however, the federal court created a multilevel (building, district, and citywide) system of citizens' advisory committees. These Boston councils have more functions and broader authority than similar committees in other cities.

STATE MANDATES
Several states have followed the lead of the federal government and have established various mandates for citizen participation, either through state law or department of education regulation. These mandates apply to programs which serve target populations, such as compensatory education for poor children, or are aimed at problems such as sex discrimination or drug abuse.

California, Florida, and South Carolina pioneered by mandating multipurpose school councils. The California and Florida approaches will be discussed later, as one promising effort to link school improvement and citizen participation. Other states have sought less prescriptive ways to foster citizen participation by encouraging school officials to consult with public in planning and carrying out programs.

In the late sixties, New York and Michigan passed legislation decentralizing the school system in their largest cities, New York City and Detroit, respectively. In each case, elected district boards assumed some of the legal authority of the central board of education and the base of citizen participation was widened.

LOCAL MANDATES
A number of local school districts have established various forms of participation. In Los Angeles, the Board of Education was threatened with legislation which would have broken the district into several strong subdistricts and given substantial authority to both the black and Chicano communities in areas in which they are geographically concentrated. In response, it adopted a form of weak administrative decentralization and created citizen advisory committees in each school building. Another local initiative in Louisville will be discussed later in this chapter. As the decade of the seventies wore on, hundreds of other districts established citywide advisory committees on a wide range of topics, and scores began building-level school councils or advisory committees.

The next five types of groups described are citizen-initiated organizations with a primary or exclusive focus on education. They include traditional parent associations such as the PTA, citywide education groups, and grassroots neighborhood education groups.

PARENT ASSOCIATIONS

The National Congress of Parents and Teachers remains the largest organization composed primarily of citizens concerned with school and youth related issues. The national PTA and its state affiliates often participate in important educational issues, but the local units have traditionally limited their functions to providing information, training (parent education), and service. With some exceptions, these groups encourage parent involvement but not participation.

CITYWIDE EDUCATION ASSOCIATIONS

These associations exist in many large cities and in some smaller towns as well. The Public Education Association of New York City is the oldest and best known. Most seek to cover a range of functions encompassing both involvement and participation, including activism in electoral politics.

GRASSROOTS EDUCATIONAL ORGANIZATIONS

In the mid- and late sixties, the civil rights movement and antipoverty programs spawned a wide variety of small, local education groups aimed at school reform, especially in black and Hispanic communities. They were often started by charismatic neighborhood leaders. Two good examples of such groups are the United Bronx Parents, founded by Evalina Antonetti in New York, and United Black Parents of the West Side in Chicago, begun by the late Ida Mae Fletcher. Such grassroots groups appear to have diminished in their levels of activity and visibility in many cities, or else they have changed strategies and now stress service delivery.

MULTI-ISSUE GROUPS

In nearly every community there are groups which devote some attention to school-related issues. Examples are: Leagues of Women Voters, Urban Leagues and Urban Coalitions, Chambers of Commerce and other business associations, taxpayers organizations, religious organizations, and local units of the NAACP or Aspira. Moreover, the past decade has seen a rapid growth of multipurpose neighborhood associations and community development organizations. These groups, in all of their widely diverse forms, are a major force in local politics, but only occasionally do they appear to assign school issues a high priority.[12] Because this type of organization offers promise as an effective form of participation, examples will be discussed in more detail later.

CHILD ADVOCACY GROUPS

The number of such groups has grown rapidly since the early 1970s. These organizations are found at the national, state, and local level. They provide both case advocacy to protect the rights and interests of individual students on a case-by-case basis and class advocacy aimed at protecting or advancing the interests of categories of youngsters such as the handicapped. The activities of these organizations usually include litigation, research, and monitoring of administrative implementation of laws or court decisions.

THE ISSUES, THE PARTICIPANTS

Just as form influences function (and vice versa), the forms and functions of citizen participation in the schools affect and are affected by the issues that arouse people to participate. These issues in turn are affected by which persons or groups are involved. Finally, all of this—forms and functions and issues and participants—is affected by the political culture. The political culture, as it is understood here, includes the local context, traditions, and political realities, and also prevailing norms and expectations about what schools can or should do and what citizen participation can or should achieve.

On both counts—expectations about schools and expectations about citizen participation—the decade of the 1960s was a watershed that brought forth new participants and new issues and generated new forms and new functions for citizen participation. As suggested in previous sections, some of these forms have worked, some have not. While the temper of the times has changed and the political realities of the coming decade are different—more austerity and perhaps less faith in social reform—the political culture of the 1980s includes expectations and claims first articulated during the 1960s.

Before the 1960s, the climate of expectations was different. As Tyack points out in Chapter 1, the professionalizing and bureaucratizing of the schools which accompanied the Progressive Reform Movement greatly reduced lay influence in matters of school budget, personnel, and program. This historical fact was legitimated by the subsequently prevailing norms about the citizen's role in educational policy making. Until the 1960s, citizens individually and collectively were most often active in performing information and public relations functions for the public schools, which were growing rapidly and required a greatly increased public investment. This requirement put a premium on generating community support, a function willingly assumed by civic activists and school boosters. More overt political participation, when it did occur, stressed electoral politics. Its underlying assumption was "elect good school board members who believe in well-financed schools and who will appoint good superintendents who, in turn, will run the schools with professional skill."

The people who were involved in school affairs were, like most civic activists and joiners of voluntary associations even today, most often white and middle-class. As Zeigler and Tucker pointed out in Chapter 2, they had much in common with teachers, administrators, and school board members—the vast majority of whom were also white and middle-class. Even more importantly, there was an assumed consensus between school professionals and parents on fundamental values and educational goals. Accompanying this consensus was a faith and trust in educators as competent, expert, and sympathetic to community interests and a tacit assumption that most decisions about school budgets, personnel, and programs were (given the consensus about values and goals) technical matters and as such best entrusted to professional educators.

In the 1960s, schools, like other public institutions, became embroiled in the general "crisis of legitimacy." This was due in part to the failure of schools to achieve in practice what our democratic traditions and, since 1954, our national policy charged them to do: overcome racial discrimination and equalize educational opportunity. It was also due in part to the entry of new participants. With these new participants, the poor and the minorities, came new issues and challenges and new forms of participation.

Leaders in the black community in New York City, along with many white liberal allies, became frustrated with endless footdragging by the school district to avoid desegregation and turned to community control as an alternative. The community control movement spread from New York to other cities, to the Chicano communities in the Southwest, and to Indian tribes.

The movement claimed the right for the community to have a strong voice in the most significant areas of schooling: budget, personnel, and curriculum. Community control advocates maintained that minority children would never be adequately educated in schools controlled by the middle class.

These new participants challenged professional hegemony over the significant areas of school governance and programs. In the absence of collaborative mechanisms for dealing with such "new" challenges, the poor and the minorities employed strategies of protest and confrontation. These were answered with increased opposition on the part of established educational interest groups, such as the UFT's response to personnel actions by New York City's community-control demonstration districts' boards (see Chapter 3). That conflict escalated into a general conflict about community control and, at the most general level, a conflict about the appropriate roles of citizens and educators in the governance of schools.

Community control efforts in other major cities were defeated, in part because of the events in New York City, and in part because in each case the same interests groups were challenged by demands for community control. However, a number of pilot efforts were initiated and have survived in one form or another. These include experiments in community-controlled schools within public school systems such as the Morgan School in Washington, D.C., the BUILD Academy in Buffalo, and a number of Indian-controlled school districts on or near Indian reservations. Some private community-controlled schools have also persisted. These include the Nairobi Schools in East Palo Alto, California, and some of the alternative schools which formed the Milwaukee Federation of Independent Schools.

The persistence of these and other models of decentralized, school-building decision making is one legacy of community control. A second legacy is a challenge to the once predominant (and now once again fashionable) explanation for student failure which puts most of the blame on the student and his or her home environment. A third legacy was to legitimate citizen challenges in areas hitherto considered a part of the professional's reserve. What were once seen as purely technical issues are now seen more correctly as questions of values—of cultural and subcultural norms. The final legacy of community control is that the appropriate roles for both citizens and educators in school policy making have not been resolved. This latter issue remains salient, especially in times of austerity, declining enrollments, and, once again, changing expectations about schools. Designing a durable and, in contrast to the 1960s, a mutually supportive set of roles for both citizens and educators involved in political decisions about schooling is the task for social inventors in the 1980s.

These inventors may learn from some of the promising practices discussed in the final section of this chapter.

PROMISING DIRECTIONS

With this survey as background and with the six proposed criteria as a framework, it is now possible to identify some promising practices and directions. There is a surprising agreement among evaluators, researchers, and observers about the inadequacy of most structures currently labeled citizen participation, when clear definitions and criteria are applied to them. So it is not difficult to separate the wheat from the chaff and identify promising practices. In the following pages, I will briefly examine two promising ideas. They are, first, school-based management and, second, citizen-initiated community development organizations working on a broad scope of social and economic concerns. An additional practice—third-party problem solvers—will be examined in the next chapter.

SCHOOL-BASED GOVERNANCE

The concept of school-based governance assumes that the school site is the most manageable unit for school decision making. As originally proposed within the context of school finance reform, school-based governance seeks to reconcile increased state funding to enhance equity with increased discretion at the building in order to encourage both administrative efficiency and diversity of program offerings.[13] As a management and finance reform tool, school-based governance or, as it is sometimes called, school site management includes: making the individual school site the cost center by means of lump-sum budgeting to the site, requiring cost-accounting and school performance reports at each site, and increasing principal accountability for individual school program budgets. As a means of educational reform, school-based governance recognizes that the individual school is also the most manageable site for introducing innovations and refinements in instructional programs.

As a form of school governance, this idea calls for a more radical and thoroughgoing form of decentralization in which important decisions are delegated to the school-building level. As such, it may include having building principals responsible for hiring, assigning, and firing school employees at the building level and allow for school-by-school curriculum planning.

The significance of school-based governance for citizen participation is fivefold. First, it brings decision-making authority down to the level at which most citizens are able and willing to participate. Second, it creates the opportunity for participation in significant issues with the possibility of tangible results. This is accomplished where the building principal's discretionary authority is explicitly shared with building level committees or councils representing citizens, parents, staff, and sometimes students. Third, by devolving program decisions down to the school-building level, school-based governance allows for local diversity. This not only allows for the legitimate expression of subcultural values but also builds support for public schools on the part of both low-income parents who may feel alienated from the kinds of programs being offered and more affluent parents who might otherwise seek alternative, private-sector schooling. School-based governance can create the opportunity for exercising choice without forsaking the public system of schooling.

Fourth, school-based governance allows for the increased state role needed to realize financial equity without jeopardizing local control. As such, it points to a way out of the dilemma implied by the work of Harmon Zeigler: the more federal and state initiatives seek to reform schools and make them responsive, the less room there is for local control.

Finally, school-based governance can improve school-community relations, especially in the current era of hard times. By placing decisions at the school-building level, it breaks down some of the barriers between lay persons and professionals, in part by making decision making visible, immediate, and vulnerable. Decisions are no longer "protected" by being hidden behind the smokescreen of district policies. School-site budgeting also brings the intense political and, in times of austerity, conflict-ridden process of resource allocation down to the one level where there is the most possibility of consensus. Choices between resource allocations at the building level are seen to be more closely tied to their impact upon children. A common concern for children can provide the basis for discussion and, perhaps ultimately, genuine collaboration between citizens and professionals.

In theory, then, school-based governance has the potential for maximizing many of the aspects of the six criteria enumerated in the first section of this chapter. In practice, it is too early to tell. School-based governance is, at present, more of an idea with a few concrete instances than an accomplished fact or even a new wave of reform. However, the three examples of this concept in practice discussed below suggest that social inventors of the 1980s can benefit from experiments with school-based governance in Kentucky, Florida, and California.

KENTUCKY: THE ROOSEVELT COMMUNITY SCHOOL IN LOUISVILLE

Unlike the other two examples which follow, the Roosevelt School is not the result of a local response to a conscious state policy initiative in the direction of school-based governance. Rather, Roosevelt is best seen as a survivor of an aborted local initiative for decentralization that was, in part, a victim of the cross-pressures created by court-ordered desegregation. In terms of its unique history, aspirations, and accomplishment, the experience of Roosevelt has much in common with earlier efforts at community control. This is useful since it demonstrates certain affinities between the idea of community control and the idea of school-based governance.

In the early 1970s, the School Superintendent in Louisville led a major effort to reform that city's schools. One of the key features of that effort was the development of a decentralized plan for school governance through the creation of mini–school boards at each school site. This plan was never fully implemented since it was resisted by other school administrators. Ultimately, the reform fell victim to a school desegregation court order merging the city and county schools.

Roosevelt was one of the few schools which did adopt the plan and its concept of mini–school boards. This school served one of the poorest areas of the city which was about 80 percent white and 20 percent black. With strong support and commitment from the community and the leadership of its principal, Car Foster, Roosevelt evolved a unique experiment in school-based governance.

Three emphases defined this experiment at the Roosevelt Community school. First was the conscious attempt to make that school a community school. On one hand, this meant reflecting community values and interests in the school program. The school building itself became a community center. It and its programs became an object of pride for community residents. On the other hand, the school utilized indigenous community resources as represented in the time and efforts of its predominantly low-income parents. The school's program included parental involvement in a score of activities including: tutoring, parental involvement as primary educators in the home, and parent education. At Roosevelt, what we have called citizen *involvement* laid the groundwork for genuine citizen *participation*.

Second, the Roosevelt experiment paid conscious attention to the realities of schools as formal organizations influenced by the informal norms of school staff and by the inevitable barriers between school professionals and citizens. This was addressed by providing training and workshops for both staff and parents.

Third, the capstone of the Roosevelt experience in school-based governance is its Community School Board composed of parents, other community residents, teachers, and other school staff. Its structure provides an arena in which citizens and educators collaborate as equals. Its functions and powers provide an avenue for significant and tangible accomplishments. As stated in its 1977 by-laws, the Board's powers illustrate the school-based governance concept in practice. The Board was empowered to:

1. Determine the types of programs or services the local school will operate.

2. Establish the broad general policies which will govern the operation of the school (truancy, absences, teacher orientation, etc.).

3. Assist in program planning and evaluation of the school program.

4. Be responsible for input in overall school affairs.

5. Insure that people in the school community have opportunities to express their needs and desires to the school administration and that their thinking is considered in the development of the school program.

6. Investigate and make recommendations regarding any existing programs within the school.

7. Establish priorities for use of funds allocated from the general budget of the Jefferson County Board of Education based on student enrollment or membership.

8. Establish priorities for use of various federal funds allocated through the Board of Education (Title I, Title II, etc.).

9. Interview and recommend the hiring of all personnel working at Roosevelt.

10. Evaluate all personnel working at Roosevelt.

11. Formulate experimental educational programs for all age groups in the community and seek federal, state, local, and private funding for same.[14]

At this writing, it is uncertain whether the Roosevelt School will survive the merger of the Louisville and Jefferson County school districts. The principal has left and the Central Board has twice tried to close the school. Nevertheless, the Roosevelt Community School and its Board have been able to muster neighborhood support and, so far, persevere. Whether it survives or not, that school has already illustrated the capacity of school-based governance to increase citizen participation and satisfy many of the criteria emphasized earlier in this chapter.

FLORIDA: MONROE COUNTY

As noted earlier in this section, school-based governance is an idea that is proving attractive to policy makers in those states seeking ways to maintain some degree of local autonomy and diversity in decision making while the state assumes a larger share of the costs of the public schools and legislatures and state education agencies exercise more power in school affairs. Following the recommendations of a governor's commission, in 1973 the Florida legislature enacted a far-reaching program of school finance reform and school improvement that included an emphasis on school site management. The program has several elements important to this discussion: state financial support based on pupil weightings with the school site as the cost center; school-by-school accounting and reporting; and advisory committees mandated to participate in the development of school instructional programs and the preparation of annual reports on school progress.

Florida's policy initiatives have been implemented unevenly.[15] This is partly because the school-based governance aspects of the program elicited little support from the Department of Education and much opposition from the statewide associations of educators and school board members. Nonetheless, full-scale pilot programs are underway in two Florida counties and several others have installed some aspects of school site management.

One of these pilots is in Monroe County, which covers a large geographical area between Key West and the outskirts of Miami with 150 miles between the district office and the farthest school building. In Monroe County, the principal has emerged as a manager with substantial discretion over budget, personnel selection, and staffing patterns. This has been accompanied by training and technical assistance for principals as they assume new responsiblities. A recent evaluation of school-based management in Florida concludes that the Monroe County program "changes the roles of the superintendent and school board to that of monitoring rather than prescribing the educational program within those schools, and it also provides for programs that serve each community better than would a district wide curriculum and staffing pattern."[16]

In addition, the experiment in Monroe County illustrates the potential of school-based governance in promoting the responsible exercise of professional expertise. It creates more opportunities for participation in significant decision making (as opposed to "housekeeping" functions) not only for principals but for teachers and school staff side by side with citizens.

CALIFORNIA

A second statewide initiative towards some form of school-based governance was undertaken in California in 1972 with the establishment of the Early Childhood Program. In 1978, Assembly Bill 65 (A.B.65) revised and extended the program to all school grades, now calling it the School Improvement Program. It also was tied to a comprehensive school finance reform measure.

The School Improvement Program (SIP) provides funds on a per pupil basis to individual schools which develop a concrete plan to carry out a comprehensive program of improvement. According to Wilson Riles, the State Superintendent of Public Instruction, these special funds are designed to "serve as a catalyst to pull together everything a school is doing to provide for more effective use of school funds and overall accountability."[17]

By 1979, SIP grants, ranging from $70,000 to $100,000 or more per school, were going to more than half of the state's schools. The program mandates school-site councils composed of an equal number of school building employees and citizens (student representation is required at the junior and senior high schools) selected by their peers. The site councils are responsible for developing the individual school improvement plan and allocating the special state funds to carry it out.

Several promising features characterize this California approach. First, it recognizes the diversity of local values and perspectives and, in fact, seeks to preserve such diversity. SIP is based on the principle that reforms can only succeed when local people feel a sense of ownership in those reforms. When those affected by a decision have a part in making that decision, changes are more likely to be implemented. Rather than imposing a master blueprint of reforms and innovations, the state plan provides local people with the money to create their own reforms.

Second, it can serve as a model for the kind of creative federalism necessary to reconcile the need for stronger federal and state action to redistribute scarce resources equitably while still maintaining local control. This is accomplished by SIP's three-tier management plan. The state sets the program's framework, general goals, and procedural requirements. The local school districts develop their own master plan and a set of criteria for evaluating participating schools. The site council is responsible for developing the site plan and allocating the special state funds to carry it out.

Third, through the mandated responsibilities of the site councils, the California approach creates an opportunity and vehicle for citizen participation and impact on significant issues. While the site councils do not have powers comparable to the Roosevelt Community school board, they are not merely advisory like some of their federal counterparts. Their scope is broad and includes most significant areas of school policy except for personnel decisions. Site councils have the authority both to develop and approve plans for school improvement.

Fourth, the combination of state funds, significant functions for the site councils, and equal representation of both educators and parents on those site councils creates the opportunity and the incentive to improve school-community relations. It is not the fact that both teachers and parents sit on the same council which is significant. Rather, the important factor is that the system is so designed that each group needs the support of the other in order to accomplish a common objective: the development of a plan with which to obtain state funding. Joint planning by professionals and laypeople and the incentives to forge parent-teacher alliances in the interest of the children are an integral part of this program.

Finally, the California approach recognizes local variations in traditions of citizen participation and offers a waiver provision schools or school districts can use to exempt themselves from an aspect of the state mandate if that aspect inhibits the intent of the mandate. One school I visited did receive a waiver from the strict interpretation of the site council mandate. It met the intent of the mandate by consolidating its preexisting advisory committees and citizen participation structures into an umbrella school-site council which includes the mandated mix of representatives for the SIP site council.

The school is in the San Jose area and serves a largely low-income Chicano population. Its council encompasses the Title I Parent Advisory Committee, the Federal Bilingual Education advisory committee, an advisory committee for the U.S. Office of Education's Follow Through program, the School Improvement Program, and the PTA. Thus, it has succeeded in integrating a number of usually fragmented committees and categorical programs within a single council with operating subcommittees to preserve the identity of the separate components. This umbrella council provides a wide variety of opportunities for parent involvement in the school, in addition to participation in decision making through the council itself. Many of the activities are in the building on weekends, as many of the Chicano mothers do not like to go into the classroom, and some work. One example is a weekly inservice program for parents on education-related topics including nutrition and how to help their children with school work at home.

Council members reported that the School Improvement Program has led to improved reading instruction, greater community interest, more support from the central school board and administration, increased parent involvement in the school, and a curriculum and building reflecting the culture and traditions of the local Chicano community. To paraphrase the earlier quote from Wilson Riles, the state's mandate for site councils has affected this San Jose school by acting as a catalyst to pull together everything the school was already doing to provide for more effective exercise of citizen participation.

On the whole, however, California's approach is but a beginning and not a model or a ready-made blue print. It represents a partial intervention rather than a full-scale reform of local school governance to increase citizen participation. It relies on incentives—the availability of state funds—but incentives alone can only go so far. For example, access to power and resources for the poor and minorities is built into the program design but not guaranteed. Furthermore, the School Improvement Program is only part of any school's experience. While it is too early for a definitive judgment, it is not clear whether the joint planning process involving educators and citizens will automatically spill over into other areas of decision making.

In light of the standards enumerated in the first section of this paper, the California approach is most shaky on the criterion of adherence to political and organizational realities. It is not clear, for example, whether the natural resistance to change and the informal professional norms which resist the participation of nonprofessionals in important areas can be overcome in a program whose funding represents only a small portion of the school budget and where the employee organizations resist building-level decision making as a threat to districtwide collective bargaining.

As can be seen from the few examples presented, school-based governance is a promising social invention. One of its primary strengths is that the concept does not claim to be the one best system for organizing and governing schools but rather offers the opportunity to devise locally appropriate alternatives. As a form of decentralization, the implementation of the school-based governance concept should be observed closely on two counts of special importance.

First, a decentralized school system is not as effective as a centralized one in redistributing resources. There is a trade-off. Centralization decreases participation but makes it possible for strong, centralized leadership to redress inequities across the system. A decentralized system increases participation (which may include increased power for the poor and minorities) but limits the scope of exercise of the power to redistribute resources. Some advocates of school-based governance respond to this dilemma by pointing out that their plan is based on another approach to educational equity. For example, a major conclusion in a recent study done for the Florida legislature points out:

> Children in different communities with a single school district have different educational needs and styles. By permitting those people closest to these communities—parents and teachers—to make more of the educational policy decisions affecting a particular school, it is hoped those particular educational needs and styles can be better served. School-based management, in other words, encourages school program diversity so as to promote equality of educational outcomes rather than inputs. Without programs tailored to serve individual students, it is difficult to accomplish anything more than superficial dollar equality among schools in a district.[18]

Nonetheless, various forms of decentralization can be asked to stand the test of their effects on equitable distribution of resources. Programs that not only provide but guarantee access to power for representatives of low-income people are more likely to be designed to pass this test.

Second, while decentralized governance may increase participation, it provides increased control over a limited and very localized part of the environment. In decentralized governance, citizen participation runs the risk of being trivial because many forces influencing that local environment are operating from the city, state, or national levels. School-based governance, as seen in our California and Florida examples, seeks to balance building, district, and state responsibilities, combining some of the best aspects of both centralization and decentralization.

Finally, however, it is important for parents and citizens participating at the school-site level to understand the limits of their scope, to identify important external forces and decision makers, and to create vertical alliances and networks that allow access to information and influence.

COMMUNITY DEVELOPMENT ORGANIZATION

The Community Development Organization, another promising development in citizen participation, might also be called "grass-roots interest groups." The latter label captures the variety of forms taken by such organizations: grass-roots, neighborhood, or block associations, federations of such organizations, and community development corporations. They have, however, several common features.

They are all citizen-initiated, private-sector, voluntary organizations. Most are membership organizations or, at the very least, serve or represent an identifiable and usually geographically bounded constituency. Unlike some traditional civic organizations, they are united around concrete, often material, and almost always local interests, such as housing or health services, rather than general causes. Unlike some urban groups of the 1960s, neighborhood interest groups are not usually protest groups. Some of these groups, like the community development corporations, perform a quasipublic function of coordinating neighborhood renewal efforts and providing services. Many are nonideological and take a pragmatic approach by playing the pluralist bargaining game in representing local interests before municipal agencies. Finally, unlike parent associations or educational interest groups, these community organizations are multi-issue oriented. They represent a community's interest in a whole range of issues which define the quality of life. Education, however, is not often a top priority for such groups.

One reason for educational issues receiving such a low priority is the lower-class constituency base of such organizations. Other more basic survival issues—jobs, housing, transportation, health—inevitably take priority, and in economically deprived neighborhoods they can be all-consuming. Moreover, concrete material interests are easier to mobilize. Finally, the interest-group approach may not be as effective in the educational arena not so much because of any inherent defects in that approach but because access for such interest groups to educational policy making and the whole process of bargaining and compromise is neither institutionalized nor accepted. This is due, in part, to the norm which dictates that educational issues are either too important to be left to politics or else are technical issues best left to professionals.

Nevertheless, some of these groups, whose activities are illustrated below, do involve themselves in public school issues. Such involvement, while rare, is significant. The significance of their involvement and its promise for increased citizen participation in educational decision making derive from several additional features common and unique to these multi-issue development organizations.

First, such organizations represent one lasting and, especially in the case of community development corporations, durable invention of the War on Poverty and Model Cities initiatives. Second, participation in voluntary, private-sector associations has been traditionally the preserve (one could say the luxury) of the upper and middle classes—the civic elites. Contemporary community development organizations are, on the other hand, one of the few private-sector associations which manage to mobilize and represent minorities, the poor, and the working class. As such, these organizations have the potential of empowering the powerless.

This empowerment can be accomplished in a number of ways. On the most general level, the mere fact that lower-class neighborhood interests are organized is one step towards influence and redistribution of benefits. Our political system at the national, state, and municipal levels is characterized by interest-group bargaining. It does not recognize or deal with abstract or individual claims for social justice. Interests which remain unorganized remain invisible and, hence, powerless. On another level, community development organizations provide services to constituencies which are typically resource-poor and underserviced. For example, the Lena Park Community Development Corporation serves a predominantly black and low-income constituency in the Dorchester area of Boston and provides job training and placement services as well as engaging in outreach for health, mental health, and recreational services. The PATCH, a neighborhood organization in the poverty-ridden Atlanta neighborhood of Cabbagetown, home of about 2,000 poor whites with strong Appalachian mountain roots, provides job training and counseling for both adults and youth. In addition, it has capitalized on local skills in such traditional Appalachian crafts as quilting and promotes the revival of interest in such crafts as part of its neighborhood economic development strategy.

On another level, these community organizations are able to define their own agendas since they are voluntary. Thus, the agendas they choose reflect the interests of the constituencies they represent. Therefore, when such community organizations do get involved in school affairs, it is often on issues that meet our criterion of significance, and their involvement produces tangible results. For example, Lena Park has been influential in important personnel decisions in some newly desegregated Boston schools. In San Francisco, SPEAK (the Sunset Parkside Education Action Committee), a grassroots group of white middle-class and working-class residents of that city's southwest and west sides, recently (in 1977) undertook a thorough study of San Francisco junior high schools, publicizing its findings in a report to parents. That study and the publicity accompanying it provided the impetus for developing a new curriculum for some 400 junior high students. Like Lena Park in Boston and PATCH in Atlanta, SPEAK also focuses on neighborhood quality-of-life issues by acting as both an advocate-interest group and a provider of services. Some of SPEAK's specific accomplishments include persuading city officials to reconstruct a streetcar line to improve public transportation in the area, obtaining city approval and action for public access to a nearby beach, and establishing a community resource group on alcoholism.

A third significant feature of community development organizations is their multi-issue focus. While this often means that other issues—such as housing and employment—override concerns with public schooling, it also means that these organizations not only mobilize and articulate interests around specific issues but that they also serve to aggregate those interests. In other words, inevitable choices about what proportion of resources to devote to schools are often rehearsed and reconciled within such groups.

This has two consequences. First, it promotes participation which can contribute to social cohesion. The consensus within such multi-issue groups is often a mirror image of the kind of consensus necessary in the larger process of allocating resources for schools in times of austerity. Often, a concern with one set of issues—housing and community development and stability—leads to a concern with schooling. This transfer of concerns makes it far more likely that these groups will see and act upon the connection between school issues and community issues.

Second, such a linkage between school issues and quality-of-neighborhood-life issues can lead to actions which create community support for schools, especially on the divisive issue of school desegregation. For example, the Heights Community Congress was a federation of over fourteen community organizations in the relatively affluent University Heights and Cleveland Heights suburbs of Cleveland. While spearheaded by white middle-class liberals, the congress included representation from minority and less affluent groups. Growing out of a concern with real estate values and community stability, the congress engaged in a vigorous program to promote peaceful desegregation of area schools.

The federated structure of multi-issue and multiconstituency organizations such as the Heights Congress also creates participatory forms which contribute to social cohesion while at the same time encouraging and, in fact, organizing diversity (the constituent organizations maintain their identity and, on some issues, their separate interests). Federated organizations can also create vertical networks across class and race lines.

A similar networking-integrating function can be performed by community development corporations given their unique position of representing a lower-class constituency while cultivating contacts with public agencies and "downtown" business elites. For example, Lena Park's board of directors contains both "civic elites" and low-income and minority people. Contacts with the former group enabled this organization to exert influence on policy and helped it to draw both jobs and services into the community.

Finally, both the structure and strategies of these community development organizations can serve as models for more traditional, single-issue voluntary education groups. This can be seen by summarizing the unique features of these organizations compared to single-issue education groups.

First, the ability to have an impact on concrete issues affecting people's lives is the primary strength of the multipurpose community development organization. Low-income people participate when the stakes are visible and tangible benefits are attainable. It is the track record of achievements—in the lexicon of this chapter, "significant results"—on the part of these neighborhood interest groups and federations which most differentiates them from single-issue education groups, both mandated and voluntary, for whom similar accomplishments in the schools are harder to define and achieve.

Second, those community organizations which have perservered have developed a mass base—that is, an identifiable constituency which either participates in, is served by, or is represented by the organization. Third, this mass base is due, in part, to the multi-issue focus pursued by community development organizations. A more durable constituency is created by organizing to meet the needs of a neighborhood as a whole rather than discrete interests of particular sets of clients, such as parents or welfare recipients exclusively.

Fourth, constituency development is further enhanced by the federated model which integrates various constituent interests under one organizational umbrella. As noted above in the description of the Heights Congress, such an umbrella organization can appeal to and include a variety of community groups: churches, block clubs, planning groups, planning associations, and PTAs. In contrast, federation building appears to be much more difficult for single-issue education groups and these groups have trouble creating adequate constituent support. While neighborhood interest groups are able to attract all community residents, educational groups, whether citywide or neighborhood-based, appeal primarily to parents or else clients of particular categorical programs.

Finally, when neighborhood interest groups represent constituents' interests to other municipal agencies, they operate in a public policy context in which the resource allocation process can be every bit as political and divisive as it is in the school policy making arena. However, this nonschool context is one in which bargaining, compromise, and access for group interests—in short, citizen participation—is part of business as usual. In education, by contrast, powerful and deep-rooted norms work against participation. One norm still dictates that school governance is not or should not be a part of "politics." Another, the norm of professionalism, dictates that all educational decisions are technical matters best settled by experts. Norms dictate practices and, so far, the practice of school governance has yet to provide citizen participation groups with a settled role as key actors in the normal way of doing business. This may explain why single-issue education groups have trouble achieving results which would in turn increase their influence (the process feeds back upon itself; success breeds more success). It may also partially explain why so few community development organizations get involved in school issues. This suggests that further elaboration and refinement of the kind of social inventions described in the previous promising practice—school-based governance—may create the kind of access for citizen participation which will serve to invigorate both mandated and voluntary forms of citizen participation.

Both forms of citizen participation are equally necessary if we take seriously the six criteria introduced earlier in this chapter. Access to decision making about significant issues with the possibility of achieving real results is enhanced by moves towards school-based management. In that context, members of a mandated school-site council actually have something to participate about. But there are some functions mandated groups cannot and should not perform. As public bodies, mandated councils cannot play a mobilizing role. They cannot do the job of organizing different constituencies and pushing particular interests. These functions are best performed by private-sector citizen-initiated groups whose nature and function allow them to organize and promote diverse perspectives. As such, citizen-initiated groups promote diversity. Mandated groups, on the other hand, can promote cohesion. They can do this through a broad-based membership which represents diverse interests and viewpoints and by taking on significant issues and decision-making roles which force these interests to reconcile. Compromise and reconciliation have the best chance of occurring when there are real issues at stake, when there are actually decisions that can and must be taken.

In short, the balance between diversity and cohesion and the other values implicit in the six criteria for judging participation has the best chance of being maximized in a situation where there are both mandated representative structures with a meaningful policy-making role and a surrounding context of vigorous, private-sector citizen-initiated interest groups. Without the latter, mandated councils would have nothing to represent and no one to keep them accountable. It is for these reasons that recognizing, strengthening, and providing access to the kind of community development organizations described above should be included in any future social inventions for citizen participation.

A FINAL NOTE

In this chapter, I have pointed to many contradictions and confusions in the current citizen participation scene. Despite much talk and activity, many of the current forms of participation in the schools are not working well at all. Both educators and citizens are dissatisfied; there is little power sharing. Most of the policies and activities fall far short of meeting the proposed criteria. Yet, there are many promising ideas and practices, such as those discussed here and in the next chapter. Social inventiveness is not dead. There is substantial hope that policies, mechanisms, and activities will be developed which will adequately satisfy the criteria proposed here.

The current hard times combined with a commitment to the importance of education in our society should press educators and citizens to become inventors of more productive and satisfying ways for communities and their schools to relate to one another through citizen participation.

NOTES

1. L. Harmon Zeigler et al., "How School Control was Wrested from the People," *Phi Delta Kappan,* vol. 58, no. 7, 1977, pp. 534–540.

2. Based on a three-year study entitled "Citizen Organizations: A Study of Citizen Participation in Educational Decision Making" conducted by the Institute for Responsive Education under contract to the National Institute of Education. Other examples and case study material discussed in this chapter are based primarily on that study. A more extended discussion of the findings pertinent to the issues raised in this chapter is contained in three reports: *Federal and State Impact on Citizen Participation in the Schools* (1978) and *Patterns of Participation* (in two volumes, 1978 and 1979). All three are published by the Institute for Responsive Education, Boston, Massachusetts.

3. Marilyn Gittel et al., *Local Control in Education,* Praeger, New York, 1972, pp. 40–65 and 120–33.

4. Robert N. Bush, "Preface" in Bruce K. Joyce (ed.), *Involvement: A Study of Shared Governance of Teacher Education,* National Dissemination Center, Syracuse, New York, 1978, p. xiv.

5. Eva L. Baker, Joan L. Herman, and Jennie P. Yeh, *Evaluation of the Longitudinal Effects of the Early Childhood Program,* University of California at Los Angeles, Center for the Study of Evaluation, 1978.

6. Some examples are, Arnold M. Rose, "Alienation and Participation," *American Sociological Review,* vol. 27, pp. 834–38; December 1962; and Arnold M. Rose, "Attitudinal Correlates of Social Participation," *Social Forces,* vol. 37, pp. 202–206, March 1959. See also, Herbert McClosky, "Consensus and Ideology in American Politics," *American Political Science Review,* vol. 58, pp. 361–382, June 1964. Much of this earlier literature is surveyed in Sidney Verba, "Democratic Participation," *Annals of the American Academy of Political and Social Science,* vol. 373, pp. 53–78, September 1967. More contemporary works which address this issue include, Richard L. Cole, *Citizen Participation and the Urban Policy Process,* D. C. Heath, Lexington, Massachusetts, 1974; Lois S. Steinberg, *Social Science Theory and Research on Participation and Voluntary Associations: A Bibliographic Essay,* Institute for Responsive Education, Boston, Massachusetts, 1977; Sidney Verba and Norman H. Nie, *Participation in America: Political Democracy and Social Equality,* Harper and Row, New York, 1972; and Robert K. Yin et al., *Citizen Organizations: Increasing Client Control Over Services,* The Rand Corporation, Santa Monica, California, 1973.

7. George H. Gallup, "English Annual Gallup Poll: Public Attitudes Towards the Public Schools," *Phi Delta Kappan,* October, 1976.

8. Dale Mann, "Political Representation and Urban Advisory Councils," *Teachers College Record,* vol. 75, no. 3, 1977, pp. 379–397.

9. Susan Heck, "Perceived Outcomes and Concurrent Conditions of Parent

Participation in School Policymaking," unpublished Ph.D. dissertation, School of Education, Stanford University, Stanford, California, 1977.

10. See Eliot Levinson, *The Alum Voucher Demonstration: Three Years of Implementation*, The Rand Corporation, Santa Monica, California, 1976; and Felix Gutierrez and Gloria Chacon, *The Educational Voucher Intrigue: An Analysis of Its Impact on the Alum Rock Community*, The Southwest Network, Haywood, California, 1974.

11. John E. Coons and Stephen D. Sugarman, *Education by Choice: The Case for Family Control*, University of California Press, Berkeley and Los Angeles, 1978.

12. Janice Perlman, *Grassrooting the System*, University of California, Institute of Urban and Regional Development, Reprint No. 139, 1976.

13. Lawrence L. Pierce, Walter Garms, James W. Guthrie, and Michael W. Kirst, *State School Finance Alternatives: Strategies for Reform*, University of Oregon, Center for Educational Policy Management, Eugene, 1975.

14. Cited in *Sharing the Power? A Report on the Status of School Councils in the 1970's*, Institute for Responsive Education, Boston, Massachusetts, 1977.

15. The original recommendations are contained in: *Improving Education in Florida*, a report of the Governor's Citizens' Committee on Education, March 1973. This report is available through ERIC, ED 078-531. The record of subsequent implementation is contained in *Improving Education in Florida: A Reassessment*, prepared for the Select Joint Committee on Public Schools of the Florida Legislature, February 1978.

16. *Improving Education in Florida: A Reassessment*, ibid., p. 41.

17. "Meeting the Challenge of Improving Education: The Perspective from California," *Citizen Action in Education*, vol. 6, no. 1, p. 11, March 1979. *Citizen Action in Education* is a quarterly newsletter of the Institute for Responsive Education, Boston, Massachusetts.

18. *Improving Education in Florida: A Reassessment*, op. cit., p. 60.

5

THIRD PARTIES AS PROBLEM SOLVERS

LUVERN L. CUNNINGHAM
Ohio State University

J ohn W. Gardner has noted, "One of the first requirements for solving our problems is that we confront them, identify them early, appraise them honestly, and avoid complacency or evasion." He added, "The second thing to be said is that social problem solving today requires a combination of technical competence and motivated people."[1]

This chapter is about problem solving in the public sector. More specifically it is about problem-solving citizens groups in education. Even more specifically it is about special problem-solving groups that have clear missions, professional staffs, high motivation, funding, and broad legitimacy.[2] It is not about the hundreds of committees, either self-initiated or institutionally named, that study and review problems, important as such groups are.[3] The problem-solving groups discussed in this chapter are composed primarily of citizens who are residents of the city involved and are not professional educators employed by the school district.

Problem-solving third parties work in different situations where problems extend beyond the problem-solving abilities of established institutions and their leadership. Often finance seems to be an issue; so are desegregation, decentralization, governance, business management, low pupil achievement or all or some combination of these.[4]

Problem-solving third parties do many of the things that traditional citizens groups of the past have done. They study, gather data, debate, and settle upon recommendations. But that is just the first part, the easy part. They then strike common cause and work with institutional authorities on implementation, on putting recommendations in place, on monitoring their recommendations' effectiveness—in fact, on solving the problem.

Several terms are used almost interchangeably to identify the functions that citizens groups can perform when they are devoted to problem solving. Third force and third sector convey essentially the same meanings as third party. Third-party activity is widespread in our society. It occurs as a part of our judicial system; it is at the heart of labor negotiations; it is essential to international affairs; it is increasingly invoked in disputes between husbands and wives; and it is employed in many other arenas of existing of potential conflict. In labor-management relationships third-party roles are formal and reasonably well understood. Mediator, conciliator, arbitrator, and fact finder are formal roles. Skilled persons occupy them. They have become professionalized, and individuals devote their lives to those careers. Furthermore, they are so specialized that individuals can and do charge generous fees for such third-party services.

Third-party activity is both formal and informal, public and nonpublic, reported and unreported. *Formal third-party activity* is legitimized and publicly accepted at a general level. That is, it is legal, sanctioned by tradition, acceptable to most people as a form of conflict resolution or problem solving. It is public, often open, certainly not clandestine. *Informal third-party activity* is not necessarily public especially in delicate international matters or domestic relations problems. Informal third-party activity often is spontaneous with few if any broadly shared prior specifications—legal or otherwise—surrounding the intervener's authority or activity.

The services of a third party can be invoked from any of several quarters. It can be as simple as carrying a message, or as involved as the work of Henry Kissinger or President Carter convening individuals and groups over time in various parts of the world with the goal of achieving an acceptable state of affairs among nations. At a more familiar level, a friend can be asked to convene husband and wife, parents and children, or next-door neighbors to settle matters at issue. The friend intervenes, fact-finds, mediates, conciliates, and helps achieve an acceptable state of affairs among family members.

Third-party activity in education (setting aside labor relations) has many of the same attributes of third-party forms described above, but it differs chiefly in the specification of the other parties. An education problem-solving citizens group may serve many individuals, many groups, many constituencies. The third party in some respects negotiates the public interest among boards of education, school employees (especially top school administrators), students, parents, citizens, the state, even federal interests. Such citizens groups occupy privileged terrain, and, because of their power and influence, must proceed responsibly. Their accountability is often questioned, and rightfully so, since their membership is not determined through traditional election processes. Their sponsorship, too, is sometimes obscure, at least to the average citizen, and their impact on many matters is not in full view, nor is it easily traced.

Third parties are usually invoked when established institutions are thought to be failing.[5] The admission of failure on the part of a school board or a city council, a school superintendent or a mayor is a serious step.

What can citizens do that trained school personnel or board members cannot do? First, they can approach problems more objectively and less passionately than those traditionally involved. Problem-solving citizens groups do not have the obligation of day-to-day governance and management. They are relatively free from the harassment of school system patrons, even students. They are remote from day-to-day problems of administration and teaching. They are freer, have more time for analysis and reflection, and are removed from the affective side of management. Citizens groups can be concerned, for example, about a teachers strike, even have opinions about it, but not be responsible for negotiation. School board members and superintendents don't enjoy the luxury of such remoteness. It seems only prudent and wise, then, to solicit help from the sources of knowledge, energy, and wisdom in the community. And that is what third parties as problem solvers is all about.

Second, a third party can be a unique catalyst to achieve the release and the integration of the unlimited energies that reside within the human community. Third-party involvement does not diminish the worth of what is in place. It does not demean. It neither defiles nor denigrates. A third party respects the legacy of the past, the efforts of the dedicated. It builds upon that legacy and refines that contribution. Its distinctive task is to integrate new energies, new wisdom, and new persons in an assault upon problems in the public interest.

The eight citizens committees listed in Table 1 are used as examples to describe the similarities and variances among problem-solving third parties. Each group was born of crisis; each was created to revitalize a public school system and enable a city's schools to deliver an improved quality of education to its students and, as a consequence, to strengthen the social and economic structures of their cities.

Each third party varies in size and composition of membership, staff, working committees, and budgets. All, however, are devoted to eradicating problems related to education that are hazardous to the life and health of the community.

The Metropolitan Columbus Schools Committee was essentially a single-purpose body created to prepare the Columbus community for school desegregation. The Dallas Alliance had a larger agenda but was responsible for developing a school desegregation remedy plan. The Detroit Education Task Force focused on many problems. So did the Los Angeles Citizens Review Committee. The Milwaukee Committee of One Hundred was to assist in the development of the Milwaukee remedy plan initially; later the presiding federal district judge added the responsibility of monitoring the implementation of the remedy plan. The St. Louis Citizens Education Task Force and the San Francisco Public Schools Commission developed and pursued comprehensive problem-solving agendas. The Kansas City Council on Education was initiated by the local Chamber of Commerce and worked on several problems including finance, school organization, and desegregation.

THE THEORY OF THIRD PARTIES

The success of third parties turns on the power and legitimacy they possess or can earn. Their power and legitimation may come from several sources. One is from the institutions they are expected to serve.

TABLE 1 CHARACTERISTICS OF THIRD-PARTY PROBLEM-SOLVING CITIZENS GROUPS

CHARACTERISTIC GROUP	SIZE MEMBERSHIP	PROFESS. STAFF	SUB-STRUCTURES	FUNDING SOURCES	STEERING AND/OR COORDIN. STRUCTURE	SCHOOL BOARD ENDORSED/ SPONSORED	MEDIA PROFILE
Metropolitan Columbus Schools Committee	open	yes	one committee	Private	Steering Committee	Neither	Low
Dallas Alliance	open	yes	Three Committees	Private	Steering Committee	Endorsed	Moderate
Detroit Education Task Force	53 1973–74 70 1974–75 40 1975–76	yes	two to five committees	Public/ Private	Steering Committee	Sponsored	Moderate
Los Angeles Citizens Management Review Committee	open	no	As required	Public	Neither	Sponsored	Low
Milwaukee Committee of One Hundred	113	no	As required	Public	Neither	Sponsored	Low
St. Louis Citizens Education Task Force	40	yes	nine committees	Private/ Public	Steering Committee	Sponsored	Low
San Francisco Public Schools Commission	25	yes	Nine Task Forces	Private/ Public	Neither	Endorsed	High
Kansas City Council on Education	open	yes	As required	Private	Neither	Neither	Low

Another is from other levels or units of government. Still another is from individuals and groups who are aware of the seriousness of an institution's difficulties and support the creation of a special group charged with problem solving.

A third party's power is its legitimation. There are many examples of well-intended, even well-funded community groups that have worked on school problems and needs without success. Such failures are essentially due to the lack of legitimacy. If they lack endorsements from key community sources of legitimation, there is little prospect that their efforts will be effective, because institutional officials can more easily resist them. The goodwill and understanding of school officials are especially essential if implementation of third-party recommendations is to occur. And unless problem-solving citizens groups stay in close touch with school system personnel (teachers, counselors, other specialists), problems will not be solved.

Problem-solving third parties have several characteristics. First, they rely on their ability to intervene in ongoing processes of the institution under review for legitimation, information, participation, suggestion, and implementation.[6] Information that is reliable, current, and accurate is essential to the study and analysis of problems. The participation of school officials and school personnel is necessary to information gathering and the review of problem-solving proposals drafted by the citizens group. Suggestions from people on the firing line are important because they more often than not know what ought to be done. And implementation can only be achieved with the cooperation and participation of the people who are paid to do the job. Second, problem-solving third parties are potentially very powerful and influential and thus must work formally and openly. They must publicly report their progress periodically, both orally and in writing, especially to those most likely to be affected directly by recommendations.[7] Third, their impartiality and neutrality must be maintained, especially during the period of agreeing upon directions and recommendations. Indeed, when a problem-solving citizens group steps off its sheltered turf and assumes an advocacy posture on controversial points or events of short-term significance, it reduces its prospects for long-term, large-scale effectiveness.

Problem solving requires broad participation. School officials, as well as other community leaders, gradually come to recognize that the solutions to problems often reside beyond school district boundaries. This acknowledgment is hard to achieve and often comes reluctantly. Third parties, especially their leaders and professional staff, must be aware that school system problems require action and resources from several places. Problem-solving groups are likely to recognize the scope of problems, their complexity, and the places where change must take place because of their diverse memberships. Many groups, best reflected in the membership of the Detroit Education Task Force, are formed to ensure representation from governments, institutions, and community sectors that can provide legitimation, linkage, support, and implementation of recommendations if problem solving requires action beyond the institution's boundaries.

Third parties must have very strong leadership.[8] Heavy demands are placed upon the persons chosen. The citizens group members, the school system served, the media, and the community at large hold high expectations for their performance. Problem solving is difficult, time-consuming, and patience-testing. There are no easy solutions to problems, and there are few short cuts. It requires painstaking care and a willingness to slug it out over time.

Two groups, the Detroit and the St. Louis Education Task Forces, adopted the principle of co-leadership. Although there were some weaknesses in placing responsibility with two or more persons, the advantages far outweighed the defects. The leadership attributes of more than one person are available and enrich the leadership resources to be applied. Multidimensional leadership is essential. Citizens group members expect leadership; the professional staff must be led as well. Leadership is essential, too, in working with school officials, the media, state and other local governments, and the public.

Third parties have varying levels of community visibility. Some seek publicity and want the citizenry to be aware of their mission and even their specific objectives. Others wish to remain in the background, to do their work quietly and without fanfare. The Columbus, Detroit, Dallas, and San Francisco groups were in the spotlight at various times. The formation of the San Francisco Public Schools Commission attracted widespread public note. So did the Dallas Alliance when Judge William Taylor, Jr. selected its desegregation plan from among several developed by other community groups and school officials.

The initial meeting of Milwaukee's Committee of One Hundred was broadcast over commercial television even though the session lasted more than three hours and occurred on the same day as Wisconsin's 1976 Presidential primary election.[9] The Los Angeles third party preferred and maintained a rather low profile in media terms. So did the St. Louis Education Task Force initially.

Relationships with the media become very important as the problem-solving efforts of third parties proceed to the point of recommending change. High public visibility elevates expectations and makes the third party's work more difficult. Extremely low visibility affects a group's credibility to some extent and reduces its political potency. Citizen leaders and professional staff must give thorough consideration to media relationships. They should consider matters of profile, sharing of published and unpublished reports and recommendations, enlisting cooperation in press conferences, and involving media leaders from time to time in the progress of the third party's work.

The presence of a prestigious and powerful citizens group presents some problems to established groups in a community. The PTA, Band Boosters, and education committees of the NAACP, Junior League, League of Women Voters, Urban League, and dozens of others have staked out their terrain and want to preserve it. Turf can be threatened; the visibility of other groups can be challenged. Even though third-party problem-solving objectives do not pertain to other groups, the work of the third party may invade arenas already well cultivated by others. Third parties should avoid "competition" with in-place citizens groups and find ways of striking common cause and enlisting the assistance of other groups.

Third parties are legitimized more quickly in times of crisis. Crisis makes legitimacy much easier to achieve at the outset but, curiously, crisis makes it more difficult to sustain. Early successes of third parties in responding to crises elevate expectations and put more pressure on groups to sustain their success record. Americans are reluctant to tamper with constitutionally and statutorily established governments and institutions. Thus permutations or extensions of traditional or established authority must be effective. If not, they are short-lived and find themselves quickly on the scrap heap of social invention.

The Detroit Education Task Force was born of crisis. The Detroit Public Schools were on the threshold of bankruptcy. They would have had to shut down unless some miracles were performed. The Detroit Central Board of Education was under pressure from New Detroit Inc. and other community groups to enlist the support of the community. After a period of resistance, the Board named a problem-solving task force to help them out of their fiscal troubles. The early weeks of the Task Force's existence were given over almost exclusively to the financial crisis. A finance subcommittee was created, made up of members of the Task Force who were expert in finance. They went to Lansing, the state capital, and met with key legislators, the Governor, the Superintendent of Public Instruction, and the State Treasurer. They gathered data, reviewed alternatives, and fashioned legislation which was introduced and passed as Public Laws 1 and 2 in the 1973 session of the Michigan legislature. The legislation would solve the immediate financial crunch, if it were judged constitutional by the Michigan Supreme Court. While the Court was making up its mind, the State Superintendent loaned the Detroit Public Schools enough money (interest-free) to complete the 1973–74 school year. The crisis was over, at least temporarily.

The Dallas Alliance focused initially on the desegregation/integration of the Dallas Independent School District. The times were troubled. The Court had requested a community response to segregated schools. The Alliance, funded by wealthy individuals and private sector institutions, got busy. It employed an energetic, capable sociologist as its Executive Director. He linked closely with the Alliance's chairperson, fashioned an ambitious community involvement strategy, and designed a desegregation strategy to present to Judge Taylor. It was chosen from among several submitted to the Court, including a plan devised by the staff of the Dallas Independent School District. When school opened in the fall of 1976, national television highlighted the peaceful desegregation of the Dallas Schools including a picture of Dallas Superintendent Nolan Estes driving a school bus on opening day. The Dallas Alliance rose to the occasion, met the challenge, and solved the immediate problem of producing a desegregation remedy plan.[10]

San Francisco offers another illustration of a problem-solving group born out of crisis. In the mid-1970s, the San Francisco Unified School District was wracked by dissension. The school district serves a city of unparalleled diversity. Local leaders spoke of thirty-seven distinct cultural and racial minorities represented in the city and in its public schools. The problems of multicultural and bilingual education were severe. Enrollments were declining, as was true everywhere, but the decline in San Francisco was aggravated by an absence of housing for middle-class families within the city.

San Francisco is one of California's "Big Five," enrolling nearly 70,-000 pupils in 1975–76. It was a wealthy city and spent a great deal per pupil. In fact it ranked just behind Beverly Hills and Pasadena in per-pupil investment. Yet, its test results were unimpressive. Pupil achievement had been going down over the years to the point where it was in the lowest decile on the state-administered tests.

In 1975, State Superintendent of Schools Wilson Riles was so discouraged by increasing expenditures and declining test results that he urged the Board of Education in San Francisco to accept a blue-ribbon group, named by Riles, to help solve the district's problems. The Board resisted vigorously, then gave in in the face of intense community support for Riles's proposal. Thus, a third party, the San Francisco Public Schools Commission, emerged because of a peculiar form of crisis—low achievement despite high public investment. The Commission set out immediately to learn why achievement levels were so disappointing and why per pupil costs were so high. The analyses of expenditures led to a series of changes intended to improve learning outcomes.

Following its initial work on finance, the Detroit group moved quickly to an examination of administrative organization at the central level. The Dallas Alliance directed its energies to achieving a constructive response to the court order. And San Francisco developed a multiple-front approach to a broad set of local educational problems. Each sustained its initial legitimacy through constructive action. But the public memory is both fickle and short. In order to retain their credibility, these groups were faced with the need to follow through quickly and effectively on other problem fronts.

And herein lies a paradox. Established high-cost institutions like public school systems can continue year in and year out with marginal-to-inadequate performance. But ad hoc, special-purpose groups such as third parties must prove themselves continuously to maintain their legitimacy. The community has little tolerance for their ineffectiveness; without approbation from many quarters, problem-solving third parties cannot function effectively.

THIRD-PARTY FUNCTIONS AND STRATEGIES

The basic purpose of third parties as they are treated in this chapter is to solve educational problems. Attention is focused particularly on those problems that have been unyielding, enduring, and especially threatening to those who enroll in schools, to their parents and families, indeed, to the community at large. In the ordinary course of problem solving, third-party groups fulfill several functions and employ numerous strategies.[11]

In one way or another, third parties pass through all the classic stages of problem solving, even to investing substantial attention to monitoring their handiwork. Considerable time is spent in locating the most important problem arenas, in isolating the issues, and in defining the problems. All problem solvers must make sure that they know what the problem is before proceeding. In Detroit, San Francisco, and St. Louis, it took many months to decide what the educational problems really were. Once defined, it took additional time to determine which were the most important and which should be attacked first. To actually solve problems a number of subfunctions or strategies are employed by a third party.

CONVENING

Convening is assembling people who, in the absence of a third party, are not likely to meet. Convening is an exercise of leadership. Inherent in convening is an enormous power potential. Assembly of media leaders for briefings on third-party progress is an illustration. Such assemblies occurred regularly in St. Louis, Columbus, San Francisco, and Detroit.

ACCESSING

Accessing involves the location and application of ideas, human resources, even dollar resources to problems which ordinarily would escape the purview of, or be unavailable to, established school authorities. The Advisory Committee from Higher Education established by the Detroit Education Task Force is a good example. This committee identified experts from the faculties of several Michigan universities and made them available (without charge) to the Detroit Education Task Force and to the Detroit Public Schools.

MEDIATING

Today's problems are often saturated with emotion and conflict. The parties involved are sometimes unable to reach satisfactory resolution. When such conflict occurs in areas of interest to third parties, mediation may be required to facilitate the work of the citizens group. The Dallas Alliance mediated many differences in the development of a desegregation plan that would be accepted by the court. Sustained and skillful negotiations were required between and among civil rights organizations, parent groups, business interests, educators, and the school board. Those negotiations involved many compromises and tradeoffs which were reflected in the school desegregation remedy plan.

LINKING

There are many examples of disjunction in modern communities. School board members and superintendents in the past were often able to communicate across many segments of the community. This was especially true among elites. Today school officials are often less able to sustain such communication even if they are able to establish it in the first place.

CATALYZING

Problematic conditions are often marked by inertia, confusion, lack of direction, even despair. A third force or party can be a catalyst, an external agent, and a motivator. Sometimes it takes little more than a nudge to get things off dead center. For example, the Education Committee of the Detroit Task Force had grown increasingly discontent with the quality of teaching in the Detroit Public Schools. When it was learned that large numbers of beginning teachers were employed from Wayne State and Michigan State Universities, members of the committee wanted to know about their programs. They were especially interested in how beginning teachers had been prepared to teach reading. Meetings were held with deans, heads of teacher education programs, professors, reading specialists, and students in training. Curricula were examined and changes urged, many of which were made.

PROXYING

Third parties and their members can on occasion serve as proxies for school authorities. The proxying function is similar to but not the same as the linking function. It calls for the group or individuals to stand in the place of others, in this case, school boards or their individual members and school administrators. Leaders for the Detroit Education Task Force in the early hours of solving the 1972–73 fiscal crisis of the Detroit Public Schools "stood in" for school leaders in negotiations in Lansing. At other times and under other circumstances school officials could have handled such matters themselves, but not in this case.

LEADING

Leading is implicit in some of the other functions described above. Convening, linking, and catalyzing are leadership acts involving initiation. Third-party problem solvers are leadership groups. They are given room to move, turf to occupy, and resources to apply. They move in on uncertainty and confusion. They mobilize energy, they capture attention, and they direct and redirect. And they do so under privileged circumstances, including the opportunity to apply rational approaches to problem solving.

REPORTING

Many communities distrust the information they received from school sources. An objective, impartial third party can assemble and disseminate information that will be believed, at least as long as the third party retains its credibility. Thus, an efficient and sustained reporting capability is essential to third-party work. The San Francisco Commission employed a full-time staff person to guide and direct the Commission's reporting activity. The Detroit group retained such a person on a part-time basis.

IMPLEMENTING

Implementing is the function that distinguishes problem-solving groups from other citizen bodies. It is an exceptionally difficult part of problem solving and requires very close collaboration with school officials even to the point of working day after day inside the school system with school personnel. Implementation requires patience, understanding, and adjustments on the part of citizens and school people if it is to occur.

These functions are described as if they were discrete, independent activities. It is useful to set them apart for the purpose of analysis, recognizing that in the maelstrom of problem solving they lose their independence. For example, an act of reporting may turn out to be a catalyst to portions of the education community. As it impacts constructively on human events, it may be seen as an important act of leadership. Convening persons who ordinarily would not assemble or collectively confront a problem (in which each has an independent stake) often has important by-products. A convening can achieve leadership, mediation, reporting, linking, and accessing—in fact, most of the subfunctions of third-party problem solving.

CONVENING: A POWERFUL TOOL

Third parties, because of their impartiality and legitimacy, have one powerful tool at their disposal. It is convening, or the assembly of individuals and groups key to problem-solving activity. Several types of assemblies have been used by third-party groups, each for a particular purpose. Colloquies, seminars, workshops, conferences, and hearings will be reviewed in terms of third-party experience.

THE COLLOQUY

The colloquy is a time-honored form of assembly. It is a formal mutual discourse involving persons possessing diverse perspectives. It was used effectively by the Detroit Education Task Force. Small numbers of citizens and professionals were invited to participate in task force–sponsored colloquies which were focused essentially on professional questions, such as the teaching of reading, about which there was intense citizen interest. They were designed to be maximally effective as adult learning enterprises. Forms of participation were differentiated and controlled by trained facilitators. Professional issues were clarified sufficiently so that lay persons could proceed more confidently with their problem-solving tasks. Colloquies were limited to single, three-hour sessions.

THE SEMINAR

Seminars are structured, disciplined forms of convening. Traditionally, they have been considered as formats for campus-based, essentially graduate study. Only recently have they been viewed as tools for citizen groups. Unlike the colloquies, citizen group seminars continued over time, with defined memberships. Emphasis was placed upon the incorporation of organized information such as expert testimony, research summaries, readings, and presentations by seminar members. Seminars were used by citizen groups in St. Louis and Columbus. In both instances, school desegregation problems and issues were the subject matter. The seminars were directed by citizens skilled in seminar leadership.

THE WORKSHOP

Workshops on governance were employed extensively by the San Francisco Public Schools Commission. They involved Commission members, staff, school board members, school administrators, citizens, even the media. Their purposes were similar to those of the colloquies in Detroit, but were conducted quite differently. They were exploratory, educative, and, to a modest extent, consensus-generating. They met many times, were less rigid in format, and were less controlled. As applied to governance issues in San Francisco, the workshops allowed intensive probing of superintendent–school board relationships. Only the Commission could convene the relevant parties on these matters because of the circumstances surrounding those relationships. No other group possessed the legitimacy or influence necessary to bring public exploration of ways to improve these aspects of the governance and management of the San Francisco Unified School District. The sustained review of these relationships through workshops and other forms of convening kept the spotlight on them and led to some improvements.

THE CONFERENCE
Conferences are ordinarily short-term. They involve large numbers and are constructed around a theme or topical agenda. Conferences meet citizen needs to become better informed and serve political and social needs as well. The conference form of convening was used by the Columbus and the St. Louis groups to heighten community awareness about the important issues of desegregation. The Detroit group sponsored a citywide conference on youth employment, an exceedingly difficult Detroit problem. Each succeeded in elevating awareness; however, none of the conferences achieved problem solutions.

HEARINGS
Hearings are used by third parties and many other groups. They are widely used in legislative processes, especially at the state and federal levels. Boards of education have adopted the hearings mechanism for public review of anticipated actions, often in regard to school desegregation remedy plans. Following the civil rights revolution of the 1960s, public bodies that were under pressure adopted the hearings format as a basis for sounding out public sentiment in regard to many issues that were before them.

Hearings are assemblies of interested persons who wish to speak on public issues to bodies that can influence outcomes. They should be formal, guided by ground rules clearly stated and announced publicly, held in settings that are familiar and known to citizens, and conducted with reason and consistency. Hearings can be incredibly valuable instrumentalities. However, most hearings processes break down when the ground rules established for their conduct are violated. They require strong and consistent chairing in reasonably formal settings that are comfortable for those who attend. Hearings should be time-bounded so that some effort is made to discipline the length of reporting.

The hearings instrument should be sheltered and protected. It is a precious form of assembly and its discreteness should be maintained.

Subcommittees of the Detroit Education Task Force and the San Francisco Public Schools Commission used hearings in a slightly different sense. They did not, in fact, meet the criteria advanced above. They were more nearly "review processes" held for the purpose of informing staff and commission members about problems and issues before subcommittees. They were, however, closely akin to conventional legislative hearings.

THIRD-PARTY EFFECTIVENESS AS PROBLEM SOLVERS

The distinctiveness of citizens as problem solvers is in problem solving itself. The appraisal of citizen group effectiveness must turn on whether or not problems are, in fact, solved and whether or not the recommendations for change are implemented and achieve the purposes for which they were intended. This is an exacting expectation which should ordinarily be applied to the problem-solving efforts of institutions themselves. Most often, however, it is not. What does it mean to solve a problem? What evidence is necessary to conclude that the problem is no longer a problem, that conditions have been altered, circumstances rearranged, difficulties removed, productivity restored or achieved? Each problem warrants individual judgment about whether or not it has, in fact, been solved.

In Detroit, for example, the early work of the Task Force's Finance Committee led to legislation (and other circumstances) which allowed the Detroit Public Schools to remain open for a full term in 1972–73. If the problem had been defined as finding ways to keep the schools open for a full school term, then the problem was solved since the schools remained open. If the problem were defined as achieving deficit financing of a 72 million dollar debt and balancing the 1973–74 budget, then the early action in 1973 failed because an October 1973 determination of the Michigan State Supreme Court declared half of the two-part legislative package unconstitutional. As a consequence, the Finance Committee had to return to the drawing boards and design a fresh approach to funding the deficit. A plan to sell deficit bonds was devised through the help of some of Detroit's financial leaders. Eventually the deficit was funded and the budget balanced. Those two issues were laid to rest; the short-run financial problems were solved.

Another problem illustrates the cumbersome and tortuous path to solution. The San Francisco Public Schools Commission in September 1976 recommended that the San Francisco Unified School District do its own purchasing rather than continue to have it done by the City and County of San Francisco. The Board of Education approved the Commission's recommendation effective July 1, 1976, contingent upon the preparation of an acceptable transition and implementation plan. The Commission then assisted school administrators with the planning necessary to achieve the changes. A Commission staff person was assigned to work with school administrators, as was a skillful executive on loan from Pacific Telephone. Five months were invested in planning. A comprehensive planning document was prepared and eventually adopted by the board. Before board approval, however, pressures from city officials who opposed the idea began to produce uneasiness on the part of some board members. The Commission found it necessary to reassure board members that their decision to assume purchasing was right, that in the long run it would improve services to children and save money. Many hours were invested by the Executive Director in blunting the pressures from city officials. And eventually the plan was adopted unanimously. The school district is now doing its own purchasing.

Implementation of recommendations designed to solve problems is actually much tougher than the analysis of problems and development of recommendations. When it appears that authorities are serious in their support of third-party proposals, opposing forces are often mobilized, and constraints emerge. Solutions to problems call for changes in behavior, reallocation of resources, adjustments in duties and responsibilities, and explicit or implied judgments about performance. The talk ends, change begins, and the status quo is disturbed.

The San Francisco Public Schools Commission intended to complete its work in eighteen months, by June 30, 1976. In May 1976, the Commission decided to extend its life until December 31, 1976. Following that decision, the Commission held a full-day workshop to plan the implementation of its many recommendations to the San Francisco Unified School District and to the City and County of San Francisco. The intent of the workshop was for school board members, the superintendent and staff, principals, teacher organization leaders and Commission members to anticipate problems of implementation and to develop ways to ensure effective implementation. Agreements were worked out which guided the work of the Commission over its remaining months of active service.

In each city, many recommendations were advanced to the respective boards and, in some cases, other agencies and levels of government.

Some were accepted and endorsed immediately and directed to appropriate administrators for implementation. Some recommendations were neither accepted nor rejected but simply "received." The implementation workshop in San Francisco described above was exceptionally significant in terms of problem solving. The Commission staff prepared materials prior to and following that workshop which aided in the review of the Commission's work and in the development of implementation strategies. The day following the workshop, the Commission staff summarized implementation agreements that had been reached. These agreements became the implementation agenda for the next several months.[12] Commission members were assigned implementation tasks, as were school district, city, and county officials. To keep a public and official focus on this phase of the Commission's work, the Commission monitored progress and reported to the community regularly on implementation.

There is an important distinction between problem solving as a basic objective of a citizens group and the constructive impact that the presence of such citizens groups have upon the educational system apart from problem solving. In San Francisco and Detroit particularly, the fact that the citizens groups were working on problems stimulated intense work on those problems within the school systems. In some cases the problems were well along toward solution before the formal advancement of recommendations by the citizens groups had occurred. There were other effects, too.

The Detroit Education Task Force (and, to a lesser extent, the San Francisco Public Schools Commission and the St. Louis Education Task Force) impacted on nearby institutions of higher education, state departments of public instruction, foundations, businesses, and industries. In Detroit, an Advisory Committee from Higher Education became the conduit for influence upon colleges of education especially. Teacher-training and counselor education programs were strengthened as a consequence of the task force's defining them as problem areas. The Detroit Task Force and its staff were major participants, too, in designing and implementing a teacher center located at Wayne State University and funded by the Michigan State Department of Education.

In San Francisco the work of the Commission affected city and county government fundamentally in the areas of purchasing, legal services, comptroller functions, recreation, health services, civil service, libraries, and ownership of school sites. The Commission's work on testing had direct relevance for the California State Department of Education, calling for a reappraisal of the statewide testing program sponsored and conducted by state education officials. The St. Louis

Education Task Force's work on vocational education involved suburban school districts and the Missouri Department of Education, setting the stage for permitting St. Louis Public School students to enroll in St. Louis County vocational programs.

STAGES IN THIRD-PARTY HISTORIES

The exposure to educational problems for competent lay people is often disturbing, if not outright unnerving. Many enter the scene with great intelligence, energy, commitment, and boundless naiveté. They expect to locate quick, if not easy, solutions. They believe that the problems of schooling will yield to science and technology. "If we can put a man on the moon, we should be able to teach poor children to read." And so it goes.

But the sustained and penetrating encounter with problems reveals their complexity and their unyielding nature. Thus, the early work of citizens, in the non-crisis arenas, becomes one of familiarization, probing, and learning what it is all about. Finance problems are in many respects the easiest to understand and solve. Pupil motivation, learning, and achievement are much more difficult. Bank presidents and insurance company executives in Detroit (ably assisted by the Citizens Research Council of Greater Michigan) were able to probe the school system's financial difficulties and systems of fiscal management and reporting in order to improve the district's record of fiscal responsibility. But other citizens wallowed in the uncertainty of teaching methods, educational objectives, counseling approaches, and teacher preparation. They were frustrated by the thousands of young people who could not find jobs, wandered the street, vandalized, and rioted. These behaviors continued after a balanced budget, which was an early task force objective, had been achieved.

Problem-solving citizens groups work simultaneously on a number of problems, each of which relates in a fundamental way to every other problem. The total set of problems is, in effect, a problem mosaic, a problem anatomy. Because there are many problems, interrelated in theory and in reality, the energies of citizens and staff are spread across many fronts at the same time. Work may be going well in some areas, poorly in others. Morale may be high among some members of the group, low among others. The feelings of achievement and accomplishment ebb and flow. The problem anatomy of a school system has no jugular.

Skillful coordination is required when subgroups of citizens' committees are proceeding at varying rates, across many fronts, employing different study processes, and reporting serially to boards of education.

Leaders of both the committee and the staff must come to understand that orchestration is necessary, especially when many problems are under review at the same time.

Time is exceptionally critical in short term, ad hoc citizen enterprises. There is never enough, and much is consumed in starting up and phasing out. Progress often becomes sluggish and is often uneven across problem areas, producing anxieties among members of the total committee. Members become anxious about completing on time and uneasy about extensions, and they want to be assured that recommendations that are as yet unimplemented will be implemented. Their professional staff have time concerns that are similar but often more personal. They carry the dual burdens of completing staff work responsibly and locating new employment for themselves.

When citizens with a problem-solving expectation confront problems, they go through rather distinct phases. Initially, there appears to be a shared confidence that problems can be defined and solved. On occasion there is anger and disappointment that the problems were not solved long ago since they seem so simple. This phase continues as citizens learn more about schools and schooling, teachers and teaching, managers and managing.

Phase two is marked by a mood of surprise and apprehension. Citizens feel less confident than they did originally. As they gather information, meet school officials, ask questions, and examine issues more thoroughly, the features of problems become clearer. More and more of the problems' dimensions become apparent. What seemed achievable, now seems more remote. Some citizens withdraw temporarily from active engagement with the issues, even consider removing themselves from the committees.

For some, skepticism about whether a citizens effort can yield results continues for months. The media and critics of the group may become impatient and publicly cast doubt on the efficacy of the effort. Such criticism affects morale and inhibits progress to some extent.

The feeling of being overwhelmed is sustained until there is a breakthrough, until the staff and committee leaders begin to put problems in perspective, establish some priorities, and develop some logical processes for problem review and analysis. With this the third phase begins. This phase is marked by renewed confidence when work is well under way in several problem areas. Consultants are developing background papers, and recommendations begin to crystalize. As soon as initial recommendations are passed along to school officials and implementation begins, feelings of progress are sufficient to carry the group forward for many weeks.

A fourth phase occurs when several pieces of work have proceeded to the point of recommendations and those recommendations have been passed along to school officials. If accepted, the processes of implementation begin in earnest. It is then that the recognition of the difficulty of implementation produces a new despair. Implementation appears more difficult than all that has preceded—problem identification, definition, study, analysis, and formulation of recommendations. Citizens, after the satisfaction of progress, run headlong into the sluggishness and seeming indifference that mark bureaucratic enterprise, and a second period of pessimism arrives.

The final phase is marked by the exuberance that comes from success. It is the sense of accomplishment, the feeling that the young people enrolled in schools are at last the beneficiaries; that the long hours and the frustrations have been worth it.

Professional staff and citizens group leaders should expect these phases to occur and not be intimidated by them. Awareness that these are natural and to some extent predictable can be helpful.

APPLICATION OF THE CONCEPT TO OTHER SECTORS

The *Detroit Free Press* urged the application of the third party notion to other public service areas in Detroit.[13] A form of third party was also recommended by Ohio's Governor James A. Rhodes in January 1979. He urged the establishment of a small citizens group to oversee the finances of the city of Cleveland.

There are large numbers of private development organizations that engage in problem solving. They are made up essentially of business people who have discovered that they cannot isolate their enterprises from social and political controversies and must increase their involvement in local public affairs. Their approaches are narrow in contrast to the third parties, but their impact can be, and often is, substantial. For example, the Allegheny Conference on Community Development was the prime mover in the physical transformation of the city of Pittsburgh.[14] There are striking similarities in how such groups and third parties go about their work. Each could learn from the other.

One needed permutation is to define problems that spill out beyond the zones of responsibility of a single institution. Youth problems are a good example where problem-solving task forces that transcend single institutions would have merit. These groups could engage in cross-sector analysis and appraise the meaning of crime and delinquency policy for education, employment policy for crime and delinquency, and educational policy for the others. There are few, if any, established mechanisms for effective cross-sector policy analysis and policy recommendation at the community level. Dedicated citizen effort directed toward large intractable problems such as youth unemployment makes sense.[15]

Nothing has been said thus far about incorporating problem-solving theory into the problem-solving activity of third-party groups. An effort was made in Detroit, San Francisco, and St. Louis to construct the work of citizens around frameworks drawn essentially from the work of Harold D. Lasswell.[16] A commitment to improve the quality of public policy, to use scientific data in problem solving, and to extend the number of citizens participating in the examination of difficult public issues in their midst was held by members of the professional staffs that served those three groups. It is likely that citizen participation in the future, whether based upon problem-solving premises or not, will involve such frameworks.[17]

IN CLOSING

Third party problem-solving experiences have provided a useful basis for comparison and contrast with other forms of citizen participation. Each form of participation has merit. But some appear to have more potential for large-scale, constructive impact than others. And these deserve careful appraisal.

Hundreds of thousands of citizens are "involved" in work with public institutions. No estimates are available of the magnitude of those contributions of time, effort, and personal and occupational sacrifice. But we know that they are substantial. Persons with academic and other interests in citizen participation owe it to themselves and to those who are participating every day to become as well informed as possible about what really makes a difference.

Advocates of involvement may be perilously close to fraud if they continue their advocacy without concern for the value or meaning of participation. Time is much too valuable to citizens and professionals to waste it on meaningless involvement. Participation of citizens must lead somewhere; it must make a constructive difference. Thus there is more and more reason why serious assessment needs to be made of the consequences of participation and the premises under which it proceeds.[18] Participation can be "institutionalized" and lose its significance. Every effort ought to be made to locate effective forms and processes of participation, including problem-solving approaches that are constructed on thoughtfully conceived premises. The academic community, despite its obvious remoteness from many dimensions of contemporary social change, has within its membership many insightful students of problem solving and institutional adaptation. The work of such persons should be carefully inspected for theories or concepts that can be used in practical settings. Such theories and concepts exist.

When they are identified, we face the task of making those involved in citizen activity aware of them. At this point in our experience with participation, it may be more important to concentrate on citizen effectiveness than on extending the numbers involved. If that appraisal is accurate, then leaders in the citizen participation movement ought to turn their energies to building awareness and understanding of the philosophies, premises, and circumstances within which participation can, in fact, be effective.

NOTES

1. John W. Gardner, *Morale,* W. W. Norton and Company, Inc., New York, 1978, p. 123.

2. The author served as Executive Director of the Detroit Education Task Force during 1973–74 and Co-Executive Director during 1974–75. Later he served as Executive Director of the San Francisco Public Schools Commission and consultant to the St. Louis Citizens Education Task Force. Each of these groups is (or was) a problem-solving body, as distinct from other citizens committees that serve essentially as study and/or advisory bodies. Frequent references are made to the work of these third-party groups. For additional descriptions of the Detroit Education Task Force see Luvern L. Cunningham, "The Education Task Force in Detroit," *Inequality in Education,* no. 15, November 1975, pp. 45–52, and Luvern L. Cunningham, "New Forms of Involving Citizens in Educational Systems," in Elinor Ostron (ed.), *The Delivery of Urban Services,* Sage Publications, Beverly Hills, 1976, pp. 103–26.

3. For a review of traditional advisory committees, especially those mandated by federal vocational and career education legislation, see Leslie H. Cochran, L. Allen Phelps, and Linda Letwin Cochran, *Advisory Committees In Action,* Allyn and Bacon, Boston, 1980.

4. The history of problem-solving activity of third parties is included in Rodney Muth and Lawrence L. Slonaker, *Toward a More Comprehensive Strategy for Strengthening Educational Leadership and Policy Making,* Volume II, Mershon Center, The Ohio State University, 1976, pp. 156–162; and in Luvern L. Cunningham, "Policy Science in the Field," *Quarterly Report,* vol. 4, no. 2, Mershon Center, The Ohio State University, Winter 1979.

5. Cunningham, ibid.

6. Ibid.

7. For example, the San Francisco Public Schools Commission published a dozen major documents which focused upon the specific problems on the Commission's agenda and included recommendations that were made to the San Francisco Unified School District and the City and County of San Francisco. Copies are available through the San Francisco Foundation, San Francisco, Ca.

8. Gardner, op. cit., pp. 132–35. In these brief pages, the leadership requirements of our society are described. They are remarkably similar to those needed by third-party leaders.

9. David A. Bennett, *Community Involvement in Desegregation: Milwaukee's Voluntary Plan,* Milwaukee Public Schools, Wisconsin, 1978.

10. Implementation of the Dallas school desegregation plan was threatened by appellate actions, its destiny resting ultimately with the United States Supreme Court.

11. Cunningham, "Policy Science in the Field," op. cit. The functions defined in this section were taken from this report.

12. See "Workshop Summary: A Progress Report on Implementation and Planning for the Future," San Francisco Public Schools Commission, June 1976, available through the San Francisco Foundation, San Francisco, Ca. (Mimeographed.)

13. *Detroit Free Press,* Tuesday, March 11, 1975, p. 8A.

14. Judith Getzels et al., *Private Planning for the Public Interest,* American Society of Planning Officials, Chicago, October 1975.

15. A proposal to establish a third-party group that would solve "cross-sector" problems was made to Mayor Kevin White of Boston. See Joseph M. Cronin, Luvern L. Cunningham, David S. Seeley, and Josh Smith, *Improving Boston Education,* Special Report to Mayor Kevin White, August 1976, pp. 11–12.

16. Harold O. Lasswell, *A Pre-View of Policy Sciences,* American Elsevier Publishing Company, Inc., New York, 1971.

17. Use of a scientific approach to planning based upon theory is described in William R. Ewald, Jr., *Information, Perception and Regional Policy,* National Science Foundation, Washington, D.C., 1975.

18. Mandated citizen involvement in Florida was assessed recently at the request of the Florida legislature. See *Improving Education in Florida: A Reassessment,* prepared for the Select Joint Committee on Public Schools of the Florida Legislature, February 1978, available through the Senate Education Committee, Senate Office Building, Tallahassee, Florida.

6

FEDERAL INTERVENTION AND NEW GOVERNANCE STRUCTURES

BARBARA L. JACKSON
Morgan State University

The decade of the 1960s saw profound change in American society. It was a time that brought together two divergent themes that have characterized this democratic nation since its founding: the steady, though halting, inclusion of excluded American citizens into the democratic process of decision making; and the constantly changing role of government, especially at the federal level, seen as appropriate by the people in order to respond to the social and political conditions of the times.

The major group seeking inclusion during this period was black Americans, the largest minority in the country and the only group that had experienced slavery followed by a system of laws deliberately preventing them from exercising the privileges of citizenship granted after the Civil War. What was different in the 1960s was the nature of the protest; a more aggressive mode was adopted that challenged the established authority of society's institutions. The response of the government, especially at the federal level, was also different. The evolving change in what was considered legitimate for government to do that had started with the New Deal in the 1930s reached fruition.

A third force emerged during this period that also influenced the response of the government—in the words of Robert Nisbet, "a quest for community." The demands of an increasingly complex modern society seemed to be destroying the primary associations, the social bonds so essential to the health of the individual and in turn the society. Alienation and isolation were developing among many groups. Nisbet defined the problem in this way:

Behind the growing sense of isolation in society, behind the whole quest for community which infuses so many theoretical and practical areas of contemporary life and thought, lies the growing realization that the traditional primary relationships of men have become functionally irrelevant to our state and economy and meaningless to the moral aspirations of individuals. We are forced to the conclusion that a great deal of the peculiar character of contemporary social action comes from the efforts of men to find in large scale organizations the values of status and security which were formerly gained in the primary associations of family, neighborhood and church.[1]

The response of the federal government, long viewed as distant and remote from the individual citizen or these primary social associations, was to promote, to sponsor, and, in some instances, to re-create intermediary groups that would serve as mediators between individual citizens and the government.

This response of the federal government to these various forces is the focus of this chapter. Education and schooling are relatively new areas for intervention by the federal government. A brief overview of the federal government's role in education in the context of the recent decade of change will be followed by a description of several federally sponsored programs that will serve as the framework for the analysis of major themes. The focus will be on programs authorized by Congressional legislation and implemented by the Executive branch through the Department of Health, Education, and Welfare. I will not deal here with governance structures mandated by court order.

A DECADE OF CHANGE

The history of America shows that, given the right combination of internal and external pressures, the government is able to shift its response to accommodate new and challenging situations. At no time in our history was this more pronounced than during the 1960s. In the words of James Sundquist:

> In the nineteen-sixties the American federal system entered a new phase. Through a series of dramatic enactments, the Congress asserted the national interest and authority in a wide range of governmental functions that until then had been the province, exclusively or predominantly, of state and local governments. The new legislation not only established federal-state-local relations in entirely new fields of activity and on a vast scale but it established new patterns of relationships as well. . . . The massive federal intervention in community affairs came in some of the most sacrosanct of all the traditional preserves of state and local authority—notably education. . . .[2]

These changes in the philosophy and appropriate role of the federal government did not occur by accident. A major factor was the change in strategies adopted by the Civil Rights movement after 1954. Up until that time, blacks through their organizations had concentrated on removing all of the legal barriers erected since Reconstruction to prevent their participation as American citizens. Once the law was clear—separate cannot be equal, and the equal protection clause of the Fourteenth Amendment included not only education but the entire system of segregation—direct action occurred on many fronts. This was a time of ferment, of boycotts, of riots, the March on Washington, Black Power, Martin Luther King, Malcolm X, the Black Panthers. Public schools in the South were extensively desegregated despite massive resistance, and there were continued court actions and increased enrollment of black students in colleges, especially in white institutions in the North. A new sense of identity emerged, symbolized by natural hairstyles and a search to discover the past—the roots of the African heritage.

While almost ten years lapsed from the time that the Supreme Court spoke in the 1954 Brown case,[3] the Congress and Executive branch finally did respond. For one of the few times in our history, a climate was created that reaffirmed the democratic ideals on which the country had been founded. All the federal branches acted in concert to implement those ideals with actions aimed not only at righting the wrongs of the past for black Americans but at creating conditions for the fuller participation of all citizens in the processes of their government.

Under the leadership of Kennedy and Johnson, the Congress passed the Great Society legislation with amazing speed. First, there was the Juvenile Delinquency Act of 1960, which made funds available to projects like Mobilization for Youth and the Haryou Act in New York—an entirely new and different approach to the problems associated with young people, for they were to be included in deciding their own future. There was a shift from blaming the victim to an assumption that "society" was responsible for the plight of many. Then in 1964 came the Economic Opportunity Act with its many programs that have now become household words: Headstart, Job Corps, Neighborhood Youth Corps, Peace Corps, Vista Volunteers, and the Community Action (CAP), all governed by the glorious phrase "maximum feasible participation." A variety of education bills was passed, greatly expanding federal support in this area. A new Vocational Education Act was followed by one for higher education creating another set of programs—Talent Search, Upward Bound, Special Services for the Disadvantaged. There were also increased scholarships and grants, financed by the federal government, for poor students. The climax came with the monumental education bill, the Elementary and Secondary Education Act (ESEA) of 1965, whose Title I authorized a billion dollars just for poor kids. It appeared that for the first time communities and their schools would have enough money to make a difference for those children who had not succeeded in the past.

Moreover, this federal education legislation was buttressed by a new Civil Rights Act (1964) and a wide-reaching Voting Rights Act (1965). These were important for schools, for they provided enforcement power so that national purposes could be implemented.

The thrust of much of this legislation was a recognition that in an industrialized, technological society, people are often the victims of circumstances beyond their control. If citizens were to be able to exercise their options, the government would have to become the protector of the rights of individuals by expanding governmental action rather than limiting what governmental institutions could do.

One way to accomplish this end would be for the government to create new structures or organizations through which citizens and groups could make the decisions that affect their lives. It was no longer sufficient for these decisions to be made by elected officials or even appointed bureaucrats responsible to these officials. What was now seen as necessary and legitimate was a more direct connection between the people, their communities, and their government.

Beginning with the urban renewal legislation in the early sixties, the role that citizens could play in government decisions steadily expanded. The Economic Opportunity Act of 1964 incorporated a "maximum feasible participation" requirement; Model Cities was a further extension with a formal structure with specific responsibilities called, in most cities, a Model Neighborhood Board. In education, several programs mandated participation, though they differed in the specific requirements. They included Head Start, Follow Through, and Title I of ESEA. These governmental actions were supported by the community control movement, found mainly in some major cities where parents and community representatives attempted to assert their right to participate in the school decisions that were being made about their children.

For a few short years, it appeared that the American dream of Jefferson and the founding fathers had been reborn, this time with the government assuming the role of protector of individual and group rights. The efforts to desegregate the schools had roused parents to take a closer look at their schools and to question the professional educators who everyone had assumed were fulfilling their obligations to educate all the children. Almost inadvertently, the federal government had addressed a fundamental cause of citizen dissatisfaction by assisting communities to create new structures through which they could take action. Even though education traditionally was the responsibility of the states and local communities, the need for re-connection still existed. To quote Nisbet again,

> ... irrespective of particular groups, there must be in any stable culture, in any civilization that prizes its integrity, functionally significant and psychologically meaningful groups and associations lying intermediate to the individual and the larger values and purposes of his society. For these are the small areas of association within which alone such values and purposes can take on clear meaning in personal life and become the vital roots of the

large culture. It is, I believe, the problem of intermediate association that is fundamental at the present time.[4]

THE ROLE OF THE FEDERAL GOVERNMENT IN EDUCATION

Under our federal system of government, only those powers that are explicitly delegated by the Constitution can be exercised by the federal executive, legislative, and judicial branches. Since education is not one of these explicit powers, the states assumed responsibility for providing public education based on the belief that an informed citizenry was essential to a democratic, representative form of government. In most state constitutions, the purpose for providing public schools is generally stated in terms of protecting the commonwealth. The actual operation of publicly supported school systems has been delegated to local government in all states except Hawaii.

However, even though there was no explicit power granted, the federal government has played some role in educational matters since the adoption of the Constitution. Through interpretation of the Constitution, most notably the general welfare clause, Congress has been able to find sufficient authorization when the public will so demanded. After the adoption of the Civil War Amendments, especially the fourteenth with its due process and equal protection clauses, additional authority for the federal government to act was clearly established. By using the violation of constitutionally guaranteed rights as a basis for change, the courts became an active partner in education and school issues.

Prior to the sixties, most forms of federal aid were through grants of land or money to the states that were then shared with the local communities. The aid was primarily to help states and local communities accomplish their objectives. In effect, the federal role was one of providing technical assistance. It did not monitor closely to see that the purposes of the grants were achieved. The legislation of the 1960s changed the philosophy, necessitating a concomitant change in the way in which the federal government related to states and local communities. As summarized by Sundquist:

> Characteristic of the legislation of the 1960s are forthright declarations of national purpose, experimental and flexible approaches to the achievement of those purposes, and close federal supervision and control to assure that the national purposes are served.
>
> In the newer model the federal grant is conceived as a means of enabling the federal government to achieve *its* objectives—

national policies defined, although often in very general terms, by the Congress. The program remains a federal program; as a matter of administrative convenience the federal government executes the program through state or local governments rather than through its own field offices, but the motive force is federal, with the states and communities assisting—rather than the other way around.[5]

In the field of education the significance of the change was not so much in the amount of money now available from the federal government, though in total it was sizable; nor in the percentage of the total education budget now coming from the federal government, for it only increased from about three to seven percent, with the state and local governments still sharing the major portion. What was significant was the recognition that problems were no longer local in the urbanized and industrialized society of the mid-twentieth century, necessitating a fundamental change in the role of the federal government.

This shift in philosophy and monitoring role was most evident in ESEA. Even though each state received monies on a formula basis, the funds were clearly earmarked to address a national problem and to achieve a national purpose:

> In recognition of the special educational needs of children of low income families and the impact that concentrations of low income families have on the ability of local educational agencies to support adequate educational programs, the Congress hereby declares it to be the policy of the United States to provide financial assistance . . . to local educational agencies serving areas with concentrations of children from low income families to expand and improve their educational programs by various means (including pre-school programs) which contribute particularly to meeting the special educational needs of educationally deprived children.[6]

Once it had been firmly established that Congress could support education and explicitly state how the funds could be used, it was an easy step to begin to add stipulations regarding other aspects of the school system as conditions for accepting the federal dollar. What gradually became a significant feature in more and more programs was the insistence on the involvement and participation of the local community, especially those who formerly had not been a part of the power structure.

The next step was a more deliberate and conscious effort to influence the governance structure. There were only a limited number of programs where the federal government attempted this more fundamental change. The lure of federal funds was combined with close monitoring to make sure that the agreed-upon changes would actually occur. Three examples of this type of intervention are the Experimental Schools Program, the Urban/Rural Development Program, and the Boston King-Timilty School Council project under Title III of ESEA. In the next section some features of these programs are briefly described, followed by an analysis of those aspects that relate directly to several of the major themes of this volume.

EXPERIMENTAL SCHOOLS PROGRAM

The Experimental Schools Program was first introduced by President Nixon in his message on Educational Reform in March 1970. According to the U.S. Office of Education, the Experimental Schools Program was to be a "bridge between basic educational research and actual school practices."[7] Congress appropriated $12,000,000 for fiscal year 1971. When Sidney Marland was appointed Commissioner of Education in December 1970, he announced that the rapid implementation of this program would be one of his highest priorities.

According to the official publication of the Office of Education,

The Experimental Schools Program itself is experimental—it is testing significant alternatives to present government and pedagogical practices. Most notably:

- Funding is for something longer than a year, allowing for continuity and internal integrity while testing and retesting possible alternatives.

- The target population is large enough to allow for sufficient experimentation but small enough to be thoroughly evaluated and documented.

- The choice of curriculum, organization, staffing patterns, and internal evaluation measures are all the choice of local personnel and the community.

- Each applicant is required initially to send in a sample letter of interest rather than a professionally prepared proposal.

- Once a letter of interest is chosen by an independent selection committee as a possible contender for an operational grant, the U.S. Office of Education provides a planning grant to allow for any necessary technical assistance.

- Instead of the evaluation and documentation coming after a project has been completed or well under way, it is an integral part of each Experimental School site from the beginning.

- Documentation includes not only the narrow components of a project, but the project itself and the total environment of which it is a part and which it is shaping.

- The independent evaluators will use anthropological and sociological measures to identify both what is appearing to succeed and what is appearing to fail, sharing both and 'hard' and 'soft' data with the U.S. Office of Education and the project staff.

- The three levels of evaluation ensure integrity in the reporting system.

- Each site will provide an informational center for visitors which will not impinge on the experiment itself yet fully inform all interested parties on the results of the experiment.[8]

It is clear that there were several features of this program that were quite different from many of those associated with the programs of the Great Society. Some features were an attempt by the new Republican administration to answer the critics of those programs; some were clearly an attempt to bring about fundamental change in the way schools were governed; other features attempted to address the larger issue of the purposes of education and the ways in which public schools could be changed to respond to those purposes. While not explicitly stated, it would also appear that these new directives might have been instituted to provide a response to the "quest for community" that seems to have emerged as a dominant force in today's society.

In response to some of the criticisms of earlier programs as well as to provide for better management, the Experimental Schools Program had a built-in planning period, financed by the federal government, when the detailed plan would be developed based on a letter of intent. This was another reflection of the change in approach of the federal government to see that the national priorities were included in the proposed activities from the very beginning.

The funding arrangement was also different. The grant was to be multi-year to allow for some advance planning. Also reflecting the national priority to induce change in the local system was the requirement for financial support for the project on the part of the local school system to be shared on a formula basis with the federal office from the beginning, with the local share increasing each year.

To counteract the criticism leveled at many programs, Experimental

Schools emphasized evaluation. It was to take place on three levels: at the project site by staff responsible to the local people; at the individual sites but conducted by a contractor external to the project staff and directly responsible to the Experimental Schools office rather than the local site; and a third level that was intended to include all of the projects, the evaluation activities, and an assessment of the total program. This third level was never implemented; extensive reports were, however, prepared by both of the other levels.

The major features that make the Experimental Schools Program appropriate for inclusion here relate to the issue of governance at the local level as well as the relation between the federal government and the local community and its schools. Unlike some of the Great Society programs that provided federal funds to local school districts through a formula incorporated in congressional legislation or through allocation by a state agency, this program was a direct link between the federal agency and the local community. The state level was bypassed by design. This was in direct conflict with the established mode of operation, and illustrated, as did some of the community action programs of the Great Society, that one national purpose was to change the power structure. Since, however, the state level still retained certifying and legitimatizing functions for schools, the local projects had to deal with their state department of education and, in some instances, the state legislature. The other dominant feature was the explicit mandate that the "community" be involved in the decisions about the use of these federal funds.

Finally, these projects established a framework within which the purposes of schooling could be reexamined. For the two described here, the issue focused around defining an alternative. How can a diverse school population be better served? Can the One Best System really provide for everyone? And who should decide? Once decided, what forms of governance are required to provide the continual monitoring to see that those purposes are being achieved? And how do national purposes and priorities become implemented without the federal government assuming too direct supervision?

The five years of the Experimental Schools Program have now ended for most of the projects and the final evaluation reports of the Level II or outside evaluators have now become part of the public record of the National Institute of Education (NIE). The turnover of staff in Washington, most notably the departure of the director, Robert Binswanger, who set the tone and established the program, may have contributed to the lack of publicity for what promised to provide "answers" to many of the issues facing public schools, especially about the process of change.

The discussion of the Minneapolis and National Urban League Street Academy Projects that follows is based primarily on the written reports of both Level I and Level II evaluators and on interviews with some of the people directly involved at the local sites. Because both sites took the assignment of documentation seriously, there is an abundance of written material on what happened and, in most instances, critical assessments of the projects during their history up until their transference or incorporation into the respective public school systems.

The two projects differ in several ways. In Minneapolis, the grant went directly to a public school system and involved a designated section of that system that provided alternatives to parents, children, and staff. The National Urban League Street Academies project involved giving a grant for both evaluation and operation to three local Leagues to operate Street Academies for high school–age children. The outside evaluation component was assigned to the Research Department of the National Urban League as opposed to a totally outside group as in Minneapolis. Both involved "community" but in different ways. Both were similar in the ultimate objective as enunciated by Experimental Schools—the incorporation of the "experiment" into the school system. In Minneapolis, alternatives did become official policy throughout the school system. In the case of the Street Academies, all three were transferred to the local school systems in terms of assuming financial responsibility for their continued operation beyond the experimental five years.

NATIONAL URBAN LEAGUE STREET ACADEMY PROJECT

In June 1972, the National Urban League entered into a thirty-month grant agreement with the Office of Experimental Schools that covered the operation of three Street Academies under the auspices of the local Urban Leagues in three different cities with an evaluation component under the direction of the National Urban League's Research Department. As stated in the agreement, the project had three fundamental objectives:

1. to give a thorough and well-researched test of the "Street Academy concept" in Oakland, California, under the direction of the Bay Area Urban League, in South Bend, Indiana, under the direction of the South Bend Urban League and in Washington, D.C. under the direction of the Washington Urban League;

2. to test the acceptance of the Street Academy by the local public school system to include as a viable alternative to the present school system;

3. to have thorough evaluation and documentation of each site and of commonalities for all three sites done by an independent agency, but one which is understanding of the Street Academy concept.[9]

The original thirty-month grant (July 1, 1972–December 31, 1974) was for $3,644,468 with $670,222 allocated for the Level II evaluation and documentation. As with the other Experimental Schools projects, there was an option for an additional thirty months of funding for the operation of the three academies providing the local school systems agreed to underwrite a percentage of the budgets during that period. Each year beginning in 1973–74 through 1976–77, the school system would increase its contribution, starting with twenty percent of the budget, then forty percent, then eighty percent, and finally in the 1977–78 school year there would be no contribution from Experimental Schools at all. It was originally intended that the evaluation component would end with a final report in March 1975. After intensive negotiation and pressure, it was agreed that a fair test of the concept should include transference or adoption by the local school system, requiring an extension for part of the staff until July 1977. Thus, the final report includes most of this critical negotiation period.

The grant agreement itself represented the first in a series of negotiated agreements that characterized Experimental Schools Projects. The National Urban League's letter of interest proposed seven cities located throughout the five Urban League regions that existed at that time. The first instance of influence, if not out-right dictation, by the federal agency was the selection of the sites. The Urban League recommendations were rejected, and three new cities proposed. Part of the rationale provided by Experimental Schools was that in these three cities there was a promise of full support from the superintendents of schools—an absolute and overriding requirement of Experimental Schools. It can be surmised that unless there was agreement on these sites, there would have been no grant to the Urban League. Whether the superintendent's involvement should have been considered so crucial is open to question, since in two of the sites (Oakland and Washington) the superintendents did not remain more than a year after the project began. It raises a serious question about placing so much emphasis on the leadership of particular people as a major criterion for funding any project. In fact, in the Washington site, there were three different superintendents during the short five years of the project. If adaptation of the system to new ways of operation is the goal, perhaps more attention should be given to the institutional arrangements than to the people present at any given time.

A second indication that Experimental Schools would have a close monitoring role was the selection of the first Director of Evaluation and the other staff members. This phase was under the auspices of the Research Department of the National Urban League, headed by Robert B. Hill, with offices in Washington. A director did not begin until October, even though the grant had been approved to begin in July, because it took that long to find someone "acceptable" to both the Urban League and Experimental Schools.

Time emerged as a potential obstacle to implementation. The planning period had to be extended in recognition of the original unrealistic schedule. At times, the Experimental Schools' staff in Washington showed little understanding of the difficulties inherent in creating any new institution, much less one that had so many new elements.

Despite the handicaps, the planning did proceed, and three new Street Academies did open: South Bend in February 1973, followed by Washington, D.C. in May, and Oakland in June. Staff had been found with both unusual teaching skills and an understanding of the Street Academy philosophy; appropriate buildings had been secured, often with the assistance of the local school systems; equipment was purchased, a curriculum developed, and students recruited. The required connection with the local school district turned out to be a real advantage. The liaison person provided invaluable assistance, especially in obtaining buildings, equipment, and materials. In Oakland, the system also provided free lunches, limited transportation, and curriculum development consultation.

This project differed markedly from the other Experimental Schools projects in the nature of the evaluation component. After six months of intensive negotiations, an evaluation plan was finally approved in June 1973. It had two major objectives:

1. to evaluate and document the impact of the Street Academy on the students, staff, and community;

2. to develop an anthropological-type case study of each of the three sites.[10]

A series of reports was to be produced to fulfill these objectives. All were completed according to the schedule.[11]

The nature of this project forced the evaluation component to assume a different role. Unlike most of the other projects that were within the context of the public school system, this project was to test the concept of something new and largely untried, a "Street Academy."

The Street Academies had their genesis in New York City as an alternative to the public school system. Their explicit purpose was to retrieve young people who had not been well served by the established school system. Street Academies were nourished in the atmosphere of the various community control movements that represented the quest for community of the sixties. What became crucial to this project, with implications for alternatives that seek public funding, was the task of defining and identifying the essential characteristics that would clearly show how a Street Academy was different from regular secondary schools. This project also had to demonstrate how such an alternative could become cost-effective and acceptable to a school system and its community.

In the Level II Final Report to Experimental Schools, the reasons for the creation of a Street Academy are stated: to reclaim and to retrieve high school–age young people who have not been well served by public school systems; they may or may not have completely dropped out of that system. Basic to this orientation is the belief

> ... that minority and low income students are educable—can be retrieved, and can be assisted by education programs. The concept refers to students, however labeled—under-achievers, dropouts or unduly hassled/pushed out of public schools. They can be assisted to acquire those coping abilities and knowledge required to successfully live as productive citizens in society.[12]

This philosophy was implemented by a curriculum that emphasized the basic skills. All of the academies used a variety of individual methods with an overriding curriculum theme. In Oakland it was called Incentive Modification; in South Bend, Survival; and in Washington, Integrated Learning. There was also an emphasis on self-development and attitudes toward self and life. The project's emphasis on evaluation and documentation led to using standardized tests as one measure of achievement, but because both staff and students felt the tests had little utility (in the words of one student, "Why test to find out what we don't know"), data from this source are minimal. But based on what was available, the Final Report makes this cautious comment:

> Our findings indicate that growth occurred in certain areas for Street Academy students as a group. Statistically significant advances were made in total reading and total mathematics. There was growth in the academic status of the students. In the area of attitudes we found that there was some growth that was indicative of increased self-esteem and efficacy. Students became less dependent on external approval of their attitudes and behaviors. They became more oriented to collective action and to organizing for making demands for rights that would affect their lives. These changes were consistent with Street Academy objectives.[13]

One essential characteristic of the Street Academy concept related to staff. Staff members were not only able to teach the basic skills, they were also characterized by their sense of personal accountability and a belief in their ability to motivate students to learn. They had to believe in the philosophy on which this alternative was based— the educability of all young people. Most also had the advantage of coming from backgrounds similar to the students' so that there was a cultural identification and understanding. Most were young. Much emphasis was placed on student-teacher interaction, which was more intimate and personal than in the public schools.

The physical location and setting of a Street Academy are also considered essential characteristics. The very name, Street Academy, carries a certain connotation from the early days when the concept first began in New York. The "street" was the place where workers found the students, where the outreach office was located. The academy was a place of reentry where the student could be reclaimed. If this were so, the place needed to be identified with a different life and not reminiscent of the unhappy life experienced in traditional school buildings. This element was fulfilled in different ways in the three sites.

In Oakland, the East Oakland Academy was housed in a building that was once a supermarket, and the Emiliano Zapata Academy in a former furniture store. The other two cities had to depend more on creating the climate and setting inside the building, for their sites were in much more traditional spaces. South Bend's building had been used by a local church for its education center. In addition, unlike the Oakland Academies, it was located downtown, outside the community where most of the students lived. Even so, the staff and students were able to create the appropriate atmosphere inside the building for a more intimate and informal interaction between students and faculty—one of the goals of the Street Academy philosophy.

Washington, D.C., also had two sites. The first was a two-story brick building that had once been a public school; it was renovated, and had a portable structure in the school yard. The interiors were particularly representative of the philosophy of street academies. The other site, Dix Street, was housed in a building that had once been a bicycle factory. In order to emphasize that these facilities belonged to the community, the buildings were used for other meetings and activities.

Another essential characteristic was the emphasis given to supportive services. Here, too, implementation differed at each site. In all cases, however, all staff saw supportive services as an integral part of their responsibility, even where specialized counselors were part of the staff. Since many of the students had children, child care became an accepted part of the supportive services.

The key to implementing the philosophy and program of the Street Academies is not these internal characteristics, which could be duplicated in a public school system, but rather the governance structure. Here was a unique arrangement: a community agency that was an advocate for a particular constituency group contracted with a local school system to operate an educational program for students whom that very system had failed. In addition, there was a third party—the Experimental Schools office in Washington—that would help set the ground rules for the partnership. Once the agreement had been signed, that third party would monitor the operation to see that the obligations were met, not the least of which would be financial support on the part of the local school system. Joint Governance Boards were formed in each of the three communities to establish the policies under which the program would operate. In practice, these groups assumed an advisory role, while the Urban Leagues through their executives and boards took responsibility for the actual operation of the academies. The appointment of a full-time liaison person from the public schools completed the governance and staff arrangements. An analysis of this arrangement and discussion of its implications for change in the public school system follow the description of the Minneapolis program.

MINNEAPOLIS SOUTHEAST ALTERNATIVES

The second illustration of federal intervention through the Experimental Schools Program is the Minneapolis, Minnesota, Southeast Alternatives. The national priority was the same as for the Urban League's Street Academies, but the differences in implementation show how national priorities are adapted to the local community.

The Minneapolis Public School System was one of eight school districts that received a $10,000 planning grant in 1970 to prepare a proposal for a single comprehensive K–12 project, the originally stated purpose of experimental schools. In May 1971, along with the Berkeley Unified School District of Berkeley, California, and the Franklin Pierce School District of Tacoma, Washington, Minneapolis received a twenty-seven-month operational grant of $3,580,877. A second grant of $3,036,722 for a thirty-month period was later approved for 1973–76.

The Minneapolis Southeast Alternatives (SEA) project covered a well-defined area in the Southeast section of the city and included all the kindergarten through twelfth grade students, numbering approximately 2,000. This section of the city was racially and economically diverse. It was described in this way in the grant agreement:

Bounded by factories, flour mills, freeways, multiple dwellings, residential neighborhoods, shopping areas and railroads, it also houses the main campus of the University of Minnesota, Minneapolis. Stately old homes, low income apartments and expensive condominiums are all located in the area. This mixture of ages, occupations, interests, and life styles supports a diversity of views about the nature of public education which the five SEA alternative schools of parent choice reflects.[14]

This area had the added advantage of several active parent and community groups that had already expressed interest in developing alternatives to the "regular" offerings of the public schools.

The central theme of Southeast Alternatives was to provide comprehensive change in the educational structure and programs for the better education of children. It offered students, teachers, and parents a choice in the types of educational programs available, involved students, faculty, and parents in educational decision-making processes, and decentralized the administrative structure of the school district to local schools.

Four major alternative school programs were offered at the elementary level and two at the secondary. Parents were involved in each to varying degrees ranging from the traditional PTA structure to assuming major responsibility for running the school. There was also an overall council. A teacher center was established with federal SEA funds to provide teachers with an opportunity to receive substantial in-service training as well as to provide an avenue for pre-service experiences. An in-service committee made up of teachers received proposals and acted on them, thus providing a direct role for teachers in the staff development activities. The University of Minnesota and Minneapolis Public Schools jointly operated the Teacher Center.

The evaluation of this project, as with all those funded by Experimental Schools, was both internal (Level I) and external (Level II). Level I was designed to provide day-to-day, responsive, formative evaluation for the program decision makers. The Level II evaluation was originally contracted to the ARIES Corporation and later transferred to Educational Services Group Inc., under the direction of Larry J. Reynolds.

URBAN/RURAL DEVELOPMENT PROGRAM

A second federal program—the Urban/Rural Development Program—had purposes somewhat similar to Experimental Schools in regard to governance. Here the decision making was to be in the control of a specially designed school/community council. While the monitoring role was somewhat different in that it was delegated to regional coordinators rather than staffed from Washington, the insistence on participation with recognition and acceptance of a shift in responsibility by the local school system was the same.

This approach was based on the assumption that changes in educational programs and in-service training would occur if there were also changes in the power of communities to plan and operate their own educational activities. Here, as with Experimental Schools, there were additional federal funds for the Council. The community and school personnel on the Council were to have parity, defined as "deliberate, collaborative or mutual, decision making on the part of those rendering services and those receiving services."[15]

According to Terry and Hess, the unique elements of this program were:

- at least half of the members of the joint governing body (the School/Community Council) are drawn from the community;

- the program for each site is planned to fit the needs and circumstances of that particular community;

- the control of funds is in the hands of the Council (with expressed concurrence of the local school board);

- the concentration is on training of educational personnel and development of community educational resources.[16]

Nine million dollars from the Education Professions Development Act was appropriated in 1971 to launch the program which was operated under the Bureau of Educational Personnel Development. The twenty- three sites that became part of the Urban/Rural Program were vastly different from one another, though the common characteristics of "economic poverty and low educational achievement may create an illusion of similarity."[17]

BOSTON KING-TIMILTY ADVISORY COUNCIL

One other program that had as its purpose a shift in decision making was the Boston King-Timilty project funded by Title III of the Elementary and Secondary Education Act.[18] It is used here as an illustration of an intervention that did not include several of the features built into both Experimental Schools and the Urban/Rural Programs. The contrast adds clarity to some of the issues of the volume as well as pointing out some of the conditions that might be necessary for federal intervention to achieve the goal of changing decision-making processes.

This project, unlike the others, did not have the unqualified support of the system—it was adopted by only a 3–2 vote of the Boston School Committee. There was no requirement in the initial agreement that the school system continue funding after the end of the three-year federal grant, and even this grant had to be renewed each year.

The two schools were located in the Roxbury section of Boston and had an almost 100 percent black student population. A parent group that predated the creation of the Council was joined by several university faculty members who assisted in securing the grant. The Council had representation from the community, with an emphasis on parents of the children in the two schools involved and school personnel from those schools, and had control over some of the grant funds—for travel, materials, and program insofar as they were additions to the standard curriculum. Little was done to examine the total curriculum, as was true in some of the Minneapolis alternatives.

Early in its existence the Council became embroiled in a citywide issue over the appointment of principals to the two schools. Without consulting the Council, two white principals were appointed in the spring at the very time the Council was coming into existence. Although jurisdiction over personnel was not spelled out as one of the Council's responsibilities, the fact that the Boston School Committee ignored their existence entirely after approving the grant (even by the slimmest of majorities) roused the Council to action. Through a variety of tactics, from negotiation to confrontation, two black principals were eventually appointed to these schools. The political activities the Council engaged in in this process did create a kind of cohesion that comes from joint action to accomplish a clearly designated goal.

Like the Minneapolis SEA, the King-Timilty Council was a part of the system. Unlike Minneapolis, where the administration supported decentralizing decision making, the Council was viewed as a source of trouble to the people in the central office. Since it did force some attention to the systemwide promotion system, a kind of tension throughout the system was created—a necessary condition for change.

I have described briefly the major features of three programs that had as one of their major purposes a change in the governance structure combined with a commitment on the part of the local school system to be a partner in that change. We now turn to an analysis of various aspects of these projects as they illustrate several of the major themes of this volume: democracy and community, including the important issues of definitions and representation; the purposes of education, especially as defined through alternatives; and finally, the role of public schools in a democratic society.

DEMOCRACY AND COMMUNITY

We often speak of democracy and community in the abstract or in terms of the individual since our society is rooted in the right of the individual to pursue life, liberty, and happiness as each individual defines that pursuit. This emphasis on individualism has been buttressed by the influence of the Protestant philosophy that salvation is not to be achieved through intermediaries but through the individual's personal relation to God. As a consequence, there has been a tendency to ignore the importance of social groups as an indispensable connecting link between the individual and society. But in today's industrialized and urbanized world—and it may have always been true despite our rhetoric—the individual makes most decisions in the context of a group, an organization, or a community. Status, position, and, often, the access to the goods of the society are determined by group membership or participation in an organization or by membership in a community.

Nisbet summarizes this important need in *The Quest for Community:*

> The greatest single lesson to be drawn from the social transformations of the twentieth century, from the phenomena of individual insecurity and the mass quest for community, is that the intensity of men's motivations toward freedom and culture is unalterably connected with the relationships of a social organization that has structural coherence and functional significance.[19]

In middle-class communities, social organizations of many types have always existed. For the poor, however, group action has not been the norm; rather a sense of powerlessness and voicelessness has permeated their lives. In the decade of the sixties both groups changed. Among those who had always felt a connection with their government, alienation and disillusionment were growing as government seemed to be getting too big and out of their control. At the same time, the Civil Rights movement demonstrated conclusively the efficacy of joint action for the poor. The intervention of the federal government through the creation of new governance structures aided both movements by attempting to return decision making to the local community.

Two issues now took on a new significance: first, how to define "the community" and, second, how that community would be represented. These were not new issues, nor have they been resolved during this period of increased citizen participation. They have, however, taken on new dimensions due to the deliberate effort by the federal government to change the power structure rather than let the natural political processes adjust conflicting values and allocate scarce resources as had occurred in the past.

Most of the community organizations or agencies created with the support of antipoverty legislation had a geographical base—the more traditional definition of community. The Urban/Rural Development Program followed this tradition:

> "Community" was defined as the area served by the school and included parents and non-parents who lived and worked within the school's boundary. This definition was most important; it delimited the universe called community and provided an operational base for the activities required to justify within the school community the introduction of another federal program.[20]

The Experimental Schools projects, however, departed from this definition and emphasized an ideological definition where people come together not because they live in close proximity and share a physical neighborhood but because they share beliefs and values. In Minneapolis the shared community for a particular alternative school was a philosophy of education and support of a particular style of schooling to implement that philosophy. In the Street Academy project, only in Oakland was the geographical neighborhood a significant influence in the definition of community. In the other sites, and in Oakland as well, the Street Academy philosophy and expectations for a different kind of education were the dominant basis for the sense of community generated.

Another example of the ideological definition of community is the Boston King-Timilty Council. While this parent-school council served two particular schools in Boston and had as its purpose the improvement of education for specific students, it soon became involved in a citywide dispute over the appointment of principals. In its confrontation with the School Committee, the Council was viewed as representing the entire black community of Boston. By assuming that role or being granted that status by the Boston School Committee, the question of whom the Council represented became a source of continuing conflict. Since some members of the School Committee were opposed to the Council and at times openly hostile, they were almost gleeful in assuming that the Council did speak for the entire black community and blamed them for whatever was done by black community activists. Thus, identification as representatives of the black community became at times a handicap, since the Council did not always agree with the strategies proposed by black leaders who were not a part of the Council. This Boston project forced the issue of who speaks for the community—a constant question when the power structure is being threatened. Thus, we see the validity of using different definitions of community that are not dependent on geography. We must look anew at the basis of representation if the efforts to expand democracy are to have real meaning.

Hanna Pitkin suggests that there are four types of representation:

> *Formalistic:* here the focus is on the arrangements through which the representation takes place, not on the acts of representation themselves.
> *Descriptive:* the critical feature is the congruence between descriptive characteristics of the representatives and the represented. . . . Whatever features of the constituency are thought to be significant must be represented among the composite of decision makers.
> *Symbolic:* is even less concerned with the substantive congruence between the representative's acts and the represented's wishes than the previous types . . . [it] refers mainly to the way people feel about representatives or a representative body.
> *Substantive:* is the heart of the matter because it deals with the actions of the representative, not the method of choice or the sharing of descriptive features or the responses evoked by facades . . . the root definition is "acting in the interest of the represented in a manner responsive to them."[21]

The recent study by the Institute for Responsive Education on the status of school councils, *Sharing the Power?*, makes it clear that the majority of citizen's councils, especially those that are government-mandated, are of the first three types. Few fit the category of substantive representation as defined above. They have not had substantive influence in the "three key areas of educational policy: the program, personnel, and the budget of local schools," nor have they developed appropriate structures to be responsive.[22] In contrast, both Experimental Schools and Urban/Rural Development programs did address these issues through a variety of new structures. In the next section, the dimensions of these new governance structures are described.

GOVERNANCE STRUCTURES

Since issues of governance—who decides what, when, and how—are basic to democracy and community, these projects provide examples of a variety of ways that government can intervene to alter traditional ways of operating schools. The Experimental Schools program was quite explicit about its views of the role of the schools. It not only recognized the continuing role of public schools but wanted to demonstrate that the system could be made to work for all children. A change in structure was needed; not just a temporary change while outside funding was available but rather a change in the governance structure that would make possible a continual reexamination of who makes decisions about education. By funding alternatives for a limited time with the provision that the local school system participate in the change process, the federal government was trying to find long-term solutions that would make the system continually more responsive. The same philosophy was evident in the Urban/Rural Development Program.

Up until the Experimental Schools Program, Street Academies had operated outside the established school system. The initial discussions of funding revealed concern about sponsorship. Could the academies be true to their beliefs and maintain their integrity and commitment to students who had been failed by the system if the community was not the sole sponsor? Would accepting the federal dollar and the condition that the local education agency (LEA) be a partner force compromises that would destroy the essence of the Street Academy?

Because of these concerns, the initial agreements between the Urban Leagues and the LEAs were careful to specify the philosophy and the essential characteristics of staff and program. During the five years of outside funding, there were some adaptations to the demands of the system, but most of the essentials were preserved. Whether this will continue now that the LEAs have assumed financial responsibility will have to await the test of time.

The mechanism created to monitor these initial agreements was a joint governance board. At the three sites they differed in numbers, but all included representatives from the Urban League, Street Academy staff, local school system, parents, and students. In South Bend, the Urban Coalition, which had previously collaborated with the Urban League, was also included. In Oakland, during the first contract year, the board's name and composition were changed to include more community representation.

In the Street Academy project, parents were not as involved as they were in Minneapolis. Some did not have the time; others did not have the inclination to be active parents. It may be that many felt that since a community agency like the Urban League was a dominant partner, their interests were adequately represented. In addition, the project involved only secondary school students, a group whose parents are always difficult to involve. In Minneapolis, too, the high school governance structure had the most difficulty becoming active.

Despite the title of governance board, the local League, usually through its Executive, and the Street Academy director played the dominant role in policy and implementation during the five years of the outside funding. The local League took the major role in the negotiations with the Washington office. The superintendents were very supportive of the project, and the school liaison officers played important roles in linking the Academy operation to the school system.

In two of the three sites, a transference committee was formally appointed by the Governance Board to work out the continuing relationship after the end of Experimental Schools support. In Washington, D.C., the negotiations were informal, due, in part, to the close alliance between the Academy staff and the school system that had existed from the beginning of the project. The end result was the same in all three sites: the assumption of the total fiscal support by the LEA. In Oakland, there was a formal contract between the LEA and the League to operate the Academy, with state monies based on average daily attendance supplying the bulk of support. In the other two cities, the budgets were absorbed as regular line items of the school system budget.

What is significant about the governance structure is that it was successfully demonstrated to the school systems in at least three diverse communities that decision making could be shared. The experience led Moore to this conclusion in his final report:

> The school systems have a five-year history of being cooperative and of keeping lines of communication open through liaison officers and personal contacts. The systems have already shared in the governance of programs and the setting of program policies. The fund of past cooperative relations gives no surface indication that future relations between the Leagues, Academies, and the school system will be otherwise.[23]

The issue of governance was different in Minneapolis in that the Southeast Alternatives Project was always an integral part of the school system. It differed also in that participation was viewed as a part of the definition of alternatives—as a right of the various groups to participate. As stated by James K. Kent, former Director of SEA:

> Alternative schools should be viewed as one sensible way to demonstrate what so many know so well—that children learn in myriad ways, that effective teaching strategies vary, and that parents, students, faculties, and staffs have a right to be involved in school decisions for, after all, we are public institutions under elected citizen boards of education.[24]

He continued,

> The local school community of students, parents, faculties and administrators are the key decision-making community and all these groups are substantively involved in the planning, development, operation, and evaluation of the schools.[25]

For Minneapolis, it was clear that "full participation in the many decision-making processes is at the heart of any open, responsive, alternative approach."[26] Within SEA, the method of involvement in decision making differed from school to school. This difference is explained partly by the conditions that existed before the creation of the particular alternative and partly by the nature of the alternative school itself.

At one end was the Free School organized by parents and faculty who shared a particular philosophy. Since the parents were intimately involved in founding the school and in the very tangible task of finding a building to house the program, their participation was viewed as legitimate and necessary from the beginning. In the early stages, the faculty person in charge was designated head teacher as opposed to principal. Their deliberation focused primarily on how to translate the philosophy espoused by the Free School Governing Board into operating programs constrained somewhat by the fact that they were part of the established school system. Some of the debates were quite similar to those of the street academies as they struggled to be a part of a system of which they were quite critical.

Another element in the Free School Governing Board that made it somewhat different from the other alternatives was the inclusion of students. There was an attempt to include students below the secondary school level, but this was soon found to be unworkable.

As the years progressed, the Free School Governing Board found it more and more necessary to have written rules and regulations not only for their own operation but for the school itself. When the North Central Accrediting Agency denied accreditation to the Free School because the head teacher did not meet the state requirements for certification as principal, the Board realized that it could be only so free and still remain a part of the established system. This was one example of the power still held by the state despite the attempt to bypass this level. With a new principal, the school did receive accreditation. But basic questions were raised, as with the street academies, about how different a school can be and still be accepted by the gatekeepers of the society. To what degree will the students and staff be willing to risk their own future to provide an alternative? In this instance, a fundamental question about change and the obstacles to it was raised. In the words of one of the Minneapolis reports, " . . . principals' associations and teachers' unions are an obstacle to hiring alternative people for alternative education programs."[27]

At another of the alternatives in SEA, the Marcy Open School Council represented all the groups involved in the school's program. By vote, these groups chose to establish an advisory rather than a policy-making governance council. In operation, however, the Council did gradually assume some policy-related responsibilities. For example, they were involved in developing the budget for the additional funds available through the federal grant and in recommending the selection of new staff members. Later, when the principal left, they were involved in the selection of a new principal.

A 1974 report of the evaluation team contained this summary comment on the role of the Marcy Open School Council:

During the 1973–74 school year the Council began an evolution away from serving merely an advisory role to the Marcy administration. Although the principal still has the legal responsibility for decision making at the school, he has worked himself into a comfortable position as an ex officio Council member, and most decisions are made by consensus of the Council members. It was found that students did not have the patience nor interest to participate on the Council on a regular basis, so official student membership on the Council was dropped with the provision that students could come to the Council at any time with their concerns.[28]

Moving along the continuum of alternatives provided through Southeast Alternatives, the Pratt Motley Continuous Progress Program provided yet another form of governance. The function of the Coordinating Committee, as the original group was named, was to coordinate the program between the two separate buildings which originally housed the program. In 1974–75, the faculty meetings for the two buildings were combined, which seemed to decrease the need for a special coordinating committee. But even after the program was combined in one building, the committee continued representing both faculty and parents, but with no officers.

According to the 1974 evaluation report, most committee members felt the committee was needed and that it should deal with day-to-day management problems as well as serving the principal as a sounding board for staff and parent opinions. The prediction was that the committee would evolve into a formal principal advisory group.

The fourth elementary alternative was the Tuttle Contemporary School. This program was more traditional in school program and in the decision-making process. The parent group retained the PTA organizational structure. Its purpose was to facilitate home-school-community communication and interaction by informing school staff about parent and community concerns, raising additional funds for the programs, and assisting in the recruitment and training of volunteers for the schools. However, the involvement of parents and staff in decision making was more extensive than in the past, though less than in the other alternatives.

The Marshall-University High School shows yet another variation in governance structures. Prior to the establishment of SEA, the high school was sponsored by the University of Minnesota and had a Policy Board that was originally intended to be a decision-making body. This objective was never reached. During the early years of SEA, various plans were developed to establish a different governance structure for the high school component that would be more in line with the community involvement at the other schools. In June 1973, a final proposal was approved, and a new Principal's Advisory Council began meeting in the winter of 1974. The Council would involve staff as well as parents and students in issues before decisions were made. It deliberately was to have a diverse membership.

In addition to new governance structures at each of the school sites, a council was established to oversee the entire SEA project. This group, known as the Southeast Alternatives (SEA) Council, was founded in the spring of 1972. The group included the director and one member representing each of the constituent members of SEA as well as the Planning Coordinating Committee and the Van Cleve Community Park. Its main function was to act as an advisory group to the SEA Director. A part of this responsibility was to conduct an evaluation of the Director. Another important function was to provide communication among and between the various components.

According to the evaluation report, most members interviewed felt that the SEA Council had impact on a variety of issues with which the Council was involved: establishment of the SEA Teacher Center; planning for the continuation of SEA for 1973–76; the superintendent's decision regarding which district SEA should join and the timing of that move; establishing council members as observers at the SEA management team meetings; establishing a procedure for evaluating the SEA Director which helped stimulate schools to set up evaluations of their administrators; and participating in hiring new administrators. The evaluator observed that:

> [One result of] this increased involvement in the decision-making process is that some Council members now find it hard to remain comfortable in just an advisory role. They find it harder to accept

the idea that the Director has the right to follow *or* reject a Council recommendation. One member felt that since SEA was an experimental program, some experimenting should be done with letting the Council make independent decisions. The experience of the Southeast Council clearly illustrates both the benefits and difficulties of increasing people's participation in the governance process.[29]

In summary, in all of the Minneapolis alternatives parents were active participants along with school people. Even though the councils differed in the extent of their jurisdiction, all participated to some degree in the three key areas of educational policy: program, personnel, and budget. Their influence over program was the most extensive. Decisions about budgets tended to be confined to the additional federal funds, but their influence was significant in that these monies supported certain program thrusts such as the community liaison positions. In personnel, all councils seemed to have some voice—whether explicitly stated or not—in the selection of the principals and other leadership personnel. Thus, what had formerly been the almost exclusive prerogatives of administrators or school people were now shared decisions. The representation was substantive, for the most part.

As the project continued, the administrators seemed to become comfortable in expanding the decision-making process even though it took more time to arrive at consensus. At the same time, all of the parent surveys indicated greater parent satisfaction with the schools as a result of SEA.

The test as to whether there had been a fundamental change in the decision-making process came in Minneapolis, as it did with the street academies, when the five-year Experimental Schools support ended. The Superintendent at the time, John B. Davis, agreed to allow the Southeast Council to participate in the deliberations and make a recommendation to him as to which area to join. The review included interviews with each of the three area superintendents to see if their philosophy was compatible with SEA. The Council's recommendation to join the West area was honored by the Superintendent even though it would not have been his choice.

In a report by the Level II evaluation team, this prognosis was made:

SEA successfully preserved the identity of its governance structure as a model for community involvement in decision-making while reorganization with the MPS system was accomplished. Although SEA lost administrative independence with the West area merger, it did not lose autonomy of internal decision making.[30]

However, there were significant changes external to SEA that dampened this positive view. Not only were the federal funds from Experimental Schools no longer available, but the regular school budget was facing an 8½ million dollar deficit for the 1976–77 school year. In addition, several major administrative changes were to take effect with the start of the 1975–76 school year: the supportive area superintendent, the citywide superintendent, and the SEA director all left the system. The question for Minneapolis is whether meaningful institutional change can occur when the leadership of particular people, considered essential to continued movement toward agreed-upon goals, is no longer present.

The Urban/Rural Development Program provides another variation of governance structure that emphasizes the concept of "parity" between community representatives and professional educators. This program was funded by the Bureau of Educational Personnel Development and focused on in-service training of teachers in poor communities. The mechanism for deciding what should be done, and how, was the creation of a community council that would represent the two major constituencies of the school community: parents, along with others in the school's community, and the staff of the schools. The concept of "parity" was defined as deliberate, mutual, collaborative planning and decision making on the part of those giving the service as well as those receiving the service.[31]

The 1975 evaluation of this program concluded, as did those reviewing the Experimental Schools programs, that changing the decision-making process was not only possible, but doing so brought about changes in the educational program itself. To quote from their report,

> The operation of the program has demonstrated, in our view, that community people can participate effectively and wisely in educational decision-making and implementation. It has also demonstrated, we think, that some time and experience are required to allow people in the community to develop competence in these tasks.[32]

IMPLICATIONS FOR GOVERNANCE STRUCTURE

Why were the Experimental Schools and the Urban/Rural projects judged "successful" in changing the decision-making process, and, further, why was there a favorable prognosis that the change would remain in the future? First, the time factor was important. In the Experimental Schools projects, for example, the special arrangement lasted for five years with outside funding and support for the "experiment." Over that period of time, community involvement could develop a high degree of sophistication and refinement such as was seen in the SEA Council's participation in the decision as to which area to join.

In addition, there was administrative autonomy and encouragement and support of top officials in the local school systems in the Experimental Schools and Urban/Rural projects. This was not true in the Boston King-Timilty Council project which was resisted by the system. Thus, support and willingness to let the separate unit work through its new processes seem to be essential conditions for change.

Moore suggests that another reason for the success of the street academies was the design of the program itself.

> Having a definite set of objectives, a schedule of events that were to occur, a timetable for their occurrence, and an external monitor whose authority was recognized, if not always welcomed, outcomes (that may well have still been mired in the discussion and resolution of issues in some cases) occurred. Knowledge of the experimental design, its expectations, and demands had a formative value for participants, especially the Urban League and the Street Academies. The design was a reminder that the demonstration project was oriented to testing the Academy concept, modes of implementation, and acceptability for adoption and transference to public school systems. It was not a demonstration of the development of self-sustaining alternative models. In this sense, the experimental design and its objectives had a unifying effect for participants who had their own specific objectives attached to the project. [33]

The external monitor may be a key component. While coercion may be too strong a word to describe its dominant mode of operation, there was ample evidence that the Washington Experimental Schools office, even with the changing program officers, was determined to have the local parties live up to their agreement to alter the decision-making process. While there was a disposition to change at the local level, the outside legitimating force may have spelled the difference.

At the same time, the constant prodding was accompanied by changes in regulations that often led to misinformation and misinterpretation. These actions by the Washington office seemed to create and to nourish conflict with the local sites. What also happened in the process, that might not have been recognized at the time, was that the local parties tended to draw closer together to "fight" their common enemy. They were forced to work through their own conflicts at the local level. In sum, what these projects may have contributed most is evidence that conflict resolution can become an accepted part of the change process; that negotiation and compromise are as necessary for the operation of schools as for any other societal institution. But what also appears to have been demonstrated is that an external force with an authority accepted by both parties may be a necessary ingredient.

In the Urban/Rural Project, the federal government, as such, was not present, but the same function was performed by the regional coordinators. In the Boston project, the third party was almost totally absent in that the federal government, once the funds were granted, was hardly visible in monitoring the project, and had little clear mandate as to arrangements for continuation. Thus, when the three-year funding ended, so in effect did the Council. It may be too much to expect that those in control will have enough initiative and courage or risk-taking ability to make fundamental changes even where the need for a change is recognized. Where those in power see no reason to include others, there is even less chance that adjustments will be made without an outside inducement. Moore would go even further in regard to the need for a third party:

> The project experiences would indicate that there should be formal policy on maintaining ties with third parties, and political ties. The success of the project was not simply based on altruistic elements nor on education elements alone. Politics was an active ingredient in the processes.[34]

These projects offer a wide variety of governance structures, all using some form of a school-community council. The intention was to reduce the previous dominance of professional educators and school board members, who should have had the best interests of the children paramount in their philosophy and programs, but who failed to produce to the satisfaction of many. These federal programs were predicated on the assumption that neither the professional educators nor the school boards—appointed or elected—adequately represented all the interests of the "community." These projects do provide some answers to whether the creation of a new governance structure can change the way in which decisions that should lead to more effective education for the children involved are made.

This statement regarding Minneapolis is equally applicable to the Street Academies and the Urban/Rural Development Program and sums up the Council's role as more substantive than symbolic:

> ... the decisions made in SEA were of greater significance than those typically made in public schools by parents, teachers, support staff, and building administrators. Typically, central office administrators retain power over decisions about budget alloca-

tions, staffing patterns, and selections, the nature and extent of in-service training, building alterations, new curriculum materials, and the basic instructional organization of teachers and pupils. These decisions were "decentralized" in the sense that they fell largely within the domain of SEA and were established within SEA. Within SEA, the building, or alternative school, became the unit for instructional decisions rather than centralized governance groups.[35]

PURPOSES OF EDUCATION AND SCHOOLING

While the governance structure received the federal government's major attention, the mission of the schools also came under scrutiny. In Experimental Schools projects, funded as they were for a limited time period with the condition that the local public school system be a partner and make a commitment to continue the program beyond the life of the experiment, the discussion of mission was framed in terms of alternatives. If the mission of the public schools is to educate all the children, then alternatives should be a part of the publicly funded system, not a luxury acceptable only in times of big budgets. But confining the discussion to alternatives is insufficient. As stated by Moore,

> Reorganization, as informed by the Street Academy experience, requires a wider definition of education and its purposes. The Street Academy conception of education entails supplying students with tools to live as productive citizens. This means reading, writing, and arithmetic. But it also means the inculcation of values, attitudes, and the necessary behaviors to cope with and change those conditions that make productive citizenship improbable or impossible. This calls for rethinking why we are schooling students. Is there any relationship between schooling and educating them? What are we educating them for?[36]

These programs recognized that purposes and goals should be decided at the local level within the context of developing the individual and meeting the needs of society. It was recognized that ways to achieve these goals might differ so that the responsibility of the national level was to assist local communities to make their own decisions and to create, in the words of Nisbet, the intermediary associations so essential to giving meaning to life.

In Minneapolis, for example, each school community—including the parents who chose that school, the faculty, and administrators—was sanctioned by the system to determine the philosophy and then implement a program to carry it out. These same people monitored the process with authority to change if necessary. In the Street Academy project, the local Urban League played the dominant role in determining the purposes and methods to achieve them. They were constantly faced with the theoretical and practical issues of defining an alternative while being a part of the very system they were opposing.

Since many systems are struggling with defining alternatives, the Street Academy Evaluation offers one framework for an exploration of the issues. There are at least three ways in which any institution can be considered alternative:

> First, as an alternative for students, in the sense that having been unable to handle the regular schooling experience, for whatever reason, students are provided with an opportunity to attend another kind of school. Secondly, they may be viewed as alternatives in structure, whether it be in the curriculum design or in methodological approach. Finally, they may be alternative in their objectives.[37]

In regard to the second definition of an alternative—curriculum design, methodological approach, or structure—the Street Academies were most successful. Even though much of the curriculum had to be predetermined if the students were to be adequately prepared to cope with the society of which they are a part, courses were offered of cultural, historical, and practical value to the populations served. The Street Academies were free to explore alternative methodological approaches which were exemplified by "high levels of one-to-one teaching, in-depth individual counseling, high levels of informal student/teacher interaction, and a general alternative in the 'climate' of the centers." Moore continues:

> The importance of such curriculum additions and climate alternation should not be underestimated. Many studies have shown that academic performance is as much affected by climate as by I.Q., socioeconomic status, and other traditionally recognized factors. For example, it is clear that the reduction of fear of failure by emphasis on effort exerted, rather than strict emphasis on raw scores, increases both the qualitative and quantitative performance of students who have been conditioned to fear failure. It is equally true that there is a relationship between self-esteem and performance, and self-esteem and social context such that a cooperative and consonant social environment makes people feel better about themselves and results in better performance. This would be particularly true of persons who were previously looked down on in regular institutions as dumb, trouble makers, etc.[38]

It is in the area of objectives that alternatives have the most difficulty in defining how they are different from the established school system. At one level the new structures would be doing a disservice to their students if they did not prepare them for the "real world" of work in the existing society. This was an area of constant tension for the Street Academies and probably will continue to be after complete transference to the school system. "They are forever dual. . . . If they fall into the dominant order with regard to curriculum, bureaucracy, climate and method of evaluation, they will lose their clientele and their purpose for existence. On the other hand, if they reject the larger objectives and throw the book away, they will lose their financial backing and be forced out of business."[39]

These theoretical issues involved in defining an alternative were reflected in the practical problems of the organizational structure of the academies. The authority structure—who makes the rules—differed at each site. Some rules and consistency in enforcement were as necessary in these small alternatives as in the larger systems. It was soon learned that when groups of people have to work together to accomplish a common goal, there must be some agreement as to how they will interact to achieve that end. There were deep-seated differences of opinion on all these bureaucratic matters. Students and a large percentage of the staff believed that these matters could be handled differently than in the public schools and that their objectives of retrieval would be undermined if they took on too many of the characteristics of the public schools' rules and regulations governing behavior. For example, accurate reporting of attendance became a major issue, as did how many absences a student would be allowed and still be counted as a student. This approach seemed inconsistent with the concept of retrieval. And yet, if funds were to be based on student attendance (and that was being argued in at least two of the sites), there had to be some records. In each instance, these issues continued throughout the life of the project as conflict areas that had to be resolved. Moore points out:

> The Street Academies, as alternative institutions, are expected by their clientele to be less regimented and regulated. As a consequence, unlike their normative counterparts, Street Academies must re-address their position on such issues as smoking, absenteeism, suspension, expulsion, grading criteria and enforcement. As institutions who service self-selecting populations who are not by law required to attend on one hand, while on the other hand being engaged in gaining the support of local educational authorities, accreditation, and the stamp of legitimacy, the Street Academy is again found in an ambivalent position.[40]

By attempting to return decision making and choice to local communities, these programs were also forcing a reexamination of the purpose of schooling. While they may not have used these words, each of these projects did seem to be addressing the same issues as Bernard Watson:

> Problems such as illiteracy, racism, and unequal opportunity are only symptoms of the deeper crisis which confronts us today. In fact, the fundamental question is whether we can survive as a nation of decent, humane, and free people. It is time that we become advocates of people rather than programs, and that we concentrate our attention on the survival of humanity rather than merely the survival of individual projects. It is clear that our educational goals must address this question and must focus on skills, empowerment, and humaneness.
>
> Skills may be defined as distinction and knowledge—as the ability to use one's knowledge effectively and readily in execution and performance. . . . This means that in developing skills, we need to prepare people for a full and productive life, not just for jobs which will lead to maintenance and bare survival.
>
> Empowerment means enablement—the process of making one able to do something. This definition implicitly requires the means and opportunity for doing. More importantly, it speaks not only to individual empowerment, but to group empowerment.
>
> Most important of all is the quality of humaneness. Education in this context is marked by compassion, by sympathy and consideration for other human beings. . . . If we strive for intellectual achievement at the expense of respect, forbearance, and a sense of equity, we will surely have failed.[41]

THE ROLE OF THE SCHOOL IN A DEMOCRATIC SOCIETY

The premise of these programs went beyond mere support of the continuing existence of public schools. They were to demonstrate that the system could be made to work for all children. To accomplish this purpose, a change in structure was needed; not a temporary change while outside funding was available, but rather a change in governance structures that would force a reexamination of who makes decisions about education and the system. By funding alternatives for a limited time with the provision that the local school system participate in the change process, the federal government was trying to find long-term solutions to make the system continually more responsive.

Furthermore, these projects demonstrated that education is neither apolitical nor nonpolitical. It is an integral part of the political process through which decisions are made about the allocation of goods, services, and values. The process of adoption and transference, in the case of the Street Academies, and expansion and reintegration into the total system, in the case of Minneapolis, were clearly political acts. They required compromise and negotiation, the accepted political processes used to reach decisions involving conflicting values and limited resources. What was remarkable is that, with so many new participants in a field where negotiations have never been the norm, the projects did not disintegrate. On the contrary, the political activity seemed to propel them closer to their goals. The evaluation reports on both of these projects make special note of the development of these political skills on the part of the citizens and parents involved in making essential decisions about education along with professional educators. Although more permanent change did not result in Boston, the members of that Council did learn how to manipulate the system.

The political activities of the leaders of these projects suggests another phase of the democratic political process—the role of leadership in effecting change in institutions. There were many strong personalities with definite views about what should be done and how. At the same time, the turnover of personnel at several critical points raises the concern of placing too much reliance on particular people rather than on institutional arrangements if a shift in the power structure is the desired goal.

At the national level, the Director of Experimental Schools, Robert Binswanger, did remain throughout most of the five-year period, providing firm direction to the development of the program. But the rest of the Washington staff changed constantly. The Minneapolis reports, for example, mention repeatedly the change in program officers. At the local level, the Minneapolis Director, Dr. Kent, remained through most of the period though principals changed at several of the schools. In the last year, there were major systemwide changes as the Area Superintendent and City Superintendent both left.

There were also changes in the Street Academy project. The original Director of Evaluation left after the first year, but her replacement was already on the staff and remained until the end of the project. Only one of the three superintendents remained throughout the project and is still there. In the other two cities, there was more than one change in the superintendency. The Street Academy directors in Oakland and Washington stayed throughout most of the period; in South Bend, the director left after the first year. The executives of the Urban Leagues, key people in the political process, remained the most stable—both the Bay Area and South Bend executives had been there before the project and are still there. Only in Washington was there a change, and that occurred in the first year, so that the present executive was in office through the crucial negotiating process for transference. The Urban/ Rural Development Program also benefited from strong, decisive leadership at the national level.

These observations suggest that while it is important to have particular people to initiate a new program, it is equally important to pay attention to changing the structure if long-lasting results are to be achieved. If anything has been learned from these studies and others, it is that dynamic leaders do move on.

CONCLUSIONS

Based on these limited case studies, what can be said about communities and their schools as a result of intervention by the federal government? First, the variety of new governance structures that emerged demonstrated quite conclusively that there is no one best way through which school-community interaction can occur. It is clear that whatever structure is adopted should take into account the political, social, and historical context of the local community. As the outside evaluator in Minneapolis noted, "The momentum of Minneapolis in moving toward alternatives, decentralization and community involvement was critical. Federal programs may accelerate momentum but it is not likely that money alone will create it or reverse it."[42]

In regard to the use of alternatives combined with a new governance structure, there is now evidence that the established system can work in partnership with new groups. The schools will not be destroyed when the decision-making process is opened to new participants. In fact, there was some evidence that satisfaction with the schools increased with the change.

Additional money was another major contributing factor. In the case of the Street Academies, they could not have been created without the federal funds. In Minneapolis, the resources made it possible to accelerate a change that was already underway. More importantly, "the increased resources provided the means to further define and develop the alternatives so that they could become more distinct in terms of instructional materials, staffing patterns, building arrangements, support staff, staff development, and evaluation services." [43] This was very important at the point of reintegration, for each alternative could now more clearly state its philosophy and program so that other parent groups could make an informed choice.

The monies were also valuable in relation to the expanded governance structure and may account for the greater difficulty experienced by government-mandated councils that have not (until recent years) had funds to use for their own development. In Minneapolis the federal funds created a "managerial overhead beyond that which would be expected in a public schools program ... [and] funded several positions, assumed by parents, to handle program management within the formal structure of SEA."[44]

What may have been equally significant was the multi-year commitment of outside funding. Even though each project had to prepare a new budget each year, they could depend on a five-year commitment of support. They also knew that the local system was required to work out a method for continued support after that period.

While there is no question that the extra funding was important and perhaps essential, especially in the case of the Street Academies, it should also be noted that, at least in Minneapolis, much of the program was not dependent upon additional funding. Some of these ideas could be duplicated in any system. The evaluation report commented:

> ... new governance structures per se cost little. Community involvement is an attitude and pattern of interaction, neither of which necessarily costs additional money. A sensitivity to the affective aspects of instruction does not require new instructional materials or new buildings. While money provides visible change in a program, the noncost factors of philosophy, attitude, and commitment give new programs their substantive changes.[45]

What seemed to distinguish these projects from other attempts to influence local schools was the recognition that change does not occur easily or rapidly in long-established organizational structures. As noted in the report on the Boston project:

> Both participation of parents and learning of students are not amenable to short-term, isolated solutions. A process for continuous dialogue and adjustment of programs is essential in order to deal with change in a bureaucratic system which by its nature becomes rigid and unresponsive to rapidly changing needs.[46]

Another important factor that all the evaluation reports comment on is the critical and necessary role played by the third party. What still needs to be tested is whether there are other groups or organizations that can play a similar role or whether the authority, along with the money, of the federal government is the critical difference.

Another factor suggested by these projects is that of size, both of the individual projects and the federal program itself. Unlike Title I, Headstart, or Follow Through, which affect a great number of school systems, these programs were quite limited. Throughout its five-year history, Experimental Schools only funded seven different projects; Urban/Rural had twenty-three sites. These are very few compared to the nearly 16,000 school districts in this country. What now needs to be tested is the expansion of these ideas to more districts. Can this be done without the same level of extra funds or the close monitoring that was possible when the programs were small?

In assessing the role of the federal government as an intervenor on behalf of communities in the operation of their schools, we are brought to the age-old question of, first, whether the schools can create a new social order and, second, how the community will be defined to address the question. While these projects are encouraging to those who believe that a sense of community can and must be developed if a healthy society is to be maintained, we need to take heed of these words of Robert Akerman so that the problem of communities and their schools will be defined appropriately:

> American cities are not fulfilling the traditional role of communities in Western civilization, and we are likely to continue to have an urban problem until we inquire into what a community is and ask whether our modern big cities can ever be the right kind of community.[47]

He contrasts the present large cities with the model of the Greek city, which "was more than just a place to work, shop or reside. It was a center of allegiance; of shared tradition; the city gave significance to the individual's life."[48]

The hope of recapturing that sense of community, of satisfying the quest for community which lay behind many of the movements of the sixties by both the included and excluded may well lie in finding ways to connect the individual with the government through the creation of the new intermediate associations. These illustrations have demonstrated that the federal government can play an appropriate role as intervenor—by providing funds, by demanding commitment, and by monitoring local action—to reverse the trend toward bureaucratic, large-scale organizations in education, where intimate involvement of all parties is most needed. Some system of publicly supported educational institutions would still seem essential in a democratic society that is predicated on the belief that citizens can decide what is best for them based on informed choices. The future may depend on guaranteeing the existence of structures close to the people where all can learn self-government.

NOTES

1. Robert A. Nisbet, *The Quest for Community*, paperback reprint, Oxford University Press, New York, 1976, p. 49.

2. James L. Sundquist, *Making Federalism Work*, The Brookings Institution, Washington, D.C., 1969, p. 1.

3. *Brown v. Board of Education*, 347 U.S. 483, 1954.

4. Nisbet, op. cit., p. 70.

5. Sundquist, op. cit., p. 3.

6. Public Law 89-10, 89th Congress, April 11, 1965, Sec. 201.

7. *Experimental Schools Program*, 1971 Experimental School Projects, U.S. Department of Health, Education and Welfare. Reprinted January 1973, p. 1.

8. Ibid., pp. 4–5.

9. Vernon Moore (ed.), *The Street Academy: The Five Year Experience*, a final report submitted to National Institute of Education, National Urban League, Inc., Research Department, July 31, 1977, p. iii.

10. Ibid., pp. 1–2.

11. Reports issued by Street Academy Project: *Evaluation and Documentation Plan*, June 19, 1973; *Periodic Report: The Planning Period*, June 30, 1978; *Instrument Selection and Construction*, September 29, 1973; *History of the Street Academy: Implementation of a Concept*, October 30, 1973; *First Period Report*, March 11, 1974; *Street Academy Goals and Objectives*, July 1, 1974; *The Essential Characteristics of Three Operationalized Programs*, September 29, 1974; *Second Period Report*, September 28, 1974; *Third Period Report*, April 30, 1975; *The Street Academy: The Fourth Year*, June 30, 1976.

12. Moore (ed.), op. cit., pp. 1–2.

13. Ibid., p. 71.

14. Southeast Alternatives Internal Evaluation Team, *SEA Parent Opinion Survey, 1974 Final Report*, Minneapolis Public Schools, May 30, 1974, p. ii.

15. James V. Terry and Robert D. Hess, *The Urban/Rural School Development Program: An Examination of a Federal Model for Achieving Parity Between Schools and Communities*, School of Education, Stanford University, Stanford, California, January 1975, p. 6.

16. Ibid., p. 2.

17. Ibid., pp. 7–9.

18. For a more detailed description of this program see Barbara L. Jackson, "The King-Timilty Advisory Council, The Black Community of Boston and the Boston Public Schools: An Analysis of Their Relationship," unpublished paper, September 1969.

19. Nisbet, op. cit., p. 230.

20. Terry and Hess, op. cit., p. ix.

21. Discussed in Dale Mann, *The Politics of Administrative Representation*, D.C. Heath and Company, Lexington, Mass., 1976, pp. 8–10.

22. Don Davies et al., *Sharing the Power? Report on the Status of School Councils in the 1970's*, Institute for Responsive Education, Boston, January 1978.

23. Moore (ed.), op. cit., p. 155.

24. *SEA Journal 1971–1976*, Minneapolis Public Schools, 1975, p. 3.

25. Ibid., p. 4.

26. Ibid.

27. Activities Report on Internal Evaluation Team, January–March 1975, p. 22.

28. Don Rawitsch, *Study of Participation in Governance by Representative Groups in Southeast Alternatives*, June 3, 1974, p. 8.

29. Ibid., p. 30.

30. Mary Mueller, *The Reorganization of Southeast Alternatives: A Working Paper on Merger with the West Administration Area*, report to National Institute of Education, Minneapolis, Minnesota, Educational Services Group, March 1976, p. 29.

31. Terry and Hess, op. cit., p. 6.

32. Ibid., p. 69.

33. Moore (ed.), op. cit., pp. 155–156.

34. Ibid., p. 156.

35. Larry J. Reynolds, *Successful Change Attempts: Lesson from the Minneapolis Experimental Schools Program*, report to National Institute of Education, Minneapolis, Minnesota, Educational Services Group, April 15, 1976, p. 17.

36. Moore (ed.), op. cit., p. 175.

37. National Urban League, "First Period Report," March 11, 1974, volume V, p. 4.

38. Ibid., p. 5.

39. Ibid., p. 6.

40. Ibid.

41. Bernard C. Watson, "Accountability in Inner City Schools Through School-Community Involvement," *The High School Journal*, vol. LX, no. 4, pp. 168–169, January 1977.

42. Reynolds, op. cit., p. 17.

43. Ibid., p. 12.

44. Ibid.

45. Ibid., pp. 12–13.

46. Jackson, op. cit., p. 55.

47. Robert Ackerman, "Face the Real Urban Question," *The Atlanta Journal and Constitution,* p. 3-C, June 25, 1978.

48. Ibid.

7

PUBLIC SCHOOLS AND TEACHERS' UNIONS IN THE POLITICAL ECONOMY OF THE 1970s

DAVID STERN AND JOHN HARTER
University of California, Berkeley

Taxpayers in the 1970s were reluctant to pay high salaries for public school teachers. Excess demand for teachers turned to excess supply, not only because the number of students stopped growing but also because the public became more skeptical about the value of education itself. Severe economic recession made taxpayers less willing and able to pay taxes in general and contributed to skepticism about the value of education in particular by creating the appearance of "overeducation" among young workers just entering the labor market. Public support for education, weakened by recession, was further strained by the aggressive bargaining strategy of teachers' unions. There is some danger that withdrawal of public support and union aggressiveness may now be linked in a vicious circle. No "technical fix" will provide the remedy. What would help is some political process that creates a clear connection between benefits to the community from public schools and material benefits for groups of teachers. One possible approach is some form of productivity bargaining.

THE REVENUE FAMINE OF THE 1970S

Public elementary and secondary schools had a much harder time raising money in the 1970s than in the preceding two decades. The number of pupils enrolled in public elementary and secondary schools rose from 25 million in 1950 to more than 45 million in 1970. In 1950, the schools enrolled about one-sixth of the total population; by 1970, almost one-fourth of the population was in public elementary and secondary schools. Personnel—teachers, principals, supervisors, and auxiliary staff—increased even faster than students, from less than a million in 1950 to more than 2.25 million in 1970. And the average annual salary per instructional staff member grew from $3,010 in 1950 to $8,840 in 1970. Allowing for inflation, the average salary rose 84 percent over these two decades. As a result of the rise in both the ratio of staff to students and the average staff salary, expenditure per pupil in average daily attendance nearly quadrupled, from $209 in 1950 to $816 in 1970. Allowing for inflation, public schools were spending about two and a half times more money per pupil in 1970 than in 1950.[1]

After 1970, however, the fiscal environment became less hospitable. Elementary and secondary school enrollments reached a peak in 1972 and then began declining by about three-quarters of a percent each year.[2] Projections indicate that this decline will continue at about the same rate through 1985.[3] Enrollments can be expected to start growing again some time between 1985 and 1990, depending on fertility rates in the late 1970s and early 1980s, when the baby-boom generation will themselves reach peak child-bearing age.[4]

Despite the decline in number of students enrolled, the number of teachers continued to grow every year (at least through 1975).[5] Curiously, the number of instructional staff in public elementary and secondary schools actually grew at a faster rate from 1972 to 1974, after enrollment had begun to fall, than from 1970 to 1972, when enrollment was still rising. The rate of increase in instructional staff was slower in the 1970s than in the 1960s, but the number still increased. As a result, the ratio of staff to students continued to rise.[6]

Salary trends, on the other hand, clearly reflect a change in fiscal climate in the early 1970s. From 1972 to 1974 the rise in average salary for instructional staff failed to keep up with inflation.[7] This reduction in real earnings offset some of the rise in staff-student ratios. The net result was that expenditure per pupil, controlling for inflation, did continue to grow from 1972 to 1974, but only at half the rate at which it grew from 1966 to 1968.

Part of the explanation for these events is that changes in the supply of teachers lag behind changes in the number of students. When enrollments were rising rapidly in the 1950s and early 1960s, there was an excess demand for teachers, so salaries grew rapidly as school districts competed for qualified people. The number of teachers also grew—and continued to grow even as growth in the number of students slowed down and finally stopped after 1970. With the new abundance of teachers, districts could keep hiring additional staff without having to raise salaries even as fast as the cost of living.

But this is only part of the story. There is no fixed, constant relationship between the number of students and the number of teachers. The demand for teachers also depends on how much the public values their services. If taxpayers feel education is important and teachers are needed, then they will be willing to have more teachers hired even with a constant or declining number of students. As long as taxpayer demand for teachers' services increases, teachers' salaries can keep rising. But after 1970 the public became less willing to pay more taxes for public education. For several reasons the social valuation of teachers' services stopped growing.

First of all, the national economy entered a period of severe recession, which sent unemployment rates up and personal income down. The overall unemployment rate, which had been declining steadily from 5.7 percent in 1963 to 3.5 percent in 1969, suddenly shot upward to 5.9 percent in 1971, on its way to more than 8.5 percent in 1975. The result of sudden softening of demand for labor was predictable: real earnings stopped rising. Adjusting for inflation, the average nonsupervisory worker in the private nonagricultural sector found his or her gross weekly earnings in 1974 only 19 cents more than in 1969. A worker with three dependents actually had less real take-home pay per week in 1974 than in 1965.[8] With unemployment worse than at any time since the Depression, and with the growth of real earnings suddenly stopped, many taxpayers were experiencing more acute economic anxiety than they had ever known.

Public school budgets are especially vulnerable in these circumstances. Like other public services financed in large part from local property taxes, they are easier targets for spontaneous local taxpayer revolts than are federal programs controlled in distant Washington. And changes in average income have been found to affect school budgets even more strongly than budgets for other state and local public services.[9] In good times local taxpayers are more likely to expand education than fire or police services, but in a crunch it is education that gets cut. Voters who had approved 70 percent of proposed bonds for school construction in the mid-60s approved less than half in 1971 and 1972.[10]

The vulnerability of public school budgets in times of recession has increased in recent years because state taxes have been paying a larger share of educational expenses. Between 1970 and 1974, the amount of money raised by state governments for public elementary and secondary schools grew by more than 50 percent, while local school revenue grew by less than 40 percent.[11] The growth in the state's share has been in part a response to the demand for property tax relief and in part a response to court-ordered reform in school finance. Following the California Supreme Court's 1971 decision in *Serrano v. Priest*, a number of courts have ruled that state constitutions require state governments to offset some of the inequality in revenue-raising capacity among local school districts. Since state legislatures are loath to require wealthy districts to reduce their spending, they have responded by raising expenditure levels in the less wealthy districts instead.[12] For example, the California legislature responded to *Serrano* in 1972 and again in 1977 after the first response was ruled inadequate. The 1977 package provides four billion dollars of additional spending over a five-year period, plus an estimated $200 million of local property tax relief, all financed by state taxes.[13] This kind of shift makes public school revenues more dependent on state income and sales taxes and less dependent on local property taxes.

The problem is that state taxes are relatively sensitive to changes in average income. While income and sales tax bases grow faster than the property tax base when average income is rising, they also shrink faster when income is falling. In a time of severe recession like the early 1970s, maintaining constant growth of income and sales tax revenues may require increasing the tax rates. This entails legislative action and will be especially difficult to enact when taxpayers are already feeling the pinch.

A legislator considering whether to raise tax rates to pay for public schools could also find a least two substantive reasons for reluctance in the early 1970s. One was the widely publicized "Coleman report," which had proclaimed in 1966 that school resources appeared to have little effect on students' academic achievement. This message was amplified and synthesized with other studies in authoritative reports by Christopher Jencks[14] and Harvey Averch.[15] The controversy about why some studies found effects and others did not became part of the evidence in several of the court cases dealing with school finance reform. Legislators could easily conclude that, since the experts disagreed among themselves, there was no strong justification for spending more money in the schools—at least not without strong "accountability" provisions attached.

The second reason for skepticism about school effectiveness was found in the labor market itself, where the possibility of widespread "overeducation" was appearing for the first time in the history of this country. Children born in the baby boom following World War II entered college in record numbers during the 1960s. The proportion of individuals between ages eighteen and twenty-four enrolled in college rose from 17 percent in 1960 to 26 percent in 1970. Because this age group itself represented a larger proportion of the population as a whole in 1970 than in 1960, the actual number of people in college more than doubled during the decade, while the total population grew only 13 percent.[16] As this horde of young college graduates began to move into the labor force after 1970, they became victims of recession. Unemployment rates went up for all young workers, including college graduates. For those young workers who did find jobs, real earnings did not compare favorably with past years, especially for the now-more-numerous college graduates.

Figures for white males show that the average income ratio of college graduates to high school graduates decreased between 1968 and 1973 for all age groups, with the sharpest drop among younger workers. In 1968, college graduates about three or four years out of school had earned 48 percent more than high school graduates with the same amount of post-school experience; but in 1973 the young college men earned only 25 percent more. The influx of young, college-educated workers also caused a somewhat smaller reduction in the relative advantage of older college graduates. Among men with about thirty years of post-school experience, the average income ratio of college to high school graduates fell from 50 percent in 1968 to 41 percent in 1973.[17] The entry of so many young college graduates into the labor market also accounts for the rising rate of unemployment, relative to the labor force as a whole, among people trained for professional and technical occupations.[18]

This kind of deterioration in the relative economic position of highly educated workers had never happened before in this country, and it challenged the traditional American belief in advancement through education. If schools can no longer guarantee large economic returns, then exactly what can they offer? This was a persistent question in the 1970s, in contrast to what now seems the naive faith in the power of education to cure social problems which prevailed in the 1960s. In 1976, the Gallup Poll found 80 percent of respondents wanted schools to give more emphasis to career preparation[19]—and Career Education has been one of the very few new federal programs in education in the 1970s.

Instead of engendering new programs, the major result of apparent "overeducation" and of the recession itself—without which the labor market could have more easily absorbed the influx of new college graduates, and taxpayers could have afforded to let expenditure per pupil keep growing at previous rates—has been to make any additional money for public schools very hard to get.

ARE TEACHERS' UNIONS TO BLAME?

Because teachers' unions grew in both membership and militancy during the 1960s and 1970s, an obvious question is whether unions are responsible in some way for the recent fiscal problems of public schools. As of August 1976, more than 1,886,000 teachers belonged to the National Education Association (NEA), and 375,000 belonged to the American Federation of Teachers (AFT).[20] More than 80 percent of teachers pay dues to one union or the other, compared to 25 percent of all workers in the private sector. Along with more organization has come increased militancy. From 1950 through 1959 there were twenty-six teachers' strikes in the country as a whole. From 1960 through 1965 teachers struck twenty-one times. Then in 1966 the number of strikes suddenly rose to thirty in one year alone. And from 1967 through 1971 there was an average of 115 strikes every year.[21]

This storm of strike activity signaled a period of upheaval and drastic changes in the public schools. Unions showed they could mobilize teachers, and teachers demonstrated a new refusal to accept passively whatever wages and conditions of employment the school board and superintendent handed down.

Starting in 1965, more and more state legislatures began to give legal power to unions representing teachers and other public employees. As of 1962 only Alaska, New Hampshire, and Wisconsin permitted teachers to bargain collectively. By 1971, twenty-six states had passed some kind of law recognizing and regulating collective negotiation for teachers.[22] In 1976, "twenty-eight states required that various aspects of management-labor relations in the public sector be negotiated and agreements set down in a contract. Sixteen states permitted collective bargaining although a formal agreement was not mandatory. Four states prohibited collective bargaining and the remaining two states had no guidelines at all."[23] Although collective bargaining may, in fact, take place despite the absence of such statutes—a study by Chambers found that school districts and teachers' unions in Missouri were bargaining collectively in 1974–75 even though it was technically against the law[24]—the sudden rush of statutes represented an important ratification of union power. As unions continue to consolidate their authority to bargain for teachers, it is evident that the shift in power will be irreversible. For the foreseeable future, unions will share the responsibility for governing public schools.

Most of the strikes called by teachers' unions have had to do with salaries. Out of 857 work stoppages from 1962 through 1971, 584 were mainly over salary. In another 112 strikes the main issue was recognition and security of the union itself.[25] The issues in this first wave of strikes indicate that unions first mobilized teachers over pay and the right to unionize.

The fact that unionization and accompanying strike activity were focused on salaries does not necessarily mean that the effort succeeded. Several statistical studies have attempted to find out whether teachers won higher salaries through collective bargaining than they would have otherwise. It is possible that the supply of teachers and the availability of revenues determine teachers salaries whether or not there is a union that bargains for teachers collectively.

Between 1970 and 1973, half a dozen studies analyzed data from various years in the middle and late 1960s. These studies all found that, on average, teachers in districts with collectively negotiated contracts received salaries that were at most only 5 percent higher than those of teachers in districts without collective contracts.[26] More recently, two studies by Chambers have found that the salary difference associated with collective bargaining is actually more like 10 to 15 percent.[27] The reason for Chambers' higher estimate is that he took account of not only whether collective bargaining occurs in a given district itself, but also whether it occurs in nearby districts. Even if a particular district does not have collective bargaining, it will generally have to pay higher salaries, if neighboring districts do, in order to compete for well-qualified teachers and perhaps also to forestall unionization. Chambers found that the salary level in a given district actually depends less on whether collective bargaining takes place in that district itself than on whether a large proportion of teachers in the region as a whole are covered by collective contracts. During a period in which some, but not all, districts engage in collective bargaining, Chambers' estimate represents a more complete accounting than the earlier studies of the salary differences associated with collective bargaining.

One interpretation of Chambers' results in that when collective bargaining is first taking hold in a region, all districts in that region grant larger than normal salary increases. But collective bargaining may or may not continue to result in larger salary increases after it becomes widespread and school boards get over the initial shock. Stiglitz compared salary levels in fifty-one large school districts each year from 1961–62 through 1969–70. She found collective bargaining was associated with higher salary levels in 1966 and to a lesser extent in 1967 and 1968, but not in 1969.[28] This indicates that unionization had a one-shot effect on salaries. After the initial effect, the presence of collective bargaining does not result in continued acceleration of teacher salaries.

A rough comparison of figures for all public elementary and secondary schools in the U.S. before and after 1966 also fails to show any persistent union effects. Since 1965 was the year in which the movement to legalize collective bargaining took hold in state legislatures, 1966 represents the beginning of the collective-bargaining era. In the six-year period from 1960 to 1966, average annual salaries for instructional staff, adjusted for inflation, grew more than 23 percent. But in the six-year period from 1966 to 1972, instructional salaries adjusted for inflation grew only 13 percent. Meanwhile, the number of instructional staff per ADA, which had grown less than 7 percent over the 1960–66 period, increased more than 14 percent in 1966–72.[29] This is surprising, because comparisons between districts at a given point in time have shown that collective bargaining not only raises teachers' salaries but also *reduces* the ratio of staff to students.[30] Therefore, the overall trends in average salary and staff-student ratios before and after 1966 do not show unionization having a dominant effect.

Similarly, in 1965–66, public elementary and secondary schools spent 64 percent of their current budget (total budget excluding capital outlay) on "instruction," which mainly consists of salaries for teachers and other instructional staff. This was the same percentage of current budget that was spent on instruction ten years earlier, in 1955–56. But ten years later, in 1975–76, the percentage of current budget spent on instruction actually fell, to 61 percent.[31] Again, this overall trend cannot be attributed to unionization, because teachers' unions tend to bargain for an *increase* in the instructional budget over other categories of expenditures.

The major trends in teacher salaries and budget allocation apparently are not attributable to the unionization of teachers but to the end of the teacher shortage and to the effects of recession. This can be seen more clearly by comparing trends before and after 1970, the year in which economic expansion halted and the unemployment rate began to climb steeply. From 1966 to 1970, the average salary of instructional staff, adjusting for inflation, grew 7.8 percent. This represents a slower annual rate of growth than in the 1960–66 period, when there was still some shortage of teachers, but it is nevertheless substantial. It is more than three times the rate of growth from 1970 to 1974, when salaries of instructional staff, adjusting for inflation, grew only 2.5 percent. As the country entered a period of high unemployment and declining real incomes, it became more difficult for teachers to win big salary increases, in spite of collective bargaining.

This was not for lack of trying. Even with recession and the revenue famine for public schools and other public services, teachers' unions, as well as other public employees' unions, continued to bargain aggressively for higher salaries. In 1975, for example, when the national unemployment rate averaged 8.5 percent, unions in some localities were able to win big raises for public employees. Los Angeles police and fire department employees won a first-year increase of 7.8 percent (after a court battle); Delaware teachers, New York police (after binding arbitration), and several categories of municipal employees in Milwaukee all won contracts with first-year pay increases of 8 percent; Chicago police and firefighters and teachers in Madison, Wisconsin, got first-year raises of 9 percent; while Baltimore teachers and Cincinnati police and fire department employees won 9.8 percent.[32] Considering that the Consumer Price Index rose 7 percent in 1975—and in some contracts there were automatic cost-of-living wage increases over and above the pay raises provided by the new settlements—these represent substantial real wage gains.

The bargaining strategy of public unions in 1975 strongly resembled that of unions in the private sector. Major collective bargaining agreements negotiated by private unions in 1975 gave members an average wage increase of 10.2 percent in the first year of the new contract, not including possible automatic gains through cost-of-living adjustments. These 1975 contracts on average provided bigger pay raises than settlements reached in 1974, which gave average first-year pay raises of 9.8 percent.[33] Apparently, unions in neither the public nor private sector were deterred by recession and the soaring rate of national unemployment.

But while unions in the private sector may not have to worry about their image, public unions do. As the public employees' unions continued to bargain aggressively for higher pay when many voters were experiencing severe economic anxiety, it became politically advantageous for elected public officials to oppose the unions and their demands. In 1975 even reputedly liberal Democratic governors, elected with the support of public and private labor unions, were taking a hard line.[34] The most severe setbacks for public unions occurred in New York City, where the municipal labor unions were forced to submit to thousands of layoffs, together with postponement of pay increases recently won in collective bargaining, before the Ford administration would provide emergency federal backing for New York bonds.[35] And the spectacle of New York elicited strong talk from public officials around the country. For example, the *New York Times* reported:

> In Seattle, Mayor Wesley Uhlman says New York's fiscal crisis is a blessing for him, because the public backs him when he says "no" to city employee unions. And even in Beverly Hills, perhaps a synonym for urban riches, there are echoes from across the continent: Many residents are asking, "Have we been too generous with city employees' retirement plans?"[36]

Similarly, when municipal unions in San Francisco went out on strike in 1975–76, public opinion clearly turned against the unions.[37]

When public employees' unions demand more money than voters expect to pay, the issue becomes whether public employees are delivering enough services in return. If voters perceive unions as attempting to raise salaries but not trying to make any corresponding improvement in the quality of services, then voters perceive the net effect of unions as negative. Thus, the 1976 Gallup Poll found that, for every three people who thought unionization of teachers had "helped" the quality of public education, there were five people who thought unionization had "hurt."[38]

As the electorate becomes less willing to grant what public unions demand, there is serious danger that a vicious cycle will set in. Withdrawal of public support can force reductions in the public payroll, either by laying people off or by not hiring new people to replace those who retire or leave for other reasons. But reducing the number of public employees creates more unemployment in the local economy, both directly and indirectly, as the smaller number of public employees now spend less money and thus create less demand for workers in local businesses. The impact can be significant. *Business Week* observed that local and state governments have become "a major deflationary force in the economy."[39] This is one rationale for "countercyclical revenue-sharing," which uses federal funds to prevent local governments from cutting payrolls when unemployment is already a problem.[40]

As the reluctance of local taxpayers to pay for public services can exacerbate local unemployment, the increase in local unemployment in turn further reduces the local electorate's ability to pay taxes. Public payroll reductions also create hostility and mistrust between public employees and employers. Unions will charge, and public officials will deny, that revenues are sufficient to avoid reducing staff or to raise salaries. Both sides accuse each other of bad faith. The result can be all-out war. Seattle teachers, for example, went out on strike in the fall of 1976, after two years of bitter wrangling over layoffs and salaries. Union spokesmen called it "one of the most successful strikes this nation has seen," and "a tremendous team effort."[41] But the price of union solidarity in this kind of confrontation is hostility between teachers and the public. A teacher who feels abused by the school board is not likely to want to render extra services to students and parents. Although striking teachers will try to enlist community support, the experience of confrontation between employees and employer will produce a lingering rancor and lower morale, making it difficult to restore good relations between public workers and the community. The result can be still further reduction of public support.

Even though the fiscal problems of public schools in the 1970s were mainly attributable to economic recession and not to the unionization of teachers, the behavior of teachers' unions has made matters worse. By continuing aggressively to demand higher salaries without trying to demonstrate any corresponding improvement in services, teachers' unions are acquiring a bad public image. This negative image in turn hardens the resistance of local taxpayers. As revenues become harder to raise, local economic conditions may deteriorate further, and relations between teachers' unions and public officials become increasingly acrimonious. Perhaps it will never be possible to break this vicious cycle. It certainly is fatuous to propose what one NEA spokesperson called "a return to the big, happy family approach of the past."[42] But a less cynical view is also possible. Labor unions in other sectors of the economy have found various ways to reconcile the material interests of their members with the goals of the employing organization. Some of these approaches might be fruitfully applied in public education.

ADAPTING THE CONCEPT OF "PRODUCTIVITY BARGAINING" TO PUBLIC EDUCATION

Raskin has argued strongly that public unions can no longer win public support without serious commitment in improving worker productivity. After documenting how public sentiment turned against municipal unions in San Francisco during the strikes of 1975–76, Raskin observes,

"A similar tide of community conviction that unions have been getting too much in collective bargaining and giving too little in job performance is noticeable throughout the country." Arguing for "vastly improved municipal management with unstinting union cooperation," he goes so far as to say,

> The survival of the cities and eventually of all government, given the mounting rebelliousness of the taxpayer, depends on getting more and better services for every dollar of wage investment. . . . .Experiments in worker participation both in this country and West Europe hint at the potentialities for city-saving along this line.[43]

Similarly, in early 1976, representatives of the major national education lobby groups met to discuss the problem of money. Their figures showed "current trends in revenue will support only a 'no improvement' program, despite declining enrollments." Robert McBride, who presented the dreary numbers, told the group that raising more money for public schools "requires more than just a brilliant sales campaign." Something must be done about "the long slide in economic productivity of school personnel."[44] But what?

Unions and management in other sectors of the economy have found various ways to increase labor productivity, or the value of output per hour of labor input. At least three of these approaches might be applicable in public education. One way is for the union simply to accept a reduction in employment, through layoffs or attrition, in exchange for improvements in pay, benefits, or job security for those workers who remain. Implicitly, this happens every time a union wins a raise in the cost of labor since the employer consequently hires fewer workers. Despite some conventional wisdom, higher pay for public employees generally does mean reduced demand for workers, just as in the private sector.[45] Sometimes the bargaining away of jobs in exchange for more pay and benefits has occurred explicitly, for example, in agreements by unions representing longshoremen and typographers. Labor-saving equipment was introduced, but existing workers were granted lifetime employment security.[46] This kind of explicit trade-off has also occurred in the public sector. For example, in Tacoma, Washington, the firefighters' union accepted a more efficient deployment pattern in return for a shorter work week.[47]

A second approach has been the establishment of formal communication channels so employees and union representatives can talk with management about work procedures. The 1976 *Directory of Labor-Management Committees* lists hundreds of unions and employers that have set up such channels.[48] These committees resemble the "works councils" created by national law in several Western European countries in the past three decades, except that these European councils often have actual authority to decide matters such as scheduling, while labor-management committees in the United States tend to be consultative only.

A third distinct approach unions and management together have taken toward increasing labor productivity has been to tie earnings to output on a continuing basis. This can be done through individual piece-rates, which unions tend to oppose, or through group bonuses like profit-sharing plans. Group incentives have been found to be more effective when the productive process requires any significant degree of cooperation among workers.[49] An interesting example of a group incentive plan for a public enterprise was implemented, after negotiation with the union, by the Swedish Tele-communications Administration.[50] Under that plan, for example, all employees in the installation department share a cash bonus each year. The bonus is bigger if more telephones and other equipment are installed more quickly and with fewer malfunctions and if fewer employee-hours are required. The formula for combining these various quantities into a single number representing productivity was negotiated with the union. A similar group bonus plan was negotiated by municipal unions and elected officials in Nassau County, New York, but has not yet been implemented.[51] On a one-shot basis, the Detroit sanitation workers' union agreed to new performance standards in return for payment of half the savings to the workers.[52]

The Scanlon Plan is perhaps the best-known mechanism devised by unions and management to improve labor productivity. More than a hundred companies in the United States are now using some version of this plan, and many others have used it at one time or another since it was first formulated in the 1930s by Joseph Scanlon.[53] The Scanlon Plan embodies all three approaches described here. An index of labor productivity is computed for some base year, and a negotiated formula determines the amount of cash bonus awarded for improvement in the index in subsequent years. The bonus is shared among all employees, possibly including management. Channels of communication are established for workers and managers to discuss suggestions for continually improving productivity. In effect, the plan gives workers an incentive and a means to suggest ways of reducing the number of workers needed to produce a given amount of output or to produce more output with a constant number of workers. Featherbedding is clearly discouraged.

Are mechanisms like this feasible in public education? A group bonus plan in education would make some material benefits for teachers contingent upon some measure of performance. This measure would have to be something teachers can actually affect and also something with positive value to students, parents, and taxpayers.

One possible precedent for tying benefits to outcomes in education is the federally sponsored demonstration of performance-contracting in twenty school districts in 1970–71. Here students' scores on standardized achievement tests were used as the measure of performance. Contractors had a direct financial incentive to try to improve these scores. The results of the demonstration were not conclusive because it went on for only one year. Also, the effects of the incentive formula by itself could not be clearly distinguished from the effects of changes in technology or in the amount of money spent per student.[54] Similar confounding of effects obscures the results from the federally sponsored demonstration of education vouchers in Alum Rock, California.

Moreover, standardized tests may not be appropriate for measuring teachers' performance, not only because of the obvious temptation to teach to the test, but also because such tests are not designed to measure mastery of skills taught in a particular school or classroom. If teachers are to receive some bonus pay or extra benefits depending on student performance, the measure of student performance must be consistent with *all* the important objectives of that particular school. The difficulty of constructing such measures explains why the customary procedure for evaluating teachers—even where a system of merit pay actually awards extra money to teachers with very positive evaluations, as in Darien, Connecticut—relies mainly on classroom observation and subjective judgment by the principal or others considered competent to recognize superior teaching when they see it.

One problem in using a measure of student performance to derive an index of teacher performance is how to adjust for differences in students' background and prior performance. This problem can be solved statistically through procedures such as regression analysis. In effect, the change in performance of students in a particular school in a given year can be compared to that of students with identical backgrounds. Such an approach was spelled out in a proposal for evaluation in New York City schools developed by the Educational Testing Service under the joint sponsorship of the United Federation of Teachers and the school board.[55] The same statistical adjustment procedure is used by the California Assessment Program in reporting test results back to local school districts. Adjusting test scores for differences in students' background is technically possible. The more difficult problem is deciding what aspects of student performance to measure in the first place, and how to relate the measurement to benefits for teachers.

This problem cannot be solved by technicians alone. Citizens—parents, students, taxpayers—must share the responsibility. Ideally, there would be ongoing dialogue between citizens and teachers on a small enough scale so that participants are dealing with their own personal and professional concerns, not merely trying to represent the "public interest" in the abstract. This means a substantial number of people would have to participate. To some extent this kind of dialogue has already been taking place in states attempting to set standards of proficiency for high school graduation and for promotion in earlier grades.

Participation in defining educational outcomes and determining how some benefits for groups of teachers might depend on performance may be exactly the kind of work that would "empower" existing citizen groups. According to Davies, there are now more than 100,000 such groups around the country, including committees at the school district level and at individual school buildings. However, Davies complains that these committees are "often empty gestures raising false hopes and contributing to what U.S. Representative Barbara Jordan has termed 'a network of illusions'." To fulfill the promise of participation, Davies recommends that citizens' committees be given staff and other support, and the authority to make real decisions over "budget, personnel, and programs."[56]

This kind of reform might also justify expenditures of the additional federal money teachers' organizations have been seeking. Beginning in 1974, the NEA Political Action Committee has been directing considerable amounts of money and effort to Congressional elections. After spending $30,000 on federal elections in 1972, the Committee increased its expenditures to $250,000 in 1974, and then to $600,000 in 1976.[57] In addition to endorsing 349 candidates for the House and Senate in 1976, the NEA also made a sufficiently visible effort in the Presidential election to win from Carter's campaign director, Hamilton Jordan, a statement that "The massive support from teachers was critical to our winning this very close election. All over the nation, we turned to the NEA for assistance. We asked for their help, and they delivered."[58] What the NEA wants the President and Congress to deliver in return, among other things, is an increase in general federal aid to education. The NEA wants the federal government to increase its share of total expenditure on public education from less than 10 percent at present to a full one-third.[59] This would mean additional federal expenditure of about $25 billion each year.[60]

It does not seem likely that taxpayers who have been resisting increases in spending for schools at the local and state levels will be any more enthusiastic about increases at the federal level— unless the new money is clearly attached to improvements in educational services. One way to use federal funds for this purpose would be to provide money to schools where dialogue is taking place between citizens and teachers about defining the desired outcomes of education. The additional money could pay participants for the time such dialogue would require and could provide staff and other support. Some new money could also be used for incentive payments to provide bonus pay or other extra material benefits to groups of teachers in schools that, in fact, achieve more of the desired outcomes. The purpose would be to encourage individual schools and communities to learn how to provide incentives for groups of teachers who do a better job.

CONCLUSION

"Productivity bargaining" in public education would involve citizens, teachers, and administrators in a process of defining educational outcomes and determining how groups of teachers can appropriately be given additional material rewards for contributing to achievement of these outcomes. Participation in such a process could help restore and sustain trust between teachers and the public, which has been eroding in recent years.

Other reforms in collective bargaining have been proposed with the same goal. For example, "final offer arbitration" and other improved impasse procedures could help prevent strikes.[61] "Multilateral bargaining" would provide a formal role for members of the community in collective negotiations between teachers and school boards. "Multilevel bargaining" would settle salary and other money matters at the level of the district or even the state, and leave matters of educational practice to be decided in individual schools or other small units.[62] These proposed reforms are not mutually exclusive; they are highly complementary. In a different way, each of these proposals would help collective bargaining between teachers and school boards evolve from an adversary process to a more cooperative relationship. Now that teachers' unions have established legitimate power and school boards have grown more accustomed to bargaining, evolution along these lines may be more likely, especially if citizens will help.

NOTES

1. *Statistical Abstract of the United States, 1976,* Table 209.

2. Ibid., Table 211.

3. *Projections of Educational Statistics to 1985–86,* National Center for Educational Statistics, 1977, Table 1.

4. Harriet Fishlow, "Demography and Changing Enrollments," paper prepared for the National Institute of Education Seminar on School Finance and Productivity, Berkeley, California, November 1976.

5. *Projections*, op. cit., Table 22.

6. *Statistical Abstract*, op. cit., Table 209.

7. *The Condition of Education 1975*, National Center for Educational Statistics, Table 32.

8. *Handbook of Labor Statistics 1975 - Reference Edition*, U.S. Department of Labor, Bureau of Labor Statistics Bulletin 1865, Table 104.

9. Orley C. Ashenfelter and Ronald G. Ehrenberg, "The Demand for Labor in the Public Sector," in Daniel S. Hamermesh (ed.), *Labor in the Public and Nonprofit Sectors*, Princeton University Press, Princeton, N.J., 1975, p. 71.

10. *Statistical Abstract*, op. cit., Table 228.

11. Ibid., Table 227.

12. See Robert O. Reischauer and Robert W. Hartman, *Reforming School Finance*, The Brookings Institution, Washington, D.C., 1973.

13. "Analysis of Assembly Bill No. 65," *Legislative Analyst*, Sacramento, Ca., September 1, 1977.

14. Christopher Jencks et al., *Inequality: A Reassessment of the Effect of Family and Schooling in America*, Basic Books, New York, 1972.

15. Harvey Averch et al., *How Effective is Schooling?*, prepared for the President's Commission on School Finance, Rand Corporation, Santa Monica, California, March 1972.

16. *Statistical Abstract of the United States 1972*, Tables 161, 162. The precise growth in college enrollment was 117 percent.

17. Richard B. Freeman, *The Overeducated American*, Academic Press, New York, 1976, p. 202.

18. *Handbook of Labor Statistics*, op. cit., Tables 64, 65.

19. George H. Gallup, "Eighth Annual Gallup Poll of the Public's Attitudes Toward the Public Schools," *Phi Delta Kappan*, October 1976, p. 191.

20. NEA *Reporter*, November 1976, p. 13.

21. Robert J. Thornton and Andrew R. Weintraub, "Public Employee Bargaining Laws and the Propensity to Strike: The Case of Public School Teachers," *Journal of Collective Negotiation in the Public Sector*, vol. 3, no. 1, Winter 1974, pp. 33–39.

22. "Summary of State Collective Bargaining Statutes Affecting Teachers," ECS *Compact*, Education Commission of the States, Denver, Co., February 1971, pp. 17–24.

23. Walter I. Garms, James W. Guthrie, and Lawrence C. Pierce, *School Finance: The Economics and Politics of Public Education*, Prentice- Hall, Englewood Cliffs, N.J., 1978, p. 99.

24. Jay G. Chambers, "The Impact of Bargaining on the Earnings of Teachers: A Report on California and Missouri," paper prepared for the UK-US Conference on Teacher Markets, University of Chicago, December 1976.

25. William D. Torrence, "Using Federal Work Stoppage Data to Develop Education and Training Programs in Labor Relations for School Managements," *Journal of Collective Negotiations in the Public Sector*, vol. 2, no. 4, Fall 1973, pp. 343–49.

26. See Hirschel Kasper, "The Effects of Collective Bargaining on Public School Teachers' Salaries," *Industrial and Labor Relations Review*, vol. 24, October 1970, pp. 57–72; Robert Thornton, "The Effects of Collective Negotiations on Teachers' Salaries," *Quarterly Review of Economics and Business*, vol. 2, Winter 1971, pp. 37–46; W. Clayton Hall and Norman E. Carroll, "The Effects of Teachers' Organizations on Salaries and Class Size," *Industrial and Labor Relations Review*, vol. 26, January 1973, pp. 8–35; David Lipsky and John Drotning, "The Influence of Collective Bargaining on Teachers' Salaries in New York State," *Industrial and Labor Relations Review*, vol. 27, October 1973, pp. 18–35; and Donald E. Frey, "Wage Determination in Public Schools and the Effects of Unionization," in Daniel Hamermesh (ed.), op. cit., pp. 183–219.

27. Jay G. Chambers, "The Impact of Collective Bargaining for Teachers on Resource Allocation in Public School Districts: The California Experience," paper prepared for the Southern Economic Association meetings in New Orleans, November 1975. Also see Chambers, op. cit.

28. Charlotte K. Stiglitz, *Wage Determination for Teachers and the Demand for Educational Expenditures*, unpublished Ph.D. dissertation, Department of Economics, Yale University, New Haven, Conn., 1976.

29. *Statistical Abstract 1972*, op. cit., Table 209.

30. Hall and Carroll, op. cit., Chambers, "The Impact of Collective Bargaining for Teachers," op. cit.

31. *Digest of Educational Statistics*, 1976, National Center for Educational Statistics, p. 72.

32. U.S. Department of Labor, Bureau of Labor Statistics, *Current Wage Developments*, March 1975, p. 24; June 1975, p. 34; July 1975, p. 34; August 1975, p. 44.

33. U.S. Department of Labor, Bureau of Labor Statistics, *NEWS*, January 23, 1976 (USDL-76-51).

34. Notably Governors Grasso in Connecticut, Dukakis in Massachusetts, Brown in California, and Carey in New York. Meager pay raises for state employees in New York and California are reported in U.S. Department of Labor, Bureau of Labor Statistics, *Current Wage Developments*, August 1975, p. 44.

35. See *Public Employee Press* (newspaper of the New York local of the American Federation of State, County, and Municipal Employees), August 8, 1975, pp. 2–4, and December 19, 1975, p. 5.

36. *New York Times*, Section 3, Part II, p. 37, January 4, 1975.

37. A. H. Raskin, "Conclusion: The Current Political Contest," in A. Lawrence Chickering (ed.), *Public Employee Unions: A Study of the Crisis in Public Sector Labor Relations*, Institute for Contemporary Studies, San Francisco, 1976.

38. Gallup, op. cit., p. 195.

39. *Business Week*, December 26, 1977, p. 23.

40. Edward M. Gramlich, "The New York City Fiscal Crisis: What Happened and What Is to be Done?" *American Economic Review*, vol. 66, May 1976, pp. 415–429.

41. NEA *Reporter*, December 1976, p. 5.

42. Gary Watts, quoted in *Education USA*, National School Public Relations Association, Arlington, Virginia, January 23, 1978, p. 160.

43. Raskin, op. cit., pp. 209, 218–19.

44. *Education USA*, National School Public Relations Association, Arlington, Virginia, April 12, 1976, p. 197.

45. Ashenfelter and Ehrenberg, op. cit.

46. "Improving Productivity: Labor and Management Approaches," U.S. Department of Labor, Bureau of Labor Statistics, Bulletin 1715, prepared for the National Commission of Productivity, September 1971.

47. Ralph J. Flynn, *Public Work, Public Workers*, New Republic Book Company, Washington, D.C., 1975, p. 48.

48. *Directory of Labor-Management Committees*, National Center for Productivity and Quality of Working Life, Washington, D.C., October 1976.

49. Edward E. Lawler, III, "Improving the Quality of Work Life: Reward Systems," report prepared for the U.S. Department of Labor, Contract No. L-74-78, University of Michigan, Ann Arbor, June 1975.

50. M. Nivert, "A New Pay System and New Forms for the Field Activities of the Swedish Telecommunications Administration," Organization for Economic Cooperation and Development, Paris, March 24, 1975.

51. Vincent J. Macri, "An Approach to Productivity Improvement in the Public Sector, A Procedural Manual," report of the Multi-Municipal Productivity Project, Nassau County, N.Y., prepared for the U.S. Department of Labor, Contract No. L-74-74, Mineola, N.Y., July 1975.

52. Flynn, op. cit., p. 48.

53. Henry Tracy, "Scanlon Plans: Leading Edge in Labor Management Cooperation," *World of Work Report*, Work in America Institute, Scarsdale, N.Y., March 1977.

54. Edward M. Gramlich and Patricia P. Koshel, *Educational Performance Contracting: An Evaluation of an Experiment*, The Brookings Institution, Washington, D.C., 1975.

55. Frederick J. McDonald and Garlie A. Forehand, "A Design for an Accountability System for the New York City School System," Educational Testing Service, Princeton, N.J., June 1972.

56. Don Davies, "Citizen Participation in Schools: A Network of Illusions," *Citizen Action in Education*, Institute for Responsive Education, Boston, Mass., January 1978.

57. Telephone conversation with staff of the NEA Political Action Committee, December 1977.

58. NEA *Reporter*, December 1976, p. 1.

59. Brochures published by NEA Political Action Committee, 1976 and 1977.

60. U.S. Congress, Congressional Budget Office, "Elementary, Secondary, and Vocational Education: An Examination of Alternative Federal Roles," January 1977, p. 46.

61. See, for example, James Stern, "Final Offer Arbitration—Initial Experience in Wisconsin," *Monthly Labor Review*, pp. 39–41, September, 1974. Also, Fred Witney, "Final Offer Arbitration: the Indianapolis Experience," *Monthly Labor Review*, May 1973, pp. 20–25.

62. For an illuminating discussion of these concepts, see Charles W. Cheng: *Altering Collective Bargaining*, Praeger, N.Y., 1976.

8

SCHOOL-COMMUNITY INTERACTION:
A Comparative and International Perspective

THOMAS J. LA BELLE AND ROBERT
E. VERHINE
University of California, Los Angeles

The purpose of this chapter is to provide an overview of school-community programs worldwide. It is our intent to offer program examples from other countries, thereby establishing a comparative and international perspective to the primarily domestic issues discussed in this volume. This is not the first time that such a global overview has been attempted, and we have drawn, where appropriate, from these earlier contributions.[1] As might be expected, however, we had to begin anew in developing a framework for discussing the many types of programs we encountered, and we necessarily developed some basic criteria for judging whether a program would be eligible for inclusion within the framework. Thus, we decided to limit our discussion to only formal (rather than nonformal) education programs, and we further decided to include only primary and secondary schools, thereby excluding all forms of higher education.

Through a rather extensive search of the literature as well as a dependence upon information from our own field research in Latin America, we developed a framework of five models of community schools: community schools for educational access, community schools to enhance learning, community schools to foster the transition between study and work, community schools as community centers, and community schools to strengthen nationalism and socioeconomic development. Each of these approaches is outlined in a separate section of the chapter. The discussion is intended to highlight both narrow and comprehensive program examples within each approach and to demonstrate interrelationships among the five approaches. It should be noted that conceptually, the first model—community schools for educational access—differs from the other four in that it focuses on community-created schools to satisfy educational demands, whereas the others stress providing relevant education for the community. Thus, while each model represents a distinctive set of goals, the final four have more in common with each other than they do with the first.

The presentation and discussion of the various school-community programs is severely limited by the quantity and quality of the information available. In some cases the information about programs is so favorable as to make an analytical assessment impossible. Some information is several years old and may no longer provide an accurate description of the current situation. Also, it was difficult to compare programs since more information was available for some programs than for others. Accepting these constraints, we have attempted to describe these programs in their own sociocultural context while attending to the issues of purpose, function, decision making, finance, social change, and so on. The reader will note, however, that due to the nature of the available data the emphasis is on a descriptive over-view of the status of community schooling worldwide rather than on in-depth comparative analysis.

COMMUNITY SCHOOLS FOR EDUCATIONAL ACCESS

A community school for educational access is one that is established and maintained by the community to provide schooling opportunities for local youth. The distinguishing features of schools in this category are their emergence as a result of community initiative and their concern with local governance and finance. Importantly, this model of community schooling places a greater emphasis on the presence of local control than on how that local control is used. Hence, in contrast to the four models to be discussed subsequently, this approach is more concerned with the school as an expression of local will than with the school as an institution serving local needs and conditions. Indeed, for reasons that will be detailed below, the programs falling under this rubric are often indistinguishable in form and content from traditional academic-oriented schooling efforts.

Although community schooling for educational access is undoubtedly the oldest form of community schooling, it has never emerged as a dominant model due to the sociopolitical and economic need in most countries for centralized educational decision making at the national level. Among the many factors contributing to this worldwide trend toward administrative centralism are authoritarian traditions in social, economic, and political life, the impact of nationalism and modernization, the use of public schooling as an instrument of national policy, and the effort to attain social goals efficiently through coordinated planning and supervision. Also, educators and social reformers have often sought greater national control over formal education in the hopes of augmenting the availability of financial resources, extending schooling to remote areas, and enforcing standards of instructional quality.[2]

Despite contributing to the quantity and quality of formal schooling, however, the centralization of authority has not enabled most so-called developing countries to construct a sufficient number of schools to accommodate those seeking access.[3] Although educational expenditures and enrollment rates in the Third World have advanced sharply since 1950, the demand-supply gap in many regions has actually widened. While demand has been fueled by rising expectations and increasing job skill requirements, supply has been constrained by dwindling financial resources, soaring educational costs, and competing social priorities. The gap is usually greatest on the secondary level where traditional practices have tended to restrict entry to a select few.

As a result, many communities in various parts of the world have taken matters into their own hands and established their own schools.

Below, we will consider three cases in which such local efforts to provide educational access have evolved into a nationwide movement. Although the three programs have emerged in different continents, have reached different stages of development, and have different relationships with their respective national governments, they are similar in that each focuses on the secondary level, emphasizes community voluntarism and self-help, and represents an important component in its country's educational infrastructure. Taken together, they offer valuable insights into the positive and negative consequences of community-spawned programs of formal instruction.

HARAMBEE SCHOOLS IN KENYA

The Kenya *Harambee* (self-help) schools are secondary institutions created and operated by rural communities without regular assistance from the national government. The first *Harambee* schools appeared in 1964, the year of Kenya's independence from Britain, and thereafter the movement spread at such a rapid pace that by 1970 it accounted for 62 percent of Kenya's secondary schools and 41 percent of its secondary enrollment.[4] The principal factor contributing to the emergence and proliferation of the Harambee schools has been the demand-supply gap mentioned above. Economic expansion following World War II coupled with a concerted effort by the colonial government to expand primary school facilities resulted in more and more people actively seeking access to secondary education. At the same time, entry was limited by a secondary system that was both underdeveloped and highly selective.[5] Under these circumstances, the creation of secondary schools by local groups has had the advantage of "combining a large expected private benefit for contributors (or their children) with a handsome political pay-off for their main sponsors."[6]

In addition, the *Harambee* movement has undoubtedly been facilitated in Kenya by the region's tradition of self-help activity. Communal forms of government have always been important in East Africa, and education has long been considered a community concern.[7] Missionaries attempting to establish schools in the early twentieth century relied heavily on local donations of land, buildings, and funds. In the 1930s the Kikuya people, reacting against the low quality of missionary schools and the pressure that the missions were placing on traditional customs, initiated the Independent African School Movement to promote indigenous-based instruction.[8] During the 1950s self-help efforts played an instrumental role in the development of Kenya's primary school system. In 1964, President Kenyatta attempted to capitalize on his nation's self-help heritage by asking communities to sponsor *Harambee* projects for the sake of social progress.[9] Later that same year the *Harambee* school movement began to materialize.

As we examine the *Harambee* schools, it is important to understand that the movement constitutes a collection of independent grassroots efforts. There is no overarching, coordinating *Harambee* structure and there is no official set of *Harambee* rules or procedures. There is, however, a degree of uniformity among the local efforts since all schools must eventually be approved by public authorities and because self-help groups want their schools to be equivalent to others already established.

The process of initiating a *Harambee* school usually begins after a small group of accepted community leaders (chiefs, primary school headmasters, and religious figures) call a meeting at which interested residents express opinions and pledge support. If those present decide to establish a school, additional meetings are held to discuss publicity, site selection, and funding and to elect a committee to supervise the self-help effort. This committee assumes responsibility for raising and budgeting funds, hiring the school staff, and securing accreditation from the Kenyan Government. According to Anderson, these school committees tend to be composed mainly of farmers, primary school teachers, and civil servants. In addition, prestigious individuals, such as country councillors and clan leaders, are generally included for diplomatic purposes. Sometimes two committees are formed, one comprised of local dignitaries and the other serving as the actual working nucleus.[10] The effectiveness of these decision-making bodies is obviously a major determinant of the success of the school.

Most *Harambee* schools initially operate in primary school facilities. However, the widespread belief among local residents that both educational quality and government approval are based on the size and appearance of the school facility has invariably created pressure for physical capital formation.[11] Thus, there has been a tendency for the original plant to be either remodeled or completely replaced by a new structure. Teachers for the self-help schools are mostly recruited from the faculties of local primary programs with additional staff positions filled on a temporary or part-time basis by those who fail to secure certificates for teaching and by vacationing students. Because of low salary scales and the general unattractiveness of rural life, the *Harambee* programs rarely secure the services of fully certified secondary instructors.[12]

The curriculum offered by the schools is academic in emphasis, with particular stress given to the arts and humanities. The self-help institutions, like the Government schools, aim at preparing students for the rigorous Certificate Examination, a vestige of British colonial rule and long a passport to social and economic success in Kenya. Hence, the major reason for the classical, academic focus of the curriculum is the structure of rewards for secondary school graduates.[13] Other factors contributing to this orientation include the high costs associated with technical-vocational courses, the traditional conception of what formal schools should teach, and the need for self-help groups to devote their innovative energies to the task of fund raising.[14] As one observer has noted, " ... people have been more concerned with the problems of expansion than with changes in content."[15]

Financing for the *Harambee* institutions is derived mainly from tuition fees, with additional income coming from such sources as cooperative societies, county councils, churches, local firms, civic-minded individuals, and the Kenyan Department of Community Development. Unfortunately, self-help financing in Kenya has proved to be both uncertain and uneven.[16] Limited local resources, a lack of local financial expertise, and the tendency for initial enthusiasm to dissipate quickly have hampered community efforts to raise and allocate funds. Moreover, many localities have been saddled with excessive educational costs resulting from an over-emphasis on school plant development. In the past, "self-help has largely been treated as a substitute for capital, not as a technique for raising it."[17] However, due to local demands for educational parity, the much-touted cost-saving potential of self-help has been severely compromised. Of course, the fact that most *Harambee* programs suffer some economic hardship does not mean that some schools have not fared much better than others. Disparities in wealth, commitment, and leadership among communities have caused the level of education inputs to vary significantly from one school to the next. These variations, along with the reliance on tuition fees for school income, suggest that the *Harambee* movement has tended to reinforce social inequalities despite expanding educational access.

From our review of the teaching, curriculum, and funding of *Harambee* schools, it should be evident that the movement has a number of problems. Indeed, most observers of the local programs agree that educational quality is generally low.[18] Although all self-help schools must eventually meet standards established by the Kenyan Government, they are permitted to function in the interim as long as they abide by health requirements and show bona fide intentions. Thus, it is common to find teachers ill-prepared, instructional materials lacking, and student-teacher ratios high. In addition, many programs suffer from mismanagement. Local administrative inexperience together with the speed with which most schools are established have produced serious dysfunctions in planning and organization. Committees have been dismissed, school sites transferred, and school names changed. In some communities, schools have become hopelessly entangled in local political and religious conflicts. In others, they have fallen into the hands of village entrepreneurs who have used them for profit-making purposes.

Given these difficulties, it is not surprising that *Harambee* school graduates tend to perform poorly on the Certificate Examination (for some schools the pass rate is zero) and that some programs have been forced to cease operations altogether.[19] Ironically, even apparently successful schools may produce negative consequences. There is, for example, some evidence that self-help schools have strained family budgets and caused funds to be directed away from more economically vital activities.[20] Also, the classical academic orientation of the *Harambee* school curriculum has contributed to an oversupply of academically trained personnel in Kenya.[21] Hence, the few graduates who do pass the Certificate Examination often fail to find expected employment opportunities. When appropriate jobs are found, they are usually in distant urban areas, thereby draining the community of local talent.

As a result of these various problems, the Kenyan Government, although a strong supporter of the ideology of self-help, has on many occasions expressed concern over the *Harambee* program. In 1967, the Kenyan Educational Commission recommended that *Harambee* school expansion be restricted because of low standards and the need for an integrated, planned educational system.[22] Although this recommendation has never been implemented, the Government has taken steps to control the movement by imposing financial guidelines, health regulations, and periodic inspections. Also, in some cases the Government has given direct financial assistance and has sponsored training programs for rural secondary teachers. These developments have led some observers to predict that the entire *Harambee* network will eventually be absorbed by the official system in the name of educational quality and integrated planning.[23] Yet, given Kenya's self-help tradition, its persistent demand-supply gap in secondary education, and the fact that Harambee groups have actually gained in political clout in recent years,[24] it seems likely that the movement will continue for some time. As we will see below in the cases drawn from Brazil and the Philippines, it is certainly within the realm of possibility for self-help schooling to achieve both permanence and legitimacy.

CNEC SCHOOLS IN BRAZIL[25]

The National Campaign of Community Schools (CNEC) is a private, nonprofit educational program which has functioned in Brazil for more than thirty years. Like the *Harambee* movement, CNEC is dedicated to expanding educational access through community self-help and has enjoyed remarkable growth as a result of burgeoning educational demand. Starting as a single one-room night school in the northeastern city of Recife, CNEC has evolved into a nationwide effort which encompasses about 12 percent of the current secondary enrollment in Brazil. It presently reaches over 300,000 students in nearly 1,000 municipalities through a network of more than 1,200 schools and 17,000 teachers. Since the Campaign has concentrated on those areas where schooling opportunities are most restricted, over 90 percent of its facilities are located in rural towns and villages, and nearly 40 percent can be found in the country's most poverty-stricken region, the arid Northeast. The program's success in extending schooling access is indicated by the fact that in 10 percent of Brazil's municipalities the CNEC school is the sole institution offering secondary instruction.[26]

CNEC schools differ from the *Harambee* institutions in two important respects. First, while the *Harambee* effort remains a loose collection of separate schools, CNEC is an integrated educational system operated under established rules and coordinated through an overarching administrative apparatus. Second, whereas *Harambee* schools often function as money-making ventures and normally charge substantial tuition fees, CNEC schools are expressly designed to serve the economically deprived and are prohibited by statute from charging any fees whatsoever. We will say more about these two distinguishing features as we briefly review CNEC's mode of operation and historical development.

The primary unit in the CNEC structure is the Local Sector. The Local Sector is officially responsible for creating and maintaining the school. It is composed of a minimum of 100 community residents who agree to make monthly financial contributions to the program. The Sector is directed by a council of seven to nine unpaid representatives elected by the Sector membership. The council's major task is to raise and allocate local funds. In addition to collecting from Sector members, it attempts to tap other sources both within and outside the community. One particularly dynamic council, for example, has acquired economic support from a school farm, a labor syndicate, a philanthropic foundation, a federal university, the Secretariat of Education, the National Congress, the United States Consulate and Peace Corps, and the State of Pennsylvania.[27] In 1972, the combined income of the Local Sectors accounted for 70 percent of CNEC's total budget of $9.7 million.[28]

The CNEC local councils not only raise funds but also control their dispersal. Hence, they are responsible for making decisions concerning plant development, supply and equipment acquisition, personnel selection, and staff salary levels. However, it should be noted that daily school administration and matters of pedagogy and curriculum are left to the school director, who in turn must act in accordance with norms set forth by the State Secretariat of Education. Like the *Harambee* schools, local CNEC programs are subjected to periodic public inspection to insure that physical facilities, curriculum content, and teacher quality are consistent with official standards.

While CNEC's local apparatus actually organizes and runs the school, the Campaign's structure includes state and national organs to provide a measure of coordination, supervision, and financial assistance. On the state level, operations center around a policy-making council composed of nine Directors who serve voluntarily and are elected every two years by representatives from the Local Sectors. Daily administrative concerns are handled by a small professional staff. The state CNEC offices are responsible for performing three major functions. The first and perhaps most important is to provide assistance to communities attempting to establish self-help schools. The process of school formation is normally initiated when a community group visits the state office and requests assistance in setting up a secondary program. First, the visitors are asked to fill out a questionnaire which enables the staff to determine both whether the community needs a school and whether it has the human and physical resources to sustain one. If these two questions are answered affirmatively, the group is sent home with instructions to organize at least 100 local residents into a Local Sector. Once this membership quota is reached, a community meeting is held and representatives from the state office explain the CNEC program—its history, goals, and organization—and present specific guidelines for creating the school. Thereafter, the state level continues to give advice and counsel to the new Sector and helps it obtain the necessary teacher certification, course approval, and school accreditation from the State Secretariat of Education.[29]

A second important state CNEC function is to oversee local operations to insure that the Campaign's goals and statutes are adhered to. Toward this end, the state office requires each Sector to submit an annual financial statement and activities report, and state staff and council members make occasional visits to CNEC school sites. If extreme irregularities in local operations are detected, the state council can authorize a representative to assume temporary control. The third key responsibility of the state organization is to procure funds from statewide entities (public and private) and distribute them among the Local Sectors. CNEC's state fund-raising efforts are generally facilitated by the fact that the state councils normally include respected educators and civic leaders. Most of the financing acquired on this level comes from the State Secretariat of Education and commonly takes the form of either teacher contracts or student scholarships. In 1972 state sources accounted for 10 percent of CNEC's total income.[30]

CNEC's national apparatus is like the state structure in that it consists of a policy-making council and a small administrative staff. The National Directorate is composed of seven members elected every two years by an assembly of two representatives from each state. The administrative staff is headed by a Superintendent and is responsible to the Directorate. The national office carries out policy formulated at the annual CNEC convention, and it seeks to synchronize the direction of the movement with the laws and plans set forth by the federal government. In addition, it interacts with the state level in much the same way that the latter interacts with the Local Sectors. The national structure helps establish new state programs, oversees state operations, and solicits and distributes funds from nationwide public and private organs. Financing from this level represents about 12 percent of CNEC's total and derives mostly from the Ministry of Education.[31] These funds are used almost exclusively to maintain the state and national administrative offices. Federal funds reach local communities only when there is a financial surplus. Communities which receive such funds are usually either in dire financial straits or are engaged in an innovative school project.

We see, then, that CNEC is a complex organization functioning on local, state, and national levels and incorporating both voluntary and professional input. Although state and national offices exercise supervisor powers, CNEC is basically a decentralized system designed to provide a framework for community self-help schooling efforts. Aspects of the Campaign which reflect its grassroots focus include the following: (1) responsibility for creating and maintaining the school rests with the Local Sector, (2) community effort accounts for 70 percent of the program's income, (3) lower levels of the organization elect the policy-making councils on upper levels, and (4) the state and national CNEC staffs are extremely small.[32] Moreover, CNEC makes no effort to plant schools in unsuspecting communities. Instead, it offers guidance and direction to community groups soliciting its assistance. Those on the local level seeking to establish a secondary program are often attracted to the Campaign because (1) it offers specific guidelines for action, (2) it serves as an intermediary in dealings with the Secretariat of Education, (3) it provides some financial assistance, and (4) it is a legitimate national entity.

The institutionalization and legitimization of the CNEC organization evolved slowly over a considerable period of time. The process was facilitated by two important characteristics of the movement: first, from its inception CNEC was a cohesive unit organized around a defined set of principles; and second, it has had remarkably dedicated, able, and permanent leadership. The movement commenced in 1943 after Felipe Tiago Gomes, a pre-law student in Recife, read John Gunther's account of Peru's efforts to utilize student volunteers as teachers in literacy programs.[33] Reasoning that the "student volunteer" approach could be used in Brazil to create tuition-free secondary schools for the economically deprived (Tiago Gomes himself was from a poor family), he convinced six of his classmates to join him in founding the *Campanha do Ginasiano Pobre* (Campaign of the Poor Junior High School Student). Three years later, after a hard-fought struggle to raise funds and acquire accreditation, the Campaign opened its first "free" school, a single class taught at night in a donated room. From that point on, the program steadily gained momentum, propelled by both a widening demand-supply gap in secondary education and a spirit of democratic idealism which swept the country in the aftermath of World War II. The movement's advancement, of course, was also aided by the untiring efforts of Tiago Gomes and his colleagues to promote their cause. The youths persistently cultivated the press, sought support among philanthropists and school teachers, and applied pressure to political figures. Hence, by 1948, the Campaign had opened five schools in as many states, and in December of that year it held a national conference to set up a formal organizational structure. Those in attendance (most of whom were university students) approved a written constitution, establishing a governing directorate (with Tiago Gomes as President), and changed the movement's name to the National Campaign of Free Schools (CNEG).[34] However, they left intact the program's emphasis on voluntarism. All positions in the organization, from classroom teacher to national President, were kept on an unpaid basis.

It was not until 1953 that the Campaign began to promote the concept of self-help school financing. By that time it had become apparent to the movement's leaders that the "voluntary teacher" was not viable on a long-term, large-scale basis. Therefore, CNEC's Fifth National Conference restructured the organization to provide the community financing through Local Sectors. Thus, we see that CNEC's emphasis on local self-help was more a product of economic necessity than, say, of any commitment to community development. Also, we should note that the strategy it employed was not uncommon to the financing of social institutions in Brazil. Hospitals, recreation clubs, and the like had long been run by voluntary, dues-paying groups. CNEC's uniqueness within the Brazilian context derives primarily from the fact that (1) it applied this approach to education, and (2) it did so on a coordinated, nationwide scale.

The legitimacy of the CNEC movement jumped marked by in 1953 when, after years of lobbying by Tiago Gomes and others, the Brazilian National Congress passed a law authorizing the Ministry of Education to give each CNEC school an annual stipend based on the number of grade levels offered. Though the amount allotted covered only a fraction of each school's operating expenses, it gave the Campaign a major boost by indicating government approval of the program and by making it economically advantageous for communities desiring a secondary institution to join the CNEC system. Several years later, in accordance with a worldwide emphasis on developing education facilities,[35] the Brazilian Government increased its support to CNEC to include special funds for school construction. As a result, the percentage of Local Sectors which had constructed, or were constructing, their own plants increased from 8.6 percent in 1961 to 81 percent in 1968. Paradoxially, although the construction funds were coming from the nation's capital, CNEC's building program helped strengthen the movement's grassroots foundation. Construction was directed by the local councils, and, since the financing was provided on a matching basis, each community had to make a substantial contribution to the effort. This contribution usually took the form of donated land and labor, so it served both to reduce monetary expense and to enhance local involvement in the school program. Moreover, since the completed buildings represented tangible evidence of accomplishment, they had the dual effect of promoting community pride and facilitating the Campaign's diffusion to neighboring localities.

Meanwhile, on the state and national level CNEC began taking steps to regularize its operations by professionalizing its administration. Beginning in 1961 the state and national CNEC councils were authorized to employ permanent staffs. Tiago Gomes, who had maintained his role as the movement's chief advocate, became General Superintendent, a powerful position which he continues to hold today.

Hence, by the late 1960s CNEC had reached a reasonably advanced stage of institutional development. The complex organizational structure had emerged, and the Campaign had become an integral component of the country's educational infrastructure. Although officially a private entity, CNEC had established a close working arrangement with the Brazilian Government, and, since the Ministry of Education tended to concentrate its resources on the primary and university levels, the movement generally complemented public school development. During the 1970s, however, there has been some deterioration in the CNEC-Government relationship. Public authorities, eager to use intermediate schooling as an instrument for political and occupational socialization, have sought to extend their control over secondary education. In line with this objective, the Educational Reform Act of 1971 dictates that all public and private junior high schools will eventually be incorporated into the primary school system. It is not surprising, then, that between 1970 and 1972 the Government slashed its regular contribution to CNEC by 70 percent and curtailed altogether the funds for construction. CNEC's response to these actions has been twofold. First, the Local Sectors, the key economic component in the organization anyway, have successfully assumed an increased share of the financial burden. Secondly, the Campaign has begun to move into other areas of education. It recently took control of a teachers college and it has also started to promote the formation of self-help community centers which offer a variety of nonformal educational activities.[36] Thus, it seems reasonable to conclude that CNEC and its brand of community-based schooling will continue to thrive in Brazil for some time to come.

Our optimistic prognosis, however, is not meant to imply that individual Sectors do not suffer severe difficulties. Indeed, the CNEC schools face problems not unlike those experienced by the *Harambee* institutions. Unquestionably the most serious of these is the uncertainty of school financing. Like their *Harambee* counterparts, CNEC's incomes tend to be restrictive in amount, unstable over time, and uneven across localities. Community fund-raising efforts in Brazil, as in Kenya, are often confounded by the nature of local economic, political, and social conditions. Moreover, CNEC institutions suffer an added hardship because they are not permitted to charge tuition fees. It is true, of course, that they have a pledge from each Sector member to make a monthly donation. However, this commitment is not legally binding and cannot be effectively enforced. Also, the fact that local programs may receive aid from CNEC's state and national offices often contributes to local economic insecurity because financial assistance tends to fluctuate with shifts in the Government's social priorities. In response to this situation, a number of schools have resorted to charging tuition fees covertly by requiring each student or his family to join the Sector before enrolling. Also, some Sectors have begun to concentrate their fund-raising energies outside the locality, soliciting aid directly from national and international firms and agencies. Naturally, the success of this latter course of action is highly dependent on the dedication, ability, and political influence of local school leadership, and so is precarious at best. Clearly, a serious weakness in the CNEC operation is that, while it has created a structure for financing, it has failed to develop a definite strategy for securing funds. The organization makes no attempt to provide its participants with fund-raising or financial-management skills.

An obvious consequence of these economic limitations is that CNEC schools, on the average, cannot match the public institutions in terms of the quantity and quality of physical and human resources. In 1969, CNEC's per-pupil expenditure was less than 25 percent of that of the public system.[37] Although this difference may in part reflect the Campaign's efficient use of inputs and its reliance on borrowed and donated resources, it also betrays the presence of substantial deficiencies in plant, equipment, and personnel. For example, the questionable quality of CNEC's teaching staff is indicated by the fact that 75 percent of its members are without full secondary-level certification.[38] The Campaign's leadership is attempting to remedy this situation by sponsoring a number of in-service training programs. However, progress has been slowed by the combination of low CNEC pay scales and competition from an expanding public system.

Another important limitation of the CNEC program is its curricular orientation. As in the *Harambee* movement, the great majority of schools in the CNEC system are heavily academic in focus. Consequently, instruction often has little relevance to the local milieu and generally leaves graduates without practical job skills. Both the Brazilian government and the national CNEC office are concerned about this problem and have strongly urged the community schools to offer appropriate vocational and commercial courses, which has met with considerable resistance from the Local Sectors. In Brazil, as in Kenya and elsewhere, the structure of the perceived opportunities, the image of what formal education should be, the desire to make the community school legitimate in terms of the wider society, and the attention which must be given to fund raising have tended to mitigate against innovations designed to adapt self-help schools to their immediate context. Of course, in some instances these pressures supporting traditional orientations have been surmounted. Several schools in the CNEC system, for example, successfully adjusted their curriculum along more practical lines long before it was a national policy to do so.[39] In fact, as we will see in the case study which follows, it is possible for self-help schooling to promote locally applicable learning through an approach which integrates fund raising and instructional processes.

THE BARRIO HIGH SCHOOLS IN THE PHILIPPINES

The *barrio* or neighborhood high schools are nonprofit, self-supporting institutions designed to extend secondary-level educational opportunities to rural youth at minimal governmental expense.[40] Like the *Harambee* and CNEC schools, they have emerged in response to demands for educational access and are established and maintained through grassroots self-help efforts. The program began in 1964 with three schools in the town of Urdaneta. By 1972 it had proliferated to 1,670 institutions with an overall pupil enrollment of about 250,000. Today there are more *barrio* high schools than public and private schools combined, and they enroll approximately 15 percent of the nation's secondary students. In recent years the movement has broadened its focus to include the formation of community colleges and nursery schools. The spirit which underlies the overall effort is illustrated in the following statement:

> The barrio high school is no longer an experiment, it is already a movement. In every sense of the word, the barrio high school is of the people, by the people, and for the people. . . . While striving to improve it, the barrio people make the most out of existing resources. This principle has generated what is known as self-help barrio high schools and has kept aflame and alive the ingenuity, resourcefulness and initiative of the people.[41]

Before reviewing the characteristics of *barrio* high schools, it must be emphasized that the Philippine self-help program differs from the Kenyan and Brazilian models in two important respects. First, the *barrio* high schools are considered a part of the country's public educational system and are therefore closely regulated by the Philippine Government. Rules concerning their formation and operation were explicitly set forth in the *Barrio* High School Charter, a legal document enacted by the National Congress in 1969. Secondly, the self-help schools make a comprehensive effort to help students and parents raise money for tuition expenses. Students are encouraged by their teachers to engage in money-making projects both at school and at home, and parents are assisted by school personnel and agricultural extension workers in improving their farm's earning potential. Hence, the *barrio* high schools offer a specific strategy for fund raising, one that not only generates school income but also contributes to individual and community development.

The *Barrio* High School Charter stipulates that a self-help school may be organized whenever at least forty students in the *barrio* are available to constitute a grade level. However no program may be established within a three-kilometer radius of an existing public or private school. The founding of a *barrio* high school is initiated when a *barrio* council passes a resolution addressed to the Superintendent of Schools indicating a willingness to support and maintain the school and containing the signatures of at least forty students and their parents. Upon receipt of the resolution, the Superintendent sends a representative to meet with the *barrio* council and inform it of the rules and regulations concerning the establishment and operation of the school.

A budget indicating estimated income and expenditures for one year of operation is then prepared, approved by the *barrio* council, and made part of the petition. A list of qualified teachers, an inventory of available rooms and facilities, and the results of a survey of potential enrollees are also attached. If the Superintendent of Schools is convinced that the proposed program will serve the public interest and can operate on the basis of the estimated budget, he will recommend it to the Secretary of Education who in most instances grants formal approval.

Unfortunately, available sources of information do not provide us with much insight into the political maneuvering and organizational activity that undoubtedly lie behind these formal procedures. We do know, however, that those providing the actual leadership usually include unemployed college graduates, the local elementary school principal, the PTA president, the *barrio* captain, and the mayor. Also, it is clear that a series of community meetings is normally held at which advocates of the program solicit support from potential students and their families. The students are recruited from three local groups: those in their final year of elementary school, those studying at a high school outside the village, and those of post-primary school age who are not enrolled in school.[42]

Once the school is established, it uses the facilities of an existing primary school and is administered through the machinery of the Secretariat of Education. Ultimate authority rests with the Secretary of Education, while direct supervisorial responsibilities are delegated to the District Superintendent of Schools. Daily school affairs are managed by the principal of the nearest complete general secondary school. The positions of assistant principal and teacher-in-charge are assumed by the principal of the elementary school where the high school holds its classes. The teachers for the *barrio* high schools are officially appointed by the Superintendent of Schools and must possess the same qualifications as instructors in any provincial, city, or municipal high school. There has to be at least one full-time qualified teacher on the staff for each grade level offered. In addition, qualified elementary school teachers—usually from the school where the *barrio* high school classes are held—are commonly employed on a part-time basis. According to Orata, the *barrio* high school approach to staffing is designed to pursue four goals: (1) economy, (2) articulation of elementary and high school classes, (3) encouragement of elementary school teachers to remain in the *barrio*, and (4) provision of employment to qualified college graduates.[43]

The curriculum offered by the *barrio* high schools is officially prescribed by the Secretariat of Education. It includes both traditional and academic subjects and at least one vocational course. The orientation of this vocational course may be determined on the local level so that it serves *barrio* needs and conditions. As we will point out below, many of the school self-help activities are undertaken through this vocational course.

The *barrio* high schools are supported largely by tuition fees paid by the students. The Charter dictates that these fees may not be higher than those charged by the provincial high schools. In practice, such fees may be very low or even nil if financing is acquired elsewhere. Other common sources of school income include *barrio* fiestas and raffles, donations by civic organizations and concerned citizens, and a percentage of the *barrio* real estate tax. In addition, over the years both individual programs and the movement as a whole have received economic aid (i.e., money, books, materials, and equipment) from international organizations and multinational firms.[44] Although the annual budget must always be approved by the District Superintendent, responsibility for collecting and administering school funds is formally vested in the *barrio* council.

The feature that makes *barrio* high school financing unique among self-help schooling efforts is that all of those participating in the local program must sign a formal agreement of school support. In it, parents promise to make every effort to increase the productivity of their farms by following the suggestions of the vocational instructor and agricultural experts. Students agree to help pay school expenses by helping their parents on the farm and by undertaking, as part of their school assignment, money-making projects. In turn, the school and lay leaders promise to secure the services of government and nongovernment experts to guide and assist students and their parents. As an incentive for complying with the agreement, students receive academic credit for carrying out their projects and parents may be issued a Certificate of Proficiency for newly acquired skills. Also, students are sometimes awarded scholastic bonus credits which reflect their parents' financial contribution. In addition, many schools soften the economic burden of school fees by permitting families to defer payment until after the harvest is sold and by adjusting course schedules to allow children to assist their parents at home.

By available accounts, the student-project approach to school financing has been very successful.[45] In 1970, 320 high schools with a total enrollment of 43,603 students produced an aggregate project value of over 1.6 million pesos. The projects include both at-home and in-school efforts and normally involve activity relevant to rural living. The most common projects include poultry and pig raising, vegetable gardening, banana cultivation, corn shelling, and handicrafts.[46] In addition, students often engage in projects directed specifically at community service. They build toilets, repair homes, build fences, plant trees, establish home and cottage industries, and maintain the school plant and premises. In most instances these activities are an integral part of the school curriculum. Not only do they form the core of vocational instruction, but they are also infused into other subjects as well. Students might write about their project in an English class, examine its social implications in a social studies session, and study its physical and biological properties in a science course. An obvious benefit incorporating projects into the curriculum is that school learning is made relevant to the local milieu. Although the schools continue to stress academic subject matter, through their projects students are able to acquire an understanding of local problems and the practical skills appropriate for local employment. In Orta's words, "They learn to earn because they must earn in order to learn."[47]

We see, then, that the Philippine self-help approach to school financing has considerable potential. Not only does it provide a strategy for school fund raising; it also seeks to augment local economic output, foster direct community service, create a basis for life-long adult education, and relate schooling content to local circumstances. Unfortunately, available evidence does not enable us to make an accurate determination of the extent to which individual programs actually attain this potential. The only evaluation available is by Pedro Orata, a founder of the movement and obviously a strong supporter. Not surprisingly, his conclusions are highly favorable. He claims, for example, that the self-help programs have enabled local residents to increase productivity and standards of living, to overcome habits of passivity and dependence, and to gain greater respect for manual labor. He further argues that they have reduced primary school drop-out rates, lowered crime rates among youth, created incentives for teachers to remain in the *barrios,* and made *barrio* life less drab and restrictive. Orata also contends that the instructional quality of the self-help schools is equivalent to that of regular secondary programs. He notes that although the *barrio* schools suffer from inexperienced teachers and inadequate supplies, they benefit from smaller classes, closer parental supervision, and high student motivation. He supports his contention by indicating that *barrio* high school graduates have done well on standardized tests and in national competitions for scholarship awards and that an estimated 54 percent of them continue their studies on the university level.[48]

We conclude this section with several observations. The fact that schools are developed through self-help and community initiative in a neighborhood setting, for example, provides several potential benefits to the populace. Such a school may open status and income opportunities for local youth. It may also contribute to local development by attracting, training, and retaining individuals with needed knowledge and skills for the community and by securing some external capital for education-related activities. The establishment of such a school may also generate feelings of pride and interest in local issues among the population and thereby promote an ongoing process of social action. This latter point, however, is not confirmed in the available case studies. Indeed, once the school is formed there is little indication of local participation in school decision making. Instead, the school is often administered by professional educators on the assumption that such individuals will bring prestige and legitimacy to the school and will keep standards of quality high. Furthermore, where communities are involved in school decision making, as was found in the CNEC program in Brazil, they tend to be dominated by one or two members.

Community schools for educational access also suffer from a series of problems which emanate from the sociopolitical and economic context within which they operate. They are often accused, for example, of reinforcing existing inequalities (because affluent communities can afford the most modern school and because affluent members of a community can afford the school fees), of redirecting local resources away from more economically productive community activity (it is not clear, however, whether schools tap unused resources or take resources away from other endeavors), and of creating an oversupply of individuals who are academically trained in low-quality programs (the schools tend to replicate traditional academically oriented educational institutions with less-qualified personnel and with minimal financial resources). The uncertain availability of sufficient funding is partly responsible for the fact that this type of school may serve the interests of the wealthy rather than those of the middle and lower socio-economic populations. It also partly explains low-quality programs. Another explanation of such outcomes can be found by assessing the attitudes and values as well as the organizational and administrative capabilities of the local population. The desire for immediate educational access, for example, may cause schools to be established hurriedly without proper planning. The belief that physical plant development is an indication of educational quality results in higher cost and a redirection of scarce resources away from curricular priorities. The notion that equates academic training with status and income opportunities also has negative consequences. The school program is left with little relationship to community needs and circumstances and may be a cause of graduates leaving the locality in an effort to seek employment and apply what they have learned.

In sum, community schools clearly help meet demands for school access and may allow for both resource economy and the use of untapped resources. However, because of the academically oriented school ethos and the desire for formal educational legitimacy they are not necessarily adapted to the current needs or projected future of the community. The community school programs to be discussed subsequently contrast with this first model in that they are specifically designed to provide locally relevant learning. Interestingly, most of these programs do not evolve from the community. They are often imposed from the outside by those who wish to promote community development.

COMMUNITY SCHOOLS FOR THE ADVANCEMENT OF LEARNING

As indicated earlier, a community school for educational access is distinct from the other models of community schooling in that the former concerns community-created schools and the latter concern schools whose primary purpose is to relate to the community. This community-relevance orientation is reflected in an approach to learning that contends that there is value in having adults and children participate together as learners and that individuals are educated most effectively when they interact with material that has the potential of immediate application in their own community. This approach is often derived from either the thoughts of educational leaders or perceived inadequacies in the way schools operate. John Dewey, for example, puts the argument this way: "From the standpoint of the child, the great waste in the school comes from his inability to utilize the experiences he gets outside the school in any complete and free way within the school itself; while, on the other hand, he is unable to apply in daily life what he is learning in school."[49] Similarly, A. S. Makarenko, the well-known Russian educator, states, "the educative process takes place not only in the classroom, but literally on every square yard of our land."[50] The learning argument also emerges in response to educational practices considered outmoded or inappropriate. Thus, cooperation between the school and community is sometimes found where there is a desire to overcome centrally formulated and abstract curricula, to replace rote learning, to encourage greater use of school facilities by community members, and to involve parents in both their own and their children's education.

BRITISH PRIMARY SCHOOLS
A current example of a rather narrow learning approach to community-school cooperation can be seen at the primary school level in England.[51] The rhetoric includes such phrases as "total learning environment" and "educative community," indicating the importance placed on drawing

from the out-of-school context.[52] The British program is based upon the influence of the educational theoretician as well as the desire for educational reform. The theory comes primarily from Jean Piaget, especially his concepts supporting highly individualized rates of development by children and the idea that work and play are not distinguishable activities for children. Although the desire for educational reform began in the 1940s with the Butler Education Act, it was not until the Plowden Report of 1967 that the thrust was clearly turned toward the need to make primary school space more open and flexible and access to the out-of-doors immediate and apparent. Parents and nonprofessionals are modestly involved in the operation of the primary schools and assist with enabling the child to function in both the school and the community.[53]

When compared with other learning approaches to school-community cooperation, the British effort tends to be a rather school-centered program with only minimal articulation with the wider society. Although it is a national effort, and therefore larger in scope than the following examples from Argentina and Israel, conceptually the British model is overly reliant on the role of the school and its personnel for creating community involvement. The case of the family schools in Argentina provides a different approach to learning and offers an example that has some potential for generalization elsewhere.

THE FAMILY SCHOOLS OF ARGENTINA[54]

Family schools have operated in the northern section of Argentina around the city of Reconquista since 1970. Each EFA, or *escuela familiar agricola,* has a team of four or five monitors who work with a council of local parents and the students to operate the school. The schools offer the first three years of secondary school. Twenty to thirty male and female students attend for one week, during which they live in and do all the upkeep with the exception of cooking. Then they return home for two weeks. Thus, the school can be used for all grades on a rotating basis (i.e., week one, first grade; week two, second grade; week three, third grade; week four, first grade; and so on). Economically, this rotating system is potentially cheaper as fewer dormitories, classrooms, and so on are needed. At the same time, however, instructional costs are not necessarily reduced as a result of the apparent need to have four or five monitors at each school.[55]

The EFA schools were begun by local individuals with the assistance of the French educator Jean Charpentier. The schools were thought to be necessary, in part, because of "generation-gap" type communication problems among adult farmers and their children. By involving parents in the educational process of their children, it was felt that some of these problems could be overcome. The curriculum, as the leadership points out, is based on questions, not answers; there exists an aversion to the encyclopedic teaching-learning process of traditional schools. There is also a belief that life outside schools is more important than inside schools and that the family must be central to and responsible for the school.

The teaching-learning model involves action, reflection, generalization, and action on a movement from the concrete to the abstract and back to the concrete. The curriculum is organized around six areas: applied science, consciousness raising, social science, physical and natural science, and communication. The sixth area of the curriculum is known as the *plan de busqueda* or independent study. Students have a list of questions to which they must find answers during their two weeks at home. The questions are generally based on themes from one of the curricular areas and may be suggested by students, teachers, or parents; they generally begin with personal and family issues and then move to those of the community, the nation, and the world.

All but two of the twelve schools operated by APEFA are in an area inhabited by about 95 percent third and fourth-generation Italians from the area of Friuli, Italy. Additionally, approximately 95 percent of the population are members of socioeconomic cooperatives. These two factors—ethnicity and community organization—are helpful in explaining the apparent success of the APEFA program. Since each community must request the establishment of a school, the ethnic and community organization characteristics mean that there exists not only a history of common values and language but also a community infrastructure within which people are accustomed to collaborating for the achievement of common goals. Whether these demographic factors or simply the EFA philosophy and operation explain the program's success is now being tested as the last two schools initiated are located outside of this ethnic enclave and are among a poorer population.

Once a community secures a school, it automatically joins the APEFA Federation which trains the teachers and supplies technical assistance to the teachers and communities that operate the schools. Each of the parents' organizations associated with an EFA is represented in the Federation. The Federation is currently faced with several issues with regard to the program. The first might be termed political, as there is pressure from educators at the national and regional levels against the innovativeness and flexibility found in EFAs. These pressures are related, in part, to the government's recent recognition of EFA graduates as having completed the equivalent of a junior high school education. The concern is that such recognition by the government will bring interference with APEFA's philosophy, methods, and goals. The second issue is related to economics. Since participating families are often unable to assist to any great extent in the financial operation of the schools, resources are scarce. Finally, it is hard to find competent teachers and train them to stay ahead of the parents in terms of flexibility and openness to new ideas and directions. Even with these problems, however, the EFAs have been successful in keeping youngsters interested and active in rural life. A recent follow-up study found that of the 177 EFA graduates through 1975, 127 were working in agriculture in the immediate area while the rest continue studying or are working in allied fields.[57]

As can be seen from this description, the family schools form a more integral part of the community and clearly represent a more holistic approach to education than that offered in the British scheme. As suggested above, however, the role and function of the family school may be of less significance in explaining outcomes than the common cultural values and history of organization characterizing the communities. This argument appears strengthened by the following discussion of education in the Israeli Kibbutz. Here is a case where education appears to permeate life both inside and outside of schools.

THE ISRAELI KIBBUTZIM

The kibbutzim are collective settlements first established in the early twentieth century by Zionist immigrants. They function as producer and consumer cooperatives in which all members share in the operation of a huge land grant constituting an almost autonomous village. The kibbutz derives its livelihood from mixed agriculture, or from a combination of agriculture and small industry. The economy is highly mechanized and carefully planned with technical and financial aid coming from a kibbutzim federation (there are four such federations in the country) and the Israeli government.[58] In the mid-1960s, while the kibbutz population comprised about 4 percent of the nation's total, it accounted for 30 percent of Israel's agricultural production and 20 percent of its industrial output.[59]

The social organization of the kibbutz is based on collectivist principles. Membership is voluntary and all property is shared. The kibbutz is entrusted with responsibility for the economic, social, cultural, and psychological welfare of its members. Every man and woman is expected to work in return for his or her maintenance. The operation of the kibbutz is in the hands of a secretariat and a network of committees, all elected by the membership and rotated every two or three years to insure democratic participation.

Formal education in the kibbutz is viewed as a mechanism for preserving the kibbutzim way of life. Schooling is designed to inculcate a sense of community membership and responsibility as well as prepare the student for productive work. Kibbutz educational programs are based on the following principles:

1. The commune has responsibility for every child from birth to maturity;

2. Children are raised and educated in small groups who live together in separate educational units;

3. Parents and teachers share educational responsibility;

4. All children receive the same basic education irrespective of scholastic standing;

5. A positive attitude toward work is stressed;

6. Classroom instructional practice is based upon a project method.[60]

Although the kibbutzim retain the family as the basic social unit, much of the socialization and education of children is entrusted to professional nurses and teachers. Between the ages of one and four, the children reside in a toddler's house where they are taught proper habits of hygiene, play, and social behavior. At the kindergarten level, ages five to seven, they are housed in a separate building and visit their parents each evening. At this level there is an emphasis on organized activity, and, at age six, the child is introduced to reading, writing, and numbers. Between the ages of seven and twelve, the children enter a "Junior Children's community," usually comprising about thirty-five students. Studies range from four to six hours daily with an additional hour devoted to manual labor, either in the children's community or on the kibbutz. The elementary curriculum includes instruction in the sciences, humanities, and the arts. In addition, emphasis is placed on understanding ecology and production processes in agriculture. There is an effort to present the academic subjects in an organically linked manner. To link learning to life, the project method is employed. Projects are generally related to the particular circumstances of the kibbutz.

The kibbutzim also offer a secondary school program. Some 150 to 300 adolescents are housed in a school adjacent to the kibbutz. The school is usually equipped with workshops, laboratories, recreational facilities, and a library. The curriculum is of a broad, general-education nature designed to develop intellectual, personal, and social traits rather than concrete vocational skills. To fill this latter void, the kibbutz offers an extensive adult education program which includes vocational training. According to Bien, this educational pattern matches the

life-style of residents since, following completion of military obligations, youth often seek vocational knowledge and training.[61] Also, it
should be noted that secondary-level students with special abilities are
sent to suitable schools at the expense of the kibbutz.

In general, then, kibbutz education reflects and promotes communal
living. Young people are prepared to contribute socially, culturally, and
economically to the kibbutz. Not only is education closely tied to the
wider community, it is in and of itself a community. Children live,
work, and play in collective children's homes. They are part of a group,
based on age, which advances through the nonselective educational system as a unit.[62]

It should be understood that community-based education in Israel
is not a dominant feature of national educational policy. The kibbutz
schools serve only 5 percent of the nation's student population.
Because of the prestige and political influence of the kibbutzim, they
retain considerable autonomy over their schooling programs. This
autonomy is not anchored in fiat but rather based on a tacit agreement
with the Ministry of Education and Culture.[63] Each kibbutzim federation has an education committee which supervises the organization and
operation of the kibbutz schools. It offers in-service teacher-training
programs, provides for the education of new teachers through kibbutz
seminaries (there are three such seminaries in the country), and establishes general curricular guidelines consistent with government norms
and the kibbutzim ideology. On the local level, each kibbutz has its own
education committee composed of teachers and parents. This committee administers the schooling program, selects and assigns teachers,
and takes responsibility for the guidance, placement, and psychological
adjustment of each member child.

The cases of England, Argentina, and Israel represent current efforts
to foster learning by emphasizing cooperation between a school and its
community. They are characterized by both common and distinct features. They all share, for example, a desire to enhance schooling by taking advantage of available community resources, to involve parents in
the educational process, and to relate what goes on inside schools to
the child's life at home and in the neighborhood. They also differ, however, in several important ways. First, one is struck by the importance
of the population's cultural background and homogeneity in the
APEFA and kibbutz examples. These populations share immigrant
status, live in confined locales, are rather autonomous in their socioeconomic activity, and represent considerable experience and history
in organizing their membership for the achievement of common goals.
Second, both the Argentine case and the kibbutzim create schools as
an integral part of their communities. Unlike the British example, nei-

ther is national in scope and neither accepts the national school system nor its dictates. In effect, both the APEFA and the kibbutz examples point to the importance of community initiative and commitment in attempting to link schooling with overall community goals. They also suggest that the more continuous the schooling experience is with the cultural values and behavior of a population, the more integral the school becomes in the support and retention of the community's goals and ideals.

COMMUNITY SCHOOLING TO FOSTER THE TRANSITION FROM STUDY TO WORK

An extension of the learning approach to cooperative community-school programs involves the preparation of youngsters for productive work in either the local area or in the nation as a whole. These school-work efforts differ from those just mentioned in that there is less emphasis on bringing the community into the school and more on preparing children for employment in the community. The importance of school-work cooperation is seen not only in the kind of curriculum the school offers, which should reflect current and future community needs, but also in the ways in which the community offers opportunities for youngsters first to experience and then pursue chosen careers. As will be seen below in the discussion of examples from Kenya, Brazil, Eastern Europe, and Cuba, several strategies are used to attempt to achieve these goals and thus to overcome the isolation of school-based training from the work place.

THE VILLAGE POLYTECHNIC MOVEMENT IN KENYA

The Village Polytechnic Movement was established in Kenya in the late 1960s to provide primary-school leavers with skill training applicable to rural self-employment. According to Court, the movement represents both a means to alleviate unemployment and a practical manifestation of official rhetoric emphasizing self-help activity.[64] The impetus for the movement was provided by a report issued in 1966 by the National Christian Council of Kenya (NCCK) stressing the serious unemployment problem among rural primary-school leavers. Most programs on the local level have been established by church groups. The effort is coordinated by a nationwide policy committee which includes representatives from the NCCK and from local ministries.[65] Between 1966 and 1972 over fifty polytechnics were established.[66] The basic funding has come from an annual NCCK grant supplemented on the local level by church collections, donations from commercial concerns and charities, contracts for sale of work, and student fees.

Polytechnics are generally directed by either a school teacher or a local craftsman, and most offer a two-year course including instruction in standard rural crafts—especially carpentry, masonry, and tailoring—as well as some academic instruction, typically in English and accounting. Court identifies five types of polytechnics: (1) conventional-vocational; (2) settlement-vocational (there is a close association between school and community and the school is used as a community center); (3) centralized entrepreneurial (the emphasis is on self-employment through commercial subjects); (4) centralized cooperative (where members of cooperatives are trained); and (5) dispersed cooperative (the intent is to create independent cooperatives from trainee work groups).[67]

A study of polytechnic graduates revealed that the program led to money-making opportunities for a sizable percentage. However, many found these opportunities outside the rural areas. Hence, the program has achieved its objectives without making major inroads into the educational and economic structure of rural areas.[68] Another study indicated that most trainees preferred to view the polytechnic as part of the academic educational system. Hence, they often demand the credentialling function of a traditional academic school and reject the "self-help" concept. Thus, a major constraint on the innovativeness of the effort is the pervasive formal school ethic. In this regard, Court concludes that the polytechnic movement " . . . will have to await modifications in the social structure linking schooling and wage incentives before it can begin to have an extensive impact on educational philosophy and practice in Kenya."[69]

The polytechnic movement points out the difficulties inherent in attempting to link vocational preparation with selected employment opportunities. Court correctly diagnoses the situation by pointing to the social structure and the nature and existence of employment incentives rather than to the schools themselves in attempting to smooth the transition between education preparation and productive work. One innovative approach toward the resolution of this dilemma can be seen in the Brazilian National Apprenticeship Service which was initiated in 1942 and has now spread throughout Latin America.

THE BRAZILIAN NATIONAL APPRENTICESHIP SERVICE OF INDUSTRIAL TRAINING

SENAI, or the National Apprenticeship Service of Industrial Training, involves the collaboration of industry and government in training the industrial labor force. The idea for such a program apparently began in 1937 when the national government found itself short of funds to expand the national education system. As a result of this restrictive budgetary situation, the constitution of 1937 included the following statement concerning the role of industry in education:

It is the duty of industry and economic syndicates in the sphere of their specialties to set up apprenticeship schools for their associates.[70]

Because the industrialists apparently did not agree that it was appropriate for them to become involved in educational programs traditionally administered and funded by the government, and as there apparently did not exist any organized pressures from the industrial working-class population for, such educational services, they did not cooperate voluntarily. The subsequent legislation creating SENAI, however, mandated such cooperation through a tax paid by employers on the total worker payroll. It is this aspect of the program, involving the maintenance of the educational programs through financial contributions of industrial employers, that establishes the SENAI effort as an innovative cooperative school-community program.

SENAI is designed to assist industry in pre-service training of new, skilled workers, advanced training of skilled workers and master craftsmen, on-the-job training of skilled and semiskilled workers, and training of supervisors and technicians.[71] In 1971 SENAI was supported by a one percent tax on the monthly payroll of industrial firms employing more than 100 people. In that year, it was (1) sponsoring thirteen industrial colleges that enrolled 2,400 students, of which six were maintained by private industry; (2) offering apprenticeship training for youth under eighteen years of age, enrolling 43,000 students in SENAI schools and about 50,000 on the job; (3) offering skills training, specialization, and upgrading of adults, enrolling 145,000 in SENAI schools and 101,000 on the job; and (4) working with several other agencies in training and upgrading industrial skills. In 1971, SENAI graduated 12,500 apprentices and trained or upgraded 154,000 adults and 330 technicians.[72]

On the basis of the SENAI experience, programs of a similar nature have been initiated during the last two decades in, among others, Colombia (SENA), Venezuela (INCE), Chile (SCT), Peru (SENATI), Argentian (CONET),[73] and, most recently, in Ecuador (SECAP). Some of these agencies have expanded their services to include basic education, agricultural technical assistance, and literacy programs. They vary in the administrative relationships between the government and industry and in the amount and conditions of the tax levied to support the programs. In terms of programs, for example, SENA in Colombia recently inaugurated a "popular professional preparation" program in both rural and urban areas of the country. Mobile units in the rural areas train individuals for the development of community enterprises, cooperatives, and entrepreneurs, whereas in the urban areas the program is designed to train both the unemployed and underemployed.[74]

Whereas Kenya and Brazil, as well as other capitalist countries, must generally rely upon incentives like wages to channel the vocational choices of students, communist countries tend to merge study and work into a single, unified process. This phenomenon can be seen in the following examples from Eastern Europe and Cuba. China, a similar example of this approach, will be dealt with in a subsequent section on cooperative school-community relations for nationalism and socioeconomic development.

COMBINING THEORY AND PRACTICE IN EASTERN EUROPE
The chief aim of education in the countries of Eastern Europe, including Poland, East Germany, Czechoslovakia, Hungary, Rumania, Yugoslavia, Bulgaria, Albania, and the Soviet Union, is to serve the needs of society over those of the individual. The emphasis is on both theory and practice through the concept of polytechnic education—the combination of school and work. Nigel Grant characterizes Eastern European education as teacher-centered and state-controlled. He notes, however, that youth organizations are strong and manifest a political and indoctrinating role and that local community groups are intended to implement policy and allocate funds. Although local communities are able to exercise these functions, the state retains actual control over the schools.[75]

Based upon Marxist-Leninist ideas regarding teaching and productive labor for the new generation, and influenced by the thoughts of A. S. Makarenko, the Soviet educational system is a fusion of family, school, and community. Schools for children of preschool age are required to be set up in every apartment house as well as in factories and collective farms employing women. As the child grows older, a factory or office will adopt a group of children as their "wards" to acquaint them with work in Soviet society. Throughout the educational system emphasis remains on cooperation between work and school and on collective discipline.[76]

The core of the Eastern European socialist system is the commune, a socioeconomic and political entity which has considerable responsibility for the school process. The commune in Yugoslavia, for example, determines the rates of taxes paid for education and allocates financial resources. It may also amend up to 15 percent of the school's curriculum to match local communal needs and problems. As with other socialist countries in the area, in Yugoslavia it is believed that the mode of production of one's material life conditions the process of social, political, and spiritual life. In education this means that it is "necessary to look for forms and methods of work, and for situations, in which young people will establish relations by working and directly participating in the life of the community."[77] The commune carries out this process by linking learning with productive labor in which the adults assist youngsters in understanding the basic principles of modern production and work.[78]

STUDY AND WORK IN CUBA

A final example of school-community cooperation, also in a communist state, is provided by Cuba, where in recent years there has been a new emphasis on work and study linked to production.[79] These programs are extensions of the earlier innovations in Cuban education of the 1960s and include "interest circle" programs built around scientific, technical, and cultural issues for primary and secondary students; worker and farmer improvement courses designed to enable the work force to complete primary school at the work site; on-the-job technical training in factories; and "people's schools" oriented to small craftsmen. Many of these programs emphasize the idea of work and study adapted to the worker's daily schedules.

The "school to the countryside" program and the "centennial youth columns" program are also supportive of these principles. In the school-to-the-countryside program nearly all secondary school youth move to rural areas for six to ten weeks per year and pursue their studies half the day and do farm work during the other half. Although centennial-youth-columns programs are primarily designed to increase productive work on a para-military, production-line basis, many youths have also been able to complete vocational education courses during the three-year period that they are in the program.[80]

Eastern European nations and Cuba, because of their authority structure and ideological base, use primarily moral and social incentives such as personal satisfaction and community betterment to encourage and foster participation in these education and work programs. Many other nations, like Kenya and Brazil, must rely on more traditional socioeconomic incentives. The major source of such incentives is jobs. As is apparent, little value can be attached to training per se until opportunities exist for the application of what is learned. Hence, in most areas of the world, individuals cannot become contributing members of the economy until structural changes are made in societies the schools are supposed to serve. In Guyana, for example, a program was begun in the David Rose Centre to train individuals for self-employment in cookery, handicrafts, leatherwork, metalwork, sewing, and woodwork. The goal was to train 800 unemployed young people through several three-month courses. After the first two courses in 1974, an evaluation was conducted and the report made these comments:

> ... no effective action was taken to rectify the main shortcoming of the first training course, *viz.* the failure to link the training in a practical way to the following production state. In other words, the training programme tended to be regarded as an end in itself, rather than as a means to an end.[81]

Cooperative school-community programs provide one, often temporary and partial, resolution to school-work transitions. The SENAI apprenticeship model appears to provide a viable relationship between education and job placement. By paying the apprentice while he is learning his trade, industry channels him into a particular position through a combination of classroom and on-the-job experience. Whether this or another alternative proves effective, however, depends primarily on the ability of both the school and the community to assess the relationship between what is learned and the opportunity for its application and use. As we shall point out later, the problem of applying and using new behaviors is central to larger and more complex programs where the goal goes beyond employment to include nationalism and socioeconomic development.

COMMUNITY SCHOOLS AS COMMUNITY CENTERS

The three forms of community schooling discussed above are similar in that each focuses on the formal aspects of education. Whether the emphasis is on providing educational access, promoting relevant learning, or integrating work and study, the concern is with the school's traditional role, that of educating the young. Hence, although the programs in these three categories are all aimed at community improvement, their effects are largely indirect and slow to materialize. Success in these cases is tied to the probability that in-school experiences will carry over into adult life and enable graduates to enhance individual and community well-being. This probability, of course, is limited by a host of sociocultural constraints. Moreover, even under the best of circumstances, this approach to community uplift may require generations to produce tangible results.

In the community-center model, the school is utilized as an instrument for direct and immediate local progress. This approach views the school as an institutional focal point from which a variety of community services can emanate. Like the learning and work-study schemes, the school community center seeks to dissolve the barriers separating the school from its surrounding milieu. However, in contrast to the other models, it is concerned more with adults than with children and it focuses more on extracurricular activities than on formal instruction. As will be shown below, the programs falling into this general category vary in both purpose and design. In some instances, the emphasis is on the community use of the school plant for social, cultural, and recreational purposes. In others, the school is utilized as a base of operations for technical experts and school personnel attempting to foster social change. In all cases, however, the school is asked to assume new functions in the name of community betterment.

SCHOOL COMMUNITY CENTERS IN ENGLAND

Probably the oldest and most common form of school community center involves the utilization of the school plant for community activities. As a public institution which tends to be centrally located and often unused in the evenings, the school has traditionally represented a natural gathering place for community residents. There exist examples from all regions of the world of schoolhouses serving their localities as centers for play, worship, social events, and meetings. Rarely, however, has this concept of wider school use reached the proportions of a nationwide effort. For this reason, the school community center in England is worth examining.

As early as 1925, the Secretary of Education in Cambridgeshire County proposed that British communities be organized around their educational institutions and that schools function as community centers serving the population of a rural region. Adult instruction, medical services, library and recreational services, prenatal and infant care, and an employment bureau could parallel the regular school program for youngsters.[82] Other communities, apparently finding such a school-community concept of interest, also initiated community-center programs. This in turn was supported by the Butler Education Act of 1944 which emphasized schools for the promotion of the social and physical training of the community. As a result of the Butler Act, the number of full-time community-center wardens increased from the prewar figure of 20 to more than 200 in 1951.[83]

The Wyndham School in Cumberland represents a relatively recent example of a British school used as a community center. It attempts to give the public "good value for its money" by making its classrooms, library, recreation area, swimming pool, and theater available for community use. In addition, the school sponsors an adult education program, a public coffee bar and lounge, a supervised youth center, and a nursery play center. In organizing the various school-community activities, the Wyndham personnel cooperate closely with local groups and associations. According to Houghton and Tregear, this program is an instance where the "community school" concept has "produced what those who know it regard as one of the best secondary schools in the whole of Britain."[84]

Although the community centers in England have undoubtedly helped meet local needs, they illustrate the limitations inherent in this general approach to social uplift. All services and activities are provided within the confines of the school plant. Instead of seeking to interject the school into the community, these centers try to attract the community into the school.[85] Hence, they are essentially passive instruments of social policy. While this strategy may foster some local melioration, it is not likely to generate community development. By failing to intervene actively in the prevailing sociocultural context, school community centers cannot hope to alter the structural arrangements which affect the character of community life. Examples of efforts to make the school an "active" center for social change include the cultural missions in Latin America and UNESCO's Fundamental Education program.

CULTURAL MISSIONS IN LATIN AMERICA

The cultural mission program was initiated in Mexico in the early 1920s. It was begun as a result of the problems encountered by primary school teachers working in federally operated schools in rural areas. Prior to the program's initiation, supervising teachers, known as missionaires, visited rural primary teachers to assist them in carrying out their instructional duties. In 1922 these supervisors met and decided that each rural school had to have arable land, as agriculture was the essential base of the rural dweller. This notion led to the first cultural mission team composed of an instructor in soap-making, a tanner, two agriculturalists, a carpenter, and a home-making teacher who, in 1923, went from Mexico City to Zacualitpan in the State of Hidalgo. In the early years the cultural missions were basically traveling normal schools that assisted rural teachers and augmented the rural curriculum. After 1943, they spent up to three years in a region or community assisting with the construction of schools and promoting community activities. By 1926, there were six missions in operation, by 1939, eighteen missions were in contact with some 4,000 rural teachers, and by 1943 there were thirty-four missions.[86] About half the missions worked with Indian populations.

The teams consisted of a director, social worker, nurse and midwife, an agriculturalist, a construction specialist, two individuals in the trades and industries, a mechanic and film-projector operator, a music teacher, and recreation specialist.[87] Their objectives included raising the rural population's standard of living, improving local educational institutions, improving occupational skills, introducing new crops and increasing the number of domestic animals, improving public health through nutrition education, increasing recreational opportunities, eliminating undesirable foreign influences, and encouraging the formation of cooperatives and self-help community action programs. In order to increase the likelihood that the work initiated by the mission would continue after its departure, attempts were made to organize and work through community committees, teams, and groups.[88]

Thus, the cultural missions of Mexico, while initiated around problems associated with rural schooling, evolved in later years into a community development program in which trained specialists promoted a variety of service and self-help activities. As a model for educational and community development, the cultural mission approach was copied in a number of other Latin American countries. In Cuba, for example, forty missions, each serving thirty to fifty rural schools, were in operation by 1939.[89] Each mission had a staff of eight including an expert in pedagogy, a veterinarian, a dentist, and specialists in farming, industrial trades, homemaking, and hygiene. The "missionaries" went from school to school, staying for a one-week period. By the 1940s, cultural missions had also appeared in Peru. As in Mexico and Cuba, the Peruvian teams were composed of specialists and worked in cooperation with the public school system. They utilized bilingual education techniques and would announce their arrival in a community with a loudspeaker attached to a station wagon.[90] Other countries that have experimented with variations of the cultural missions model include Venezuela,[91] Guatemala,[92] Costa Rica,[93] and Brazil.[94]

UNESCO'S FUNDAMENTAL EDUCATION PROGRAM
The mission approach with its reliance on specialists from outside the locality is not the only form of "active" community center. A second widely used development strategy focuses on the teacher as an agent for change. In this model, the teacher is expected to foster community uplift by organizing and conducting basic education classes for adults, by involving students and parents in neighborhood improvement projects, and by organizing local residents into self-help organizations. Teachers are assumed to be ideally suited for the role of community development worker because (1) they tend to be progressive in outlook, (2) they interact with parents and local leaders on a regular basis, and (3) they are trained educators, and development is essentially an educational process.

Although UNESCO did not invent this approach, it did much to popularize the concept by making it an integral part of the worldwide program known as Fundamental Education. Initiated by UNESCO in the late 1940s, Fundamental Education constituted the educational arm of the general United Nations program for social and economic development. In the words of Laves and Thompson, it was "a self-sufficient program for rural development, mainly through education supplemented by technical services in such fields as agriculture and health."[95] Its goals included the provision of communication, vocation, and domestic skills as well as the improvement of health and moral standards for participants.[96] As an international effort emphasizing self-help through broadly conceived education, Fundamental Education set the stage for the community action movements of the 1950s and 1960s.

To implement this ambitious program, UNESCO established a number of training centers to prepare teams of Fundamental Educators. Six Regional Training and Production Centres were created to service major world regions, and a number of smaller, more localized centers were set up in cooperation with national governments. According to Laves and Thompson, most of those attending these regional and national centers were selected by Ministries of Education, and a large percentage were school teachers. In Liberia, for example, a UNESCO training program was designed to produce graduates who "would act as teachers in rural primary schools and as fundamental education field workers, linking the improvement of community life with the expansion of elementary schools."[97] A UNESCO training center in the Andean Altiplano had a similar result, " . . . the teacher became part community organizer as well as part teacher."[98] In the Phillipines, the Phillipine-UNESCO National Community School Training Center was established for the expressed purpose of preparing teachers for community school service. As emphasized by the Chief of the UNESCO Mission in the Philippines, " . . . the teacher must be prepared to tie her teaching into action programs geared to community improvement."[99] Hence, the Center's standard course consisted of lectures, discussions, preparation of plans and programs, project studies and experiments, observation of ongoing community development programs, and actual work in surrounding communities. Case studies conducted in Philippine communities indicate that the Center's graduates helped provide adult instruction, initiate self-help projects, and organize and advise *Puroks* (neighborhood organizations).[100]

The overall impact of the cultural mission and Fundamental Education efforts is difficult to ascertain. Since these two programs have involved direct interventions into community life, it seems reasonable to conclude that their efforts have been greater than those of "passive" school centers. However, it is important to note that substantial evidence indicates that the cultural missionaries and Fundamental Educators often failed to reach their goals. For example, Whetten, who studied rural communities in Mexico during the 1940s, reveals that the missions had problems recruiting trained personnel and that the teams were often viewed with suspicion by local residents and parish priests. He concludes that the stigma of being an outsider, along with the long, tedious, and complex nature of the work, meant that the missions seldom accomplished all that was intended.[101] Redfield, who studied rural communities in Mexico during the same period, tends to support Whetten's observation. Returning to the village of Chan Kom in 1949 after a fifteen-year absence, Redfield learned that a cultural mission team had been in the community for a year and a half in 1944 and 1945. He found that little remained of the team's work. In Redfield's words,

> ... not one of the little raised stoves of lime cement which the mission taught people to build is now in use, nor have any of the privies built been kept in repair. In the less practical, more purely expressive arts, the enduring accomplishments of the missions are almost nil.[102]

Some of the problems inherent in the mission model may have been avoided in the Fundamental Education strategy because teachers tend to be respected and permanent members of the community. Thus, they should have a distinct advantage over the cultural missionaries in initiating and institutionalizing change. Nevertheless, they too appear to have experienced very limited success. In fact, a large number of UNESCO's Fundamental Education projects were outright failures, and by 1965 the general program was no longer considered viable.[103] Some evaluations have placed the blame upon the teacher, noting that he or she simply did not have the time, energy, or motivation to work both as a formal instructor and as a community development worker.[104] Other appraisals, however, have questioned the general strategy of using education as an agent for change. This concern over the basic premise of Fundamental Education is reflected in a recent comment by Anibal Buitron, a UNESCO representative.

> The fact that the literacy campaigns and community development projects have been running year after year in practically every developing country without much apparent gain is, in my opinion, a clear sign of their failure. ... The first and most important mistake we have made, and continue to make, is, in my opinion, our belief that we can solve all the economic, social, cultural, and political problems through education alone.[105]

This viewpoint applies to the cultural mission approach as well. Indeed, a mission project described by Whetten graphically illustrates the structural obstacles confronting any educationally based development program. The project was undertaken in 1944 in the community of San Pablo del Norte near the City of Puebla. The intent of the mission was to organize the tortilla makers in the community into a large cooperative. Mills for grinding corn would be purchased cooperatively, machines for making tortillas mechanically secured, a station wagon would haul the tortillas to Puebla and bring back corn, and small stands would be erected in Puebla for selling tortillas. It had been customary for up to 1,500 women from San Pablo del Norte and adjoining villages to carry their corn daily to one of fifteen or twenty small mills, return home to prepare tortillas, and then walk or ride a bus six miles to Puebla with twenty-five to fifty pounds of tortillas to sell in the market where each had to pay a fee for the privilege of selling. Whetten describes the results of the project:

> This scheme would obviate the necessity for all the fifteen hundred women to make the trip and sell the product individually. The director of the mission talked the proposition over with the responsible state authorities, who, in turn, advised him to consult the cacique, since such a scheme might interfere with the latter's established business. Vested interests prevented the formation of the cooperative. The cacique threatened to fight the proposal to the bitter end. It is said that he has a monopoly on transportation and owns the buses which run between San Pablo and Puebla and which now carry full loads. He charges a fee for each person and each basket each way. Obviously, any proposal to substitute other forms of transportation or even to curtail the number of passengers would seriously interfere with his business. The owners of the corn grinders also objected strenuously, since their grinding fees would be curtailed; the City of Puebla objected because, instead of collecting marketing fees from fifteen hundred people, they would be able to collect from only a limited number. Even the consumers objected that machine-made tortillas might not taste so good as hand-made ones.[106]

Clearly, efforts to generate change through community organization and the transmission of skills and information can be thwarted by social structural factors. Hence, even when removed from the classroom and directed at adults, education represents a dubious instrument for direct and immediate community improvement. We suspect that only when incorporated into an overall social strategy integrating diverse, yet functionally interdependent, sectors will the community center model of community schooling fully attain the intended effects. The reasons for our suspicion will be more apparent after considering three community schooling programs expressly designed to foster national development.

COMMUNITY SCHOOLS FOR NATIONAL DEVELOPMENT

The nationalism and socioeconomic development argument underlying school-community cooperation is concerned with raising a national identity and consciousness among students and members of the community, encouraging the use of the school as an agency of community change and development, and preparing youngsters to occupy economically productive roles in the community and nation. The learning approach to school-community relations attempts to move from the known to the unknown by complementing the knowledge, skills, and values that the student brings with him to school, and the schoolwork approach fosters employment and productive work. The development argument, like the change-oriented community center, emphasizes the social, political, and economic role of the school in fostering local and national progress and change. It posits that schools can affect these wider spheres by transmitting selected values and practical skills as well as by taking an active role in leading the nation toward needed social change. These national development programs represent the most broad-based community schooling efforts discussed thus far and encompass aspects of the learning, school-work, and community center approach.

Community schools for nationalism and socioeconomic development have most often been characterized by an attempt to decolonize education, promote indigenous culture, and generate local and national change in ways meaningful to a peasant agrarian society. They are generally sponsored by an important national leader whose support is part of a social philosophy that emphasizes the preservation of traditional values, the importance of "community" to psychological and social well-being, and the need to rely on self-help for local and national progress. The focus is usually on the primary level of schooling, where the curriculum utilizes the community as a resource, stresses local needs and problems, is designed to provide vocational skills appropriate to the local milieu, and encourages students to undertake community projects that contribute to social and economic welfare. The approach also offers adult education and recreational programs. The school and its personnel are intended to serve the cause of community development by providing leadership and by involving the entire community in planned change activities. The schools themselves are usually part of a national educational system with a centralized administrative apparatus. They foster little if any involvement by students and adults in school-community decision-making processes. These cooperative school-community characteristics can be seen in several nations. The discussion which follows outlines the examples of India, Tanzania, and China.[107]

INDIA

The concept of community schooling, known in India as Basic Education, was put forth by Mahatma Gandhi in 1937. Following a decade of experimentation and Indian Independence, it was accepted as the national system of education for children six to fourteen years of age. Schemes for establishing new Basic schools, reconverting existing schools, training administrators and teachers, and developing curriculum materials were formulated around the following basic tenets: (1) seven years of schooling for each child were to be free and compulsory; (2) the mother tongue was to be the medium of instruction; (3) instruction was to focus on manual and productive work related to handicrafts; and (4) the curriculum was intended to correlate with the child's physical and social environment. By 1956, Basic Schools had been assessed by a national committee and were found to suffer from poor facilities and inadequately trained teachers, and, in many cases, were identified as traditional institutions.[108] Ten years later, the Indian Education Commission echoed a similar theme:

> In the average school today, instruction still conforms to a mechanical routine, continues to be dominated by the old besetting evil of verbalism and therefore remains as dull and uninspiring as before.[109]

Today, despite official acceptance of the concept Basic Education is no longer operational. What prompted Basic Education to emerge and why did it fail? The answers are complex. Basic Education was both a product of conditions in pre-Independent India and an expression of Gandhi's thought. In the 1930s, when Basic Education emerged, the Indian struggle for independence was at a zenith. Nationalism permeated the country and everything foreign, particularly the British-based educational system, was suspect. Hence, Indian leaders attempted to formulate a new system suitable for Indian conditions. Of the various plans proposed, Basic Education was accepted because it was harmonious with Indian culture and it promised to make schooling free and universal at minimal expense. Moreover, it was cloaked in the philosophy of India's greatest leader, Mahatma Gandhi.

Gandhi believed that society should move toward a human brotherhood, toward a universal community of free persons without artificial barriers of caste, color, creed, wealth, and power. He believed that India could attain this goal by emphasizing its traditional values of nonviolence and truth. This required that the country preserve its rural, peasant focus. Rather than relying on the western formula of industrialization, he felt that India should be developed around thousands of self-contained, self-sufficient villages.[110]

Gandhi's educational beliefs have been described as forming the dynamic side of his general philosophy.[111] He saw social progress and educational reconstruction as intimately linked. He recommended that schooling be given a rural focus, that it emphasize service to the community, that it be "for life, through life, and by life," and that it center around handicrafts. Thus conceived, primary education could act "as a spearhead of a silent social revolution . . . and thus go a long way towards eradicating some of the worst evils of the present social insecurity and poisoned relationships between classes."[112]

The most salient characteristic of the scheme was the focus on learning crafts appropriate for the local milieu. Particular emphasis was given to skills suitable for cottage and small-scale industries. Gandhi believed that craft instruction would allow for a balanced general education in which intellect, body, and spirit would develop as a natural harmonious whole.[113] His ideas closely resembled those of progressive educators in the West in that he saw activity as the essential aspect of childhood and believed in developing the "whole" child. A second justification for the craft emphasis was that it would allow the student to serve the community. Gandhi believed that individual development and social progress were interdependent and felt that schooling should inculcate within students a desire for social service.

> The end of all education should surely be service, and if a student gets an opportunity of rendering service even whilst he is studying, he should consider it as a rare opportunity and treat it not really as a suspension of his education but rather its complement.[114]

A third and related reason for centering education around crafts was to provide a solution for the nation's economic problems. Developing appropriate manual skills was expected to promote the growth of cottage industries, thereby reducing rural unemployment and uplifting the quality of rural life. Finally, teaching crafts in schools was viewed as a mechanism for making the schools self-supporting. Gandhi and public officials recognized that a practical way of making education available to all was to meet operating expenses through the sale of craft work done by students. Gandhi wrote:

> I am very keen on funding the expenses of a teacher through the product of the manual work of his pupils, because I am convinced that there is no other way to carry education to scores of our children.[115]

As noted above, despite governmental support, Basic Education in India has been generally recognized as a failure. Most evaluations of the program focus on problems in administration and implementation.[116] They note that there was a lack of commitment on the state level, that administrators and teachers were poorly prepared, that objectives were never clearly specified, that there were inadequate equipment, facilities, and financing (self-sufficiency was never realized), and that there was little articulation between Basic schools and higher educational levels. Both Thomas and Zachariah have noted that the root causes of these problems reside in the larger cultural context.[117] Essentially, Basic Education was at odds with major trends and aspirations operating within the country. It never received full-scale support on the state and national level because it was incongruous with efforts to promote industrialization and national integration. On the village level, local elites were threatened by the classless orientation of the program. Perhaps most importantly, parents perceived Basic Education, with its rural craft focus, as being inferior and less legitimate than traditional academic instruction. It was seen as limiting rather than promoting mobility opportunities, a viewpoint strengthened by the fact that Basic schools operated only in rural areas and were poorly articulated with secondary institutions. It should be noted that the failure of Basic Education in India does not necessarily portend a similar fate for community schooling elsewhere. Although Basic Education constituted a national policy in India, the individual states were given responsibility for implementation. As we will point out below, community schooling in such countries as Tanzania and especially China is a more unified and integrated national effort.[118]

TANZANIA

Before beginning the discussion on Tanzania, it is useful to provide a brief historical overview of community education in Africa. In the early twentieth century schooling in Africa was controlled almost exclusively by missionary groups and was based on the European, academic model. During the 1920s, the Phelps-Stokes Foundation, in cooperation with the International Education Board, set up two commissions (1921 and 1924) to study education in Africa at the request of the Foreign Missions Conference of North America. The Conference wanted an investigation completed before further expanding missionary education in Africa.

The report suggested that in rural communities every part of the school curriculum should contribute to increased respect for and interest in the rural environment and that activities should be organized to "blend intimately with the life of the groups from which pupils came."[119] Based upon this report, in 1925 the British colonial government issued a memorandum of official education policy advocating integrating schools with the communities they purported to serve. The memorandum stated, " . . . education should be adopted to local conditions in such a manner as would enable it to conserve all sound elements in local tradition and social organization, while at the same time functioning as an instrument of progress and evolution."[120] This initial impetus toward education for the community was strengthened in 1935 when a colonial office memorandum, titled "Education of African Communities," urged that "the education agencies should be brought closely in relation with all of those agencies which make for the general welfare of the people."[121] However, these ideals were never implemented.[122] There was little coordination among agencies and a lack of financial resources.

After World War II the British government began actively to promote community development activities. There was a general feeling among Africans, however, that community development was designed to keep them in a traditional, backward state. Since formal academic education was viewed as an escape route from rural drudgery, it continued to be held in much higher regard by the local population than were community development programs.

In 1967, when President Nyerere put forth his program of "Education for Self-Reliance," Tanzanian education was characterized by the formal, academic, European schooling model. Nyerere asserted, "There must be a parallel and integrated change in the way our schools are run, so as to make them and their inhabitants a real part of our society and economy. Schools must, in fact, become communities—and communities which practice the precept of self-reliance."[123] Nyerere proposed that the educational system inculcate a sense of commitment to the entire community and prepare students to work in a predominantly peasant economy. Primary schools were to be thoroughly integrated into village life so that the pupils would remain part of the community.

Secondary schools were to have a vocational focus relevant to the local milieu. Every type of school was to contribute to its own upkeep by not only having a farm but by being a farm run by its own pupils.[124] Nyerere saw his program as a mechanism for developing a socialist and independent country. He saw a reorganized and reoriented educational system as the basis of an agrarian revolution in a peasant society. Hence, Nyerere employed the term "Self-Reliance" in several different contexts. Through education, he saw Tanzania becoming self-reliant among nations, communities becoming self-reliant in the countryside, individuals becoming self-reliant in their communities, and the school becoming self-reliant in terms of financing.

The emphasis is on integrating the school and community and linking learning experiences with practical everyday problems. Schools are to lead the student into rather than out of the community. Instruction has been fused with socialist thinking and enriched with practical experience and self-reliant activities. On the primary level, five hours per week are devoted to Self-Reliance. Students keep school gardens, raise poultry, maintain school buildings, and participate in community development projects. In addition, the school is expected to serve as a community center and the head teacher is given responsibility for adult education. In operationalizing the "self-reliance" approach, the Ministry of Education reserved 200 places in two training colleges for retraining teachers in "self-reliant" methods. Following training the Ministry makes a concerted effort to place teachers in their home localities. Also, the Ministry has urged communities to establish school committees of parents, teachers, and officials to plan and coordinate school-community projects.[125]

Although both the Indian and Tanzanian cases demonstrate strategies through which charismatic leaders have sought to use education to foster nationalism and socioeconomic development, one is struck by the problems that interfere with the achievement of such plans. For example, community members often seek access to academic credentials rather than vocational skills as they desire to leave their local environments. In effect, individuals realize that vertical mobility will be enhanced more if they associate with urban industrialization than if they engage in rural crafts. Hence, schooling becomes an adjunct to the worldwide trend toward both urbanization and urbanism as a way of life. These and similar incongruities underlie the lack of success encountered in India and may yet appear in the more socialistic orientation of programs in Tanzania. Is it possible that schooling can only function in accord with the sought-after community-school rhetoric where the entire fabric of society is based on labor-intensive cooperation as a way of life? The following example of China suggests that the nature of society and not the desires of the educator dictates the long-term success of school-community programs.

CHINA

Probably no country gives community schooling a greater emphasis than does China. Indeed, community-based education, as we have characterized it here, constitutes a central theme of the "educational revolution" emerging out of the Cultural Revolution. The community focus is closely in line with Mao's educational philosophy which gives emphasis to rural development, productive endeavor, community service, decentralized decision making, and the viewpoint that the whole society is a school.[126]

Although community schooling in China was not implemented on a wide-scale basis until after 1966, it was apparent in a number of earlier experimental efforts. When the Communists were based in Yenan Province before the Revolution, Mao and his associates experimented with such educational innovations as integrating theory and practice, shortening the period of schooling, emphasizing local control and financing, and establishing flexible programs such as winter schools and half-day schools.[127] Most of these efforts were directed at adults and would fall under the rubric of "nonformal education." However, the formal schooling sphere was also affected. At Kang Ta, a military and political college in Yenan which today is held up as a model of Maoist thought, "students engaged in production to support themselves, they dug caves to build dormitories, and they wasted no time in theoretical studies not directly related to practical needs."[128] On the primary level, emphasis was given to the principle of *min-pan-kung-chu* (management by the people and government assistance). Local communities were to establish, administer, and finance their own schools while the government (Communist Party) would assist in making policy and defining goals. According to Chen, this policy served the dual function of making schools more responsive to the local needs and freeing the Party from a major financial burden.[129]

Between 1949 and 1966 the Chinese educational program reflected the efforts of national leaders to create an industrial, technological society. Essentially, there were three types of schools during this period: Full-time schools, which were academically oriented and conventional in approach; and spare-time and work-study schools. These latter efforts were directed at urban workers and focused on political, literacy, and technical training either after normal working hours or on a shared-time basis during the working day. Spare-time and work-study schools were generally operated within economic units (factories, mines, offices) and directed by local committees in line with Party directives from above.[130] They never gained the prestige and respect afforded the full-time schools, however, and a dual educational system prevailed.

An exception to this basic trend came in the late 1950s during the "great leap forward" initiated by Mao. Spare-time and work-study schools experienced increased support and growth in the industrial sector while, for the first time, the rural areas began to experiment with half-work, half-study programs directed at illiterate adults. During this period the commune movement was initiated and there was an effort to shift the delivery of educational services from the schools to other social institutions.[131] However, the economic setbacks of 1959 curtailed the general movement and the educational experiments associated with it. Between 1960 and 1966 there again was an emphasis on more traditional educational practices, resulting in disaffection between educational authorities and local communities, increased wastage as students dropped out rather than risk failure, and discontent among students and teachers.[132]

The Cultural Revolution caused the schools to close for several seasons. When they reopened in the late 1960s, they were significantly restructured. In terms of administration and organization, the emphasis was now on decentralization of control to the local level. The Draft Program for Primary and Secondary Schools in the countryside declared that the reopened schools "are a new type of socialist school directly managed by the poor and lower-middle peasants under the leadership of the Chinese Communist Party."[133] In accordance with this dictate, urban schools are managed by factories and neighborhood organizations and rural schools are operated by agriculture production units. The schools in both urban and rural areas are operated by "three-in-one" committees composed of students, teachers, and party representatives. In addition to handling daily administration, these committees select curriculum materials which are developed locally by collective teams of students, teachers, and workers. Financing is also a local responsibility. The official slogan is "run schools by self-reliance, diligence, and frugality."[134] Both students and teachers farm small plots to raise school funds. They also work together to build desks and stools, and local production brigades subsidize the remaining costs. Despite this emphasis on local control, however, the Communist Party, largely through its influence on members of the local committees, continues to establish basic educational goals and policies.[135] There seems to be some disagreement among scholars over the precise rationale for the decentralization effort. Hawkins views local control as an essential element of Maoist educational philosophy while Chen sees it as an effective method for reducing the state's financial obligations.[136] Both writers agree, however, that decentralizing educational administration has caused primary education to take a variety of forms reflecting local conditions. Mobile teaching centers, half-day classes, evening instruction, and the adjustment of scheduling to planting and harvesting needs are examples of efforts to expand educational opportunities without upsetting the economic routine of village life.

Closely related to the emphasis on decentralization is what has been called the "open-door" policy in China. This policy attempts to remove the barriers between school and society and "to make the entire society a classroom." Students work part of each day in the factory or on the farm, and they are also expected to participate actively in local political affairs. At the same time, workers and other adults are involved in the formal teaching process. This compensates for a lack of trained teachers and also provides an environment for social interaction and "skill exchanges" between different age and occupation groups. Consistent with the open-door policy is an emphasis on practical, vocational skills. Mao has stated that while the main task of students is to study, they should not only learn book knowledge, but they should also learn industrial production, agricultural production, and military affairs.[137] Although the skills learned are generally those applicable to the immediate environment, children in urban areas are expected to obtain some rural knowledge. A number of urban schools have set up branch schools in the countryside where students and teachers learn about farming and then relate their knowledge to farm practices.

The middle schools, like the primary institutions, are based on local control and financing. Scheduling, curriculum, and teaching materials are guided by local needs. Indeed, many are geared exclusively to meeting immediate manpower shortages. For example, in Kwantung Province four types of middle schools have been established: industrial schools in factories, agricultural schools in communes, health schools in hospitals, and normal schools in educational establishments. Each type emphasizes needed technical skills and is based on the work-study format.

The integration between school and community in China is augmented by the rule that graduates of the nine-year primary/secondary cycle may not immediately pursue higher education. Rather, they must spend at least two years working productively in a task related to their occupational interest. In line with Mao's philosophy, the emphasis here was on working in the rural sector. Mao's position was that it is absolutely necessary for educated young people to go to the countryside to be reeducated by the poor and lower-middle class peasants.[138] This program, then, was designed to contribute to the economic development of the rural areas as well as to the political growth of the urban intelligentsia.*

These three examples of school-community programs for nationalism and socioeconomic development are as bold and broad as any that have existed during this century. They reflect a concern with forging a new national identity, one that favors indigenous traditions and opposes colonial and imperialist influences. The school is viewed as a major vehicle to socialize a new generation and to reeducate the old. The three cases also demonstrate the importance of a charismatic national leader, not only to articulate the philosophical and ideological position that undergirds the program but to demonstrate how the school-community linkages are to achieve the goals sought. Learning, work, and social change are intimately related as the approach attempts to motivate a population to progress while relying upon a collective commitment.

The weaknesses in these efforts are generally lodged in this overdependence on self-motivation and self-help among the populations involved. Hence, the strategy for change is one which, as in the Indian and Tanzanian cases, assumes that if people want to help themselves, they must simply make such a decision cognitively and then manifest the behavior to achieve their goals. We have referred to this approach elsewhere as the "man-oriented" model for fostering social change.[139] Its basic tenet involves the assumption that change is derived from the internal psychological state of man. Hence, acquiring new knowledge and attitudes is assumed to be the necessary precursor to changing behavior. While there is little evidence to support this assumption, it remains the most predominant strategy for carrying out social change programs. The problem with this orientation is that it fails to recognize and deal with the socio-structural obstacles in the wider society. In most countries, rigid social stratification systems, discrimination among ethnic groups, inadequate technology, scarce financial resources, and so on prevent even the most highly motivated individual or community from carrying out desired intentions. The need, therefore, is to go beyond the man-oriented or psychological approach and toward a more social systemic approach in designing school-community programs.[140] Briefly, this approach views change as resulting from either conflict and inequality emerging inside the system or from some innovation impinging on the system from outside. The system accom-

---

*This chapter was originally written in 1976. Obviously much has happened in China—and in other countries discussed—since then, so the programs described may have changed greatly in the intervening period.

modates to these interventions by seeking a state of equilibrium. The potential result is a new articulation among the society's various components and structures.

This socio-systemic orientation to cooperative school-community programs assists in explaining why, for example, the Indian Basic School movement failed to achieve its objectives. Taking this perspective, one would not attribute blame to the lack of desire or interest expressed by the Indian population or to the inadequacy of the schools, but instead one might look to the lack of support received from the state and national levels in augmenting the availability of credit, technology, technical assistance, and financial resources upon which the program depended. The fact is that schools are simply not powerful enough to carry out social change efforts in the absence of other institutions that are supportive of such change. Schools tend to mirror or reflect the larger society rather than act as catalysts to change. Depending upon them to promote change even when there is a motivated community to offer support is an insufficient strategy given the overwhelming socio-structural obstacles existing in the wider society. It is for this reason that the Chinese case is of interest. Here we can see how the entire society is supportive of the goals established for education. Schools become an adjunct to the process rather than the dominant institution involved in the effort.

In reviewing these school-community programs involving access, learning, work, center, and development approaches, it is possible to see how this holistic model is associated with the more innovative efforts. Within the learning approach, for example, the British and, to some extent, the Argentines depend on the school as the major catalyst to community cooperation and activity. Likewise the school-work approach in Kenya and, to a lesser extent, in Brazil places a heavy reliance on the school to resolve manpower shortages. In Brazil the attempt is to guarantee employment through cooperation with industry, while in Kenya the individual is left on his own to secure such employment. Similarly within the community center approach, the Mexican cultural missions program and UNESCO's Fundamental Education effort were unsuccessful in creating local community change as the strategy employed did not emphasize sufficiently the articulation of education with other institutional resources. All of these efforts can be juxtaposed against those of China, Israel, Eastern Europe, and Cuba, where schools complement wider societal efforts and are not viewed as the major mechanisms to resolve societal problems.

The case studies presented here clearly demonstrate that schools cannot lead the community unless the wider society, through political, cultural, and social patterns, is prepared both to assign the school such responsibility and to support its efforts. The school emerges as little more than a pawn that reflects the dominant interests either in the community or in the wider society. At the community level this often means that there is an emphasis on traditional academic curricula rather than on the needs of the local community, and at the societal level this means that there is a tendency to move toward a centralization of decision making and a standardization of curriculum. In both cases the community-school concept is weakened, if not defeated. Local school democratic decision making does not appear frequently, and the scarcity of financial resources often leads to further government encroachment.

These observations should not lead to a complete disillusionment with the community-school concept. Instead, they should assist in pointing to the problems inherent in fostering school-community programs in light of the interests of local elites and of the nation-state. The community school concept will have difficulty functioning when the wider society does not itself operate through institutions based upon the primacy of individual and institutional cooperation.

NOTES

1. See, for example, Pedro T. Orata, *Community Education Abroad,* UNESCO Philippine Educational Foundation, 1954; T. R. Batten, *School and Community in the Tropics,* Oxford University Press, 1959; Nelson B. Henry, Community Education, *Principles and Practices from World-Wide Experience,* The Fifty-eighth Yearbook of the National Society for the Study of Education, Part I, University of Chicago Press, 1959; Clifford P. Archer and others, "The Role of the Community School Throughout the World. Improvement of Rural Life," National Education Association, Department of Rural Education, Washington, D.C., 1960; Harold Houghton and Peter Tregear (eds.), *Community Schools in Developing Countries,* UNESCO, Institute for Education (International Studies in Education, 23), Hamburg, 1969.

2. Isaac L. Kandel, *Comparative Education,* Houghton Mifflin, Boston, 1933; I. N. Thut and D. Adams, *Educational Patterns in Contemporary Societies,* McGraw-Hill, New York, 1964; Edmund J. King, *Other Schools and Ours,* Holt, Rinehart and Winston, New York, 1973.

3. Philip H. Coombs, *The World Educational Crisis: A Systems Analysis,* Oxford University Press, New York, 1968; E. Faure (ed.), *Learning to Be,* UNESCO, Paris, 1972.

4. Kabiru Kinyanjui, "Education, Training and Employment of Secondary School Learners in Kenya," in D. Court and D. Ghai (eds.), *Education, Society, and Development,* Oxford University Press, Nairobi, 1974, pp.243–274.

5. Ernest Stabler, *Education Since Uhuru. The Schools of Kenya*, Wesleyan University Press, Middletown, Conn., 1969; E. M. Godfrey and G. C. M. Mutiso, "The Political Economy of Self-Help: Kenya's Harambee Institute of Technology," in David Court and Dharam P. Ghai (eds.), *Education, Society and Development: New Perspectives from Kenya*, Oxford University Press, Nairobi, 1974, pp. 243–74.

6. Godfrey and Mutiso, ibid., p. 246.

7. John Anderson, "The Harambee School: The Impact of Self-Help," in Richard Jolly (ed.), *Education in Africa: Research and Action*, East African Publishing House, Nairobi, 1969, pp. 103–34.

8. Michael H. Kovar, "The Kikuyu Independent Schools Movement: Interaction of Politics and Education in Kenya," unpublished Ph.D. dissertation, University of California at Los Angeles, 1970.

9. *Harambee* literally means "Let's pull together." Although it pertains specifically to community self-help activity, it also has a symbolic component denoting national unity and vigor. See discussion in P. M. Mbithi, "Harambee Self-Help: The Kenyan Approach," *The African Review*, vol. 2, no. 1, June 1972.

10. Anderson, op. cit.

11. Ibid., and John Anderson, *The Struggle for the School*, Longman, London, 1970.

12. Anderson, "The Harambee School," op. cit.; A. Njunji, "Transformation of Education in Kenya since Independence," *Education in East Africa*, vol. 4, no. 1, 1974; pp. 107–126; and Stabler, op. cit.

13. Godfrey and Mutiso, op. cit.

14. Anderson, "The Harambee School, op. cit.; Anderson, *The Struggle*, op. cit.; and Kinyanjui, op. cit.

15. Kinyanjui, op. cit., p. 48.

16. Anderson, "The Harambee School," op. cit.; Anderson, *The Struggle*, op. cit.; and Njunji, op. cit.

17. Anderson, "The Harambee School," op. cit., p. 113.

18. Ibid.; Anderson, *The Struggle*, op. cit,; Njunji, op. cit,; Stabler, op. cit,; and Sheldon Weeks, *Divergence in Educational Development: The Case of Kenya and Uganda*, Teachers College Press, New York, 1967.

19. Anderson, "The Harambee School," op. cit,; Njunji, op. cit.

20. J. M. Gachuhi, "The Role and Impact of Self-Help Schools on a Kenyan Community Chinga," unpublished Ph.D. dissertation, State University of New York at Buffalo, 1970.

21. Godfrey and Mutiso, op. cit.

22. See Anderson, *The Struggle*, op. cit., and Stabler, op. cit.

23. Weeks, op. cit., and Stabler, op. cit.

24. According to Godfrey and Mutiso, op. cit., the absence of a strong political party with a systematic ideology has caused political power in post-independence Kenya to devolve from the center to the periphery (i.e., to tribes

and provincial administrations) with the result that local *Harambee* activity has become an important arena within which political leadership on the local level is determined.

25. Unless otherwise noted, the information provided on the CNEC schools is the result of field research conducted by R. E. Verhine in 1973–1974.

26. H. F. Oliveira, and G. F. Lewis, "Nonformal Education and Human Resource Development in Brazil," background paper, USAID/HRO, Rio de Janeiro, 1973.

27. The Sector in question is located in the town of Itirucu, a community of about 3,000 residents situated in the interior of the State of Bahia.

28. Oliveira, op. cit.

29. Each state CNEC office employs a "pedagogy technician" to serve as a liaison between the Local Sector and the State Secretariat of Education.

30. Oliveira, op. cit.

31. Ibid.

32. For example, in the State of Bahia, where there are 161 local CNEC programs, the state staff number nine—including secretaries and drivers.

33. For the historical development of CNEC, see Feilipe Tiago Gomes, *Escolas da Comunidade,* CNEC, Bonsuccesso, G. B., Brazil, 1973.

34. The Campaign did not adopt its current name until 1968. However, in discussing the program before that date, we will continue to use the acronym CNEC (rather than CNEG) to avoid confusion.

35. See Coombs, op. cit., and Faure, op. cit.

36. The first CNEC community center was opened in Ceilandia, a suburb of Brasilia in 1972.

37. USAID, *Brazil Education Sector Analysis,* Human Resources Office, USAID/Brazil, November 1972.

38. Oliveira, op. cit.

39. One such school is the *Colegio Normal e Agricola* in Itirucu, Bahia. This school's efforts during the 1960s to give its curriculum an agricultural focus attracted national attention, and in 1968 it served as the site for a nationwide conference on rural vocational education.

40. Pedro T. Orata, "Community Schools in the Phillipines," *Prospects in Education,* 1969, pp. 52–56; Pedro T. Orata, "Do It Yourself Schools in the Philippines," UNESCO *Courier,* vol. 25, June 1972, pp. 24–27; Pedro T. Orata, *Self-Help Barrio High Schools: The Story of 250,000 Students Earning Their Education and Preparing Themselves for Life,* Eastern Universities Press, SEAMEO Regional Center for Educational Innovation and Technology, 1972.

41. Orata, *Self-Help Barrio High Schools,* ibid., p. 74.

42. Ibid.

43. Ibid.

44. Ibid., and Orata, "Community Schools," op. cit.

45. Ibid., and Orata, "Do It Yourself Schools," op. cit.

46. Orata, *Self-Help Barrio High Schools,* ibid.

47. Ibid., p. 27.

48. Ibid., and Orata, "Community Schools," op. cit.; and Orata, "Do It yourself Schools," op. cit.

49. John Dewey, *The School and Society,* McLure, Phillips, and Company, 1900, p. 89.

50. A. S. Makarenko, *His Life and Work,* Foreign Languages Publishing House, 1963, p. 273.

51. Phillip H. Woodruff, "British Primary Education—Components of Innovation," Bureau of Education Personnel Development (DHEW/OE), Washington, D.C., August 1971. (ERIC EDO81765)

52. Betty Demarest, "Community Schools in England," in Institute for Education Leadership, *Impressions of Education in Great Britain,* The George Washington University, Washington, D.C., 1974, pp. 25–32.

53. Nicolaus Mills, *The Lion and the Bear: A Children's Story for Adults,* ERIC Clearinghouse on the Urban Disadvantaged, 1974. (ERIC ED 103528, Microfiche)

54. Unless otherwise noted, the information provided on APEFA schools is the result of field research conducted by T. J. La Belle in 1975.

55. APEFA, *Otra Escola en America Latina,* Associación de la Familia Agrícola) Enfoques Latinoamericanos No. 18), 1974.

56. Jean Charpentier, "Las Escuelas de la Familia Agrícola (E.F.A.)," Conferencia efectuada en el Ministerio de Agricultura y Ganadería de Santa Fe, Santa Fe, Argentina, 1968. (Typewritten)

57. The family school movement in Brazil is similar to that of Argentina. Known as MEPES *(Movimento de Educacao Promocional do Espiritu Santo),* it was begun as part of a wider community development program in 1968. While the curriculum is organized into only three areas and based primarily on agriculture, the same philosophic tenets and independent-study-oriented alternating curriculum are present. The emphasis on community development and augmenting agricultural productivity appears to be greater in the Brazilian program than in the Argentinian and is likely to be explained through the program's initial community activities. Similar to APEFA, the MEPES program was begun by an Italian priest and the area is about 80 percent inhabited by individuals of Italian descent. See Thomas J. La Belle, *Nonformal Education and Social Change in Latin America,* University of California, Los Angeles, Latin American Center, 1976.

58. Shmuel Golan and Zvi Lavi, "The Kibbutz and Communal Education," in Peter B. Neuberger (ed.), *Children in Collectives: Child-rearing Aims and Practices in the Kibbutz,* Charles C. Thomas, Springfield, Ill., 1965, pp. 323–29; A. F. Kleinberger, *Society, Schools and Progress in Israel,* Pergamon Press, Oxford, 1969.

59. Archer, op. cit., and Yehuda Bien, "Adult Education in Kibbutzim (col-

lective settlements) in Israel," Israel Government—Authority for Education and Research, Jerusalem, July 1966.

60. Randolph L. Braham, *Israel: A Modern Educational System,* U.S. Government Printing Office, Washington, D.C., 1966.

61. Bien, op. cit.

62. Braham, op. cit.; Archer, op. cit.; and Golan and Lavi, op. cit.

63. Kleinberger, op. cit.

64. David Court, "Dilemmas in Development: The Village Polytechnic Movement as a Shadow System of Education in Kenya," *Comparative Education Review,* vol. 17, no. 3, 1973, pp. 331–49.

65. J. R. Sheffield and V. P. Diejemaoh, *Nonformal Education in African Development,* African American Institute, New York, 1972.

66. Court, op. cit.

67. Ibid.

68. Ibid.

69. Ibid., p. 342.

70. Jayne Abreu, "Craft and Industrial Training in Brazil: A Socio-Historical Study," in Joseph A. Lauwerys and David G. Scanlon (eds.), *World Yearbook of Education, 1968: Education Within Industry,* Evans Brothers, London, 1968, pp. 210–25.

71. Ibid.

72. USAID, op. cit.

73. Pan American Union, *Servicios de Educacion Tecnica y Formacion Profesional en Argentina, Brasil, Colombia, Peru y Venezuela,* Pan American Union, Depto. de Asuntos Educativos, Washington, D.C., 1965; and Abreu, op. cit.

74. An extension of the industrial collaboration with the education model of SENAI was created in Brazil in 1946. Known as SENAC, or the National Service of Commercial Training, it is subordinate to the National Confederation of Commerce in Brazil and is characterized by a financial structure similar to that of SENAI. The training in SENAC is aimed at the commercial sector of the economy and includes basic subject matter areas like secretarial and business education, typing, and beautician training along with more peripheral areas like coffee tasting, USAID, op. cit.

75. Nigel Grant, *Society, School and Progress in Eastern Europe,* Pergamon Press, Oxford, 1969.

76. Mills, op. cit.; and O. A. Chernik, "The School and the Collective Farm in the Labor Education and Vocational Guidance of Pupils," *Soviet Education,* vol. XVII, no. 9, July 1975, pp. 56–72.

77. Stevan Bezdanov, *A Community School in Yugoslavia Experiments and Innovations in Education,* no. 6, UNESCO, Paris, 1973, p. 6.

78. In the German Democratic Republic, schools are also linked with industrial and commercial enterprises as well as construction, trade, and other organizations. Since 1970, these institutions have been paying approxi-

mately 60 percent of the cost of operating the educational programs. Pupils receive stipends for a three-year period during their training. See G. Zelenskii, "Vocational-Technical Training in the German Democratic Republic," *Soviet Education*, vol. XIV, no. 7, May 1972, pp. 34–41.

79. Rolland G. Paulston, "Cuban Rural Education: A Strategy for Revolutionary Development," in Philip Foster and James R. Sheffield (eds.), *The World Yearbook of Education 1974: Education and Rural Development*, Evans Bros., Ltd., London, 1973, pp. 234–260.

80. Arthur Gillette, *Cuba's Educational Revolution*, Fabian Society (Fabian Research Series, No. 302), London, June 1972.

81. F. C. R. Pollard, "Evaluation of David Rose Centre Training for Self-Employment Project," University of Guyana, Georgetown, (Third Progress Report, typewritten), November 1974.

82. Pedro T. Orata, *Community Education Abroad*, UNESCO Philippine Educational Foundation, Manila, 1954.

83. Godfrey N. Brown, "The Problem of Community in English Education," *Social Education*, vol. XIX, no. 5, May 1955, pp. 207–217.

84. Houghton and Tregear, op. cit., p. 75.

85. A somewhat similar community-school concept, designed for youth and young adults, is the folk high school which originated in Denmark in 1844. Folk high schools are boarding schools. Students may attend for a three to ten-month session. Their purpose has generally remained one of providing youth with an understanding of their national heritage leading to "good citizenship." See H. Engberg-Pedersen, "Danish Folk High Schools in the New Industrial State,"*Convergence*, vol. 3, no. 1, 1970, pp. 84–88; and Ole B. Thomsen, *Some Aspects of Education in Denmark*, University of Toronto Press, Toronto, 1967. Such schools can be found throughout the world but especially in the more industrialized nations of Northwestern Europe, the United States, and Canada. The Canadian folk school puts some emphasis on promoting community change and community cooperation. Orata, *Community Education Abroad*, op. cit.

86. Guillermo Bonilla y Segura, *Report on the Cultural Missions of Mexico*, U.S. Government Printing Office, U.S. Office of Education, Bulletin 1945, No. 11, Washington, D. C., 1945.

87. R. E. Ruiz, "Mexico: Indianismo and the Rural School," *Harvard Educational Review*, vol. 28, no. 2, Spring 1958, pp. 105–119; and N. L. Whetten, *Rural Mexico*, University of Chicago Press, 1948.

88. Segura, op. cit.

89. Severin K. Turosienski, *Education in Cuba*, U.S. Government Printing Office, Office of Education, Bulletin 1943, No. 1, Washington, D.C., 1943.

90. Cameron D. Ebaugh, *Education in Peru*, U.S. Government Printing Office, Office of Education, Bulletin 1946, No. 3, Washington, D.C., 1946.

91. See Delia Goetz, *Education in Venezuela*, U.S. Government Printing Office, Office of Education, Bulletin 1948, No. 14, Washington, D.C., 1948.

92. George K. Benjamin, "Community Goes to School in Guatemala," *Educational Outlook*, vol. 26, no. 3, March 1952, pp. 91–101.

93. See Manuel Alers-Montalvo, "Cultural Missions in a Costa Rican Village," unpublished doctoral dissertation, Michigan State University, 1953.

94. Jose Arthur Rios, "Co-operation and Integration in Community Development: Brazilian Experience," *Fundamental and Adult Education,* vol. 9, no. 2, April 1957, pp. 66–71.

95. Walter H. C. Laves and Charles A. Thompson, *UNESCO: Purpose, Progress, Prospects,* Indiana University Press, Bloomington, Indiana, 1957, p. 157.

96. UNESCO, *Fundamental Education: Description and Programme,* Monographs in Fundamental Education, No. 1, Paris, 1949.

97. Laves and Thompson, op. cit., p. 161.

98. Houghton and Tregear, op. cit., p. 69.

99. Quoted in Bernardino, 1958, p. 94.

100. Ibid.

101. Whetten, op. cit.

102. Robert Redfield, *A Village that Chose Progress; Chan Kom Revisited,* University of Chicago publications in Anthropology, Social Anthropology Series, University of Chicago Press, 1950, pp. 146–147.

103. La Belle, op. cit.

104. Bernardino, op. cit.

105. Anibal Buitron, "Adult Education and the Second Development Decade," *Convergence,* vol. 4, no. 1, 1971, pp. 35–39.

106. Whetten, op. cit., pp. 445–446.

107. Among other programs for national development, the Philippine community schools deserve mention. They are promoted by the Ministry of Education, use teachers as change agents to work with parents and children for community development, and attempt to foster curricular relevance to community needs and interests. Like their *barrio* high school counterparts, they involve students in community service projects. The community schools are not, however, characterized by either self-financing or local control. See, for example, UNESCO, *National Commission Report on Six Community Schools of the Philippines,* Bureau of Printing, Manila, 1954; Isabelo Tupas, and Vitaliano Bernardino, *Philippine Rural Problems and the Community School,* Jose C. Velo Publishing House, 1955; and Bernardino, 1957.

108. *Basic Education in India: Report of the Assessment Committee on Basic Education,* Ministry of Education, Government of India, New Delhi, 1950.

109. *Report of the Education Commission 1957–1966: Education and National Development,* Ministry of Education, Government of India, New Delhi, 1966, p. 224.

110. M. S. Patel, *The Educational Philosophy of Mahatma Gandhi,* Navajivan Publishing House, Ahmedabad, 1953; D. M. Datta, *The Philosophy of Mahatma Gandhi,* University of Wisconsin Press, Madison, 1953;

Mahatma K. Gandhi, *Basic Education,* Navajivan Publishing House, Ahmedabad, 1951; and Mahatma Gandhi, *Toward New Education,* Navajivan Publishing House, Ahmedabad, 1953.

111. T. M. Thomas, *Indian Educational Reforms in Cultural Perspective,* S. Chand and Co., Delhi, 1970.

112. Quoted in Basic National Education, 1938, p. 10.

113. Mahatma Gandhi, *True Education,* Navajivan Publishing House, Ahmedabad, 1962.

114. Gandhi, *Toward New Education,* op. cit., p. 39.

115. *Educational Reconstruction: A Collection of Gandhiji's Activities on the Wardha Scheme,* Hindustani Talimi Sangh, Wardha, 1950, p. 63.

116. Bakhshish Saini, "Administrative Problems Connected with the Gandhian Plan of Education in India," unpublished Ph.D. dissertation, University of California, Berkeley, 1966; G. Ramachandran, "Practical Difficulties in Basic Education," *Journal of Mysore State Education Federation,* vol. 1, May 1956.

117. Thomas, op. cit., and M. Zachariah, "Public Authority and Village Reconstruction: The Case of Basic Education in India," *The Journal of Educational Thought,* vol. 4, no. 2, August 1970, pp. 94–106.

118. Another example of community schools for national development are the *Taman Siswa* schools of Indonesia. They began as an independent school system in 1922 and were designed to provide an indigenous response to Dutch colonial education. The mandated curriculum is community-centered at the lower levels and there is an emphasis on self-instruction and vocational skills as well as on instilling pride in one's national heritage. In recent years, a growing number of schools have come under the direct control of the government. See Arthur H. Pickard, "Taman Siswa and the Among System," unpublished Ph.D. dissertation, University of California, Los Angeles, 1971.

119. A. B. Eafunwa, *History of Education in Nigeria,* Allen and Unwin, London, 1974, p. 122.

120. Ibid., p. 124.

121. Ibid., p. 134.

122. J. Cameron and W. A. Ward, *Society, Schools and Progress in Tanzania,* Pergamon Press, Oxford, 1970.

123. Quoted in ibid., p. 225.

124. Ibid.

125. Laura S. Kurtz, *An African Education: The Social Revolution in Tanzania,* Pagenat-Poseidon, Brooklyn, 1972.

126. John N. Hawkins, "Deschooling Society Chinese Style: Alternative Forms of Non-Formal Education," *Educational Studies,* vol. 4, no. 3, Fall 1973, pp. 113–123.

127. T. Hsien Chen, *The Maoist Educational Revolution,* Praeger, 1974.

128. Ibid., p. 24.

129. Ibid.

130. R. F. Price, *Education in Communist China,* Praeger, New York, 1970.

131. Hawkins, op. cit.

132. Ibid.

133. Chen, op. cit.

134. Hawkins, op. cit.

135. Chen, op. cit.

136. Ibid., and Hawkins, op. cit.

137. Hawkins, op. cit.

138. Ibid.

139. Thomas J. La Belle and Robert E. Verhine, "Education, Social Change, and Social Stratification," in Thomas J. La Belle (ed.), *Educational Alternatives in Latin America, Social Change, and Social Stratification,* UCLA Latin American Center, Los Angeles, 1975, pp. 3–71.

140. Thomas J. La Belle, "Alternative Educational Strategies: The Integration of Learning Systems in the Community," in John I. Goodlad (ed.), *Alternatives in Education,* McCutchan Publishing Co., 1975, pp. 165–188.

9

COMMUNITY EDUCATION AND COMMUNITY SCHOOLS

JACK D. MINZEY
Eastern Michigan University

Whether "community education" is a new educational phenomenon or an idea of long historical standing depends on who is telling the story. To some, community education's first beginnings can be traced to biblical times, and certain vestiges can be found throughout history. These community educators claim, for example, that the essence of the concept can be found in writings such as Plato's *Republic* and Sir Thomas More's *Utopia*. To others, community education is of more recent vintage.

Over the past half-century, the writings of Henry Bernard, Joseph K. Hart, and Elsie Clapp developed an awareness of the potential of community education, and the works of John Dewey also focused attention on this area. The National Society for the Study of Education, Fifty-second Yearbook, Part II, published in 1953, has become a classic in the community education field, and in 1959, the same society's fifty-eighth yearbook focused on the international aspects of community education. As pointed out in Chapter 8, many countries have developed some type of community education, and most states in the United States have had at least one community education project.

THE FLINT STORY

The community which has received the greatest recognition for its identification with community education is Flint, Michigan. While this acclaim is not based on originating the concept, Flint is credited with developing and generating a community education program which is more nearly complete and of longer duration than any other. The Flint community-education program is also more sophisticated than many others. Its historical development demonstrates an important change in community education which not only illustrates the maturation of the concept, but also accounts for some of the more recent interest in this idea.

The Flint story began in the 1930s with the employment of Frank Manley as physical education director in the Flint Schools. Manley was concerned about the juvenile-delinquency problem in the city and felt that developing a recreation program for the youth of the community, using the schools as recreation centers, would result in a solution. He was able to enlist the financial assistance of Charles Stewart Mott, a Flint industrial leader, and a recreation program was begun.

Unfortunately, a simple solution to the juvenile delinquency problem was not forthcoming. However, during the ensuing years, the concept moved from a program of recreation for children and youth to activities for all community members, over and above the regular school program and primarily based in the schools.

This accretion of programs did provide for some very definite community needs, and the offerings expanded from recreational activities to avocational and leisure-time activities and, eventually, included adult high school–completion programs as well as courses teaching adults to read and write. In fact, the general idea was to attempt to provide programming for all types of identified community educational needs.

One of the most important aspects of the Flint community schools was their impact on other communities throughout the United States. It became the goal of the Mott Foundation, a philanthropic organization created by C. S. Mott, to develop the community school concept to the ultimate in Flint and to bring interested persons to Flint to observe this program so that they might take some of the ideas back to their own communities.

This plan proved to be quite successful. Since the 1950s, literally thousands of people have visited Flint, and many of the existing community school districts credit Flint with some degree of influence on their community education programs.

The Flint story has one other interesting aspect which is more recent in development but which has the potential for making still another contribution to the concept of community education. For the first forty years of its operation, community education in Flint was primarily programmatic, offering various kinds of classes and activities to the community. In 1972, the school board moved to make community education a more integral part of the school system. The Board of Education identified two goals for the Flint community schools: to help every citizen of Flint become the best person he is capable of becoming, and to help every neighborhood become the best community possible. To do this, they have made the goals of the school district compatible with the goals of community education and have expanded the programmatic part of the community school to embrace other, more recently, identified aspects of the concept, such as agency interaction and community council development. This action by the Flint School Board has moved these activities from programs of an add-on nature to an idea which suggests a new role for the public schools—a new concept of public education.

CURRENT STATUS OF COMMUNITY EDUCATION

The community education movement grew slowly between the years 1930 and 1965. In the late 1960s, however, the number of school districts identified as being involved in community education began to multiply at an ever increasing rate, and by 1977 there were in excess of

1,000 such school districts. This resulted in over 5,000 separate school buildings identified as community schools with the accompanying number of staff, participants, and expenditures. There were also over 100 "Centers for Community Education" which included universities, state departments of education, and other regional centers for dissemination, implementation, and training related to community education. National publications such as *Phi Delta Kappan, Community Education Journal, National Elementary Principal, National Association of Secondary School Principals Bulletin, Leisure Today,* and *The Journal of Teacher Education* have all devoted entire issues to community education, while other publications have given the concept considerable visibility. A national community education organization was begun in 1966, and by 1977, thirty-eight state or regional organizations were affiliated with the movement. Also, by 1977, eight states had supportive community education legislation and another six states were strongly considering such legislation. Federal supporting legislation was passed in 1974, and the first-year funding resulted in the addition of thirteen community education projects in institutions of higher education, forty-eight programs in local school districts, and state department of education positions for community education in thirty-three states. Each successive year of funding has seen continued growth nationally at both the state and local level.

The obvious rapid increase in community education, particularly over the past ten years, has caused many people to speculate on the reasons for such growth. Of course, one must recognize the contributions, both motivational and financial, of the Mott Foundation. It seems unlikely, however, that the total growth of the movement can be explained entirely on this basis. More likely, it is a combination of things related to several factors.

One of these contributing factors has to do with the complexity of modern society. The German sociologist Ferdinand Tönnes suggested that two types of societies exist, the *Gemeinschaft* and the *Gesellschaft*.[1] The *Gemeinschaft*, he believed, represented the simple small-town relationships of people, and the *Gesellschaft* the complex, and often distant, urban relationships. In the old *Gemeinschaft* society, the community had certain advantages simply because it was small. People interacted on a more personal basis, and there was truly a "sense of community." Such communities were characterized by kinship, informal controls, many community activities, belongingness, participation, identity, and a secure community base which made it possible to deal effectively with other communities.

However, our social structure has gone through many changes in which the underlying assumption is that "bigger is better." This has resulted in large, complex, urban communities characterized by indifference, anonymity, rigid formal controls, impersonal relationships, anxieties, and alienation. This larger *Gesellschaft* society has also been identified with many of the current problems plaguing society, such as poverty, unemployment, bad housing, and high crime rates. It is the feeling of many community educators that if we could recapture the feelings and characteristics of the smaller *Gemeinschaft* type of society, we would have reidentified that unit of community which results in the positive characteristics so essential to good community development.

Another factor related to the current interest in community education has to do with participatory democracy. It is the contention of those who support this argument that we do not presently have a democracy but an oligarchy in which opportunities for input are based on two characteristics: wealth and education. While it does appear that there is limited involvement on the basis of the larger community, participation at the neighborhood level is missing. People who advance this line of thinking see community education as a method of returning participatory democracy to the neighborhood, much in the same vein as suggested by Eric Hoffer who said:

> It remains to be seen whether it is possible to have a society free from want in which most people feel that they are growing, that they are realizing capacities and mastering skills, and have neither the time nor the inclination to do harm to their fellow men. My guess is that the unity of creative society will not be a county or a parish but a school district. The country will be divided into thousands of school districts, each responsible for the realization of the natural and human resources within a relatively small area.
>
> The unfolding of human capacities requires a social unit in which people of different pursuits, interests, skills and tastes know each other, commune daily with each other, emulate, antagonize and spur each other.[2]

A third argument advanced for the growth of community education is that for the public school it really implies a return to the role which schools used to play in society and one which communities would still like them to provide. Schools have always been expected by their communities to help strengthen the community and assist in solving community problems. As school districts have grown larger and become more bureaucratized, they have adopted management styles and procedures which have removed schools from their identification with the community. Proponents of this argument point out that the community education idea is gaining acceptance because communities are anxious to remove their schools from the hands of the professional educator and return them to the goals which reinforce community identity and community values.

Still another argument explains the growth in terms of community demands for attention to broader community needs which are going unattended. This argument, like the previous one, points to the increasing number of citizens committees and councils and cites community education as an outgrowth of insistence by communities that education be more accountable to the community it is supposed to serve. Education is charged with foisting many hypocrisies on society in which the actions of the schools do not reflect the goals which they purport to support. Communities are aware that schools talk of relevancy but are really quite removed from the realities of life; pay lip service to community involvement but only get involved with very symbiotic community organizations; speak of the children as a *gestalt* but operate as though all their educational life occurred inside the walls of the school; and promote education as a lifetime process but imply that that lifetime exists only between the ages of five and eighteen. In light of these inconsistencies, communities are demanding an elimination of these hypocrisies as well as attention to some things which schools have not typically provided in the past. They are asking for greater public use of school facilities, education for adults, assistance by the schools in the solution of community problems, attention to the special needs of segments of the community other than children, elimination of duplication of services, and community involvement in decision making. To many people, community education stands as a possible technique for getting schools to be more responsive to a wider range of demands by the community.

Of course, there are other reasons for this increased interest in community education, including some ulterior reasons held by school people themselves. Whatever the reason or combination of reasons, however, there is a considerable amount of evidence to suggest that the community education concept has captured the imagination of many communities throughout the United States.

WHAT IS COMMUNITY EDUCATION?

Like other ideas, community education suffers from the many attempts to define it. Community education is a term which denotes different things to different people, and the fact that it has been used synonymously with programs such as adult education, recreation, community service, and community development has caused consternation to many people. The resulting confusion has tended to retard the potential of its development.

There have been many attempts to define community education over the years. The following are some examples:

Elsie Clapp, 1939:

> First of all, it meets as best it can with everyone's help, the urgent needs of people, for it holds that everything that affects the welfare of the children and their families is its concern. Where does school end and life outside begin? There is no distinction between them. A community school is a used place, a place used freely and informally for all the needs of living and learning. It is, in effect, the place where learning and living converge.[3]

Jack Minzey and Clarence Olsen, 1969:

> Community education is a process that concerns itself with everything that affects the well-being of all citizens within a given community. This definition extends the role of community education from one of the traditional concept of teaching children to one of identifying the needs, problems, and wants of the community and then assisting in the development of facilities, programs, staff and leadership toward the end of improving the entire community.[4]

National Community Education Association, 1968:

> Community School Education is a comprehensive and dynamic approach to public education. It is a philosophy that pervades all segments of education programming and directs the thrust of each of them toward the needs of the community. The community school serves as a catalytic agent by providing leadership to mobilize community resources to solve identified community problems. The marshalling of all forces in the community helps to bring about change as the school extends itself to all people.[5]

Maurice Seay, 1945:

> Community school is the term currently applied to a school that has two distinctive emphases—service to the entire community, not merely to the children of school age; and discovery, development, and use of the resources of the community as part of the educational facilities of the school.[6]

Maurice Seay, 1953:

> In a community school the problems of the people and the types
> and nature of resources available become the core of the educa-
> tional program. Thus, education is put to work; it is seen as a
> power in the solution of the problems of people.[7]

Jack Minzey and Clyde La Tarte, 1973:

> Community education is a philosophical concept which serves the
> entire community by providing for all of the educational needs of
> all of its community members. It uses the local school to serve as
> a catalyst for bringing community resources to bear on commu-
> nity problems in an effort to develop a positive sense of commu-
> nity, improve community living, and develop a community pro-
> cess toward the end of self-actualization.[8]

The formal definitions of community education tend to have a high
degree of similarity. The problem with community education seems to
occur in the implementation of the concept. The difference between
concept and practice is frequently epitomized by a heavy emphasis on
program development without equal development of the community
aspects of community education, such as citizen involvement and community problem solving.

The problem in defining is also compounded by interchanging the
terms "community education" and "community schools." While many
persons have not been discriminating in the use of these terms, it is
important that the relationship between them be identified in order to
understand the concept properly. It is true that at one time the two
terms were used to describe the same phenomena. This has changed.
Community education now refers to the education beyond what is traditionally meant by that term. In the past, the word education has been
used synonymously with schooling, which implies a very specific kind
of education. In the present interpretation of education, the term is
defined as any experience which helps an individual cope with other
activities which he encounters. The term community education, then,
applies to all of the resources of the community which have an impact
on the education of the community and its members toward the end of
meeting all community needs and helping the community to grow.
These resources include the formal, informal, institutional, and individual programs and processes.

In the community education concept, all agencies, institutions, and individuals have a role to play in helping the community to grow educationally. Each must identify its role in terms of community needs and decide how they might best apply their expertise in concert with all of the other resources.

The community school is one of the institutions which must reidentify its appropriate role under the concept of community education. It is not the only institution to be concerned with community education nor is it to be the dominating force in this movement. The school functions within the philosophy of community education by doing what it does best while at the same time maximizing the efforts of others seeking to accomplish the goals of community education. Community education is the concept and the community school is one of the mechanisms for implementing this concept.

Community education has evolved from a series of programs added on to the traditional school to a philosophy of education which implies an expanded new role for public schools. This new role continues to be concerned with the traditional role of educating the typical school-aged child but, in addition, accepts some responsibilities which have not previously been perceived as public school responsibilities. To state this in another way, it might be said that public schools which have accepted the community education concept have also accepted an accountability model that includes areas of responsibility far greater than those generally assigned to schools in the past.

DESCRIBING RATHER THAN DEFINING

In order to get a better understanding of community schools, it may be helpful to examine these new areas of responsibility in more detail. In fact, an examination of the components of a community school will probably provide more understanding of community schools and their role in community education than can be gained from an examination of various definitions.

A school district which commits itself to community education and the development of community schools accepts the following six responsibilities:

1. *An educational program for school age children.* This component refers to the traditional programs offered by all school districts. It is frequently called the K–12 (kindergarten through twelfth grade) or day school program. This, of course, is a vital part of the school educational program, and every attempt should be made to expand and improve it. Of particular importance under the community education concept would be the stress on relevance, community involvement, and the use of community resources to enhance

classroom teaching. This program will be greatly strengthened if it is tied in with the other components of a community school. As contrasted with the typical view of public education, the K–12 program is a vital part but not the *only* part of public education.

2. *Maximum use of school facilities.* School buildings, usually the most costly facilities in the community, are often used only a small percentage of the time they could be available for student and community use. Many times, new buildings are constructed for community centers, recreation centers, or boys' clubs while school buildings stand idle. School facilities should be used for all types of community needs and their maximum use assured before new facilities are constructed. New school construction or renovation of old school buildings should be based on community specifications so that school buildings reflect the needs of the total community. A corollary idea considers maximum use of all other community buildings as well, such as fire halls, churches, civic buildings, and recreation facilities.

3. *Additional programs for children and youth.* This aspect of a community school presumes an increasing need for additional educational activities for school-age youngsters. Despite the ever-increasing amount of knowledge available to our society, students are exposed to formal education for shorter periods of time than they were fifteen years ago. The reduction in the school day and school year has resulted in students being forced to make choices in their educational programs rather than being able to pursue the kinds of educational experiences they both want and need. For example, students frequently must decide between band or gym, art or foreign language, choir or science, and so on because there is not enough time in the school day to accommodate all of the educational experiences they would like to have. By expanding the educational and activity offerings before and after the regular school day, on weekends, and during the summer, students have an opportunity for enrichment, remedial and supplemental educational activities, as well as recreational, cultural, vocational, and avocational experiences. These expanded program offerings can serve not only in-school youth, but preschool children and out-of-school youth as well.

4. *Programs for adults.* An important aspect of this component of a community school is that educational programs are recognized as being as important for adults as they are for the traditional school population. Included would be such programs as basic literacy education, high school completion, recreational, avocational, cultural, and vocational education. The student body, for educational purposes, would be all the people who reside in the community.

One additional advantage of this component of a community school is that through the education of adults, the schools will have an increased impact on the traditional school-age youngster in terms of better educational attainment and attitudes. We have known for many years that much of what our children learn comes from the community. By influencing the education of the adults in the community, schools can have a substantial influence on a child's education, over and above that which they already have.

5. *Delivery of community services.* One of the key problems in providing community services is that there is an expectation that people will come to where services are offered rather than taking the services to where people are located. Existing services of all kinds are encouraged, whenever possible, to use the school as a distribution point. The school would not provide the service, but would offer space in the school so that agencies, governmental units, and other groups can bring their services as near to the source of need as possible.

6. *Community development through community councils.* This phase of a community school has often been described in relation to "participatory democracy." The purpose is to assist people in a particular neighborhood in dealing with their own problems. The school aids in the development of community councils and provides the training and leadership necessary to help these councils become viable organizations which can deal with both problem identification and problem solving.

HOW DOES THE SCHOOL FUNCTION IN THIS NEW ROLE?
The basic unit for the successful operation of a community school is the elementary school. A fundamental premise underlying the community education concept is the belief that the deterioration of our communities is an outgrowth of the increase in size of these communities. As our communities have grown larger, they have lost many of the benefits which occurred naturally in smaller communities. The assumption is that we could make larger communities more viable if we could break them into smaller communities which are of such a size that human interaction and community identity can more appropriately take place. There is a kind of social-geometric principle implied which assumes that the larger community is equal to the sum of its parts. If the parts are developed to their maximum, the larger community will be better as a result.

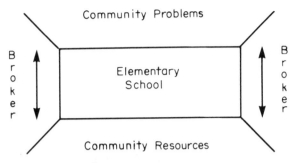

Figure 1 - Role of a Community School

Since most communities are already divided into smaller communities identified as elementary school attendance areas, it is suggested that this become the basic unit for the development of community education. The role of the elementary school in this setting becomes one of applying the components of a community school to the neighborhood community. This is shown graphically in Figure 1.

The elementary school serves as the facility from which the community school staff operates. The principal of the building is accountable for all six components of a community school. He or she will have additional staff to assist in carrying out the responsibilities involved. Additional staff may consist of a community school director, paraprofessionals, volunteers, and perhaps other professional personnel. By means of various techniques, and particularly through the development of a community council, problems within the community are identified. Resources available to the community are also identified. These resources include such things as health services, governmental services, recreation services, adult education programs, community colleges, universities, private schools, kindergarten through twelfth grade services, library services, and all other agencies and groups available to the citizens in that area. Also included should be the human resources of the community. The main function of the community school is to provide the leadership and the catalytic role necessary to relate the problems of the community to the resources available.

The result is a system which operates in the following way. When problems are identified for which resources are already available, the method of operation is simply one of making the existing resources aware of the problems. It is then the responsibility of these resources to provide their expertise to help solve the problems. While the description seems overly simplistic, the fact is that many community problems are not being resolved primarily because the servicing agencies are not aware of the extent of existing problems or the location of persons eligible for their services.

In other instances, there will be problems identified which are not being met by the agencies which are supposed to be responsible. The community school will make these agencies aware of the problems, and the agencies will be expected to provide solutions or coordinate their services with others in order to develop appropriate programs to solve the identified problems. The important point is that the responsibility for service is placed with the agency or group which has the appropriate expertise. This provides a system which makes community members aware of those responsible for serving them. It also means that services will be organized around existing needs rather than perceived needs.

In still a third situation, problems will be identified for which there are no agencies either willing or able to help. The local community, through its own resources, will now have to develop its own programs to meet these needs. This allows the community to take action without waiting for long periods of time before their problems are treated by a larger governmental unit. People will also engage in the gratifying process of dealing with their own problems through community action. Thus, communities are able not only to get maximum service from existing agencies, but they are also able to deal more effectively with their own problems when no appropriate resource exists.

EXEMPLARY PRACTICES

Prior to 1965, there were probably no more than a dozen communities which operated as community school districts. By 1977, however, there were more than 1,000 school districts supporting the idea of community education and expanding their areas of responsibility to encompass this philosophy.

While these districts represent varying degrees of development and maturity in relation to community education, there are several that might be listed as exemplary and scores that could be rated as good or even outstanding. The following have been randomly selected from the many which have been identified as exceptional. The programs are described as they existed at the time this chapter was written. Changes may have taken place since, but the examples are still informative as illustrations of school districts which have adopted the community education concept.

Flint, Michigan, continues to be perceived as *the* community school district in the United States. This is the result of a combination of the length of time Flint has spent developing this concept, the fact that the school district leadership has continued to be identified with community education, and the generous funding or community education by the Mott Foundation. In excess of 10,000 people a year come to Flint to observe the Flint community schools, and many of the community schools in the country received their inspiration from what they have observed in Flint.

Flint is an industrial community, the second largest city in Michigan and the birthplace of General Motors. It is currently highly identified with the automobile industry and has been since the early 1900s. The city of Flint has 193,000 residents, of which approximately 30 percent are black.

Community schools in Flint had their beginning in 1935 when Frank J. Manley convinced Charles Stewart Mott to provide funding for a recreational program in the schools as a means of taking young people off the streets. These programs evolved so that eventually hundreds of programs were offered to persons of all age groups in the city. These included career education, alternative education, compensatory education, special education, enrichment, remedial education, recreation, and cultural programs. The range of programs offered to the community presently numbers about 3,500 and has become as extensive as anywhere in the country. Enrollments in programs other than the regular day school often exceed 90,000, and enrollment in the adult high school is greater than in any of the city's four regular high schools.

For the first several years of operation, the programs were primarily an appendage to the regular instructional program. In 1972, the Flint Board of Education decided to integrate the K–12 in-school programs with their community education program. This new direction is best described by the following statement from the Flint community school catalog:

Community education runs through the entire fabric of the Flint Community Schools as it attempts to improve the quality of living in Flint. More than an extension of the traditional school system, community education is a sustained attack on community problems and concerns that affect the learner. Community education recognizes that life experiences are an important part of education and that a school system cannot effectively operate isolated from life. The providing of recreational, adult and continuing education, as well as a variety of community and social services, is part of this positive influence. But more importantly, community education attempts to involve citizens of all walks of life in identifying conditions and resources as the central means for uplifting the community. In Flint, community education is viewed as an evolving lifelong process, wherein the school and the community join hands to meet the needs of the individual and the community.[9]

In addition to the multitude of programs which have continued to develop in Flint, community councils have also been established. In 1972, a citywide task force developed guidelines for establishing local community councils at each school within the district and in 1974, these councils developed their own goals and objectives, identified their membership, and began operation. These councils have not only been involved with the traditional educational needs of the community, they have also dealt with such neighborhood and social problems as housing, traffic safety, drug abuse, unemployment, crime, and school integration. Basically, the main function of these councils is to study the problems and needs of their community and plan cooperative action to deal with these problems.

Brockton, Massachusetts, is an urban area with a population of 96,-000 people and a school population of 21,500. This community became interested in community education in 1969 and, through their community school committee, developed a program which began in 1970. They have developed a policy for public use of facilities and have organized hundreds of classes for people of all ages. They have encouraged inter-agency cooperation in their district, and have a community education coordinator and a community council at each of their neighborhood schools.

The Springfield community schools of Springfield, Ohio, have been in operation since 1966. This community of 90,000 people has 14,000 students in its school system. Starting with six community schools in 1969, there are now community school programs in twenty-four of the twenty-nine school buildings. Like other community school districts, Springfield has extensive programming for both youth and adults. Springfield was one of the first districts to ask the community to finance the community school program from local tax monies, and the community passed such a request in 1969. School officials feel that the positive attitude generated by community education had much to do with the passage of a 12.7 million dollar bond issue in the spring of 1976.

The St. Louis City School District in St. Louis, Missouri, became interested in community education in 1966. At that time, representatives of the Board of Education, the Health and Welfare Council, and several other agencies traveled to Flint to view their program. In January 1968, the Board of Education allocated $40,000 for the implementation of community education at one St. Louis school. This program has now grown to ten schools and encompasses all of the aspects of a community school: programs, cooperation with agencies, and local community councils.

The Jefferson County School System in Alabama serves a population of 350,000 people and got its start in community education in 1972. Thirteen community schools were in operation in 1977, and Jefferson County is moving toward identifying its schools as "Human Resource Centers." The school system has not only used its own facilities in meeting program needs. Apartment complexes, churches, houses, and industrial buildings have also been identified as sites for community education activities. The school board has also approved the policy of providing a gymnasium and community facilities for each elementary building. One hundred fifty-eight different agencies and organizations are officially listed as groups which cooperate in the community school program. There is an advisory committee at each of the community schools, and representatives from these councils serve on the regional and systemwide councils.

Many other large school districts across the country have received recognition for the quality of their community school programs. Detroit and Grand Rapids, Michigan; Miami, Florida; Minneapolis, Minnesota; Charleston, West Virginia; and Ogden, Utah, are but a few.

However, community education has not been just a large–school district phenomenon. Actually, in total numbers, more smaller school districts have adopted this concept than large ones. For example, the Ishpeming and Negauenee school districts have combined to form a joint community school operation. These two districts in the Upper Peninsula of Michigan have a student population of 1,800 and 1,900 respectively and serve an area of 800 square miles. The program began in 1968 and has grown rapidly since. This program emphasizes community use of facilities, programs for children and adults in the area of recreation and enrichment, and numerous cultural activities. Adult high school and adult basic education are offered along with special activities such as "Big Brothers" and senior-citizen activities. One very special activity is the "Winter Olympics" which includes all the communities in the Upper Peninsula and attracts thousands of participants and spectators each year. Several agencies are also cooperating with the schools, and this has had a significant impact on the traditional school program.

The Comal Independent School District in New Braunfels, Texas, is another example of a small school district which has developed an enviable community school program. This rural community is a consolidated school district with a student population of 3,400 and a total population of 14,000. Their program began with adult education and, in 1973, expanded into a community school program. This district uses the schools, churches, and some industrial facilities and offers programs to all age groups. The problems in scheduling are somewhat different than in larger communities, since there is no public transportation, and 80 percent of the students ride a school bus. Various community agencies use the school facilities, and much of the programming is for people who do not have children in school. Special projects have included bringing the services of the Community Action Agency and Mental Health Services to the community. There has also been a major effort to provide the community with preventive health services. Neighborhood advisory councils are an integral part of the program, and each facility has an advisory council. In addition, a communitywide advisory council is utilized for project planning, implementation, and evaluation.

Still another example of a smaller community with community education is Bedford Township, Michigan. Bedford covers thirty-nine square miles and is located in the Southeast corner of Michigan. It is a "bedroom" community with many of its residents working in Toledo, Ohio.

The Bedford School District came about as a result of the consolidation of three rural communities. During the early 1950s, rapid growth doubled the student population from 2,400 to 4,800 with the following results:

1. Half-day sessions for thirteen years
2. Distrust of governmental units and newcomers
3. Failure of bond and millage issues
4. Poor teacher salaries and inadequate educational programs

In 1968, under the direction of a new superintendent of schools, efforts were begun to change the image of this community. One of the techniques used was the adoption of community education. A number of advisory groups, commissions, and committees were established, and the result was the Bedford community school curriculum which consisted of the following:

1. Pre-school programs
2. Student education, enrichment, and recreation
3. Adult education, enrichment, and recreation
4. Senior-citizen programs
5. Community services

The program is staffed by both professionals and paraprofessionals, backed by a cadre of 250 volunteers. There are approximately sixty formal programs throughout the year. A summer program involves most of the community and operates through eight community centers. Building usage has greatly increased, and the community school budget has grown from under $20,000 to over $275,000. The program has proved to be so successful that hundreds of people come to view it each year, and some of its programs and goals were used to develop parts of the federal guidelines for community education legislation.

It would be wrong to leave the impression that the communities described are the most outstanding or are the only districts with recognized community school programs. As mentioned earlier, in excess of 1,000 school districts in 1977 were identified as community education districts, and hundreds of these are worthy of review. The districts mentioned here were somewhat randomly selected as examples of community education school districts. Other programs, many of them exceptional, can be identified through the National Community Education Association, State Departments of Education, or the several Centers for Community Education located at various institutions of higher education across the country.

SOME FAILURES

It would also be wrong to imply that community education has not had its failures. To be sure, the implementation and continuation of community education in the school districts described above have not been without some degree of frustration and confrontation. There have been challenges from several groups and apprehension expressed by many, generally in the form of listing all the reasons why schools should not and cannot engage in such activities.

Some community school programs that were started were later aborted. The failures have been few, however. In one region of the United States, the number of school districts beginning community education grew from 7 to 120 over a ten-year period. Of that number, only three subsequently dropped their identity with community education.

Certain factors that may account for the failures seem to appear in each of the districts which did eliminate community schools. In each case, there was not total awareness of the potential of community education nor a commitment to the concept by the top leadership or board of education. As a result, the kind of support needed, both professional and financial, was not forthcoming.

A second reason for failure has been the haste with which the concept was implemented. Effective change requires adequate time for moving in new directions, including giving people an opportunity to understand the change and to learn how to adjust to it. In the case of some of the failures, the program was investigated, announced, and operational in a few short months. As a result, it did not have time to develop a comfortable relationship with people in the community, and its rapid implementation caused it eventually to be rejected.

A third reason for failure has been the reluctance of those promoting community education to gain the support of the school staff and provide in-service training. Since community education has been primarily promoted as "school based," it becomes very important that school personnel, such as principals, teachers, and auxiliary staff, understand and support the concept. Many school districts have begun community education in spite of school personnel and, as a result, have seen their efforts sabotaged, not by direct confrontation but by more subtle and passive techniques.

A fourth reason for failure has resulted from employing poorly trained personnel to direct the program. Untrained persons, not grasping the total meaning of the concept, develop programs that are not based on community needs, fail to involve people in a meaningful way, duplicate programs of other groups and agencies, and antagonize the traditional school staff. The constant negative ramifications of such an approach soon destroy any possibility the program might have had for success.

In the vast majority of cases, however, community education through the schools has succeeded and is continuing to flourish. Probably the primary reason for this is community support. Without question, the group most credited with bringing the community education concept to the schools is the community.

Granted there has been some community resistance from community groups who lack confidence in their schools and who object to giving schools a broader role, but these groups are often speaking for vested interests rather than for the community at large. Typical of such community challenges are statements that schools should not be all things to all people, that the only role of the school is to educate children, and that community education, with its emphasis on neighborhood, cannot co-exist with the idea of busing school children for integration. While these are certainly legitimate and often emotion-laden issues, they do not often deter community support of the community education concept.

To understand why, it is important to review again the purposes of community education through community schools. The school is attempting to bring more effective education to the community. It is not designed to solve all the problems of society or, for that matter, all the problems of traditional kindergarten through twelfth grade programs. Instead, it is an expanded role for the public schools which, if carried out, would result in better services to, and more involvement of, the community than at present.

More specifically, the school accepts the responsibility for making greater use of its facilities for community activities as well as student activities, for providing educational programs for both children and adults above and beyond what is already being provided, for serving as a clearinghouse for people with needs to locate resources responsible for serving them, and for helping neighborhood communities develop local councils for the identification and solution of their problems.

Recognizing that 80 percent of the adults who live in a community do not have children in the public schools and that an even higher percentage do not have children in the local elementary school, it becomes apparent why this concept appeals to most community members. It is very likely that many community members have some interest in the educational programs and problems of the local schools. However, they also have a keen interest in their own needs, many of which could be greatly aided through the community school approach. As educational costs spiral upward and their own needs go unattended, they are more often asking, "What's in it for me?" They do not see their requests for attention to their needs infringing on the rights of traditional students. In fact, there is substantial evidence that the problems of the traditional schools are more appropriately addressed through community schools than by the current method of school operation.

IMPLEMENTATION OF COMMUNITY SCHOOLS

Of course, community support by itself is not enough. Procedures for implementation are also important. During the past ten years of intensive development of community education, several principles have been learned which, while not assuring success, at least tend to offer a greater chance for the acceptance of a community education program in the local school district. These principles are described in the following steps:

Step 1: Exploration of the concept with the school administration and school board is important. Both groups should allocate enough time so that they have a complete understanding of the concept and its ramifications. If they are not ready to provide both personal and financial support to developing such a program, then it is probably premature to proceed. If they do find that they can give such support, then they should move to Step 2.

Step 2: A task force should be appointed by the board to develop a plan for the district. This task force should be representative of the community and should be charged with the responsibility of developing a proposal for the board of education.

Step 3: Through in-service, materials, visitations, and exposure to professionals and practitioners, task force members should develop a sophisticated understanding of the concept of community education and the role a public school can play in such a concept. They should also develop an understanding of their community through data collection and an exposure to various segments of the community.

Step 4: While the task force is at work, efforts should be made to expose the community to the concept of community education and its implications for their schools. This can be done by circulating materials, using the news media, and making presentations to various community groups. It is important that the community be prepared for the work the task force is doing.

Step 5: On the basis of their knowledge of community education and the community, the task force prepares a proposal on community schools and submits it to the school board. Included in the proposal would be such things as current community education activities, resources, strategies for implementation, financing, staffing, and organization.

Step 6: If the proposal is accepted by the board of education, then the plan is implemented. The adoption of the proposal is quite likely if the preceding steps have been followed properly.

These steps have not been arbitrarily selected. They are the result of lessons learned through several years of working with school districts by scores of Community Education Center Directors located at many universities and state departments of education. The procedure does tend to deal with the problems identified earlier related to lack of support from the top, awareness by the community, and lack of understanding of the concept. It should be pointed out that this procedure is time-consuming and will eliminate the problem of programs begun in haste. It also provides for uniqueness of programs and thus eliminates the pitfalls of copying someone else's plan.

PROBLEMS AND ISSUES

Community education, like any concept, is not without its share of problems. Some of these were alluded to in the previous discussion of reasons for failure of community education in some school districts. However, it might be helpful to explore these problems in more global terms.

One major issue that continues to plague community educators has to do with defining the concept. The problem seems to center around the failure of those involved with community education to conceptualize the magnitude of their idea and the extent of its potential. In general, many community school directors tend to identify with portions of the concept rather than the concept itself; to be satisfied with a part rather than the whole. Instead of stressing their role as energizer or facilitator for other resources, they often attempt to become the resource itself. Thus, many programs called community education are in reality adult education or recreation programs or projects operated by community development proponents. While these activities are certainly valuable to the community, they often result in the perception that community education is synonymous with adult education, recreation, or community development. Frequently the community school directors themselves seek identification with these groups and agencies which results in the loss of the uniqueness of the community school.

Another problem is resistance from traditional institutions and agencies to the changes they perceive will be brought about by community education. In addition to the normal fear related to something new, a number of agencies and organizations feel that community education will eventually result in their responsibilities being taken away from them and operated by the schools. A part of this feeling is due to misunderstanding of community education, and part is due to the fact that some community school directors, as mentioned earlier, are in reality operating other agencies' programs rather than carrying out their appropriate role as facilitator.

Interestingly, the one organization which seems to be most threatened is the school itself. Despite what appears to be an exciting and challenging new role for the public schools, there is a reluctance on the part of school administrators, boards of education, and teachers to change their current roles. Instead of expanding the present responsibilities of the schools, as suggested by the community education concept, the public schools tend to reject any responsibility except that dealing with cognitive learning skills for school-aged children.

Gaining adequate financial support is also one of the current problems, and this problem is at least partially related to the hesitation of the school system to legitimatize community education. Most community school programs are expected to provide their own funds and not to infringe on the regular school budget. This is a result of the view that the things happening in community education are of an add-on nature rather than an integral part of the school program. As a result, community school directors are constantly forced to solicit funding from many sources, and the time spent raising such funds takes away from time which might be spent in more completely developing the concept of community education.

Fortunately, some inroads into a more dependable means of funding are being made. Federal legislation has provided some risk capital for experimental programs. In addition, state funding has become more prevalent with several states providing monies for school districts operating under a community education philosophy.

The most logical method for funding, however, is to use the same combination of state and local sources that finance other educational activities in the community. This does not rule out the use of funds from grants, fees, foundations, and fund raising, but it does suggest that community education is a legitimate role of the school, and, as such, should be funded on a more permanent basis rather than with the "soft monies" which have often been used in the past. Many communities have accepted the idea of funding community schools by more typical educational funding methods. An increasing number of community education school districts receive some of their dollars from the general school budget, and many have categorical monies voted solely for that purpose.

Another problem relates to staffing. This problem deals not only with the assignment of staff but also with training. Various titles have been used to describe the people who carry out the community education responsibilities in the school: Community School Director, Community Education Director, Community Education Coordinator, Community Agent, Facilitator, Energizer, and Community Organizer. In some school districts, the responsibility for achieving the goals of community education has been assigned to the building principal.

The title, however, is not the problem; the assignment of the person is. In order to carry out the responsibilities of a community school most completely, the most effective organizational unit is a primary community. Primary community implies one in which the number of residents is small enough that face-to-face relationships can take place, maximum participation can be achieved, and two-way communication is possible. One of the premises of a community school is that the one unit of operation in our society where this can best happen is the elementary school. Therefore, in order for community education to work most effectively through a community school, the personnel for carrying out the functions, as well as the accountability, for such a program should be located at the elementary school building.

In practice, some school districts have organized themselves so that the base of operation is either the high school or the school district. The result is often a system which cannot get neighborhood input or a feeling for neighborhood needs. This leads to a highly programmatic operation with little possibility for community development at the level where it is most needed.

A second problem with staffing is the failure of school districts to adapt staffing needs to community school needs. In most cases, organizations tend to identify what the needs are and then determine how many staff members (professional, paraprofessional, volunteer) are needed to do the job. Too frequently in the case of community schools, the staffing patterns are determined by what has been done in the past, what others have done, or by a general belief that employing one person as the director for the school district is adequate. Unfortunately, these methods of determining staff often assure a minimal set of programs and limit the potential for growth of community education in that community.

As for the training of community school personnel, there is great diversity. Some school districts are using untrained persons, volunteers, and paraprofessionals whose selection is based on a willingness to do the job and ability to relate well to the community. At the other end of the continuum are staff members who have graduate degrees and sophisticated training. The discipline involved in the training, however, may range from courses stressing teacher certification or school administration, to those dealing with social work or recreation. This disagreement as to what should be the basic discipline or appropriate training content creates problems because practitioners tend to base their view of community education on the discipline from which they come.

THE POTENTIAL OF COMMUNITY EDUCATION

Community education has the potential to make a great impact on the public school and the community. For the teacher, it offers the possibility of introducing real relevance into the classroom. By using the community as a resource for students, teachers can enrich the educational programs and expand educational opportunities beyond the limitations of the regular school. Teachers will find many advantages to being a part of a community-oriented school.

For the school administrator, community education will mean new roles and subsequently new areas of accountability. Taking administrative responsibility for the development of a community school will result in a larger staff, new perceptions about the administrator's role, and more community involvement. In order to accommodate these new responsibilities, administrators will soon recognize the need for new skills, particularly in regard to working with community groups.

Traditional students will acquire advantages as a result of community education. The community orientation of their teachers and administrators will result in programs more relevant to their needs. They will also find that they have many more learning opportunities available to them, and their ideas about what education can be, particularly as it relates to lifelong learning, will be enhanced. In addition, the closer relation between community and school, two important aspects of their lives, will tend to promote a more positive climate for students.

For the community there will also be many advantages. Adults will now have attention given to their educational needs. They will also benefit from the coordination of community services, increased usage of school facilities, more direct contact with schools, and involvement in school matters. More important, however, the development of community councils will involve communities in community problem solving and potentially move these communities in the direction of more meaningful participation in those things which affect their lives.

Community education, through the community schools, offers a potential for social change which is appealing to community members. Currently, the most resistant forces appear to be school boards, school administrations, teachers, and custodians. Community education, however, is growing at such a rapid pace that the likelihood of some type of community education through the public schools seems assured. Unfortunately, it is an area which is very threatening to the status quo posture of many public school educators.

It is true that community education still needs shaping and polishing, both as an educational concept and as a program in the local setting, but it is an educational innovation which cannot, and should not, be ignored. The logic of its application to the public schools including its components, its acceptance by many school districts, its appeal to many communities, and its potential for community improvement are factors which must be strongly considered by public educators. Exploring it, reviewing it, and redirecting it are all appropriate actions for the educators in our public schools, but rejecting it or ignoring its existence will not assure the demise of community education. On the contrary, it may insure that the key role which might be played by the public schools in this concept will pass from public educators to some other more perceptive and sensitive group within our communities.

NOTES

1. Ferdinand Tonnës, *Gemeinschaft and Gessellschaft—Community and Society,* translated by Charles Loomis, Michigan State University Press, 1957.

2. Eric Hoffer, *The True Believer,* Harper and Row, New York, 1951.

3. Elsie Clapp, *Community Schools in Action,* The Viking Press, New York, 1939.

4. Jack D. Minzey and Clarence R. Olsen, "Community Education: An Overview," in H. W. Hickey, C. Van Voorhees and Associates (eds.), *The Role of the School in Community Education,* Pendell Publishing Co., Midland, Michigan, 1969.

5. Resolution passed by the National Community Education Association Board of Directors, 1968.

6. Maurice F. Seay, "The Community School Emphasis in Postwar Education," in N. B. Henry (ed.), *American Education in the Postwar Period: Curriculum Reconstruction,* Forty-fourth Yearbook, Part I, National Society for the Study of Education, University of Chicago Press, 1945.

7. Maurice F. Seay, "The Community School: New Meaning for an Old Term," in N. B. Henry (ed.), *The Community School,* Fifty-second Yearbook, Part II, National Society for the Study of Education, University of Chicago Press, 1953.

8. Jack D. Minzey and Clyde LeTarte, *Community Education: From Program to Process,* Pendell Publishing Co., Midland, Michigan, 1972.

9. *The Flint Community Schools Catalog,* Flint Community Schools, Flint, Michigan, 1975, p. 9.

10

EXCHANGING SCHOOL AND COMMUNITY RESOURCES

PEGGY ODELL GONDER

M any schools seem content to "run the public's business" without bothering to involve the public. By isolating themselves from the community, schools create some problems and aggravate others. One particularly troublesome problem is a lack of confidence in the schools. It was first demonstrated in the widespread failure of bond issues and tax levies. The next wave came with the minimum competency movement. Uneasy with the caliber of high school graduates, parents and the business community asked the legislature—not the schools—to set some minimum requirements for the performance of high school graduates.

One powerful way to counter this lack of confidence is to open the school doors and create opportunities for involvement. Volunteers who spend time in classrooms generally find things are not as bad as they seemed in the headlines. Volunteers also stretch resources at a time when every dollar counts. Volunteer tutors and aides lower the pupil-adult ratio in large classes. Guest speakers bring career knowledge and other useful information into the schools at no additional cost. Executives from the business community can contribute valuable management expertise through task forces and advisory committees.

Isolation is also reduced by using the community as a classroom. Students can gain valuable skills by doing research and interviews in the community. Internships and work-study programs give students a first-hand look at a career and access to equipment the school could not afford. And classes in hospitals, museums, and other community settings provide the variety often needed to spark interest in students bored with traditional instruction.

One criticism the business community often levels at the schools is that students are ill-equipped to enter the job market. The mismatch between school preparation and job-market needs benefits no one. Because technology constantly changes those needs, schools must establish relationships with business and labor that keep career education programs on the right track.

School districts across the country have begun dealing with the problem of isolation in various innovative ways. While no one district has all the answers, their approaches provide useful models for bridging the gap.

VOLUNTEER PROGRAMS

The most common form of community involvement is through school volunteer programs. These range from the time-honored "home room mother" who bakes cookies and helps with field trips to sophisticated programs encompassing a variety of auxiliary services. Trained volunteers in Houston, for example, screen kindergarteners for vision, hearing ability, language development, and social maturity. "Picture Ladies" in the Peoria, Illinois, public schools teach art appreciation by taking art prints into the classroom and discussing them with students. Volunteers in the Lower Merion, Pennsylvania School District work in a resource center to create educational shoe box games and instructional materials for use in individualized, open classrooms.

Traditionally, a school's volunteer pool consisted of white, middle-class mothers who did not work outside the home. This stereotype is neither appropriate nor adequate to serve the needs of the average school district today. For one thing, many of those mothers are no longer at home, having long since returned to work to meet the grocery bills. Also, children in most classrooms come in many colors besides white. The sensitive school district tries to recruit volunteers from all races and ethnic groups to serve the needs of their students. Another rich source of volunteers is the retired community. Older persons have both the time and a lifetime of skills and experience to share. In today's mobile society, they are often the children's only contact with their grandparent's generation. Students and employed persons are also willing to volunteer.

One of the largest volunteer programs in the country has successfully recruited from all these sources. The Los Angeles Volunteer and Tutorial Program involves more than 30,000 volunteers. They are divided by age group into three divisions: School Volunteers are adults working during the school day, the Youth Tutorial Program uses students from elementary through college age, and the Dedicated Older Volunteers in Educational Services (Doves) tap those aged sixty and older. According to Sarah Davis, program director, most volunteers help with tutoring in basic subjects, such as reading, math, and language arts. The interesting exceptions include an eighty-three-year-old woman who teaches water ballet and a group of parents who converted a school room into a multicultural art museum ephasizing black heroes.

Successful volunteer programs place a high priority on recruitment. This is especially important with minority groups because many remember negative experiences from their own school days. Others who work may be unwilling to take what little time is left away from their families. Another problem with all volunteers is the cost of child care for the children still at home. "We could involve more parents if we could provide babysitting," Davis says.

To compensate for these barriers, Los Angeles hires recruiters from minority communities. These "community representatives" must be active in the schools and be residents of the community they serve. Most are former PTA members, former school volunteers, or members of a local school advisory council. Los Angeles is divided into ten administrative areas. The program hires three recruiters for each area: one for School Volunteers, one for the Youth Tutorial program, and one for Doves. The racial or ethnic composition of the administrative area determines the type of recruiter hired: if the area is predominately black, all three recruiters are black. The first recruiters were paid with federal manpower funds. Now, the program is supported through the district budget and through fund-raising efforts of the Friends of the School Volunteer Program, Inc. Davis says the proportion of minority volunteers parallels the student enrollment in the district. Because of the growing number of Oriental students in the schools, she predicts the program will begin hiring Oriental as well as black and Hispanic recruiters.

One problem that can scuttle a new volunteer program is opposition from the teacher union. The teachers may feel threatened and fear that either the volunteer will try to run things or will become "scab labor" during a strike. One way to avoid resentment is to assign volunteers to a school only upon request of the principal and to a classroom only on a teacher's request. The National School Volunteer Program, a membership organization made up of volunteers and staff of volunteer programs, discourages the use of volunteers during strikes. Such a policy, adopted at the outset, can go a long way to dispel distrust that could develop between teachers and volunteers.

Volunteer programs are also vulnerable during controversies. Davis feared a mass exodus of volunteers the year Los Angeles began busing for desegregation. Instead, the program lost no more volunteers than any other year. One policy that helped was that parents were allowed to ride the bus and volunteer at the school their child attended. The program also urged the parents to volunteer an additional day at their neighborhood school. This was encouraged because more black parents than white were willing to ride the bus away from their neighborhood.

Valle del Sol, a community organization in Phoenix, takes a different approach to involving minorities in the school. As an advocacy group, Valle del Sol seeks to involve parents in projects that will give them the confidence to take on larger issues of school governance. Using parents as volunteers, paraprofessionals, and aides puts parents in a subservient role, says Pepe Martinez, education director of Valle del Sol. Instead, the organization sponsored "Oro del Barrio" (gold from the neighborhood), a project to preserve neighborhood folk tales within the elementary school curriculum.

Storytellers who were highly respected in their communities were brought together for a work session to share folk tales. A librarian from Tucson and several community members wrote the tales in Spanish and translated them to English. Other community members edited the stories and bound them together into booklets which were left at the schools. The project was a success, not only because it enriched the schools but because it showed the parents they could affect the curriculum. This gave the parents self-confidence and credibility with school officials. "These are parents who are also fighting for new schools in their neighborhood," Martinez explains.

INVOLVING BUSINESSES

Volunteers can also be found through businesses that "adopt" local schools. In these programs, a business is paired with a specific school for the benefit of both. The students hear guest speakers, tour facilities, and participate in innovative programs. The businesses boost their public image while giving their employees an outlet for community services.

In Denver, the adoption process starts with a request for help from a local school. The Adopt-A-School staff gives teachers a questionnaire to determine their needs and then seeks a company that can meet those needs. At Lake Junior High, for example, the teachers decided they needed to motivate the students to attend school and to set longterm goals. The first adopting company was Rocky Mountain Empire Sports, owners of the Denver Broncos football team and the Denver Bears baseball team. One strategy being considered is to reward good attendance with "field goals" and "touchdowns." Students with the best scores would then have lunch with some of their football heroes. The franchise also plans to send their trainers to speak on nutrition to home economics classes and about athletic equipment and safety to gym classes. The students at Lake are predominately Hispanic. Their second adopting company is Mastercraft Industries, a successful cabinet-making firm owned and operated by Hispanics.

Adopting businesses also provide experiences for students in the community. Mountain Bell has built an extensive medical laboratory in Denver for employee physical examinations. Ninth-grade medical-science students from Kepner Junior High toured the facility and tried out the electrocardiogram, treadmill, and other sophisticated machines. After Stevens Elementary was adopted by Neusteter's Department Store, the students got a behind-the-scenes tour of the store's advertising, marketing, and data-processing departments. The cosmetics manager taught a charm and grooming minicourse for interested Stevens students. In keeping with the Adopt-A-School philosophy that pairings should be reciprocal, Stevens students painted jungle and spring scenes for use in Neusteter's display windows.

Adopt-A-School business consultant Jane Kerr says she has no problem finding willing businesses. It is an opportunity for them to make a public statement about their commitment to the community, she explains. The school involvement also serves as a training ground for employees being considered for promotion. The activities give employees a chance to demonstrate leadership skills, creativity, and other traits that may not be part of their present job responsibilities.

The program obviously benefits teachers by giving them professional contacts in the community. The contact, however, can be an advantage for the company, too. Denver Brick and Pipe has worked closely with ceramics students at Manual High School. Robert McNamara, lab director at the company, is glad he has a working relationship with ceramics teacher Roger Beasley. "Who knows when we'll have a problem that Roger Beasley knows something about," McNamara explains.

Adopt-A-School was born in Denver as a positive response to desegregation. Denver's business community issued statements supporting desegregation, but they had little direct contact with students following the 1974 court order. Instead, the task of promoting a peaceful transition fell to People, Let's Unite for Schools (PLUS), a coalition of some 50 community groups. PLUS hired Ann Fenton, a parent and former teacher, to coordinate parent and community involvement in schools paired for desegregation. Fenton heard about the Adopt-A-School concept at a conference. The PLUS board of directors then applied for and received a $58,000 Emergency School Aid Act grant for 1977–78. After the one-year grant ended, Adopt-A-School continued with support from participating businesses, foundations, and individuals.

Fenton believes Adopt-A-School programs work best when run by an agency that has no direct ties with the school system or the business establishment. If the organization is an arm of business, teachers think the adopting companies are trying to tell them how to do their job. Conversely, businesses are unwilling to work through bureaucracies the size of a large city school district. The Denver program's independent status also enables it to serve as a neutral broker. "Business people and educators think differently, act differently, and react differently," says Fenton. For example, educators can "meet all day," while a business executive wants meetings to be quick and to the point. "Such differences in temperament are one reason why there's an estrangement between business and the schools in the first place . . . why Adopt-A-School is needed," she adds.

Each partnership has three coordinators: one at the business, one at the school, and one for parents. In some programs, parents appear to play only supportive roles, such as helping with field trips. In others, parents are an integral partner. For example, Teller Elementary is paired with the East Denver Kiwanis Club. Three Fridays of the month, parents and Kiwanians teach minicourses on subjects ranging from cooking to drama to bookkeeping. On the fourth Friday of the month, a combination of Kiwanis members and parents comes to Teller to be interviewed about their careers. Student representatives from each fourth-, fifth-, and sixth-grade class interview the adults and present an oral or written report on the career to their classmates. The Kiwanis Club sponsors a Key Club at a nearby high school. The Key Club members plan to tutor and teach an introduction to computer programming at Teller.

"The hardest problem (in the Adopt-A-School program) is getting teachers to use the business resources," says Fenton. "It's a lot easier just to stay in your classroom," agrees Ruth Jeffs, school coordinator at Lake. "It's a constant job for me to get the teachers excited enough to want to participate."

A potential pitfall is that teachers can get sidetracked from the primary purpose—tapping human resources in the community—and alienate the business by asking for money. This happened in one adopting school, and it was "almost a disaster," Fenton says. The central Adopt-A-School office can act as a safety valve in such cases, suggesting other projects and activities. Conversely, the Adopt-A-Schools staff can relay ideas that originate in the business community but would not be accepted by teachers if they came directly from the source.

SPINOFF BENEFITS
Once the schools and businesses begin cooperating, the contacts and chemistry can produce exciting results. Two teachers at Manual High School were concerned that no students were signing up for economics courses. Colorado National Bank, one of Manual's adopting companies, was concerned that most young people have a poor understanding of economics and a low opinion of business and the free enterprise system. The bank, the two teachers, and the Colorado Council on Economic Education collaborated on an innovative new course that features simulation games and interviews in the community.

In one of the first games, called Mr. Banker, the students study loan applications and determine which ones should be granted. Some of the loans go sour and they have to decide which of several alternatives to take. To prepare for the game, the students read about the role of the Federal Reserve and study how banks operate as profit-making businesses. While playing the game, they write down questions they want answered. Next, they visit the Chairman of the Board of Colorado National Bank and the top officer of the Federal Reserve in Denver for answers to their sophisticated questions.

In all, there are eleven simulations, followed by community visits to hear two opposing points of view. After the game on the role of government in the economy, the students talk with the regional head of the Department of Health, Education, and Welfare and with a conservative business executive. Many of the business contacts work for companies participating in Adopt-A-School.

The bank provided the teachers with an office, a WATS line, and access to the typing pool to develop day-by-day lesson plans for the course. Most of the simulations were purchased from companies who developed them to train their own employees, says Richard Jordan, one of the teachers. Jordan says Colorado National gave him complete freedom to order materials and bill them to the bank. He estimates the bank contributed more than $1,000 to develop the course. The Colorado Council on Economics Education paid a college economics professor who helped the teachers make sure the activities were representative of current economic theory. The Council also acted as a liaison for various curriculum groups the teachers contacted.

The class was first offered in the fall of 1978. It was so popular that a second section was added during the spring semester and there was still a waiting list. Jordan has applied for a grant to train other teachers and expand the course to other high schools. The class succeeds because it is exciting. "How can you turn on electronically-oriented kids with books and chalk?" asks Ann Fenton. "Teachers need business expertise and resources to be able to do it."

The main danger with such collaboration is that the end product can look like pro-business propaganda. The Denver program has seemingly avoided this problem by gearing the course to producing well-informed, skeptical students. But the danger of bias is real and causes most teachers to view industry-produced materials with distrust.

In fact, distrust bordering on hostility has been a major barrier in bringing educators and businesses together. "Business and labor unions have been very eager to participate in career education programs," says Carol Andersen, legislative analyst with the Education Commission of the States Career Education Project. But teachers—especially secondary and postsecondary—have suspected their motives. Some education materials produced by business are very good, she adds. The solution is to view such materials with discrimination. If the material is basically good with some bias, the teacher can deal with the bias as part of the classroom instruction.

GOVERNMENT-INITIATED INVOLVEMENT
Government programs, such as Title I and Head Start, have often been a catalyst for involving parents in the schools. Head Start is a preschool program for children three years and older that provides medical and

educational benefits to disadvantaged children. Title I funds help students with reading, math, and language arts. The funds are given to schools with a high proportion of low-income students. Within the school, the help is given to those with greatest educational need.

In both programs, parents play key roles as members of advisory councils. The parents must comprise a majority of the council, and the school district or agency providing the program must give training to the parents. The training explains the law to the parents and their role on the advisory council. Many schools also provide training in child development. Parents are encouraged to volunteer in the classroom and many become paid classroom aides. Head Start requires one paid aide, one volunteer, and one teacher for every fifteen students. Title I regulations permit hiring of aides but do not require it.

Training Title I parents yields several benefits, says Helene Amos, program specialist with the Department of Health, Education, and Welfare. Parents from poverty backgrounds often have a low self-image which may be transferred to their children. The parents increase their self-esteem by receiving training and positions of influence on advisory councils. The children are proud of their parents, which helps the children's self-concepts. Also, the parents may become better parents (through the child development training), and this, in turn, can help with school discipline. Parents who become aides sometimes are motivated to go back to school and become teachers. Parents serving on advisory councils have also been elected to school boards.

One disadvantage, according to Amos, is that heavy involvement by parents can cause friction if administrators feel intimidated by the advisory council. "In some cases," she explains, "parents become so sophisticated, they know more about the program and law than those running it." Educators who would normally disregard advise from parents are even more resistant to advice from poor parents, says Amos, because they consider the parents unsuccessful.

The principal plays a key role in successfully involving parents. If he or she supports the advisory council, the rest of the school staff usually goes along. The principal can also help to make parents feel welcome in the school. As the school professionals have more contact with parents, the barriers begin to break down, Amos adds.

While Head Start and Title I sometimes provide upward mobility for parents, another federal program specifically helped parents and citizens climb the educational career ladder. The Career Opportunities Program (COP), was initiated in the early 1970s by the U.S. Office of Education to provide college training to minority and low-income persons working in local school districts.

Through COP, community persons were hired as instructional aides and were encouraged to enroll in college degree programs. At its best, COP sites created career ladders that gave the aides more responsible tasks as they gained experience and advanced training. During the seven years of the program (1970–76), some 14,000 aides were trained, some to become credentialed teachers, others to remain as paraprofessionals with associate degrees or some college training.

In addition to providing upward mobility to disadvantaged persons, COP was intended to help the students by providing positive role models in the classroom. An aide from the Crow Indian reservation in southeastern Montana, for example, was likely to have more success motivating a Crow student than the Anglo teacher. The program provided the additional advantage of helping rural economies by upgrading the skills of local residents.[1]

The relatively small scale of the program and its short life span of only about six years prevented COP from having lasting effects on education nationally. Its legacy, however, of recruiting community persons to work as classroom aides has been continued in some schools through the federal Education for All Handicapped Children Act. The Tucson Unified School District has one of the largest such programs, called Paraprofessionals in Adaptive Education. Supported by federal and state funds, the program pays aides to work in resource rooms and self-contained special education classrooms. The aides can upgrade their skills through in-service training at the district and special education courses at a community college. In 1979, more than 100 of the 325 aides were taking college courses at the community college or the University of Arizona.

When the program began in 1976, director Vera Yager contacted local agencies working with disadvantaged and minority unemployed and told them to send interested persons to her. About 37 percent of the aides come from these categories, which roughly parallels the proportion of disadvantaged and minority special education students in the district.

To Yager, the Indian, Hispanic, and black aides play a vital role in the education of the students. One junior high Indian boy in a resource room was totally unresponsive, she says. An Indian aide was able to establish rapport with him and give him the self-confidence he needed to start performing and learning. Often, bilingual students in the severe oral-language–handicapped class will not be proficient in either English or Spanish. Most of the speech therapists are not bilingual. Under these circumstances, bilingual aides play a vital role because they can work with the students until they are proficient in one language before work begins on the other. One black paraprofessional has developed a successful behavior modification program in which the parents reinforce what the student learns at school. Black parents agree to participate, Yager explains, because the aide "speaks the same language they do."

The aides also play a key role in helping handicapped students adjust to the regular classroom. If a teacher is hesitant about accepting a handicapped child from a resource room, the aide remains with the student until the student and the regular teacher are comfortable.

In addition to helping the students, such aide programs provide upware mobility and the opportunity to try a new career. Many applicants come to Yager unsure of what they want to do. By working as an aide, the adults learn whether special education is for them before they have invested years in a degree. The Tucson program contains a career ladder that points the way for participants who want to advance beyond their present responsibilities. Career education and job training for adults are not typical roles for the public schools, but they are roles more and more districts are assuming.

SCHOOL-FAMILY CONTRACTS

One valuable resource parents can give schools is concern for the progress of their own children. Too often, parents assume that education is entirely the school's responsibility. Malpractice lawsuits such as the Peter Doe case in California demonstrate that the student and parent, as well as the school system, bear responsibility for success in school. Teachers can only do so much if the student is unwilling to learn. And parents affect the students' willingness by their own attitudes toward education.

Some school districts are beginning to recognize formally this shared responsibility through printed contracts. Orr Junior High in Las Vegas developed "An Accountability Agreement" that spells out responsibilities for three groups: Orr teachers and staff, parents, and students. The agreement was written by teachers, administrators, and the school's parent advisory committee. According to Orr principal, Frank Lamping, the impetus came from the parents who wondered what they could do to help with their children's education. The parent group paid for the printing.

The agreement has a very formal, legal appearance. The Orr staff pledges to monitor each child's attendance and progress closely and notify parents through failure notices, report cards, and telephone calls. The fifteen responsibilities for staff include such obvious requirements as providing textbooks, a library, and a "nutritious breakfast and lunch each day." Parents have twelve responsibilities, including providing a time and place free of distraction for homework. Students agree to nine provisions, including coming to school each day, knowing school rules, and becoming involved in school activities. The contract was mailed without warning to all parents. According to Lamping, the stark, legal appearance of the document led many parents to read and learn about district policies they had ignored in a more conventional format.

Orr Junior High is near the Las Vegas strip and many residents are single parents who work odd hours. Lamping says a chronic problem at the school has been a lack of parental supervision. After the contract was mailed, attendance at Orr rose from mediocre to one of the best in the district.

The contract was not well received by everyone. A few months after the contract was mailed, Orr sent an attitude survey to parents. Responses were about equally divided between positive and negative. One of the strongest negative responses said a majority of teachers lacked interest in the children. It added, "You've now made parents *completely* responsible for their child's education. When do you do *your* job?" This parent evidently interpreted the agreement as a threat and overlooked the responsibilities assigned to the schools.

An essential ingredient to a successful contract is a cooperative spirit among the parties involved. The Oakland, California, Unified School District developed a three-way learning contract that was highly acclaimed and generated much interest among educators nationally. Unfortunately, the contract was distributed in the schools right after a teachers' strike when the word "contract" was a sore point with the teachers. Because of the resentment generated, the contract was sent back to the drawing board and emerged in a watered-down form.

The original brochure, developed by a citywide instruction committee of students, parents, teachers, and administrators, describes responsibilities for students, parents, and teachers. It was handed out to parents at a Festival of Learning night at each school. In addition to the contract, parents received sheets of "learning expectations" that specified what students at each grade level were expected to know in language arts and math. The parents also heard about a new assessment program that would give information about their child's progress.

According to Barbara Whitman, acting assistant director of community relations, the contract was well-received by parents and the business community, but resented by teachers. Turnout at the Festival of Learning was low because teachers did not encourage parents and students to attend. Teachers were angry with the administration over the strike, Whitman explains, and they resented the fact that no responsibilities were spelled out for administrators. Many felt teachers should have had a larger part in determining the language of the contract, and they were leery of signing a "contract" because of legal implications.

The revision removed the word "contract" and provisions for signatures from the participants. Instead of a three-way contract, the "Learning Guidelines" address five groups: students, parent/guardians, teachers, site-administrators, and area/district administrators. A note from Superintendent Ruth B. Love describes the brochure as a "good faith agreement" that is "not legally binding." The brochures are sent to principals for distribution as they see fit.

The concept of learning contracts is a good one for communicating the message of shared responsibility. As the Orr and Oakland experiences demonstrate, however, the method has drawbacks as well as advantages. To avoid misunderstanding and resentment, the provisions of such an agreement must be developed with adequate opportunities for all parties to contribute. When the agreement is distributed, the school should carefully explain the reasons and purpose for it. And timing of the distribution is critical. With these safeguards, the learning contract can be a powerful tool for community cooperation.

LINKING SCHOOLS AND BUSINESSES

Schools can gain powerful allies by forging ties with the business community. Through such working relationships, influential community leaders learn about the district's strengths and its needs. When those leaders become advocates of the schools, the fruits are increased prestige and political clout.

In Dallas, close ties with the business community have produced a model career education program, a smooth transition to desegregation, and support for school bond issues and for the general educational program. This seemingly blissful relationship has not always been the case. In 1965, the schools were jolted by a series of newspaper editorials that blasted the Dallas Independent School District (DISD) for not providing adequate career opportunities. The superintendent approached the education committee of the Dallas Chamber of Commerce for help in identifying vocational education needs. Once the needs were identified, seperate advisory committees were set up to shape the curriculum and plan the facilities and equipment. Having been involved in the planning, the business community turned out to support a $21 million bond issue to build the vocational center. In 1968 a new superintendent, Nolan Estes, proposed that the concept be expanded from vocational education to career education. Today, more than 300 professionals serve on advisory committees for 25 "clusters" or families of careers.

The clusters are taught at the Skyline Career Development Center and at various magnet high schools. They range from fashion and manufacturing to cosmetology, computer technology, and advanced mathematics. According to center manager Weldon Griffith, the advisory committees arrange for speakers, field trips, internships, and summer jobs for the students and job placement for the graduates. They also review the curriculum and donate equipment to make sure the students are learning the techniques that will be needed after they graduate. Dallas is a center for large electronics companies. When a piece of new equipment moves from design to production, the company will often give the prototype to the center for instructional purposes.

Advisory committee members are also active as counselors. Although the ratio of teachers to students in a cluster is 1 to 500, advisory committee members, through their contacts in industry, are trying to match students to working adults in a one-to-one ratio. In some clusters, one or two students may visit an adult to talk about his or her job. In other clusters, the counseling is a more extended "buddy" arrangement, where the student can call the adult for advice. Committee members have also arranged for teachers and students to attend seminars on the latest developments in their field.

Most career sequences last two years. After a year and a half, the student seeks on-the-job training that often leads to a paid summer job with the same company. Each cluster course is performance-based. Students work at their own pace to master objectives that have been set by the business community.

Because of the close ties with business—and in the academic clusters, with the academia—career center graduates have enjoyed notable success. Texas Instruments, which had been hiring persons with associate degrees, tested students in the DISD electronics cluster. Based on the students' high test scores, the company revised its employment policies to permit hiring career-center graduates. One bright student who participated in advanced math and science clusters received forty-five quarter-hours of college credit when he enrolled at the University of Oregon.

State and federal vocational education programs have often been criticized for failing to serve the students who really need the training—the economically and educationally disadvantaged who are unlikely to go to college or any postsecondary training institutions. Abuses of federal vocational funds led Congress to amend the vocational act in 1968.[2] Programs that receive federal funds must enroll at least 15 percent who are educationally disadvantaged and 10 percent who are handicapped. Title IX of the Education Amendments prohibits sex discrimination in federally funded programs.

The Dallas program receives no direct federal funds so it does not tabulate its enrollment according to these categories. However, Griffith says enrollment is close to 50 percent female and there are "some" handicapped, including students in wheelchairs and deaf students. Although there is no tally of disadvantaged students, the center's track record for attracting minorities made Skyline a model for magnet high schools required in the desegregation order. Students apply to Skyline based on attendance and academic achievement. If the student has a poor discipline or achievement record, he or she may still be admitted upon the recommendation of a teacher or counselor. "Lots of kids who don't do well in academics do tremendously in some of our programs," Griffith adds.

Dallas's success in career education has led to school-business collaboration in other areas. Superintendent Estes challenged businesses to help the schools become more efficient. For two years, some 50 business persons examined the district's personnel procedures, food service, purchasing, distribution, and management systems. In a case study on the project, the Chamber of Commerce of the United States estimated that businesses contributed about $125,000 worth of consulting time. The school board adopted most of the recommendations. The effort not only made the district more efficient, it boosted public confidence because taxpayers could see the district was concerned that their money was spent wisely. The task forces also involved other segments of the business community who continued their interest in the schools.

In April 1976, the court ordered Dallas to desegregate its schools by the following fall. A key portion of the plan was the creation of magnet high schools to attract a racially balanced mixture of students. Estes appealed to the business community to help develop the magnet sites, find jobs for magnet students, and create a marketing program to recruit students and parents. The first year, four schools were developed out of clusters that already existed at Skyline. As much as possible, the magnets are situated to take advantage of community resources. The business and management school is downtown and the health professions magnet is next door to Baylor Medical Center. Students work in the hospital, and doctors and staff from the medical center serve on the school's advisory committee.

Once planning was completed, the task changed to "selling" the community on the court order. A local advertising agency donated time to create a campaign. According to Rodney Davis, director of public relations for the district, the Chamber and local businesses contributed $100,000 to create two professional-quality films. The first described the magnet schools and was used to attract students. The second, "Keep it Together, Dallas!" stressed the quality of education in the district and included on-camera endorsements of the schools by community leaders. It was simulcast on the major local television stations in a half-hour broadcast.

In addition to the films, a massive print campaign was coordinated by the Chamber and the school district. The Chamber asked businesses to explain the court order in employee publications and to distribute printed material through envelope stuffers and bulletin boards. The materials were produced by the school district and distributed to about 700 businesses. Chamber staff also asked businesses to "adopt" a school that would be receiving bused students.

Prior to the court order, community and religious groups formed a Committee for a Smooth Transition. The committee set up a speakers bureau and information network to disseminate facts about the court order and plans for the actual implementation.

In December 1976, less than four months after desegregation, Dallas voters approved an $80 million bond issue for renovation and construction to complement the desegregation plan. Defeating bond issues is one of the easiest ways voters can express dissatisfaction with the schools. The passage of this bond issue testifies to the strong economic and political support Dallas has achieved by involving the community.

THE CONSORTIUM APPROACH

While the Dallas schools–Dallas Chamber of Commerce collaboration is a useful model, it is not necessarily right for every community. A small school district, either in a suburb or rural area, may not have access to a well-organized chamber or a centralized business community. In some large cities, past hostilities may stand in the way of using traditional channels for school and business cooperation. The two sided model can also leave out important constituencies, such as labor unions, nonprofit organizations, and community colleges.

The three-sided Adopt-A-School model was described earlier. In addition, about 30 local communities and states have been experimenting with another approach: the work-education council. In most cases, the council is a central coordinating group composed of representatives from the schools, the business community, labor, and government agencies. Often, the councils do not conduct career education programs themselves. Instead, they bring the interested parties together to solve problems and identify needs. For example, the Trident Work Education Council in Charleston, South Carolina, conducted a survey on the patterns of youth unemployment. Council member Jack Henty explains that the only information available was federal statistics and the council wanted to know the facts for their particular area. With the information, the council or its individual members could then design programs to benefit those most in need.

The councils are part of a network known as the Work Education Consortium. Each receives funds from the U.S. Department of Labor through one of three nonprofit agencies: the National Manpower Institute, the American Association of Community and Junior Colleges, and the National Alliance of Businessmen. Each council is tailored to the needs of the local area, but they share one goal: smoothing the transition from education to work.

Work-education councils are needed because responsibilities for education, vocational training, job counseling, and placement are often spread among many government, educational, and private agencies. Without coordination, some services may be duplicated while other needs are not met. Public school guidance counselors often have materials for the college-bound student but lack vocational information. The counselor may not have time to seek out job information under an increasing caseload of students with social, academic, or emotional problems.

On the other side, businesses may be willing to help but have no contacts within the educational system. In the meantime, as each agency operates in isolation, the low-income person leaves school with no relevant job experience, no training in how to find a job, and no clear idea what he or she wants to do. If the student has worked, it has likely been mowing lawns or other tasks that do not lead to permanent jobs.

The Work/Education Council of Southeastern Michigan saw a need to have a central listing of jobs along with salary ranges, the education and training required, and the sources where the education and training could be obtained. Two federally-funded agencies on the council paid to have the information put on a computer and to purchase 50 computer terminals. The terminals are placed throughout the county in school counselors' offices, public libraries, and state employment offices. In its present form, the computer provides up-to-date information about careers students may be considering. Eventually, the system is expected to contain actual job openings from the state employment office and the local youth employment office.

Students are not the only ones who benefit. After the Livonia, Michigan Public Schools laid off 350 teachers, the Livonia Education Association came to the Work/Education Council for help. The council, the association, a college career center, and the chamber of commerce sponsored a career planning workshop for 80 of the pink-slipped teachers. The three-day meeting included panels on alternative careers and a resumé-writing session that stressed translating teaching skills into traits that are necessary in other careers. The teachers were also videotaped in mock interviews. After the first successful workshop, the Michigan Education Association contracted with the council to conduct similar workshops around the state.

The Community Careers Council (CCC) of Oakland is a cooperative effort of the Peralta Community College District, Oakland Public Schools, and the New Oakland Committee, a coalition of business, labor, and minority leaders working to revitalize the city. According to executive director José de la Isla, the CCC serves three functions: as a forum or "middle ground" for traditional adversaries, as a source of information, and as a clearinghouse to connect the education and business community. Through a needs survey, the council learned that counselors, teachers, and community groups did not know how to contact employers. "Everyone had a Rollodex with the same 100 names," Isla says. In its first six months, the CCC clearinghouse linked nearly 1200 young people with employers. Most contacts were informational interviews, in which the youth learned about the employer's job.

Federal law encourages greater collaboration between schools, agencies, and businesses. Agencies receiving federal Comprehensive Employment and Training Act (CETA) funds must spend at least 22 per-cent of their youth employment allocation on in-school youth in cooperation with local school districts. Most CETA-school agreements provide work experiences for students, but they do not have to be limited to that. Central Texas Manpower, for example, serves twenty-six rural districts with a variety of programs, ranging from providing field trips and occupational information to administering standardized tests. Many services can be provided for all students, but work experiences are available only to disadvantaged students. Although CETA sponsors would like to award academic credit for work experiences, many state laws require that credit be given only by certified teachers. Some CETA agencies have overcome that barrier by hiring a teacher to run the work-experience program.

CAREER EDUCATION IN THE COMMUNITY
Work experiences provided by CETA are not the only way students can gain academic credit in the community. The Experienced-Based Career Education program in Greenville County, South Carolina, provides credit for career exploration to high school juniors and seniors. Students can sign up for one or two semesters. The first semester gives students a chance to explore three to four jobs. The student who wants to explore a single career in greater depth can then sign up for an internship for the second semester.

The career exploration course begins with a two-week orientation. Students complete self-awareness exercises to determine interests and skills. Next they learn about clusters of careers and are guided in relating their interests to a career choice. The step includes career counseling to ensure that students make realistic choices on careers. The students then read about their chosen careers to gain some background and learn some of the jargon they are likely to encounter on the job.

They must pass a proficiency test to indicate they have read and understood the material.

The program was developed with the aid of an advisory committee representing business and industry, says Alice Badenoch, project coordinator. The required reading was added after it was discovered that students with no preparation soon run out of things to talk about with their employer/teacher. After the orientation, the students spend six hours a week for nine weeks at each site. They observe and talk with their mentor and help with job-related tasks. Students who choose the second semester internship sign a learning contract developed by the school guidance counselor.

Badenoch says the program is popular with employers because it teaches social responsibility to potential employees. The program enhances the morale of the employer/teachers because their job is considered important by the school district and by the student. Other employees are proud that their company is contributing to the community.

The program is open to students of all ability levels but does not admit those with discipline or attendance problems. While career exploration might motivate such students, the school district is unwilling to risk alienating the business community by sending students who could be disruptive.

THE COMMUNITY AS A CLASSROOM

The local community offers a rich resource that can augment the types of experiences offered in the classroom. The new settings offer variety to the students and access to materials unavailable in the school house. One of the oldest experiments in using the community as a classroom is the Parkway program in Philadelphia. Students are based at one of five rented townhouses and take most of their courses in the community. The program was created in 1969 to serve two needs, according to Parkway director James Lytle. Politically active students were critical of the rigidity of traditional high school education. At the same time, the district needed more high school classrooms. One district administrator suggested using space in the community instead of building a new school.

About half the classes are held in church basements, YWCA buildings, and other institutions that do not charge the district. These are generally regular courses, taught by certified Philadelphia teachers. Other courses take advantage of the special learning opportunities of specific locations. History classes, for example, are taught at Independence Historical Park. During the fifteen-week course, students spend alternate weeks in Constitution Hall, Betsy Ross's house, and other spots where historical events actually happened. Two Philadelphia teachers are assigned to the park full-time, primarily to give tours to elementary students. Parkway scheduled the history classes in the afternoon to take advantage of the teachers' availability. The local utility company teaches a basic electricity course to Parkway students at the utility building. And the biology teacher schedules some of her classes at a nature center on the outskirts of Philadelphia.

In addition to course work, Parkway students gain academic credit for volunteer work in hospitals, museums, and local businesses. A student working in the hospital animal lab receives credit in biology, a student working for a community newspaper receives English credit, and a student working in the hospital's bookkeeping department earns secretarial credit. Community credits are generally given for course work beyond the minimum required for graduation. Lytle says Parkway has had no problem with colleges accepting these credits. In fact, some students take college courses in the community.

Although a few classes are offered in Parkway's rented townhouses, most meet in scattered community locations. Some classes, such as Algebra I, look no different from the Algebra I class at a traditional Philadelphia high school. Advantages, other than cost savings, include a treasured privacy for the teachers. "There are no bells, no principals peeking in the doors," Lytle explains. The program also has "virtually no discipline problem" because there are no hallways or bathrooms to patrol. "If the student wants to smoke between classes, he can smoke as he's walking down the street."

The main problem with such freedom is that some students are overwhelmed by it and "forget to go to school for a while," Lytle adds. Parkway tries to avoid this problem through an orientation for students and their parents that stresses the self-discipline required. Students are selected to attend Parkway strictly by an open lottery. Some students who can't handle the freedom voluntarily transfer to other schools. For the others, the staff seems to tolerate some class-skipping in hopes the students will realize the need for personal responsibility. This laissez-faire attitude seems fairly effective. Instead of having a problem with dropouts, Parkway's primary concern is that many students are graduating in three years rather than four. Lytle says the school is reexamining its minimum course requirements.

The other drawbacks, according to Lytle, are that the district refuses to purchase the townhouses, and lost leases cause lots of moving. Students often have to walk to class in the rain, and a janitor occasionally forgets to unlock a donated classroom, forcing last minute readjustments. "But the advantages far outweigh the disadvantages," he adds.

THE COMMUNITY AS TEXTBOOK

The community offers resources other than classroom space and teachers. The people, history, and culture of a community can provide rich source material for a magazine published by students. In the process of collecting information, students polish such skills as interviewing, photography, writing, editing, and paste-up. At the same time, they learn about their heritage and share this information with the rest of the community. Student magazines chronicling local history and culture first began in the late 1960s and have grown to a movement known as "oral cultural journalism." By far, the most successful venture is the magazine, *Foxfire*, which is published quarterly by students at Rabun County, Georgia, High School.

Begun in 1967 as an after-school project, *Foxfire* has grown to a paid staff of ten and a constellation of school courses. With camera, notebook, and tape recorder, students capture the lives of colorful local characters like Aunt Arie, an eighty-five-year-old woman who still fetches her own water. Others write series of articles on a single theme, such as banjomaking or blacksmithing. All serve to preserve the heritage of this corner of Appalachia in a positive and creative way.

The success of *Foxfire* has led to a series of books published by Anchor/Doubleday that contain selections from the magazine. *The Foxfire Book* and *Foxfire 2* through *5* are already available, and contracts are signed through *Foxfire 7*. Royalties pay the salaries of seven teachers who teach such courses as Photography, Folklore and Appalachian Music, Record Production, and Video Journalism. The magazine itself is the focus of two courses. *Foxfire 1* introduces students to interviewing, transcribing, grammar, and techniques such as writing description. Students write the magazine articles in Foxfire 2, a course they can take up to four times.

The project publishes a newsletter, *Hands On*, that exchanges information on publishing with 150 similar projects around the country.[3] *Foxfire* is also the subject of *You and Aunt Arie*, a textbook on cultural journalism.[4]

Cultural journalism is not without its hazards, according to *Foxfire* originator Eliot Wigginton. Districts are liable for any accidents that occur to students during school hours. Some schools require that students carry their own insurance, while others cover the students in an overall district policy. *Foxfire* is able to afford its own multimillion dollar policy. Other problems can be caused by errors in a story or telltale comments that the source regrets sharing with the student. To avoid hard feelings, the magazine requires students to show the completed article to the source and get written permission to publish it. An article can also cause friction at home if the topic is controversial and the student is on one side and parents are on the other.

In Rabun County, the problems pale in comparison to the benefits. *Foxfire* staff member Margie Bennett points out that the county is poor and would not be able to afford the magazine-related classes without the book royalties. The project also works with drama classes and is paying to import a theater group from Atlanta. While most schools could not hope to generate royalties from nationally distributed books, the potential is present in every community to produce a magazine based on local heritage.

LEARNING FROM VOLUNTEERING

Volunteer jobs for students provide another source of learning in the community. In fact, nineteen schools across the country have begun offering a credit course in volunteering. The course was written by the National Information Center on Volunteerism (NICOV) and is taught through the schools in cooperation with community groups. Students attend class part of the week and spend the rest of the class time volunteering in the community. According to project director, Mary Ann Ganey-Wieder, the course teaches students about the economic role of volunteers, provides career exploration and job-seeking skills, and gives students a greater understanding of their community.

The program is run in each community by a three-person team: a teacher, a staff member of a volunteer bureau, and a member of a community service organization such as Junior League. The course is part of the teacher's regular load. The volunteer bureau places the students in the community and the community organization serves as a resource for the teacher, supervising students in volunteer placements and fund raising where necessary.

The curriculum begins with a discussion of who volunteers, with an eye to breaking down stereotypes. Next, the students explore volunteer possibilities, are interviewed by the volunteer bureau, and complete an application form—all skills important to successful job seeking. The volunteer bureau guides the student to think in terms of personal goals or ways the student can gain from the experience. Guest speakers can range from a Junior League volunteer to the director of a hospital's volunteer program to the associate director of the United Way.

After students begin volunteering, they meet about every ten days in "reflection groups." The students are asked what they are learning about themselves, about other people, and about the community. For example, students volunteering at the Red Cross are asked to look at how volunteers fit into the agency's bureaucracy. They are expected to know the goals of the Red Cross and how the volunteer helps the agency fulfill those goals. Other questions examine the differing roles of board members and staff in community organizations.

Another unit of the course examines the role of volunteers in the economy. "In 1974, volunteers contributed $34 billion in services that were not counted in the Gross National Product," says Ganey-Wieder. "What would happen at a hospital if one day none of the volunteers showed up?" The students discuss the implications for a hospital's budget and the impact volunteering can have when local taxes are slashed. Students also learn how volunteer positions can help them select careers. Advocacy groups, such as Sierra Club and Common Cause, are discussed as another form of volunteering.

Students volunteer in a variety of ways. A St. Louis resident who lives in a housing project tutored young children at a nearby community center. Her work led to a summer job at the same center, where she arranged field trips for the children. "She took them to the zoo, the art gallery, the Museum of Science—places she'd never been," says Ganey-Wieder. Organizing the activities and supervising the children "really helped her grow," she adds.

Although most programs involve high school students, the Kalamazoo volunteer project includes one junior high and a school for the mentally impaired. Volunteer activities for the retarded focus on practical applications of skills they learn in school. Some, for example, tutor younger retarded students in how to make change. Others answer telephones at the school or deliver hot meals to senior citizens through the Meals on Wheels program. The students gave a Christmas party at a nursing home, which gave them experience talking with adults they did not know. Ganey-Wieder says volunteering is valuable for the self-image of a retarded person because it gives them a chance to contribute instead of always receiving help from others.

The community benefits from the program in several ways. First, the program provides an immediate supply of volunteers and the prospect that the students will continue to volunteer for the rest of their lives. One of the goals of the program is to show students they get as much out of volunteering as they put in. "Volunteer bureaus are willing to place kids, but there is often no mechanism to get to them," Ganey-Wieder says. The three-way team "creates a bridge into the school for the community." The program also provides the community with a chance for meaningful participation. "Advisory committees often become a rubber stamp for the (school) administration," Ganey-Wieder comments. By contrast, the volunteer program brings together teachers, volunteer bureau staff, and community volunteers as equals.

Teachers cannot run the program alone, she adds. They often do not live in the community and have not worked in social services, so they do not know where the volunteer opportunities are. Teachers also don't have time to make "thoughtful placements" that give students the best possible experience.

One drawback is that some would criticize devoting an entire course to volunteering, given the other requirements students must fulfill. Ganey-Wieder notes, however, that volunteer tutors are generally more motivated in their class work and students who volunteer for career exploration begin to take their other courses more seriously.

NICOV developed the curriculum and trained the participants through a three-year grant from the Kellogg Foundation. The curriculum will be available for purchase in 1980.[5]

YOUTH IN NEW ROLES

One of the primary reasons for involving students in the community is to provide an opportunity for growth. To make the transition from dependent child to independent adult, adolescents must have an opportunity to take responsibility and make decisions. The National Commission Resources for Youth operates a clearinghouse for projects that involve young people in meaningful, innovative ways. Commission members visited many projects around the country and described them in the book, *New Roles for Youth in the School and the Community.*[6] They identified projects where students created curricula, tutored other students, and counseled troubled peers. In the community, some young people operated businesses and others educated tenants on their rights under the law. The common thread binding all the examples was that students took responsibility for solving a problem or meeting a need. In many cases, the students made a significant contribution to the community while learning from the experience.[7]

In Moraga, California, for example, Campolindo High School students have contributed to the community's awareness and understanding of the problems of pollution. Also, recycling equipment purchased by the students attacks the problem of solid waste in the community. The recycling center is run by a loose-knit club known as EARTH— the Ecology Movement. The club began in 1969 as an adjunct to an ecology unit in a twelfth-grade government course. The club's first emphasis was on problem solving. In its earliest days, one of the club's most significant activities was presenting testimony at a conference convened by the Department of the Interior's Federal Water Pollution Control Commission.

According to *New Roles for Youth:*

Earth representatives gave the assembled delegates a real shock. (They) called attention to a federal law that limits the use of federal waters to owners of 160 acres of land or less; they analyzed the implications of this law; and then requested a congressional investigation to determine why the law was not being enforced. Their presentation ... stirred up considerable controversy. Although this law remains unenforced, the Campolindo students opened many people's eyes to the opportunities already available for fighting the continuing misuse of natural resources.

Over the years, the focus of EARTH has changed from problem solving and research to advocacy and protest. The two social studies teachers who were the original advisers have left the school and the ecology course was cancelled in the wake of Proposition 13. Under the guidance of science teacher Tony deBellis, the students are demonstrating against nuclear power plants and fund-raising for Greenpeace, an organization dedicated to saving whales. The students have used some of the recycling income to subscribe to publications from the Solar Heating Association, the Sierra Club, and Greenpeace. They have installed a solar collector as a demonstration project and hope to build an electric car.

All club decisions are determined by a majority vote of the members, an exercise deBellis terms "practical democracy. It's slow and painful, but it works." The club also serves as an outlet for upper-middle-class students who view their San Francisco suburb as a "white ghetto," deBellis adds.

EARTH has been criticized by some parents for its activist stands, particularly against nuclear power. Their complaint is that schools, as tax-supported institutions, should not take stands on controversial issues. DeBellis points out, however, that the club is self-supporting. He is somewhat concerned that the school district may take over the recycling center for the income it produces.

While the club is run by students, it is inevitably influenced by the adults who volunteer their time as advisers. DeBellis regrets that the students have abandoned the problem solving, saying that is not his strength. "I wish other teachers would come on board," he concludes, "but they won't. It's too much work."

STUDENT ENTREPRENEURS

Students can gain both insights and skills from the experience of running their own business. At Manual High School in Denver's inner city, principal James Ward helped students establish several companies in order to build a house. The purpose was not only to train students in various building trades, but to teach them aspects of managing and owning their own business. The students formed the Manual High School Realty Corporation and bid on a plot of urban-renewal land close to the school. Ward accompanied the students to the bank, helped them apply, and co-signed the loan.

Three more student companies were formed to complete the project. The Architectural Company designed the building, the Manual Accounting Company paid the bills and maintained the books, and Thunderbolt Construction Company supervised the building. Students in English classes drafted the contracts and wrote correspondence. Building trades students did all the labor—except plumbing and brick-laying—under the guidance of twenty-six cooperating labor unions. According to Ward, the plumbers were unwilling to work with the students unless the school installed a full apprenticeship program. The school did not because instead of training plumbers, the purpose of the project was to give the students enough experience at a trade to determine whether they wanted to pursue further training. Some students continued in the building trades after graduation while others learned they would rather do something else. However, all students learned valuable skills they can use in their own homes. According to *New Roles for Youth,* participating students had better attendance and lower drop-out rate than the school average.

Families from the surrounding community bid on the house when it was complete. Although it sold for less than the students spent, the students were very proud they had provided a home for a family who otherwise would have been unable to afford one.

The four student companies were merged into one that signed contracts with Denver Urban Renewal Authority (DURA) to design mini-parks, install sidewalks, and rehabilitate homes in the area. Under another contract, English classes prepared booklets that explained DURA programs to neighborhood residents. According to Manual assistant principal Galen Vanderlinden, the sidewalk installation was a profit-making venture that subsidized the other work. The student-run corporation, Creative Urban Living Environment (CULE), paid students a small salary during the school year. During the summer, some workers made minimum wage while other more experienced students made higher wages. Students were slower at the more difficult home-building jobs, so each of those projects lost money. Overall, however, the corporation broke even.

With a change of superintendents, the district decided to dissolve the student corporation because of concerns over liability. In essence, students ran the corporation, but the district was liable for any injuries without technically having control over the decision making. Another significant change is that the program has moved from Manual to a central career education center. Since desegregation, Manual has gained many more middle-class students who are not interested in the building trades. Also, the career center offers students a chance to sign up for a course for larger blocks of time. One of the last contracts involving Manual students was with Historic Denver, a nonprofit preservation group. Students had two hours to spend at the site, but by the time they were transported to and from the houses, they only had about one hour to work. Historic Denver was forced to recontract for the second and third houses because the refurbishing was taking too long.

Building trades students now work as subcontractors who do labor but do not play a role in managing the projects. The emphasis, however, is still on making a contribution to the community. The district is negotiating with Brothers Redevelopment, a nonprofit agency, to have the career education students rehabilitate a number of low-income houses on Denver's west side.

ARCHEOLOGY IN THE COMMUNITY

An archeological find in Cobb County, Georgia, led to an unusual cooperative arrangement between the high school and professional archeologists. The find was actually discovered by a high school student who had been doing volunteer work on a nearby dig. He noticed fragments of pottery on a twenty-two acre yard adjacent to Pebblebrook High School and mentioned it to the archeologists. They determined the area to be of archeological significance. At the same time, the archeologists learned that a six-foot pipeline was about to be installed through the middle of the site. Because time was short, the archeologists asked the principal about using students as volunteers. The school board accepted the proposal and students were interviewed. The project accepted only students who had two study halls, and they worked half a school day for four weeks. The archeologists and a graduate student in anthropology supervised the students. A history teacher served as the project's liaison with the school system.

"The students were both enthusiastic and careful," says *New Roles For Youth*. "They asked pertinent questions and never complained." One archeologist even commented that the students "were more able than most older people to evaluate their discoveries because they were less easily shocked by the differences between contemporary civilization and the culture they were uncovering."[8]

Although the students did not receive academic credit, there was a purely educational side to the project. Lectures and slide shows were presented on such subjects as cultural geography, environmental ecology, and primitive economics. A geologist interpreted geological formations and other specialists analyzed the soil.

At the end of the four weeks, the student participants and their teachers answered questionnaires. According to *New Roles For Youth*, students said, "I have learned to be more observant" and "I have learned to make better use of my time. It helped me to develop into a more responsible person." Teachers reported improvements in grades, attention span, and attitudes, with the greatest improvement occurring among the poorest students.

At the time of the excavation, Cobb County was growing rapidly and much construction was underway. As other threatened sites were uncovered, other Cobb County schools began archeology programs. At Pebblebrook, the success of the first project led to a pass/fail credit course for participants. Excavation was done during fall and spring, and many students signed up for an optional anthropology class during the winter term.

During the years the excavations were underway, 142 Pebblebrook students participated directly, and nearly 1,000 students heard lectures or saw exhibits. According to *New Roles,* "the archeologists observed growth in all intellectual traits that mark successful archeological work: patience, careful elaboration of argument, sensitivity to detail, and adherence to logic combined with respect for intuition."[9] Students gained social skills by working in teams that often paired "A" students with "D" students in an activity where both could excel.

Of course, not every school will have access to a prehistoric site. Even where sites are available, they may contain artifacts too insignificant to warrant the time and energy required. But when the opportunity presents itself, such a project gives youth an opportunity to make an important contribution to their community while learning a great deal about themselves and our past.

SCHOOL-COMMUNITY COLLABORATION

In an era of declining resources, schools need to develop other forms of community cooperation. Tax-supported institutions, in general, are under fire from citizens who feel they are not getting their money's worth. In this climate, it behooves schools to try to eliminate duplication and cooperate with other government agencies wherever possible.

In Cambridge, Massachusetts, the city school district and Department of Health and Hospitals have collaborated to combine school nursing services with neighborhood health centers. The results have meant not only a saving of money but improved health care for the low-income residents of Cambridge. The program operates at five schools in low-income areas of the city. Instead of a regular school nurse, the school is staffed by a pediatric nurse practitioner who is supervised by a pediatrician from Cambridge City Hospital. According to Dr. Philip Porter, one of the originators of the program, the nurses deliver routine service that would be given in a pediatrician's office.

The clinics are open to children from birth through adolescence.

When complications arise, the children are brought into Cambridge City Hospital or the intensive care unit of Massachusetts General Hospital. Because the staff physicians at Cambridge Hospital are the nurses' supervisors, they are likely to be familiar with the case. These physicians are also on the staff of Massachusetts General, which makes for a free flow of information at all levels of the system.

The conversion to neighborhood health centers was made in 1968, and the program was evaluated after ten years. The doctors found that 90 percent of the children who live in the area are using the clinic, indicating high public acceptance of the program. Ninety-eight percent of the children were also immunized. Over the ten years, the incidence of iron deficiency and high levels of lead in the blood had decreased. Before the program began, Cambridge City Hospital had a serious problem of low-income persons coming to the emergency ward for minor problems. After the neighborhood clinics were established, inappropriate use of the emergency ward dropped 50 percent. This change meant the emergency ward was less crowded and could more effectively serve true emergencies, so the saving was in human terms as well as dollars, Porter said.

In Cambridge, the school district and the hospital are both departments of the city, which made the merger easier than it would be in most communities. To effect the change, money was reallocated from one area of the budget to another. According to Porter, however, the proposal encountered "all the political problems you can imagine." Some people opposed the idea merely because it was a change, while others opposed it because they were affected. The janitors union was up in arms, for example, because the clinics stay open until 5:00 P.M., while school ends at 2:30. Objections were also raised because the clinics are open year-round while school is out over the summer. Planning for the change began in 1965, and Porter spent three years determining what the community wanted. Although the program appears to have high community acceptance, Porter says political problems have been "continual."

Political problems all but obliterated a program of shared resources in Bethlehem, Pennsylvania. The Bethlehem Area Community Education Project combined the resources of the school district, the city recreation department, local nonprofit agencies, and a number of state agencies. In essence, the school provided space and coordinators to run the programs, local agencies provided the services, and state agencies provided the funds. Four schools throughout the city participated, offering hot lunch programs for senior citizens, a daycare center, dental clinics, a well-baby clinic, recreation programs, and adult education classes.

The project lasted two years, then was dropped by the city and school district through budget cuts. According to one administrator, however, the problem was more political than financial. "The community supported it but the leadership did not," says David Shelly, principal of Donegan Elementary. One fatal flaw was that four of the five persons hired to run the program were from outside the community. "They did not know which strings to pull," says Shelly. "It took a year or two to find out, and by that time, they'd done the wrong thing." One sore point was that the project coordinator was paid a higher salary than some directors of nonprofit agencies received. The local teachers' union was miffed because the project asked teachers to lead night classes for less than the union's hourly scale.

Community education survived in modified form at Donegan Elementary, one of the four original schools. The largely Hispanic community formed Community Schools, Inc., to run the programs through a neighborhood council. From 1977 to 1979, the council received federal manpower funds and local donations to pay a director and an outreach person. Programs included establishing a community garden plot, training minorities to take the city civil service exam, and providing day care, night classes, and a well-baby clinic. Since manpower funds were running out, the council approached a local community college about continuing the program. The college has applied for federal community education funds.

One hurdle that faced the first Bethlehem project was coordination between a large number of entities. In an era of scarce tax resources, mammoth projects are more difficult to sell. A more modest proposal that has worked well in Englewood, Colorado, involves cooperation between city and school libraries. The Denver suburb is geographically small and has only one public library building. From 1973 to 1979, a public library employee operated a school library in each quadrant of the city four nights of the week (one night at each library). Adult patrons could read the school library's magazines and could check out volumes from shelves reserved for public library books. The librarian rotated the collection periodically and would bring books from the public library on request.

The program has changed for several reasons. Now, the public library uses only one of the buildings four nights a week. The change was made in 1979 after Sharon Winkle became director of the city library. She explained that night usage of the four school libraries was low and she hoped to increase usage by concentrating the service and publicizing it in a single neighborhood.

The school building chosen, Scenic View, had been closed by the Englewood Schools. The building is now rented by a regional education cooperative that offers adult education. Although the relationship is no longer with Englewood schools, the shared use is still with a publicly supported education entity. Winkle said she chose Scenic View because it is the farthest neighborhood from the central library and because it is the most geographically dintinct area in the city (it is surrounded on three sides by Denver and another suburb). The regional service agency operating programs at Scenic View has specialized libraries, such as one concentrating on career education, that complement the public library's collection. Winkle stressed that the change from four libraries to one was not made because of problems or conflicts with the schools, but merely in an effort to build usage of the satellite library.

The city library and the Englewood schools do continue to cooperate in two other ways. The city children's librarian visits the schools to talk with teachers about ways the library can provide them with services. Also, the city-operated bookmobile makes regular stops at many Englewood schools. Each stop attracts both children from the school and adults from the neighborhood. The bookmobile librarian visits classrooms and gives "book talks" to stimulate children's interest in reading. She also supplies teachers with sets of books or specific resources not available in the school library.

Public uses of school buildings are often the first to go when school budgets are cut. The added utility and janitorial costs are difficult to justify because they are not directly related to the education of children. In cases where the after-school user is another tax-supported institution, however, there are sometimes reciprocal benefits to compensate for out-of-pocket expenses. At the very least, when such cooperative arrangements eliminate duplication, the district demonstrates it is a careful steward of public funds. It also gives the schools a chance to serve childless taxpayers who otherwise receive no direct benefits from the district.

CONCLUSION

Many of the problems schools face are caused by their isolation from the community. The examples in this chapter illustrate promising practices where schools are overcoming that isolation. But the examples represent the pioneers rather than the norm. A number of obstacles block efforts at collaboration. Teachers and principals may be reluctant to involve the public for fear they will lose power. If volunteers converge on the schools in large numbers, they reason, they may start telling school people what to do.

A chasm of suspicion and lack of respect separates the schools from the business community. Employers who encounter unqualified job applicants blame the schools for doing an inadequate job. And teachers blame "big business" for polluting the environment and compromising the political process. Educational materials coming from such a source are bound to be "tainted."

Perhaps the biggest obstacle to collaboration is apathy, on the part of both the schools and the community. Teachers find it easier to stay in their classrooms and do things the old way, rather than try a new approach. Parents are wrapped up in their own problems, and members of the community think it is pointless to try to make a difference.

To maintain the status quo is the easy way out. It takes hard work, initiative, and some risk to begin cooperative arrangements. But the benefits in improved education, increased public confidence, and more efficient use of resources make the task well worth the effort.

NOTES

1. George Kaplan, *From Aide to Teacher: The Story of the Career Opportunity Program,* U.S. Government Printing Office, Washington, D.C., 1977.

2. Massachusetts Advocacy Center, *Equal Opportunity Denied,* Boston, 1976.

3. Subscription information is available from *Foxfire,* Rabun Gap, Georgia 30568.

4. Published by IDEAS, Dept. N, Magnolia State Rte., Nederland, Colorado 80466.

5. Request from the Natitnal Information Center on Volunteerism, P.O. Box 4179, Boulder, Colorado 80306.

6. National Commission on Resources for Youth, *New Roles for Youth in the School and the Community,* Citation Press, New York, 1974.

7. Ibid., pp.138–139.

8. Ibid., p.78.

9. Ibid., pp. 80–81.

11

EDUCATION, SCHOOLS, AND A SENSE OF COMMUNITY

JOHN I. GOODLAD
University of California, Los Angeles and
/I/D/E/A

Throughout this volume are assumptions about the meaning of education and community and the role of schools in both. My central assumption is that schools are in varying degrees learning communities with unique potential for developing a sense of community. Of primary importance is whether schools are contributing significantly to a sense of community—in effect, whether they are doing what no other existing institution in our society is as well equipped to do.

My position has been so effectively stated by Schwab that I quote at length:

> First, community can be learned. It is not primarily a matter of place, of village or small town, but a body of propensities toward action and feeling, propensities which can be expressed in many social circumstances.
>
> Second, human learning is a communal enterprise. The knowledge we learn has been garnered by a community of which we are only the most recent members and is conveyed by languages of word and gesture devised, preserved, and passed on to us by that community. . . . Even "experience" as a form of learning *becomes* experience only as it is shared and given meaning by transactions with fellow human beings. . . .
>
> It should be noted that though communal propensities, once developed, can find expression in many social circumstances, they cannot develop in *any* such circumstance. They require rewarding collaboration, communication, helping and being helped, toward goals we have set ourselves, or which have been set for us by need and want. Among these goals, learning stands high. . . . It follows, then, that a school of some sort constitutes the social climate in which the propensities toward community can best develop. The American public school can and should become such a school.[1]

The need is great. There has been a withering of community. There has been a steady, accelerating erosion of the educative function of the school. Ironically, the latter has transpired in part out of efforts to use the school to buttress the community.

Ideally, "community" and "school" can be seen as concepts as well as places. In concept, the two are very similar; both imply people coming together because of common traits, interests, activities, or goals. Members of some of the strongest intellectual communities or schools are scattered around the world, coming together only occasionally and in different settings. I deal in what follows with communities and schools as places, too. But it is my contention that preoccupation with them as places has taken our attention away from the essence of both—

namely, that a sense of community is learned and schools are for learning. To intervene in either "place" without this basic understanding, however noble our intentions, is to increase the prospect of a further withering of community and continued erosion of education in schools.

The reader might readily infer, now, another assumption which I hasten to eschew. It is that schools as institutions are the *only* learning communities and, therefore, the sole bastions and purveyors of education. Much education goes on in places other than schools and more should—as some community educators contend. The ideal educative community or society is not, for me, one where the school has expanded upwards, downwards, and sideways to embrace the whole of educating. Rather, the educative community or society is one in which all institutions play their educational roles to their full potential. The school does educationally within the community ecosystem that which no other institution is as well equipped to do.

THE WITHERING OF COMMUNITY AS BOTH PLACE AND CONCEPT

People need a sense of belonging to something larger than themselves that has a past, present, or future: family, neighborhood, town, city, nation, world, humankind. One feels at home, without alienation, in an expanding array of diverse groups. Individuals and the human community benefit mutually. After his year at Walden (interspersed regularly with visits to and from friends and neighbors), Thoreau saw more clearly than before the need for three chairs: one for himself, one for a friend, and one for civilization. What has withered most across this land is the spiritual, not the physical, essence of community.

The physical decay of urban communities has been well documented, as has been the mixed bag of efforts to rehabilitate them. But too little attention has been given, outside of academic circles, to the human perceptions leading to accepting, or contributing to, this decay. Residents of relatively stable communities commuting daily to downtown Chicago on the Illinois Central, *circa* the mid-1950s, exchanged horror stories as they sped by the newly built high-rise housing project located south and a little west of the city's Loop: of garbage and defecation in hallways, of defaced elevators, broken windows, smashed doors. "How could people do this to their own homes?" inevitably was the query of ultimate incredulity. Their own homes? Were they?

The Chicago scene was played and replayed in city after city. The signs of decay—deteriorating buildings, poverty, and violence—for the most part intensified. Rapid decline in a sense of community, interlaced with racial intolerance, was rapidly producing what Conant referred to as "social dynamite."[2] The proposed solution was education. Behind the Elementary and Secondary Education Act was the idea articulated in President Johnson's 1965 message to Congress that education is at the heart of and the solution to all our problems. We would go down in history as the nation that used its educational system to solve the problems of unemployment, poverty, crime, and even world peace. The schools were to be thrown into every breach.

There is little doubt that the human and monetary resources directed to these problems defused some of the social dynamite. Just how much worse off we would have been without them is impossible to determine. Schooling and social engineering together accomplished more than many people are willing to concede. But much of the effort was firefighting for which schools in particular are poorly equipped. The result of using our schools for what they are ill-suited to do was not just disillusionment with schools as agents for firefighting but loss of confidence in schooling. From expecting too much of schools we went to expecting too little.

The issue, however, is not one of how much to expect of education and schooling but what. From our understanding of education should emerge our views on the uses of schools.

There were two major misunderstandings or misinterpretations of education underlying at least the rhetoric of the 1960s regarding the social uses of schooling. The first was that education can solve social problems in the short run—for instance, in the two-, four-, or six-year term of political office holders. Education is a long-term solution to society's ills. Schools always have been asked to serve social purposes and always will. But they must have time to convert them to educational ends and means which have a degree of detachment from immediate problems likely to be more amenable to social engineering.

The second misinterpretation also is instrumental in nature: Education is something done to people. They are "processed" for their own and society's good. The extreme but nonetheless widely accepted view is that schools are factories: "Like a factory, education takes raw materials (students) and processes them through its operations (curriculum) to satisfy demands for products and/or success (jobs) in society."[3] The task is finite and gratifyingly definable: "The public education process culminates when the student leaves the institution to accept a permanent job for a specified salary."[4] I turn later to the educational corruptions stemming from these instrumental views.

But, first, I return to the commuters' shocked commentary on people destroying their own "homes." They mutilated their places of abode, perhaps, but not their homes. Whatever sense of home most of the inhabitants of this housing project once had was of another place and time. Now, they felt no sense of power and control, no sense of identity with their environment. Abusing it was one of the few ways available to put their mark on it. Defecating in the hallways was infantile, perhaps, but nonetheless an explicit way of simultaneously demonstrating contempt and a measure of power.

We are learning, slowly and painfully, that paternalistic interventions, however well-intended, do not assure either better physical communities or a sense of community. The goal should be to foster increased confidence, power, and action on the part of those who inhabit a geographic area. This is what education, viewed both developmentally and ecologically, can do. "It begins where people are and assists their intellectual, social, psychological, cultural and political growth, using their environment as a basis for development."[5]

These words slide past us comfortably and easily. They appear eminently sensible and have constituted the rhetoric of progressive and alternative education. But the course of action they imply is difficult for both educators and social engineers. This is in large part because professionals grossly underestimate the feelings of powerlessness possessed by large numbers of the people they want to help, having themselves been largely protected from the worst effects of social powerlessness. Actions designed to improve local circumstances too often assume a higher level of confidence and so reach those already relatively adept at helping themselves. The problem is to reach also those who feel least control over their personal lives and develop in them the confidence they need to board the train.[6]

Just a short time ago, the answer to reaching black children through the schools was more black teachers and administrators. The general effect probably was positive, especially when "black is beautiful" was the rallying call for developing self-respect. But many black educators have pulled away or are far removed—economically and socially—from the circumstances and perceptions they were to remedy. The educational principles relevant to increasing the independence, power, and autonomy of people transcend color and race.

Educators often have difficulty beginning where people are because of traditional stereotypes regarding the teaching role. We see Mark Hopkins on one end of the log and the tutee on the other. Or, the teacher is at the front of rows of desks imparting knowledge to passive pupils. The idea of beginning where individuals are, with their diversity of problems, needs, and interests is downright scary. It is so much easier to wall off these realities with the curriculum, the course, and lists of required readings. For such a reason, not the irrelevance or unattractiveness of the ideas, progressive education (for me, the word progressive coupled with education is a redundancy) has not yet been seriously tried in the public school system.

It would be a mistake to conclude from the foregoing that education and schools are all that are required for the development of a sense of community and the concurrent greening of communities. The process of developing a sense of community is itself communal; it is difficult to bring people together if they are afraid to walk to the place of meeting. Consequently, studies of the environment and the use of physical, civil, and social engineering must accompany education and be guided by the same principles of ecology and learning.

While the commuters in Chicago viewed with dismay a foredoomed housing project, a quite different kind of rehabilitation activity was under-way just a few miles away. Solutions were being sought not in federal or local governmental offices but in the kitchens and sitting rooms of houses in the vicinity of the University of Chicago. The residents of the area and the administration and faculty of the university (many of them the same people) decided that they had had enough of breaking and entering, stolen cars, muggings on the streets in front of their homes, and more serious crimes.

The fact that people who perceived themselves as having unique capabilities and power increasingly found themselves powerless and frightened is significant. Imagine, then, the plight of those who chronically regard themselves as powerless in the face of community deterioration.

The university intervened directly by providing low-interest loans to enable more faculty families to buy houses in the area and by purchasing land for purposes of constructing quality, low-cost housing. But these efforts, themselves a gamble, would have fallen far short if they had not been accompanied by enlightened efforts to sustain a long-standing sense of community. Those efforts began with environmental realities, recognized growing feelings of fear and impotence, and employed enlightened educational techniques honed in the laboratories of social science. The effect was purposeful, resourceful, and sustained.

Students, professors, and anyone desiring to live in and use the community simply had to learn to go and come together, to accompany and be accompanied, as had not been necessary in earlier years. There were those who believed that baseball bats were a desirable added precaution. But to go armed against marauders and assailants is no way to maintain a sense of community. Growing confidence that the community still had a future brought to the fore a latent desire to serve even at considerable personal risk. A professor walking his dog in the evening, accosted suddenly by two armed youths, hesitated not a moment in agreeing to accompany the police on a search for his assailants in nearby bars. Acts of crime in the neighborhood became increasingly less tolerable to the potential victims and less attractive to those accustomed to executing them. With the conditions for basic survival improving, residents became willing to make long-term commitment and investments. New fences, neater yards, and remodeled houses increasingly marked the neighborhood. The community and the university stabilized and survived together.

The story is one of long-term struggle, not unblemished, quick success. Most of the success must be attributed to two interrelated factors. One played to the self-interests of landlords, storekeepers, the university, and those who simply did not want to move or lose their equity in their houses. The other played to that sense of community which is basic to humans and which is a spirit shared. Both relied on essentially the same networking technique—persons of common predicament and varied feelings of powerlessness coming together out of desperation and slowly learning to support and share with one another.[7] These factors and the principles implied are basic, whatever the particular characteristics of a given location.

At the time, what was then referred to as group dynamics was emerging as a technique by which people learned from one another through discussion. The development of mutual understanding and respect characterized a problem-solving process in which no one person such as a teacher possessed all the answers. A leading theoretician, researcher, and exponent of the movement, Herbert Thelen, was a University of Chicago professor, community resident, and dedicated leader-participant. His ideas and techniques, on the frontiers of educational thought, proved to be of utmost practicality in a situation where nobody had the answers. They contributed strategically to the necessary growth of a sense of community.[8] He contributed significantly, also, to the special and necessary rhetoric which is " . . . not the traditional address of the one to the many but the discourse of exchange, of conversation, of discussion, through which persons, face-to-face, came to understand each other, understanding not only what each means but why they mean it—the kind of understanding that makes possible conjoint decision and action."[9]

WHAT EDUCATION AND SCHOOLS SHOULD PROVIDE

Cremin has defined education as " . . . the deliberate, systematic, and sustained effort to transmit or evoke knowledge, attitudes, values, skills, and sensibilities."[10] A sense of individuality inextricably coupled with a sense of community are the quintessential sensibilities to be developed through education. The latter by definition implies a core of shared knowledge, attitudes, values and, to a lesser degree, skills. The former implies deviance, unique abilities, and the possession of uncommon knowledge. The lower schools were created to assure that which is thought to be commonly required, either as double insurance or because of the unlikelihood of its being learned elsewhere in the community—hence the concept of the common school.

The more simple and homogeneous the community, then, the less the residents feel a need for schools.[11] Parents and tribal elders are role models for what is to be learned in common—especially moral values. Individuality, to the degree valued, finds expression in competing with peers in hunting, fishing, and fighting—pursuits related to the survival of the community. But this comfortable coupling of communality and individuality is strained as communities grow larger and more complex and schools take on a larger share of the educating. The more schools seek to teach what is thought to be commonly needed for a community extending far beyond the immediate neighborhood—to the nation as a whole or a global community—the more parents see schooling as vying with or a threat to the moral prerogatives of the family. The guilt of the college graduate who can't go home again after having been financed for years by hardworking parents and the anguished parents who can't comprehend what has happened were the stuff of many American novels throughout the rapid expansion of our system of higher education.

The desired balance between what Schwab refers to as the centrifugal tendencies of homes (differing in ethnicity, national origin, religion, and social class) and the centripetal tendencies of schools (pressing toward greater homogeneity)[12] has been severely upset in recent years. Individuals and groups not seeing their values and interests embodied in the school have sought to impose them. Demands have ranged from matching the color or ethnicity of teachers and administrators with that of the students, to parental choice of teachers and principals, to bilingual or multilingual instruction, to parental selection of alternative schools. With the human community growing more interdependent— albeit fragmented—and with an encompassing sense of community needed as never before, community as a concept has been ravaged by rampant parochialism. The withering of community and erosion of the common school have gone hand in hand:

> ... The community became people of my race, my neighborhood, my economic class. The rhetoric of the community now asserted that the schools belonged to the community, as redefined. "Pluralism" became a popular war cry. The black and white racists, the poor and the rich, the city dweller and the suburbanite all demanded that the schools their children attended should be theirs.... The neighborhood school, meaning a school that ignored the existence or importance of the wider political community, became a sacred object.[13]

While some segments of the population sought to have the school reflect their particular values and interests, another segment began to question whether a common system of schooling was even needed. This was made up of people who had seen their interests reflected in the school and had profited most from it. For them, the work of the common school was done—particularly if gaining access to it meant busing. Ironically, then, as those who now saw the school to be of potential benefit to them increasingly were gaining the power to influence it, those who had gained the most from the common school were ready to give it away. For the latter group, the voucher plan loomed as an attractive alternative. It appears to offer, next to tutoring, the greatest opportunity to secure compatibility between the values taught in the home and those supported in the school. But serious questions must be raised about maintaining a productive tension between the centrifugal moral force of the home and the centripetal moral force of schools with the public system dismantled and replaced by a voucher plan.

Not surprisingly, while these pressures have been tearing away at the common school, much of the rhetoric of school improvement and some of the substance have stressed those goals appearing to be most value-free—vocational training and the fundamental tools of learning. A back-to-basics movement finds a rather congenial climate when those groups whose values have provided the central thrust of schooling begin to get uneasy about the infusion of new values. But there is no such thing as value-free instruction. Old-style didactics, drill, and order in the classroom carry with them moral baggage stressing competition rather than collaboration and individual effort rather than group problem-solving. Values are being taught and learned in schools at all times without benefit of an explicit course in them.

The salient issue, then, is not whether but what values will be taught in schools and how. The more complex and diverse the community, the more challenging the task of maintaining a sense of community and the greater the need for the school to perform its common, unifying function. This is not easy because it means to a considerable degree resisting the instrumental, processing role which the business and industrial segments of the community in particular seek to impose upon it—and schools have tended to reflect and respond to surrounding pressures.

If we no longer see the need for a common school, no longer expect schools to educate beyond limited competencies, and want these competencies taught cheaply and efficiently, we would be well advised to seek an alternative to the system we now have. We must admit that the response of schools to the vocational interests of business and industry is anything but an unmitigated success story. The poor fit between workers needed and workers trained through the schools is cost-ineffective. Business and industry can and should do a better job of vocational training. It is not the task of the public school to shape human "raw materials" for vocational slots and in so doing create the next generation of unemployed. Vocational training is the worst kind of vocational education, leading to the absurd notion that persons with the most general, liberal education are miseducated or overeducated. If job training is what schools are for, they are not necessary.

The real scandal, however, is in the limited array of opportunities presented to students of low socioeconomic status who are literally tracked into self-fulfilling prophecies of limited futures. School-based vocational training programs are necessarily restricted to a limited segment of the jobs now available in our society. The early tracking of young people into just a few vocations is an injustice, a self-fulfilling prophecy by which those of low socioeconomic status leave school early and rarely return for more education. The home gave up vocational training because it could not provide for the growing employment opportunities in an increasingly industrialized society. Now it is the school's turn to do the same.

Vocational *education* is another matter. It is less reasonable to assume either willingness or readiness on the part of private enterprise to take this over. But in an educative community, business and industry have a responsibility, in collaboration with schools, to introduce the young to many aspects of the world of work and finance. Tax rebates for participating businesses would be an appropriate incentive.

I shall eschew the temptation to elaborate here[14] on Cremin's definition of education and settle for Peters' distinction between education and training:

> I have argued elsewhere that much of the confusion about "aims in education" comes through extracting the normative feature built into the concept of "education" as an intrinsic end. Given that "education" suggests the intentional bringing about of a desirable state of mind in a morally unobjectionable manner, it is only too easy to conceive of education as a neutral process that is instrumental to something that is worthwhile which is extrinsic to it. Just as gardens may be cultivated in order to aid the economy of the household, so children must be educated in order to provide them with jobs and to increase the productivity of the community as a whole.
> But there is something inappropriate about this way of speaking; for we would normally use the word "train" when we had such a specific extrinsic objective in mind. If, however, we do specify an appropriate "aim" such as the development of individual potentialities or the development of intellect and character, then

the aim would be intrinsic to what we would consider education to be.[15]

What many people, including educators, fail to see is that the more we use our schools simply to reinforce parochial values and serve employers' interests, the less our need for them and the greater our need for some other institution to develop sensibilities such as a sense of community transcending "my race, my neighborhood, my economic class." In which direction lies the answer—in the creating of new institutions or in assuring a common school that will be predominately educational in what it does?

There need not and probably will not be an either-or answer to the question posed. Communities differ in their resources for education and training and in their coordination and utilization of them. The context of which schools are a part will significantly influence the extent to which they can be predominantly educational. A basic assumption is that schools (or educative institutions with other names created to replace them) should do educationally that which no other institution does or appears to have the potential for doing equally well.

This does not rule out the addition of education-related services and custodial functions. Since communities differ in their ability to provide education, education-related services, and custodial types of care, schools will and should differ in what they provide beyond education. It is reasonable to assume that a variety of patterns of education and schooling might exist at any given time across this vast land.

THE SCHOOL AS COMMUNITY CENTER

An appropriate pattern for schools in some communities is to provide education-related services beyond the educational program strictly defined. But none of this should be conducted at the expense of the school's central educative task. While simultaneously decrying the school's performance in teaching even the fundamentals of reading, writing, and mathematics, various groups see it as the logical vehicle for doing almost everything else—and without added time and resources. The net effect has been both to burden the school and to cause other institutions either to give up or fail to assume responsibility for anything appearing to require education or special training.

The traditional concepts of a nine-month year, five-day week, and six-hour day make no sense for an institution seeking both to educate the young and to be the focal point for all education-related activities and a host of community services. If this expansion in functions is what we want, then schools must expand in time and resources as these demands increase, ultimately becoming full-year, full-week, full-day institutions run according to principles relevant to such a concept, not the principles normally associated with operating schools.

A comprehensive K–12 school located in one of the most impoverished sections of Tehran, Iran, provides an interesting illustration of what happens when an institution dramatically expands its scope without simultaneously modifying its operating procedures. The school, when I visited it, was administered by a principal who spent almost all her time in the community and a vice-principal who managed the school's internal affairs. The buildings contained the usual classrooms but a significantly greater variety of laboratories, shops, rooms for arts and crafts, and so on than one usually finds. In addition, there were dental, medical, and counseling facilities not only for the students but also for adult members of the community and their preschool children.

The school, I was told, was virtually the sole agency for providing whatever educational and additional human services this otherwise destitute community enjoyed. Adult counseling, for example, ranged from parental, to personal, to economic.

During my visit in early June, I remarked on the general absence of students in a school purportedly enrolling five thousand. And I noticed that equipment and supplies were being boxed and stored away. Oh, I was told, the summer vacation is beginning and the school is about to close. But what about all of the people being served? I asked. Do they not have dental, physical, emotional, and personal problems during the summer? My puzzlement brought forth only puzzled looks in response. The institution was a superb example of a school serving as a community center—but on the school's terms and schedules, not in sensitive response to the realities of the community problems it was seeking to address.

Here in the United States, persons who take most advantage of, for example, adult education classes provided by the local school tend to be those who are most mobile and with incomes well above the poverty level. Indeed, those who take most advantage of all available community services tend to be those who already have and feel considerable control over their own lives. Studies of community educational and other services generally report only numbers (e.g., of courses and enrollees), not more qualitative data on who attends and what role these services play in their lives.

The idea of a school as a twenty-four hour every day community center has much to commend it. There is, however, real danger that the centripetal tendencies of the school will dominate to the detriment of the balance referred to earlier. There may not be enough opportunities for pursuits not infused by those characteristics seemingly unique to schools. The problem is the reverse of that resulting from schools being torn by special interests until they serve no common functions. The apparent safeguard is vigilance to assure that principles we tend to associate with schooling are not allowed to pervade the entire enterprise. Indeed, it probably would be a marked advantage if the school's educative functions, too, were conducted according to only those principles of schooling which have survived the most careful scrutiny.

THE EDUCATIVE ROLE OF THE SCHOOL

Communities vary widely in their access to and development of the components of a comprehensive program of education. Most have untapped potential for job training and inducting the young into the conventions of daily living. Television can and does do more than entertain; we have scarcely begun to exploit its educational possibilities. But neither business, industry, television, newspapers, nor families provide today that deliberate, systematic, sustained effort we associate with educating. With the family itself in trouble and looking to the school for "discipline," the necessary supportive tension between home and school in rearing the young has seriously eroded. School-like institutions are needed, even if a large part of what they now do were taken over elsewhere in the community. They are needed to develop both a sense of selfhood and a sense of community.

To repeat, an institution devoted exclusively to education should do only that which other community institutions do not or probably could not do well. Even those other institutions with a relatively enlightened sense of community do not go far beyond training or demonstrating what is essential to their own self-interests. When businesses think they need employees who follow rules and regulations, it is somewhat incongruous to look to them to teach divergent thinking. As part of its selection process in seeking managers of new outlets, a major brewing company administered a test which included the question: "What would you do if confronted with a problem for which we had not prepared you—nothing, call the head office, or be creative in finding a solution?" The second choice was considered the correct answer. Selecting the third answer would have lost you the franchise.

Schools are needed for assuring attention to problem solving, developing sensitivity and compassion, exploring the world of ideas and human relations, developing self-understanding and a sense of community—the higher literacies. As we come to understand what a sense of community is—a felt membership in an expanding array of human groups—we come to understand not only why we need schools but also why it is difficult for schools to go beyond indoctrination and inculcation and why they must be protected against the endless encroachments of parochialism. Schwab's list of what must be internalized in achieving a sense of community defines what education can do and provides justification for schools:

1. A propensity to find, with others, joint needs and wants which confer on self and others a sufficient identity of purpose and endeavor to constitute an immediate group.

2. A propensity to see others as affording states of character, competence, and habit which complement one's own, thus making each person a part of another who is distinctly other:

    a. Other children differing in ethnic-religious-social class styles, attitudes, and values, as well as children of different talents and abilities.

    b. Other adults differing in the same ways and affording a variety of models.

3. A propensity to seek realization of the complementarities of self and others by welcoming problems which call for the joining of diverse talents and attitudes.

4. A propensity to recognize other and different groups as bearing the same relations to one another that diverse members of an immediate group bear to one another, and to seek similar realization of the complementarities of these groups.

5. A propensity toward reflection—alone, with another, in a group—on past actions and consequences: their circumstances; the means employed; the desirability of the ensuing gains and losses.

6. A propensity toward service, toward the giving and receiving of comfort in disappointment and congratulation on achievement, a propensity deriving from past actions undertaken and undergone with others.

7. A propensity toward accrual of symbols of past achievements and disappointments of a group, and of past members of it; and the celebration of these persons and moments by way of the symbols accrued.[16]

These sensibilities go far beyond the trivialized ends and means now mandated by states for schools. A slow rage begins to build up inside me when I contemplate the limited expectations for schools set by some in leadership positions.

Human societies are most dynamic and self-renewing (and most clearly see the need for education) when there is a productive tension between their present conditions and visions of more desirable conditions. The desire to close this gap must exist or be engendered locally. When states prescribe and mandate minimums, they tend to reduce the gap by lowering visions and not stimulating local initiative. Indeed, they provide the very rhetoric of diminished expectations, simultaneously fueling parochialism. What states have suffered from most in recent years is leadership (sic) unable to transcend the parochialism of special groups and interests perceived by most legislators to be their constituency. State mandates directing schools to do little more than train is a parochially inspired misinterpretation of what communities most need and, I believe, what parents want.

Over a period of more than three hundred years, the rhetoric of what is possible has steadily expanded the educational (and other) expectations for our schools. From a little learning sufficient " . . . to read and understand the principles of religion and the capital laws of the country," these rhetorical expectations not only have expanded but also have received widespread endorsement. Indeed, even those states with the most clearly mandated minimums include somewhere in their stated commitments to education the full range of educational goals that have emerged over three centuries: intellectual/academic, vocational, social/civic, and personal.

Some polls and newspaper stories notwithstanding, recent evidence suggests that parents have much higher educational aspirations for their schools and children than is implied in the back-to-basics movement some politicians seem to find so attractive. In A Study of Schooling, my colleagues and I found each of the four goal areas listed above selected as desirable by parents, teachers, and students with such frequency as to imply the need to set all of them as appropriate guidelines for their schools.[17] McIntire's findings were similar.[18] Indeed, not one carefully done study with contrary findings has come to my attention. The fact that parents want and expect their children to read, write, spell, and compute does not mean that they reject for schools instruction in science, social studies, and the arts.

If schools accepted and committed themselves to carry out these goals, they would provide comprehensive educational programs for the intellectual, vocational, social, and personal development of all children and youth. The rhetoric is familiar; such schools are not. If the rhetoric were translated into practice, we would have the *common* school we've never had. The school has not been common because it has not been commonly attended, or clients left before they had satisfactorily gained what was commonly intended, or students were tracked or elected themselves into things uncommon. Much of this has occurred in the name of individualization but, in truth, as often as not it has resulted from giving up on individuals. By narrowing and segmenting the learning community in schools, even while achieving near-universal secondary schooling, we curtailed development of a universal sense of community at the time we needed it most.

Even a commonly attended school with a comprehensive program encompassing all four sets of educational goals is not necessarily a common school. It can be, and often is, so internally compartmentalized and segregated that students experience little in common, maintaining most of the same divisions characterizing their geographic community. In the thirteen high schools examined in A Study of Schooling, eight were tracked in the four basic subjects and the remaining five were tracked in three of those four subjects. Those students taking a preponderance of vocational courses would have difficulty transferring to an academic curriculum; most would find the switch impossible after the sophomore year. A desegregated school may be virtually devoid of interactions likely to foster multi-ethnic understanding and appreciation. What contribution to a sense of community is made by schools which are not themselves communities? The schools we need, it seems to me, are neither alternative schools nor schools seeking to provide alternative experiences for diverse individuals and groups. They are schools seeking to provide at least a core of educational experiences for students in common.

"But people are different, they do not learn equally well, they have differing interests," go the counter arguments. Of course, but these are not sufficient arguments to warrant abdication of what a common school should imply. What has happened to our enthusiasm for Bruner's thesis that " . . . any subject can be taught effectively in some intellectually honest form to any child at any state of development?"[19] Why have we paid so little attention to the possible implications of research of Bloom and his associates? "Most students become very similar with regard to learning ability, rate of learning, and motivation for further learning—*when provided with favorable learning conditions*" (italics mine).[20] We seem to have chosen the simpler alternative of providing curricular options when we should have been creative in coming up with more favorable learning conditions, whether seeking to teach fundamental skills or cultivate the higher intellectual processes.

In recognition of the planning principals should be doing, most school districts now employ them for at least a month longer than the instructional year. But the need is for entire staffs to be employed for this additional period for purposes of planning programs of instruction commensurate with the four sets of goals enunciated earlier. There should be at hand a body of data on present curricular options in each school and patterns of student movement through them. The challenge to the staff is even greater than assuring a comprehensive, institutional curriculum. The challenge is also to assure that each student secures the broad education to which he is entitled and is not given up on and tracked early into what is likely to become a self-fulfilling prophecy of inadequate personal fulfillment and societal contribution. Are we willing, as a people, to bear the financial costs of full-time, full-year employment for those who bear the most responsibility for creating the schools we require?

AN ECOLOGICAL PERSPECTIVE

Among the utopias envisioned, education—but not necessarily schools—plays a large part. The educative society or community is one in which virtually everyone educates. The rearing of the young is a communal, not just a parental, responsibility.

Usually, there are schools. Schools emerge to do that sustained, systematic, educational task which dynamic societies seem always to require. In an educative community, the school is just one of several or many agencies in an ecosystem.

The theoretical perspective of the school in such a context is quite different from the production model described earlier. Schools are not factories processing raw materials for society's needs. Nor are they the dumping ground for difficulties other institutions confront in performing their functions. One would not say that the school is either the sole cause of or the only vehicle for correcting adolescent misbehavior. One would be concerned, rather, about the prevalence of juvenile delinquency in the community and seek to understand the genesis of the problem. What opportunities or support systems for the young might have been eroding in recent years? Is institutional policy making so dominated by aging adults that the community no longer reflects youth interests? Are children and youth not developing or are they losing a sense of community?

The perspective in this kind of thinking and questioning is an ecological one. It guides one to the feelings individuals have about belonging and having some control over their lives, to the responsive rather than the bureaucratic role of institutions, and to the interplay among institutions and between people and institutions. Clues for diagnoses and cues for actions are derived from this total context. The scapegoat or bad-guy theory, so often applied to schools, is eschewed as simplistic and counterproductive.

We have relatively little difficulty with this kind of thinking in many aspects of daily life. If the pressure in the water tap drops suddenly, we do not immediately conclude that more pressure should be created at the other end. Our first thought is of a break in the pipe or line. Or, perhaps, the pipes are frozen. It is taking us longer to learn that a decline in lumber production does not necessarily mean that lumbering activity should be increased. We have even more difficulty applying the ecological principles involved to social, institutional, and particularly educational affairs. But there has been a beginning, especially in such fields as criminology and mental health.

If we were to apply seriously such principles in taking steps toward community improvement and simultaneously seek to teach them in schools, both the withering of community and the erosion of education in schools could be turned around. Let us apply the theoretical perspective involved just to the educational part of the ecology of communities. First, we no longer equate schools with the whole of educating. Second, we look to see what other institutions educate or might potentially educate. Third, we consider the possibility of creating new settings to take over functions interfering with the ability of existing institutions to perform their primary functions well.

It soon becomes apparent that schools have expanded upward, downward, and sideways to perform educational functions, assume social functions not easily converted to educational ones, take on training functions more appropriately handled elsewhere, and increase their custodial function to make up for the declining ability of the home to provide it. Ironically but not surprisingly, schooling has lost some of its primacy as educator. With so much to do, schools have tended to lose their sense of central purpose. And, with states specifying precisely the proficiencies to be developed in children and youth, there is scarcely any felt need for educators and concerned citizens to ask first questions about the aims of education, the goals of schools, and what knowledge is of most worth.

It follows that school "leaders" soon find themselves spending more time on transportation, food services, inventories, purchasing, public relations, and paper work than on curriculum planning. Inevitably, teachers spend increasing amounts of time on such activities, too. And the more the work of teachers mirrors the work of administrators, the worse the quality of education provided.

As stated earlier, schools always have taken on and always will take on functions in addition to education. But the persons responsible for schools always should take these on thoughtfully, meanwhile shedding with similar reflection functions no longer needed. The central question always is: What should the school be doing in light of what other institutions are ill-suited to do? The answers vary from community to community and school to school.

Again, as stated earlier, during these concluding years of the twentieth century, what more and more communities should be able to do without schools is to provide specific job training and an introduction to the mechanics of learning. What schools should provide above all else is the development of problem-solving abilities, interpersonal relations, self-understanding, syntheses and integrations of life experiences, a sense of community, and an inquiring intellect. The challenges and difficulties involved in achieving such schools are great. But the task will be somewhat easier if we think of schools as having a particular educational job to do and not the whole. In doing their unique job, schools share with all other institutions some of the responsibility for what is conventionally referred to as discipline—that is, schools must conduct their good work responsibly.

Television vies with schooling in the amount of time it occupies in the lives of the young. It entertains but it also educates, in the domain of values and attitudes as well as information. We must become more acutely aware of television as educator, currently and potentially, assuring for it an appropriate place in a healthy education ecosystem.

With the school regarded as just one of many education-related institutions, albeit with the most sustained educative role to play, the appropriate chief administrative officer would be a commissioner of education (and, perhaps, culture), not a superintendent of schools. He or she would cultivate and to the degree possible coordinate the educational roles of all institutions and agencies in the total ecosystem. The persons in charge of schools would have the responsibility for assuring healthy[21] schools that perform the educational functions not promoted elsewhere in this system.

The possibilities for effectively employing a *limited* voucher plan now begin to be apparent. A mark of a sound educational program is its contribution to one's ability to make increasingly wise, independent judgments about one's own education. That is, one finds and sets new goals as an aspect of the educational experience, as part of one's personal growth. Dewey expressed this idea as follows:

> Since growth is the characteristic of life, education is all one with growing; it has no end beyond itself. The criterion of the value of school education is the extent to which it creates a desire for continued growth and supplies means for making the desire effective in fact.[22]

Attendance at a school should foster, then, not only a desire for advanced school-based education but also for educational experiences in other settings. In a healthy educational ecosystem, we should expect schools to assure what Dewey described. But young people might attend schools for varying periods of time at different stages in their lives—perhaps more in the early years than in the later ones. Then in consultation with counselors and parents (and with such consultations probably declining in successive years), children and youth would make use of vouchers in seeking to satisfy interests stimulated by education in school. Increasingly they, not their parents, would make their own educational decisions. Ideally, they would expand both their ability to take advantage of an array of educative institutions and their sense of community.

With a common school—educating and not merely training—at the center of the educative community, we need fear less the potential divisiveness of a limited voucher plan. Indeed, it might serve to increase our awareness, development, and use of the full range of educational capability existing to varying degrees in each community.

A RESEARCH AGENDA

My bias in the foregoing is clear. I favor movement toward educative communities in which all institutions and all individuals to a degree educate and feel a responsibility to do so. Within this total context, schools play a unique and largely nonduplicated role. Whether schools do more or less than educate will depend on the degree to which other institutions both educate and perform their other functions adequately.

We have tended to think of our institutions singly and not as the skeletal and organic structure of our civilization. Our intellectual orientation and accompanying inquiry tend not to be systemic and ecological. And so, we extend schooling downward because "schooling is good" without much thought to the impact of such policy and action on the family which also is "good." Efforts to improve human services in interrelated, coordinated ways require conceptualizations, research, and data of a kind we have had only rarely and on a limited basis. This chapter concludes with some brief thoughts on what an educational agenda for inquiry and research into communities might look like.

First, it would be interesting to select widely varying localities in the United States for purposes of examining their present and potential educational resources. One would want to go beyond mere identification and description into analyses of functions, services, and activities.

This kind of descriptive and analytical work should be accompanied by a more person- and less institution-oriented type of survey. One would want to sample individuals from all socioeconomic, ethnic, and racial groups to determine their use of available resources. The inquirer would not only examine who is using what resources and why but also seek to gain insight into reasons for non-use. It would be fascinating to probe into the question of why some people either do not wish to board the train or see themselves as denied access.

It would be useful, then, to sort out the institutions seeming to have "reaching power" to determine the key elements in their success. What lessons might be learned from them?

From such data, one could begin to conceptualize differing patterns of educational services, employing in the ecology both existing institutions and agencies to be created. Cost analyses would help in deciding whether functions should be added to what now exists or whether to seek a new kind of setting. It would be useful to have knowledge of differing models of coordination. Where are schools dominant and why? Are there examples of other agencies successfully coordinating many institutions, including schools? Are there any flourishing community education programs in which the schools play only a minor role? In those instances where large numbers of students are transported from many communities by bus, how do those communities without schools provide educational services?

Beyond these macro-studies are literally hundreds of others requiring relatively fine-grained analyses. Important among these are inquiries which examine not only what institutions provide for individuals but what they take away. An expanding school system that makes it less necessary for parents to assume their appropriate share of educative and custodial care can hardly be considered an unmitigated blessing. New educational services in which the personally and financially secure participate first are not what most communities need. Research that simply counts numbers of participants tells us nothing about who is left out or the degree to which those seemingly reached are meaningfully involved.

CONCLUDING COMMENT

The alienation of individuals from society and the withering of community go hand in hand. One of the conditions contributing significantly to alienation is an all-encompassing school system not committed to retaining all of its clients. "The schools have become one of the most potent breeding grounds of alienation in our society. For this reason it is of crucial importance for the welfare and development of school-age children that schools be reintegrated into the life of the community."[23] Schools can be only incomplete learning communities when segments of the age-group rightfully to be served are missing.

We have so lost sight of the mission of the common school that not all of us wince when national commissions propose removing from school those who do not adapt readily to it. Some have recommended that school-leaving age be lowered to 14 in order to expedite the departure of those for whom schooling is not meaningful. Where are they to go? Into a society where achievement in school eases passage into jobs and other institutions? Into other institutions requiring adaptation to fixed principles rather than institutions prepared to adapt to individuals? Communities and a sense of community will continue to wither so long as our institutions, educational and other, are preoccupied with their own survival rather than with the human conditions and needs they are supposed to serve.

More than money, we need a different way of viewing the problem—an alternative perspective. This perspective causes us to see individuals and institutions as part of the same environmental matrix. When abrasions and disjunctures occur between individuals and an institution created to assist in their development, it is inappropriate to assume that the institution is uncaring and individuals are sick or delinquent. Rather, something has gone wrong in the ecological relationship and that relationship could include another institution.

For example, when schools take on more functions or more of the community's educational responsibilities, they also take on a greater moral prerogative, since values are built into all that they undertake. As discussed earlier, the necessary balance between home and school is upset. Simply to increase pressure on the school for "discipline" is to further this imbalance, endangering both institutions. An ecological perspective turns attention not just to the relationship between individuals and one institution but to the health of the relationships among individuals and institutions.

The most promising direction for the future is in strengthening these relationships, not in extending the control or operating principles of any one institution to the others. The best schools are those that play a distinctive, not an exclusive, educational role. With other institutions, they share a sense of community and educate for development of this sense. Such schools are themselves learning communities.

NOTES

1. Joseph J. Schwab, "Education and the State: Learning Community," *The Great Ideas Today,* Encyclopaedia Britannica, Inc., Chicago, 1976, p. 235.

2. James B. Conant, *Slums and Suburbs,* McGraw-Hill, New York, 1961.

3. Bruce Gunn, "The System is the Answer!" *Florida School Administrator,* vol. 2., no. 3, April 1979, p. 33.

4. Ibid.

5. Paul Fordham, Geoff Poulten, and Lawrence Randle, *Learning Networks in Adult Education,* Routledge and Kegan Paul, London, 1979, p. 191.

6. Ibid., p. 235.

7. Herbert Thelen, *Dynamics of Groups at Work,* University of Chicago Press, Chicago, 1954.

8. Ibid.

9. Schwab, op. cit., pp. 247–248.

10. Lawrence A. Cremin, "Further Notes Toward a Theory of Education," *Notes on Education,* vol. 4, 1974, p. 1.

11. For further discussion, see Alicja Iwanska, "The Role of the Curriculum Maker in Cross-Cultural Perspective," in John I. Goodlad and Associates, *Curriculum Inquiry: The Study of Curriculum Practice,* McGraw-Hill, New York, 1979, Ch. 10.

12. Schwab, op. cit., p. 243.

13. Robert M. Hutchins, "The Great Anti-School Campaign," *The Great Ideas Today,* Encyclopaedia Britannica, Chicago, 1972, p. 154.

14. For such elaboration, see John I. Goodlad, *What Schools Are For,* Phi Delta Kappa Educational Foundation, Bloomington, IN, 1979.

15. R. S. Peters, *Ethics and Education,* George Allen and Unwin, Ltd., London, 1966, p. 27.

16. Schwab, op. cit., p. 246.

17. A Study of Schooling is an in-depth study of a small sample of elementary, middle, and senior high schools. It is supported by a consortium of philanthropic foundations and federal agencies and administered by /I/D/E/A/ (John I. Goodlad, project director). Although other findings are referred to in this chapter, the Study is not further referenced.

18. Ronald G. McIntire, "The Development of a Conceptual Model for Selection of Optional Educational Programs in an Elementary School," unpublished doctoral dissertation, University of California, Los Angeles, 1976.

19. Jerome S. Bruner, *The Process of Education,* Harvard University Press, Cambridge, Mass., 1960, p. 33.

20. Benjamin S. Bloom, *Human Characteristics and School Learning,* McGraw-Hill, New York, 1976, p. x.

21. For an elaboration of the use of "healthy" rather than "healthful" in the ecological context, see John I. Goodlad, *The Dynamics of Educational Change,* McGraw-Hill, New York, 1975.

22. John Dewey, *Democracy and Education,* The Macmillan Co., New York, 1916, p. 53.

23. Urie Bronfenbrenner, "The Origins of Alienation," *Scientific American,* vol. 231, no. 1, August 1974, p. 60.

12

THE PAST— AND PRESENT— AS PROLOGUE

MIRIAM CLASBY
*Boston University and
Institute for Responsive Education*

Within the Navajo tradition, the ritual of sandpainting holds a place of special reverence. To drive away disease, heal the sick, and bring blessings to the tribe, the shaman or medicine man becomes an artist, using colored sand ground from rocks or brought from the Painted Desert. Sifting the grains onto a bed of sand, he forms a replica of a plant god, a water god, or a god of healing. The age-old ceremony of ministering to the sick never changes and, in the tribe, medicine, like education, links the individual to a fixed world of custom and behavior. Moreover, the ritual is for the tribe as well as for the individual; the illness of one is the illness of all. When one member suffers, the well-being of the whole community is threatened.

In modern technological societies such as ours these rituals and the static worldview they express seem alien and irrelevant. To reflect on action, to probe the meaning of experience, to review the past for clues to understanding the present and making wise decisions about the future—these are tasks unique to mature men and women in the modern world. They assume a world forever changing, a society ever "becoming," an unknown future to be created.

The chapters of this book stand as testimony to an energetic and determined effort to interpret what has been happening in schools and communities and what these events may mean for the future. But, because we are not easily liberated from legacies of the past and from mindsets cemented by tradition, the search for understanding ourselves and our lives is inevitably marked by ambiguity and uncertainty. So these chapters also reveal the incompleteness of any single effort to capture the full significance of a range of complex events. Perhaps most of all, they reveal ways in which reality outstrips our tools—our concepts and our words—for interpreting experience.

Schools represent ways in which our society chooses to prepare our children for the life they will live as adults and for the world they will live in. One way to reflect further on the significance of the activities described in these pages and their implications for the future is to explore some of the changes in the concept and experience of "community."

Historically, the word "community" has embraced two distinct dimensions: one refers to a rational organizational structure—a geopolitical unit providing all that residents need for day-to-day living; the other refers to the bonding among individuals—affiliations rooted in shared value commitments. In tribal life, such as the Navajo's, these two dimensions were totally integrated—living space and loving space were one and the same and they were controlled by the tribe. In modern technological societies, because of changes in the character of the places where people live their day-to-day lives, the two dimensions have become separated. We travel to different places for work, for recreation, and for worship, and interact with different groups of people in those places, leading to a privatization of experience and a reliance on the nuclear family as the source of bonding. In addition, though we still cling to the term "community," dramatic changes in political, economic, and social structures have transformed the nature of life in local communities. These transformations are intimately related to three historical trends or forces: urbanization, "nationalization," and internationalization.

URBANIZATION

Of the three forces, urbanization has the longest and most visible history in the United States. For more than one hundred years, the growth of cities has defined the lot of the poor—displaced persons from foreign countries, from plantations, from mechanized farms. Although the neighborhoods they formed created "communities of the spirit," the poorest had no control over decisions that determined the kind and quality of housing, jobs, social services, or schools available to them. The poorest residents of core cities were virtually disenfranchised from local politics, a situation that continues for the new groups that moved in to take their place. Furthermore, life conditions typically expose them to the poorest (by any national standard that can be used) in housing, jobs, schools, health, and child care. Those living in the wealthiest locales have had exactly the opposite experience. The richer the place, the greater the power to control real estate, the type of population, and the schools (and the less the need for employment and social services). Social commentators have sharply observed that those who most value place—often all they have—have least control over it, while those whose work and recreation cross local, national, and international boundaries have most control over their local space. Such contradictions are unlikely to be easily resolved.

Every statistical projection for the future points to increased urbanization; urbanologists foresee metropolitan areas expanding to "urban fields" holding most of the nation's population. Such expansion will not address the problems of the poor in cities. Recent interventions to revitalize core cities, accelerated by the return of middle-class professionals, are likely to exacerbate the problem. In this real life game of Monopoly, the poor, treated as the most expendable, can only be dispersed to new ghettos, and the public schools serving their children will share their plight.

For the first time in our history, all school-aged children are expected to be in school and 80 percent of them remain through graduation. Concurrently, for the first time in history, public schools have been charged with serving the total population—poor, bilingual, handicapped, pregnant teenagers or unwed mothers, boat children as well as children of international graduate students. These special populations, with all their individual needs, are concentrated in cities, and city schools strain under the burden of attempting to understand and to respond to the challenge. At worst city schools may collapse under the strain, precipitating radical changes in the structure of public schooling in this country. Except in special wealthy enclaves with prestigious public schools, the rich have always shunned public education. Substantial withdrawal of white middle-class populations from city schools can only lead us back in history to the days when public education sponsored "schools for the poor." At best some teachers and administrators will develop schools and classrooms appropriate to the challenge—only to find that the students and their families have been forced to move to some other, presumably unprepared, school system.

The poor have a unique dependence upon public schools because they have no other choice. Despite a decade of federal stimulus for parental involvement (characterized by strong rhetorical support and marginal tangible support), neither "communities of the poor" nor the individual schools that serve them have any effective voice in those critical local political, economic, and social decisions that determine their future. Thus, we are forced to conclude that local control of schools, if it exists at all, is primarily a function of wealth and of the ability to control who lives where.

"NATIONALIZATION"

The second influence on communities and their schools tends to be hidden rather than immediately obvious. We have no good word to capture the phenomenon. The term "nationalization" will be pressed into service to refer to those forces shifting decision-making power to the national level—the centralization of influence.

National economic policies which determine rates of unemployment and inflation, trade and investment practices, and import and export patterns substantially affect the lives of citizens in local municipalities. Yet representatives of city and town governments have little involvement in the formulation of those policies. Federal Reserve Bank decisions about the flow of money are far more likely to reflect judgments of representatives of banking interests than of municipal governments.

In addition, our national economy is structured so that one-fifth of our population receives less than 5 percent of our national income, while the top fifth receives more than 40 percent. This pattern has persisted, through boom years and recessions, since statistics were first kept in 1906. It is reinforced by patterns of structural unemployment impacting heavily on minority youth. In a democratic society, this pattern ostensibly reflects choices we, as a society, make about the ways we wish to allocate our society's resources. But as long as this pattern continues, some urban center, somewhere, will always, willingly or unwillingly, host "communities of the poor" and thus bear differentially the burden of responding to their needs and to the conditions in which they are forced to live.

Also in our economy, we have seen the shift from a visible agrarian world of farmers and small-business entrepreneurs to an invisible network of interlocking corporations. In addition to operating with all the rights of private property once assigned to farmers, the top five hundred corporations control two-thirds of our total national labor force. The production system which has evolved concentrates heavily on automobiles and armaments. Again, in a democratic society, these priorities should reflect the choices of citizens about the kinds of things we want our society to produce. Instead, local governments and their citizens depend for employment and development on corporate decisions to consolidate, to mechanize, to relocate—decisions dictated primarily by the goal of maximizing profits. These decisions enrich some locales while they strip others. Local elected officials can, at best, respond to these interventions; fortunes of local areas are determined by forces beyond the control of local governments.

This powerlessness is intensified by the expansion of federal initiatives and by formal and informal networks of national power. Increased federal activity in housing, transportation, health, welfare, and education can be explained by the high percentage of individual tax dollars flowing to the federal level. Yet recipients of services, both individuals and local governments, have little voice in the formulation of policies or the design of programs, and chaotic patterns of bureaucratic implementation breed hostility and resistance.

Less visible and therefore less directly felt are the thousands of national-level groups which formulate policies for nationwide action. National meetings of governors and large city mayors, labor and professional unions, spokespersons for consumer, environmental, women, or minority concerns emulate the practice of corporate giants whose top executives meet at the Business Round Table to develop a common voice for public information and private lobbying. The groups vary enormously, however, in the weight brought to bear on national policies: advocates for consumer protection discover themselves overpowered by representatives of the U.S. Chamber of Commerce, and leaders of Action for Children's Television move at a snail's pace to change practices of commercial networks and their advertisers. Furthermore, this process for influencing national political, economic, or social policy is simply additive, introducing in serial and fragmented fashion a variety of specialized interests or concerns. Rapid proliferation of pressure groups in recent decades tends to obscure two fundamental facts: first, the potential pool of special concerns is unlimited—new needs can always be identified and new groups will continue to gather strength to articulate these needs as others fade from public attention; second, the sum of the parts is not equal to the whole—no simple aggregation of individual or group concerns can adequately address the complexity and interrelatedness of problems experienced by local citizens in cities and towns across the nation.

In this welter of national-level pressures one anomaly stands out. Federal intervention—both legislative and judicial—can be interpreted as fulfillment of constitutional responsibilities for the common good and general welfare, as well as for guaranteeing constitutional rights. Especially during the sixties, federal policies affirmed the Fourteenth Amendment rights of the poor, minorities, handicapped, women, and other populations excluded from the benefits of full citizenship. In particular, actions asserting the rights of blacks marked a significant step in a century-long struggle to redress injustices borne by those in double jeopardy because of color and former slave status. But these social policies, like our standard economic policies, rely on a "trickle-down" theory which assumes that what is perceived as good by those at the top will be good for those at the bottom. At least in the area of social policy, the near-bankruptcy of that theory becomes clear as evidence shows that federal mandates may be necessary, but they are certainly insufficient to redress inequities.

If the twenty-five years since the *Brown* decision stands as any indication, the values affirmed by civil rights interventions find little resonance in cities and suburbs. Threatened with apparent loss of decision-making control, with imposition of new social values and new standards of behavior, citizens and their elected officials rally to define their territory, to exclude the stranger, and to protect their perceived interests. The belief in local control of schools remains as the last vestige of local autonomy and that control is exercised most effectively at the current time to resist efforts to ensure Constitutional guarantees of equal rights under law.

INTERNATIONALIZATION

The final trend, internationalization, is more recent. In 1945, the United Nations Charter set forth a set of common purposes for world nations:

> To reaffirm faith in fundamental human rights in the dignity and worth of the human person, in the equal rights of men and women and of nations large and small, and
> To establish conditions under which justice and respect for the obligations arising from treaties and other sources of international law can be maintained, and
> To promote social progress and better standards of life in larger freedom, and
> To practice tolerance and live together in peace with one another as good neighbors, and
> To unite our strength to maintain international peace and security, and
> To insure, by the acceptance of principles and the institution of methods, that armed force shall not be used, save in the common interest, and
> To employ international machinery for the promotion of the economic and social advancement of all peoples. . . .

The United States has generously underwritten a substantial portion of the cost of the organization and, despite overt war in Southeast Asia and covert tactics in Chile, has publicly espoused these purposes. Sometime in the near future, we are expected to ratify the international Covenants on Human Rights already signed by forty-six nations. In addition, through satellite and newsprint, we as a people have witnessed efforts—some weak and some strong—to address apartheid in southern Africa, famine in Bangladesh and Cambodia, hostilities in the Mid-East.

In October 1979, first Pope Paul II and then Fidel Castro (speaking for nonaligned nations) addressed the United Nations Assembly and called for redistribution of world resources to alleviate the desperate poverty of two-thirds of the world's population. There is some irony that this call to the "haves" to care for the "have-nots" was delivered in the United States—the richest industrialized nation in the world, where no major political party or leader in recent history has proposed income redistribution to relieve structural poverty within the country. Ironically, too, it is not the food-poor but the oil-rich nations who press in on our daily lives. And that pressure brings new knowledge—of multinational corporate power, of the critical role of the balance of trade in causing inflation, of extravagant consumption of the world's nonrenewable resources. The pressure also alerts us to some of the interdependencies among nations, reminding us, however painfully, of the necessity of a world community.

If we define "community" as that space providing all that people need for day-to-day living, we know now that we must enlarge our traditional sense of boundaries. We have only one planet with its minerals, water, and air; we know now some of the limits of these resources, the dangers of destroying them as well as the dangers of the struggle to control them. But "community" also includes bonding and affiliation and this holds out hope that changes in perceptions of boundaries and of common needs for survival may bring changes in perceptions of "neighbor." Founded on a dream of unlimited opportunity and infinite resources, we grew from colony to nation without reshaping our concept of community, without adjusting boundaries, without shifting to define "neighbor" by inclusion rather than exclusion. The hard fact of the interdependency of world nations, the obvious need to learn to share because sharing is essential for survival—these realities of life towards the end of the twentieth century offer an opportunity to reshape our understanding of community. A vision of community as "world community" enables us to shed the myth of self-sufficiency for local "communities" and to transform our perceptions of the ways in which we live in our cities and towns, in our nation, and in the world.

This vision of a possible future, remote and difficult to attain as it seems, is already present in multiple ways. It is being shaped or destroyed by individual, corporate, or national responses to the claims of third-world people reaching out to take what is rightfully theirs. Today, for example, poor nations demand that communication bands be reserved so that airwaves will be available to them in twenty years when they need them. That demand will be accepted or rejected by international regulatory agencies dominated by industrialized nations. The vision is being shaped or destroyed by the schooling offered in every locality. Children born this year will leave their teens to walk into the twenty-first century and their schooling will prepare them either to enhance the world community or diminish it. From this perspective the case could be made that sound educational practice requires every children to have an opportunity to learn with children of different racial, ethnic, or economic backgrounds as necessary preparation for adult life.[1]

As fragile as the vision of a world community may be in the face of old loyalties and traditional practices, it gains credibility and strength from the fearfulness of the opposite vision. Because of urbanization and "nationalization," local "communities" are at risk in profound and disturbing ways. Discussions that assume that localities can function as isolated or independent units simply misrepresent reality. Even the title of this book, *Communities and Their Schools,* can be misleading if it seems to legitimate autonomous entities. Unless considerations of schooling are placed within the contexts of education in the larger society and the world society, they run the danger of unwittingly affirming a past that no longer exists. Careless perpetuation of the myth of local control of communities and their schools can only propel us headlong into that world described by Thomas Pynchon in *Gravity's Rainbow* where community exists only as "shared victimhood."

But the past also offers ground for hope. No matter how distant in time or place, we all have roots in a tribe and we still have before us symbols of societies where living space and loving space are one. Like the Navajo shaman, in touch with sand, water, and air, making sand-paintings to heal the sick and bring blessings to the tribe, these cultures build their lives on a vision of unity—on a worldview in which the well-being of the community depends on the well-being of each individual person. This worldview, present through history, found still in lifestyles of Africa and principles of both Eastern and Western religions, provides a solid base for a vision of a world community. We need such a vision to understand the deepest meanings of these chapters, to help us gauge how far we have come and what remains to be done to change the structures that diminish our lives. We need such a vision lest we—and our children in ghetto, barrio, and village—perish.

NOTES

1. The nature of this kind of education and the issues involved in achieving it are addressed in James M. Becker (ed.), *Schooling for a Global Age,* McGraw-Hill, New York, 1979.

INDEX

Monroe County (Florida), 107–108
Montana, 307
Moore, Vernon, 175–179
Moraga, Calif., 321–322
Moore, Thomas, 271
Morgan School (Washington, D.C.), 103
Mott, Charles Stewart, 271–272, 283
Mott Foundation, 272–273, 283

NAACP (National Association for the Advancement of Colored People), 75, 100, 129
Nairobi schools (East Palo Alto), 103
Nassau County (New York), 202
National Alliance of Businessmen, 314
National Apprenticeship Service of Industrial Training (Brazil), 238–240, 242
National Association for the Advancement of Colored People, 75, 100, 129
National Campaign of Community Schools (Brazil), 218–225, 230
National Campaign of Free Schools (Brazil), 222
National Christian Council (Kenya), 237
National Commission Resources for Youth, 321
National Community Education Association, 276, 287
National Congress of Parents and Teachers, 100
National Defense Education Act (1958), 26
National Education Association, 21, 25, 195, 200, 204
National Information Center on Volunteerism, 319–320
National Institute of Education, 95, 155
National Manpower Institute, 313
National School Volunteer Program, 301
National Society for the Study of Education, 271
National Urban League, 100, 129, 156–161, 168–169, 175, 178
Navajos, 30, 357, 364
Negaunee, Mich., 285
Neighborhood Youth Corps, 149
Nevada, 308–310
New Braunfels, Texas, 285–286
New Deal (1930s), 147
New Hampshire, 196
New Oakland Committee (Oakland, Mich.), 314
New Roles for Youth, 321, 323–325
New York, 21, 99
 Buffalo, 103
 Nassau County, 202
 New York City (*see* New York City)
 Skipwith decision, 67

New York City, 18, 88, 198–199, 203
 community control in, 93–94, 100, 102–103
 decentralization in, 25, 61, 64, 66–75, 77–78, 81
 Street Academies in, 158–160
"New York City Project" (N.Y. Board of Regents), 73
Nisbet, Robert, 147, 150–151, 165
Nixon, Richard, 153
North Central Accrediting Agency, 170
Nyerere, Julius K., 253–254

Oakland, Calif.:
 school-family contracts in, 309–310
 Street Academies in, 156–160, 168–169, 181
Oakland, Mich., 314–315
O'Bryant, John, 80
Ocean Hill-Brownsville school District (New York City), 61, 67, 74, 77
Ogden, Utah, 285
Ohio:
 Cincinnati, 198
 Cleveland, 115–116, 141
 Columbus, 125–128, 131, 134–135
 Springfield, 284
Olsen, Clarence, 276
Orata, Pedro, 227, 299
"Oro del Barrio" project (Phoenix), 301
Orr Junior High School (Las Vegas), 308–310

Paraprofessionals in Adaptive Education (Tucson), 307
Parent advisory committees, 88, 98, 110
Parent-Teacher Associations, 100, 110, 116, 129, 162, 227, 300
Parkway Program (Philadelphia), 316–317
Pasadena, Calif., 130
PATCH Program (Atlanta), 113–114
Peace Corps, 149, 219
Peak, G. Wayne, 27
Pebblebrook High School (Cobb Co., Ga.), 324–325
Pennsylvania, 219
 Bethlehem, 326–327
 Lower Merion, 300
 Philadelphia, 74, 316–317
 Pittsburgh, 141
People, Let's Unite for Schools (Denver), 303
Peoria, Ill., 300
Peralta Community College (Oakland, Mich.), 314
Peru, 222, 239, 245
Phelps-Stokes Foundation, 253
Philadelphia, Pa., 74, 316–317

Philippines, 218, 225–231, 246
Phoenix, Ariz., 301–302
Piaget, Jean, 232
Pierce, John, 15
Pierce, Lawrence C., 51
Pitkin, Hanna, 167
Pittsburgh, Pa., 141
Planning Coordinating Committee
   (Minneapolis), 172
Plato, 271
Plowden Report (Britain, 1967), 232
Poland, 240
Porter, Philip, 325–326
Pratt Motley Continuous Progress
   Program (Minneapolis), 171
Public Education Association (New
   York City), 73, 100
Puebla (Mexico), 248
Puroks (Philippines), 246
Pynchon, Thomas, 364

Rabun County (Ga.), 318–319
Raskin, A. H., 200–201
Recife (Brazil), 219, 222
Reconnection for Learning (Bundy
   Commission Report), 67, 74, 78
Redfield, Robert, 247
Reissman, Frank, 64
*Responsiveness of Public Schools to
   Their Clientele, The* (1975), 36–38,
   40, 42, 47
Reynolds, Larry J., 162
Rhode Island, 15
Rhodes, James A., 141
Riles, Wilson, 108–109, 130
Rodriguez decision (1973), 53
Roosevelt Community School (Louis-
   ville), 105–107, 109
Rough Rock Demonstration School
   (Arizona), 29–30
Rumania, 240

St. Louis (Mo.), 74
   Citizens Education Task Force,
      125–126, 128, 131, 134–135,
      138–139, 142
   community education in, 284–285
*San Antonio Independent School Dis-
   trict* v. *Rodriguez* (1973), 53
San Francisco, Calif., 199–200, 322
   community development organiza-
      tions in, 89, 114
   Schools Commission, 125–126, 128,
      130–131, 133–138, 142
San Jose, Calif., 110
San Pablo del Norte (Mexico), 248
Sayre, Wallace, 20
Scanlon, Joseph, 202

Scanlon Plan, 202
Scenic View school (Englewood, Colo.),
   327–328
Schattschneider, E. E., 38
School Committee (Boston), 74–80,
   164, 166
School community centers (Britain),
   243–244
School Department (Boston), 78–80
"School Improvement Plan" (Edmonds), 73
School Improvement Program (Califor-
   nia, 1978), 108–111
School Volunteers (Los Angeles),
   300–301
Schools Commission (San Francisco),
   125–126, 128, 130–131, 133–138,
   142
Schools Committee (Columbus), 125–
   126, 128, 131, 134–135
Schwab, Joseph J., 333, 339, 345
Seattle, Wash., 199–200
Seay, Maurice, 276–277
Serrano v. Priest (California, 1971), 53,
   193
Shanker, Albert, 61
Sharing the Power? (Institute for Re-
   sponsive Education), 167
Shelly, David, 327
Shields, James, 65
Skipwith, In re (New York, 1958), 67
Skyline Career Development Center
   (Dallas), 310–313
South Bend, Ind., 156, 158–160, 168, 181
South Boston High School (Boston), 29, 61
South Carolina, 18, 99
   Charleston, 313
   Greenville County, 315–316
Southeast Alternatives (Minneapolis),
   156, 161–177, 181–183
Soviet Union, 231, 240
SPEAK Program (San Francisco), 114
Special Services for the Disadvantaged
   programs, 149
Springfield, Ohio, 284
Stevens Elementary School (Denver), 302
Street Academy projects, 156–161, 166,
   168–169, 175–179, 181–183
"Study of Schooling, A" (Goodlad),
   346–347
Sundquist, James, 148, 151–152
Sunset Parkside Education Action
   Committee (San Francisco), 114
Supreme Court, U.S., 97
   Brown v. Board of Education (1954),
      24–27, 149, 361
   and prayer in public schools, 26
   *San Antonio Independent School Dis-
      trict v. Rodriguez* (1973), 53